WINDOWS 95
IN A NUTSHELL

A Desktop Quick Reference

RETURN OF ARCADE
25239-274-1372985-62772

WINDOWS 95
IN A NUTSHELL

A Desktop Quick Reference

Tim O'Reilly & Troy Mott

O'REILLY™

Cambridge · Köln · Paris · Sebastopol · Tokyo

Windows 95 in a Nutshell

by Tim O'Reilly and Troy Mott

Copyright © 1998 O'Reilly & Associates, Inc. All rights reserved.
Printed in the United States of America.

Published by O'Reilly & Associates, Inc., 101 Morris Street, Sebastopol, CA 95472.

Editor: Tim O'Reilly

Production Editor: Nancy Wolfe Kotary

Printing History:

> June 1998:   First Edition.

This book is printed on acid-free paper with 85% recycled content, 15% post-consumer waste. O'Reilly & Associates is committed to using paper with the highest recycled content available consistent with high quality.

ISBN: 1-56592-316-2

Table of Contents

Chapter 4—The Control Panel 75

Part III: Under the Hood

Part IV: Appendixes

Preface

It's easy to get started with Windows 95. The user interface is fairly intuitive, especially for today's more sophisticated user, who has been working with computers for years. But getting really proficient with the system is pretty hard, especially since Microsoft has apparently decided that the graphical interface and online help make good documentation redundant.

Windows 95 is a complex system. There are a lot of ways to do things. It's hard to remember the location of the specific user interface element you need to accomplish a particular task, and there are many features that are completely hidden if you rely on the graphical interface alone.

There are many books on Windows 95, but most of them suffer from a step-by-step tutorial organization that makes you wade through too many words to find what you need.

That's where this book comes in. It provides a condensed but thorough reference to Windows 95, with an organization that helps you get right to the information you need.

We don't document every element of the graphical interface, but we tell you how to get to each important dialog box, and what you need to know about it that isn't obvious from the labels and instructions embedded in the interface.

We do document hidden programs, and provide a wealth of useful tips. Think of this book as a cross between *Windows 95 for Non-Dummies*, *The Windows 95 Resource Kit*, and *Windows 95 Secrets*, boiled down to the essence, and you have the general idea.

Our focus is on user applications, though, not on system or network administration. While we give you a basic understanding of these deeper levels and what's available, specific installation details and detailed configuration information for system and network administrators are largely beyond the scope of the book.

Especially with networked systems, there are also settings that are dependent on decisions made by your network administrator or Internet Service Provider. Whenever possible, we give you the information you need, but at times, all we can tell you is where to go for additional information.

We have tried to speak universal truths about Windows 95 itself, but sometimes we inevitably have fallen into describing Windows 95 as it happens to be installed on our particular machines. While Microsoft has tried to limit the number of different versions of Windows 95, the truth is that, for better or worse, each user's machine represents a slightly different installation of Windows 95 (see Chapter 2, *Versions of Windows 95*). Of all the code and data that Microsoft ships on the Windows 95 CD-ROM, only about half is used in a particular user's configuration. So what we say about Windows 95 may or may not be quite true about Windows 95 as it's installed on your system.

Also, for all the statements (from Microsoft and others) that Windows 95 is "integrated" and "seamless," the fact is that the system is actually amazingly modular, customizable, and "seamy." This is a good thing, not a bad thing. This book shows a lot of different ways to modify Windows 95 to suit your needs; also check out the book *Windows Annoyances*, by David Karp (O'Reilly & Associates). But this almost infinite customizability and modularity of Windows 95 also means that many of our statements about the product—such as, for example, that the Control Panel includes a Multimedia applet, or that the Desktop corresponds to the *Windows\Desktop* directory, or that Windows 95 even *has* a Desktop—are, strictly speaking, false, or at least serious oversimplifications.

The point is simply that this book sometimes describes a Platonic ideal of Windows 95, and sometimes describes a fairly random thing that really could be called *Windows 95, as it Happens to Look on the Authors' Machines, in a Nutshell.* This sort of thing is true of any book on Windows 95. Windows 95 is a platform and set of capabilities, not a single stable product with a fixed set of features.

Organization of the Book

This book is broken into four parts.

Part I: The Lay of the Land

This part of the book is designed to give you the big picture. It consists of two chapters:

Chapter 1, *Using Windows 95*, gives a brief review of the Windows 95 Graphical User Interface (GUI) and other elements of the system, aimed mainly at people who are new to Win95.

Chapter 2, *Versions of Windows 95*, gives a brief history of Windows 95, with pointers to locations on Microsoft's site where you can get more detailed information about the contents of each version.

Part II: Alphabetical Reference

This part of the book contains alphabetically organized reference pages for each major element of Windows 95. Once you're at a given point in the system, what can you do there?

For GUI-based applications, we don't document every menu, button, and dialog box—the GUI is often self-evident. Instead, we focus on non-obvious features, and provide helpful hints about power user features and things that will make your life easier.

For command-line–based programs, we cover every option, since these programs are not as obviously self-documenting (though many do support the conventional / ? command-line option for help).

This part is divided into five chapters:

Chapter 3, *The Windows 95 User Interface*, provides a detailed reference page for each major element you'll see on the Win95 Desktop.

Chapter 4, *The Control Panel*, provides a detailed reference page for every Control Panel dialog box.

Chapter 5, *Commands and Applications*, provides a detailed reference page for each utility, accessory, and application included with the system. Both GUI-based and command-line applications are documented here. Users may be surprised to find that many applications that they know in the GUI form also have command-line equivalents, and that there are many powerful commands available to a user who is willing to step beyond the GUI. This is really the heart of the book, providing documentation that is hard to find anywhere else.

The division between Chapters 3 and 5 is sometimes arbitrary. In general, if the primary way to access something is through a top-level Desktop interface, we've put it in Chapter 3. But if its Desktop interface is an entry in the Start menu, and it's often easier to invoke by typing a command name, we've put it in Chapter 5.

Chapter 6, *The Batch Language*, describes the commands that are used to write batch files—scripts that can be used to automate repetitive processes.

Chapter 7, *Dial-Up Networking*, describes the configuration dialog boxes used by communications facilities such as Internet Explorer, MSN, and Dial-Up Networking, plus the script language used to write login scripts for automatically logging in to remote systems that don't understand standard authentication protocols.

Part III: Under the Hood

This section describes some of the underlying mechanisms in Windows 95. It is strongly suggested reading for anyone who really wants to understand how the system works. "Give a man a fish and he will eat for a day. Teach him how to fish, and he will eat for a lifetime."

Chapter 8, *Inside Windows 95*, gives a more detailed look at the architecture of Win95. It is written from a programmer's perspective, but should be accessible to most readers. It lays out some underlying factors in the Windows 95 design that have ramifications throughout the system.

Chapter 9, *Windows Startup*, outlines the Windows 95 startup process and discusses the various points at which you might want to intervene. It also describes the format and contents of important system configuration files, and documents several commands that can be issued only from within these files.

Chapter 10, *The Registry*, describes the organization of the Registry, the central Windows 95 configuration database, and lists some of the most interesting entries it contains. It also describes how to use *regedit*, the Registry Editor.

Part IV: Appendixes

This section includes various handy quick reference lists.

Appendix A, *Keyboard Accelerators*, gives a list of keyboard accelerators (also known as hotkeys and keyboard shortcuts).

Appendix B, *Filename Extensions*, gives a list of standard file name extensions and associated programs.

Appendix C, *System File and Directory Organization*, gives an annotated listing of standard system files and directories. A more extensive description of some of the most important files and directories is given in Chapters 9 and 10.

Appendix D, *Special/Reserved Characters*, gives a list of the characters that have special meaning in Windows 95.

Appendix E, *Task Index*, helps you find things. One of the big problems with graphical user interfaces is remembering just where some vital control can be found. Where was that dialog box you stumbled across last month that let you change the default window background? This appendix gives you shorthand instructions for how to do many common tasks in both the GUI and the command line.

Conventions Used in This Book

The following typographical conventions are used in this book:

`Constant width`
    is used to indicate command-line computer output, code examples, Registry keys, and keyboard accelerators (see "Keyboard Accelerators" later in this section).

`Constant width italic`
    is used to indicate variables in examples and in Registry keys.

`Constant width bold`
    is used to indicate user input in examples.

Italic
    is used to introduce new terms and to indicate URLs, variables or user-defined files and directories, commands, file extensions, filenames, directory or folder names, and UNC pathnames.

<brackets>

are used to indicate variables or user-defined elements within italic text (such as path or filenames). For instance, in the path \ *Windows\<username>*, replace *<username>* with your username—but without the brackets.

Path Notation

Rather than using procedural steps to tell you how to reach a given Windows 95 user interface element or application, we use a shorthand path notation.

So we don't say, "Click on the Start menu, then click on Find, then Files or Folders. You'll see a dialog box that allows you to specify what you want to look for. Enter a filename in the Named: field." We simply say: Start → Find → Files or Folders → Named. We generally don't distinguish between menus, dialog boxes, buttons, checkboxes and so on, unless it's not clear from the context. Just look for a GUI element whose label matches an element in the path.

The path notation is relative to the Desktop, or some other well-known location. For example, the following path:

Start → Programs → Windows Explorer

means "Open the Start menu (on the Desktop), then choose Programs, then choose Windows Explorer." But rather than saying:

Start → Settings → Control Panel → Display → Appearance

we just say:

Control Panel → Display → Appearance

since Control Panel is a "well-known location" and the path can therefore be made less cumbersome. If the item in question is visible on the Desktop, no path is shown, but we may show keyboard accelerators that can be used to open or activate it.

Paths will typically consist of clickable user interface elements, but they may include text typed in from the keyboard, as in:

Start → Run → `telnet`

or:

`Ctrl-Alt-Del` → Shut Down

There is often more than one way to reach a given location in the user interface. We often list multiple paths to reach the same location, even though some are longer than others, because it can be helpful to see how multiple paths lead to the same destination.

The following well-known locations are used as starting points for user interface paths:

Control Panel

Start → Settings → Control Panel

Context menu

Right-click on an item to display this context-specific menu

Explorer

> The two-pane Explorer file view; Start → Programs → Windows Explorer.

My Computer

> The My Computer icon on the Desktop

Network Neighborhood

> The Network Neighborhood icon on the Desktop

Properties

> Context menu → Properties

Recycle Bin

> The Recycle Bin icon on the Desktop

Start

> The Start button on the Desktop Taskbar

xxxx menu

> Menu *xxxx* on a window's menubar (e.g., File, Edit)

Keyboard Accelerators

When keyboard accelerators are shown (such as `Ctrl-Alt-Del`), a hyphen means that the keys must be held down simultaneously, while a space means that the keys should be pressed sequentially. For example, pressing `Ctrl` and `Esc` simultaneously (`Ctrl-Esc`) pops up the Start menu, but you then pick an item by typing the underlined letter in its name. So, for example, the sequence to reach the Control Panel using a keyboard accelerator (Start → Settings → Control Panel) would be represented as `Ctrl-Esc+S+C`.

Even though we show an accelerator character (such as the C in `Ctrl-C`) as uppercase, you don't need to type the `Shift` key. In fact, in some cases, the accelerator will have a different meaning if `Shift` is held down at the same time, so we'll always mention it explicitly if it's needed.

Command-Line Syntax

The conventions used for representing command line options and arguments are described in the introduction to Chapter 5.

We'd Like to Hear from You

We have tested and verified all of the information in this book to the best of our ability, but you may find that features have changed (or that we have made mistakes). Please let O'Reilly know about any errors you find by writing:

> O'Reilly & Associates, Inc.
> 101 Morris Street
> Sebastopol, CA 95472
> 800-998-9938 (in U.S. or Canada)
> 707-829-0515 (international/local)
> 707-829-0104 (fax)

You can also send us messages electronically. To be put on the mailing list or request a catalog, send email to:

nuts@oreilly.com

To ask technical questions or comment on the book, send email to:

bookquestions@oreilly.com

Request for Comments

We've tried to include as many useful tips as possible in this book, but we can always use more. If you spot an error or have a tip we might include in the next edition or in our upcoming *Windows 98 in a Nutshell* book, please let us know. If we use your information, we'll give you a free copy of the next edition or any other In a Nutshell or Annoyances book of your choice. To submit suggestions, please navigate to *http://www.oreilly.com/catalog/win95nut/* and click on the Conference link.

Acknowledgments

Andrew Schulman was instrumental in helping get this book off the ground. He taught both of us most of what we know about Windows 95, and his sensibility informs much of this book. It was Andrew who insisted on the importance of the command line and argued that the command reference should include both DOS and Windows commands rather than segregating DOS into a ghetto of its own. He convinced us by showing the magic he could make happen in the user interface by typing a few seemingly arcane incantations at the DOS prompt.

Andrew also did much of the detailed research for the book, providing not only important technical direction but also many of the web references we point you to for additional information. He also wrote the majority of Chapter 8, which is quite possibly the most interesting chapter in the book.

That being said, any mistakes that remain are our own. Andrew's role was largely advisory, and he did not have the time to review everything we wrote or repair any inaccuracies that we introduced.

Gordon McComb worked on an earlier draft of this book, before a detached retina forced him to withdraw from the project. The majority of Chapter 9 is based on his work. The "The Windows 95 Scripting Language" section of Chapter 7 is adapted from *Windows NT in a Nutshell*, by Eric Pearce (O'Reilly & Associates).

David Karp, the author of *Windows Annoyances* (O'Reilly & Associates), also made major contributions to the book. He was a swift and tireless technical reviewer, and often answered our queries with detailed paragraphs that we dropped in almost verbatim. Ron Petrusha, Mark Bracewell, Eric Pearce and Susan Peck also provided technical reviews. As with Andrew, any errors that remain are our own.

We are also indebted to the generosity of hundreds of Windows 95 users who've created web sites to share tips, insights, and detailed documentation on particular aspects of the system they've uncovered. We refer to some of these sites in the book, but there are many others that also contributed to our understanding of Windows 95, taught us useful tips, or corrected our assumptions.

A special thanks also goes to Nancy Kotary, who was responsible for taking this book from the manuscript stage into something suitable for final printing. Nancy went above and beyond the normal role of the production editor, jumping in while the book was still under development, merging her copyedits with tech review edits and new writing until some of the pages looked like palimpsests. She was unfazed by anything we could throw at her, and makes us look better than we have any right to.

Thanks also goes to Sheryl Avruch, for managing the production team; Ellie Maden, Ellie Cutler, and Jane Ellin, for proofreading and quality control; Robert Romano, who created the illustrations; Seth Maislin, who wrote the index; and Marie Rizzo and Seth, who wrote the Task Index (Appendix E). And also thanks goes to Katie Gardner for all her help with the initial formatting of the manuscript.

Troy adds: I'd like to thank Tim for giving me the opportunity to co-author this book, and would especially like to thank my loving wife Lisa, who gave me a tremendous amount of support and tolerated my absence for the many nights and weekends I spent working on the book.

Tim adds: It's been a long time since I've written a book, and I'd almost forgotten how all-consuming it can be. I'd like to thank my wife Christina, since, like Lisa, she put up with a terminally distracted husband for many months. I'd also like to thank the many people I work with at O'Reilly & Associates, who kept the company running smoothly while I had my head down writing the book.

PART I

The Lay of the Land

CHAPTER 1

Using Windows 95

While this book is not a tutorial, this chapter provides a quick overview of the features of the Windows 95 user interface, which should be sufficient to get oriented and make the most of the system fairly quickly. If you're already familiar with Windows 95, you can probably skip this chapter, but you may be surprised by how much you can still learn. You might find the section entitled "The Command Line" particularly illuminating. If you're familiar with other Desktop GUIs, such as the Macintosh, Windows 3.1, or the X Window System, you should at least skim this chapter to find out what is different.

If you're a complete computer novice, you should probably pick up a Windows 95 tutorial. Even though this chapter is more introductory than the rest of the book, it still moves pretty quickly. Or just take your time, try a few things, and maybe you'll find you don't need step-by-step instructions after all.

The Desktop

Like the Macintosh and Windows 3.1 before it, Windows 95 uses the metaphor of a Desktop with windows and file folders laid out on it. This Desktop metaphor is provided by a program called the Explorer (*explorer.exe*). Windows 95 is set up to run this program automatically every time you start Windows 95.

Figure 1-1 shows the main features of the Windows 95 Desktop. The callouts in the figure highlight some of the special-purpose icons and buttons that appear on the Desktop. Each of these is described further in Chapter 3, *The Windows 95 User Interface.*

Point and Click Operations

If you are one of the few computer users who haven't used a graphical user interface before, here are some things you need to know:

* PCs usually come with a two-button mouse (unlike the one-button mouse used with the Macintosh). Some PCs come with three-button mice, as well as

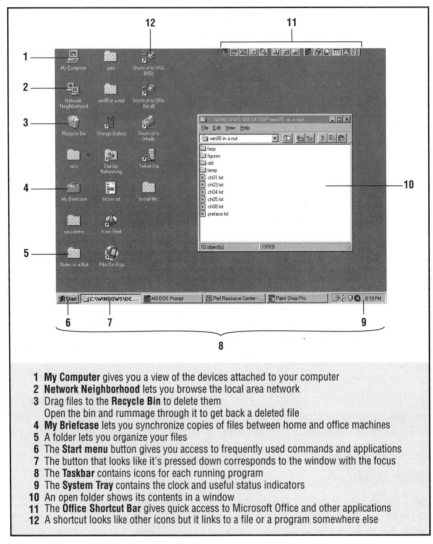

1 **My Computer** gives you a view of the devices attached to your computer
2 **Network Neighborhood** lets you browse the local area network
3 Drag files to the **Recycle Bin** to delete them
  Open the bin and rummage through it to get back a deleted file
4 **My Briefcase** lets you synchronize copies of files between home and office machines
5 A folder lets you organize your files
6 The **Start menu** button gives you access to frequently used commands and applications
7 The button that looks like it's pressed down corresponds to the window with the focus
8 The **Taskbar** contains icons for each running program
9 The **System Tray** contains the clock and useful status indicators
10 An open folder shows its contents in a window
11 The **Office Shortcut Bar** gives quick access to Microsoft Office and other applications
12 A shortcut looks like other icons but it links to a file or a program somewhere else

Figure 1-1: Windows 95 Desktop features

touchpads, trackballs, and other input devices. "Click" means to move the pointer to the desired screen object and click once with the button on the left. "Double-click" means to click twice in rapid succession with the button on the left. (Clicking twice slowly doesn't accomplish the same thing.) "Right-click" means to click with the button on the right. If your mouse has three buttons, you should just use the buttons on the left and the right, and read your computer's manual to find out how to use the button in the middle. (You can program the middle button to take over functions like double-clicking, cut and paste, and so on.)

- As in previous versions of Windows, double-click on any icon on the Desktop to open it. If the icon represents a program, the program is launched (i.e., opened). If the icon represents a data file, the file is opened by the associated program. The associations between files and programs are controlled by the filename extension (e.g., *.xls* for an Excel file, *.doc* for a Word file, *.htm* or *.html* for an HTML file, *.txt* for a text file, and so on). By default, the extensions don't show up on the Desktop, but they are part of the underlying file system, and can be viewed either with the Windows Explorer application or in a DOS window. If the icon represents a folder, a window opens, and the contents of the folder are shown as icons within the window, just as in Windows 3.1 or on the Macintosh.

- Single-click on an icon to select it. Click again (but not so quickly as to suggest a double-click) on the text, and the name of the icon will be highlighted, with a text insertion cursor showing. Type new text to rename the object represented by the icon, or click yet again to place the cursor and edit the name. You can also rename an icon by selecting it and pressing F2, or by right-clicking on it and choosing Rename.

- Click the right mouse button on any icon to pop up a menu of other actions that can be performed on the object. The contents of this menu vary depending on which object you click, so it is typically called the "context menu." The context menu for a file includes functions such as Open, Print, Delete, Rename, Create Shortcut, and so on. The context menu for the Desktop itself includes functions such as Arrange Icons or New (to create new empty files or folders). See Chapter 3 for additional details.

- Click and hold down the mouse button over an icon while moving the mouse to "drag" the object. Drag a file icon onto a folder icon to move it into the folder. Drag a file icon onto a program icon to open the file with that program. Drag it onto another file icon to rearrange the order of icons on the Desktop. Drag an open window by its title bar to move it around the Desktop. To copy a file rather than move it, press Ctrl while you drag the file to a new folder.

- By dragging a file with the right mouse button instead of the left, you can easily control whether you want to copy, move or create a shortcut with the file. With the release of the button, a small menu will pop up providing you with a set of options (Move Here, Copy Here, Create Shortcut(s) Here) to choose from.

- Hold down the Ctrl key while clicking to select an additional item. Anything already selected remains selected. You can select a group of files to delete, for instance, then drag them all to the Recycle Bin at one time. Hold down Shift while clicking to select a whole group of items at one time. Think of the first selection as an one endpoint, and the second selection (the Shift-click) as the other. Everything in between will be selected. The actual result depends a bit on the arrangement of items to be selected. If the items are in a linear list, the result is obvious, as is the case if they are in a neat rectangle, but if they are in some other geometric layout, you may need to experiment to get a feel for exactly what may be selected. For example, in Figure 1-2, clicking on My Briefcase and then Shift-clicking on the Win95 folder selected *outfile* and the *Notes in a Nut* folder, but not the file *andrew.txt*. Once you have selected a group of items, you can Ctrl-click on individual items in the group to deselect them.

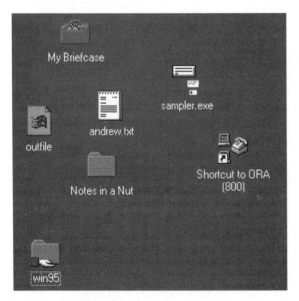

Figure 1-2: Selection techniques in the Explorer

- You can also select a group of icons or other graphical elements by starting a drag on the background of the window (rather than on a particular item). A rectangular "rubber band" outline will stretch from where you started holding down the mouse button to the point where you released it, and anything touching the rectangle will be selected.

- Ctrl-A will select everything in the folder (or on the Desktop, if that's where the focus is). This corresponds to Edit → Select All. (See "Windows and Menus" later in this chapter if you don't know what we mean by the term "focus.")

Starting Up Applications

Windows 95 has more ways to launch a program than almost any other operating system. You can:

- Double-click on a program icon.

- Pick the name of a program from the Start menu. (See "Start Menu" in Chapter 3 for details.)

- Type the name of a program in the Run dialog on the Start menu, or keep a DOS window open and type the name of the program at the DOS prompt. (Start → Run → command will open a DOS window.)

- Click on a program's icon in the Microsoft Office Shortcut Bar to start it. (The Office Shortcut Bar is available only if Microsoft Office is installed.) It can include icons not only for MS Office applications, but also for other programs whose shortcuts you install there.

- Double-click on a file associated with an application to launch that application and open the file.

- Right-click on a file, executable, or application icon and choose Open.

- Create shortcuts to files or applications (including DOS commands). A shortcut is a kind of "pointer" or link—a small file and associated icon that simply points to a file or program in another location. You can put these shortcuts on the Desktop, in the Start menu, and in many other "active locations." Double-click on a Desktop shortcut to launch the program. To launch programs automatically at startup, just place a shortcut in the startup directory (*Windows\Start Menu\Programs\StartUp*). Shortcuts are one of the really nice things about Windows 95. They are a key to much of its flexibility, so you should be sure to become familiar with how they work. See "Shortcuts" in Chapter 3 for more details.

Some programs are really "in your face." For example, if you install AOL 4.0, it puts an icon on the Desktop, in the Office Shortcut Bar, on the Start menu (in two places, no less!), and even shoehorns an icon into the System Tray, which is normally reserved for system status indicators. Other programs are fairly hard to find. Without this book, you might spend hours poking around in the Explorer trying to find a particular program.

Chapter 5, *Commands and Applications*, solves that problem. It includes a complete alphabetical list of almost every application and command that comes with Windows 95. The introduction to that chapter gives a bit more background about each of Win95's ways to launch programs, and a few hints about the best way to customize them for your use.

Windows and Menus

Any open window contains a frame with a series of standard decorations, as shown in Figure 1-3.

If multiple windows are open, only one has what is called the *focus*. The focus window is the one that will respond to keystrokes, mouseclicks, and so on. The window with the focus will usually be on top and will have its titlebar highlighted or colored in some way. To give a window the focus, just click on any visible portion of it, and it will pop to the front. Also, within a given window, only a single control has the focus—shown on buttons by an outlined focus rectangle, or in edit boxes with a blinking insertion point.

In addition, a window gets the focus any time you pop it up from the Taskbar. (More on that later.)

Often, new users are confused when they try to type into a window and nothing happens. It might be in front but still not have the focus, or the wrong control has the focus. (For example, a click on the Desktop might have moved the focus there.) Check to see that the desired window's titlebar is highlighted: for example,

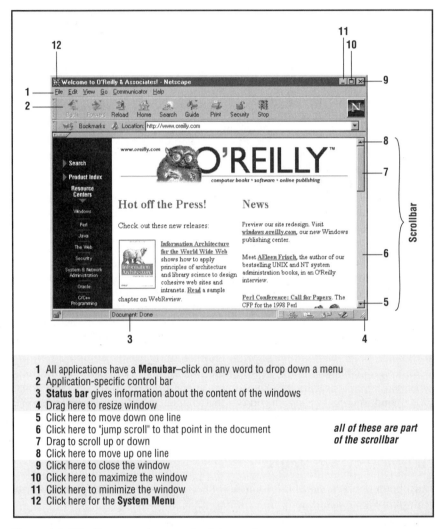

1 All applications have a **Menubar**–click on any word to drop down a menu
2 Application-specific control bar
3 **Status bar** gives information about the content of the windows
4 Drag here to resize window
5 Click here to move down one line
6 Click here to "jump scroll" to that point in the document   *all of these are part*
7 Drag to scroll up or down   *of the scrollbar*
8 Click here to move up one line
9 Click here to close the window
10 Click here to maximize the window
11 Click here to minimize the window
12 Click here for the **System Menu**

Figure 1-3: Window controls—standard decorations

the focus window's titlebar might be bright blue rather than light grey. But, like many other elements of Windows 95, the colors here can be specified by the user. See Control Panel → Display → Appearance → Inactive Title Bar.

Some windows can be set to have the property Always on Top. This means that when you drag another window into the same space, the one with Always on Top set will slide on top of the other window, hiding part of its contents. For example, the Taskbar is often set to be Always on Top. Note that a window can be on top without having the focus.

Almost every window has a few standard drop-down menus (File, Edit, and Help) as well as any application-specific menus. Click on the menu title to drop it down.

Click on an item in the menu to execute it. Any menu item whose name ends with . . . pops up a dialog box that asks you for more information. Any menu item with a right-pointing arrow leads to a cascading menu with more options, as shown in Figure 1-4. Note that depending on the screen layout, the menu may cascade to the left instead of the right, even though the arrow points to the right. If you decide not to execute any item on the menu, click anywhere else in the window to make the menu disappear.

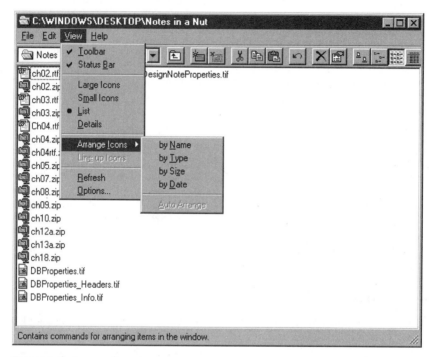

Figure 1-4: A cascading menu

You can also use keyboard accelerators to execute almost any menu item. See "Keyboard Accelerators" later in this chapter for details.

One thing that is often perplexing to new Windows 95 users is the dynamic nature of its menus.

As on the Macintosh, menu items that are grayed out are temporarily disabled. (For example, you can't delete or rename a file from a folder's File menu if no file is selected.) But Windows 95 goes one step further. Depending on what is selected in a window, you may see completely different items on the menu. See "Network Neighborhood" in Chapter 3 for an example.

Each window also has a "system menu" hidden behind the little icon on the left corner of the titlebar (see item 12 in Figure 1-3). You can also pop down the System menu by pressing Alt-space. The System menu duplicates the function of the maximize, minimize, and close buttons at the right end of the titlebar, but it also lets you move or resize the window without the mouse. (See "Keyboard Accelerators," the next section, for details.) There's also a Restore menu item, which is used to restore a maximized window to its normal open view on the Desktop. Sometimes the System menu adds other interesting functions. (For example, the system menu for non-graphical programs, such as the MS-DOS prompt or *xcopy32.exe*, provides Edit, Toolbar, and Properties menu items.)

The scrollbar sometimes appearing on the right of windows contains a rectangle called the *slider*. If you drag the slider up and down, the contents of the window move in the opposite direction. The arrows at the top and bottom of the scrollbar move the contents a line (or some similar increment) at a time. Clicking once in the empty area of the scrollbar causes the screen to scroll one screenful; clicking and holding scrolls until the slider reaches that point.

When you open a folder, the default behavior is to open a new window. You end up with an overlapping pile of windows on the Desktop. (Maybe that's why they call it the Desktop.) You can change the default behavior by choosing View → Options → Folder → single. With this setting, opening a subfolder within the current folder will open it in the same window. An icon on the window's toolbar lets you "back up" to previous folders. (See "Toolbar and Status Bar" later in this chapter for details.) This is a useful global change and will affect all folders. You can still open a folder in a separate window by holding down the Ctrl key while double-clicking on the folder you want to open.

Keyboard Accelerators

While the Explorer and many other Windows 95 applications provide graphical controls for most common operations, these programs also support an extensive array of *keyboard accelerators*. (We prefer this term to *keyboard shortcuts*, the term Microsoft uses, since they also use the word "shortcuts" for the ubiquitous link files that allow programs to be accessible from many different points in the system. Keyboard accelerators are sometimes also called *hotkeys*.) Some of these keyboard accelerators (such as F1 for help, or Ctrl-C to copy and Ctrl-V to paste) date back to the days of DOS; others are specific to Windows 95.

Appendix A, *Keyboard Accelerators*, gives a complete list of keyboard accelerators; some of the most important ones are:

Menu navigation

When the focus is on a window, press Alt followed by the underlined character in any menu title, followed by the underlined character in any menu item, to activate that menu and menu item. For example, Alt-F+O (that is, pressing Alt and F together, followed by an O) will select Open from the File menu, if the application has one. The underlined character will usually be the first character in the menu or menu item name, unless there is more than one item with the same name, in which case the program's author will have chosen some other letter. The menu pops up as you type the menu's accelerator, so you can see the item accelerators. You don't need to remember anything.

There are two exceptions to `Alt` as an initial character. Use `Ctrl-Esc` to pop up the Start menu, and right-click on an item to pop up its context menu. Once a menu is visible, typing any of the underlined characters will choose the corresponding item. In the Start menu, most items don't have underlined accelerators; just use the first letter.

Note that once a menu is visible, you can mix pointer clicks and keystrokes. For example, you could pop up the Start menu with the mouse, then type `S` for settings, then click on Control Panel. Or you could type `Ctrl-Esc`, click on Settings, and type `C` for Control Panel.

If there is a conflict, and multiple items on a menu have the same accelerator key, pressing the key repeatedly will cycle through the options. You must press `Return` to make a selection. Press `Return` when the correct menu item is highlighted.

In addition, pressing `Alt` or `F10` will select the first item on an application's menubar. Use the right and left arrows to move along the menubar and the up and down arrows to move to a specific menu item. Press `Enter` to execute the selected item.

Window manipulation without the mouse

`Alt`-space will minimize the system menu. The menu items all have individual accelerators. Accordingly, `Alt`-space+N will minimize a window; `Alt`-space+X will maximize it; `Alt`-space+R will restore a maximized window to its normal Desktop view, and `Alt`-space+C will close it. `Alt`-space+M will move a window and `Alt`-space+S will (re)size it using the arrow keys rather than the mouse. In either of the latter cases, the cursor will change to a little four-pointed arrow. Use the arrow keys to move or resize the window in the desired direction, and press `Enter` when you're happy with the result. Press `Esc` to cancel the operation.

Editing

In most applications, `Ctrl-X` will cut a selected item to an invisible storage area called the Clipboard, `Ctrl-C` will copy it to the Clipboard, and `Ctrl-V` will paste it into a new location. `Delete` will delete the selection without saving it to the Clipboard. There is a single system-wide clipboard shared by all applications. This lets you copy something from a document in one program and paste it into another document in another program. You can paste the same data repeatedly until it's replaced on the Clipboard by new data. (An optional application called the Clipbook lets you save a selection in the clipboard to use at a later date. See Chapter 5 for details.)

While you probably think of cut and paste operations as something you do with selected text or graphics in an application, the same keys can be used for file operations. For example, select a file on the Desktop, type `Ctrl-C`, move to another folder, type `Ctrl-V`, and you will have made a copy of the entire file, not of just its icon.

Ctrl-Alt-Del

Pops up a Close Program dialog box that allows you to interrupt a program that is "wedged" (not responding to its normal controls) or to reboot the system.

Alt-Tab and Alt-Esc

Let you switch to another application that is running or folder that is open. `Alt-Tab` pops up a little window with icons representing the open programs, so that you are in effect choosing from the open applications or folders; `Alt-Esc` cycles directly among the programs themselves. (More specifically, it drops the active window to the bottom of the pile.)

Tab and arrow keys

Within a window, `Tab` will move the focus between fields. Use `Shift-Tab` to move backwards. A field may be an individual data item or a list. For example, in a folder window, `Tab` will switch between the drop-down list in the toolbar and the file display area. Use arrow keys in either area to make a new selection without moving the focus. Sometimes a dialog box will have one or more regions, indicated by a rectangular box within the dialog box. The arrow keys will cycle through buttons or fields only within the current regions. `Tab` will cross region boundaries and cycle through all the buttons or fields in the dialog box.

Common Controls

Many application and system windows use a common set of controls in addition to the ubiquitous titlebar, menubar, system menu, and scrollbars. This section describes a few of these common controls.

Figure 1-5 shows some of these common controls in Control Panel → Display → Screen Saver and the additional dialog box that pops up from its Settings button.

Some of these common controls are as follows (see Figure 1-5 for an illustration of these controls):

1. Tabbed dialogs

   Settings may be grouped into separate tabbed dialog pages. For example, see Control Panel → System or Control Panel → Display. Click on any tab to bring that page to the front.

2. Radio buttons

   Radio buttons are used for mutually exclusive settings. Clicking on one causes any other that has been pressed to pop up, just like on an old-time radio. The button with the dot in the middle is the one that has been selected. Sometimes you'll see more than one group of buttons with a separate outline around each group. In this case, you can select one radio button from each group.

3. Drop-down lists

   Any time you see a downward-pointing arrow next to a text field, click on the arrow to drop down a list of other values. Often, a drop-down list contains a history of previous entries you've made into a text entry field. The down arrow (or `F4`) will also drop down the currently selected list. The arrow keys

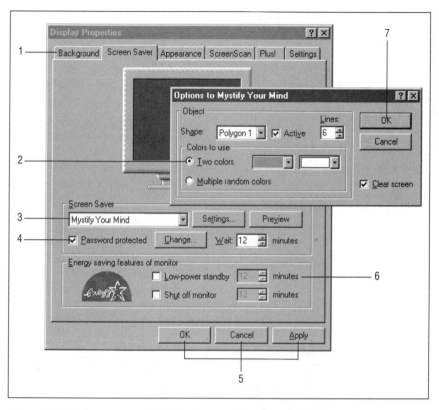

Figure 1-5: Common controls in Windows applications and dialogs

will scroll through the stored entries, even if the list is not already dropped down. Microsoft sometimes calls these lists "Look In Lists." For example, see Start → Find Files or Folders → Name & Location.

4. Checkboxes

Checkboxes are generally used for on/off settings. A checkmark means the setting is on; an empty box means it's off. Click on the box to turn the labeled setting on or off.

5. OK, Cancel, Apply

Most dialogs will have at least an OK and a Cancel button. Some also have Apply. The difference is that OK accepts the settings and quits the dialog, and Apply accepts the changes, but doesn't quit. (This is useful in a dialog with multiple tabs, so that you can apply changes before moving to the next tab.) Cancel quits without making any changes. If you click Cancel after clicking Apply, your changes will probably already have been applied, and will not revert to their original settings. But don't be surprised if some applications respond differently! Microsoft has never been clear with application developers about the expected behavior of these buttons.

6. Counters

You can either select the number and type in a new value, or click on the up or down arrows to increase or decrease the value. Any control like this one that is grayed out is disabled, being set first, or because the underlying operation is not currently available. In the dialog box shown in Figure 1-5, you need to click the "Low power standby" checkbox before you can change the counter.

7. The default button

When a set of buttons is displayed, the default button (the one that will be activated by pressing the Enter key) has a bold border around it. The button or other area in the dialog box that has the additional dashed outline has the focus. You can move the focus by clicking with the mouse, typing the underlined accelerator character in a button or field label, or by pressing the Tab or arrow keys.

In some dialog boxes, the default button (the button the Enter key presses) is "hard-coded"—it will always be the same. But in others, the default button follows the focus from button to button. For example, right-click on the Taskbar and select Properties. The Options tab (Figure 1-6) has the OK button hardcoded as the default. Note that the bold border will stay on this button even when you move the focus among the checkboxes. The Start Menu Programs tab (Figure 1-7) does not have a hard-coded default button. As you move the focus between buttons, the default button highlight moves with it. In Figure 1-7, the Add button currently has the focus and is accordingly the button that will be activated by pressing Enter.

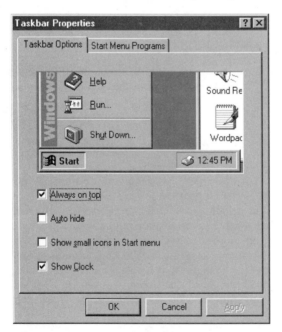

Figure 1-6: A tab containing a hard-coded default button

Using Windows 95

Figure 1-7: A tab without a hard-coded default button

Regardless of which button is the default, pressing **Esc** always has the same effect as clicking the Cancel button: it cancels the dialog box.

Two more common controls not shown in Figure 1-5 are:

Expand/collapse tree buttons

Hierarchical lists are often presented with small plus sign (+) buttons. Clicking on the + expands an item to show one additional level of detail. Clicking a – sign "collapses" (hides) all subsidiary details. For example, see *regedit* in Chapter 10, *The Registry*, or Control Panel → System → Device Manager.

Column headers

Sometimes Windows 95 presents ledger-like lists of items with multiple columns; each column has a header. For example, use Start → Find → Files or Folders to search for something like **.doc* (all files with a *.doc* extension). The returned list uses the Column Heads format, with headers such as Name, In Folder, Size, and so on (if you can't see them all, maximize the window with **Alt-Space-x**). Clicking on a column heading makes that column the basis for sorting the list; clicking again in the same column reverses the sort order. If icons are displayed in the list, the items are *active*; that is, you can click, double-click, or right-click on them to open them or perform some other action. Drag the lines dividing the headers to resize the width of columns or drag the headers to rearrange them. Double-click on column header separators to size columns automatically to the widest contents.

Views of Folders

The contents of a folder can be shown using large icons, using small icons, in a list, or in a list with details. Which view will be the default for a given window depends to some extent on the application developer. For folders, the default view is using large icons, but you can almost always use the View menu to change the viewing preferences.

If you want more information about files than their names, one of the most useful view is the Details view, which will show you not only the name of each file it contains but also its size, type, and the last date and time it was modified. The List view is the default choice for the Explorer, My Briefcase, and many other programs that list detailed information about files or system characteristics. Figure 1-8 shows the Details view of a folder.

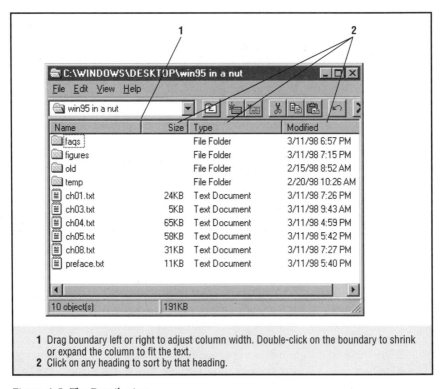

Figure 1-8: The Details view

Toolbar and Status Bar

By default, any folder has a visible Status bar at the bottom, which shows the number of items in the folder and the amount of disk space they occupy. Click View → Status bar to disable this display.

You can also turn on a Toolbar, using View → Toolbar. The Toolbar gives you all kinds of nifty navigation and data manipulation tools. These all duplicate function-

---

ality that you get from various menus and keyboard accelerators, but they are arranged in a handy palette.

Figure 1-9 shows the buttons on the Toolbar for a folder.

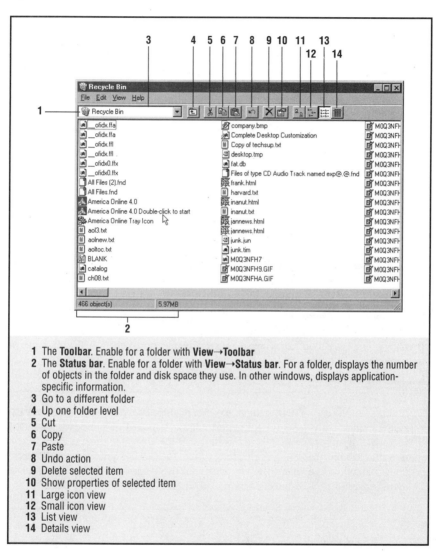

1 The **Toolbar**. Enable for a folder with **View→Toolbar**
2 The **Status bar**. Enable for a folder with **View→Status bar**. For a folder, displays the number of objects in the folder and disk space they use. In other windows, displays application-specific information.
3 Go to a different folder
4 Up one folder level
5 Cut
6 Copy
7 Paste
8 Undo action
9 Delete selected item
10 Show properties of selected item
11 Large icon view
12 Small icon view
13 List view
14 Details view

Figure 1-9: Toolbar and Status bar on a folder window

The Command Line

Many beginning Windows 95 users think that they have left the command line behind. Advanced users realize that the command line is often the quickest and most powerful way to get what you want. To create a *Hover* directory on your *C:*

drive and copy the necessary files from the Win95 CD-ROM to run the Hover game, for example, it is quicker to type:

```
C:\>mkdir \hover
C:\>copy d:\funstuff\hover\*.* \hover
```

than to click on My Computer; then click on the icon for your CD-ROM drive (containing the Windows 95 CD-ROM); then navigate to the folder *\FunStuff\Hover*; select all the files, then click File → Copy (or Ctrl-C); then navigate to a new location—either on the Desktop, or via the Explorer or My Computer, some other folder on your hard disk; then right-click to get the context menu; then click New → Folder; then type the folder name; then open the folder; and then click Edit → Paste (or Ctrl-V) to copy in the files. That's a heck of a sentence, and a heck of a lot of steps for what ought to be an easy task.

Once you learn the real name of a program rather than its Start menu shortcut name, it's almost always easier to start it from the Run prompt than it is to navigate the Start menu hierarchy. Which is really easier?

> Start → Programs → Accessories → System Tools → Backup

or:

> Start → Run → backup

The latter method is much faster, especially since, in the former, you're carefully dragging the mouse through cascading menus, where a slip of the mouse can have you getting somewhere entirely different than you planned.

Finally, there are many useful programs that don't appear on any menu. Once you know what you're doing, you can put shortcuts to them on the Start menu of the Desktop—but once you know what you're doing, you might just find it easier to type the program name!

Internet Explorer 4 (IE4), which has been shipped with all Windows 95 systems since early 1998 (OSR2.5) and will be standard in Windows 98, lets you type system commands as well as URLs into its address bar (the movable toolbar that can be "docked" to the Taskbar). If you're using IE4 as your primary system interface, our focus on the command line makes even more sense, since a command line will always be available on the Desktop.

Files, Folders, and Disks

Files are the basic unit of long-term storage on a computer. Files are organized into folders, which are stored on disks. (Under DOS, Windows 3.1, and Unix, folders were more often referred to as *directories*, and both terms are still used.) This section reviews fundamental filesystem concepts, including file and disk naming conventions and file types.

Disk Names

Like Windows 3.1, Windows 95 retains the basic DOS disk naming conventions:

A: Represents the first "floppy" (usually 3.5-inch) disk drive on the system

B: Represents the second floppy disk drive, if present

C: Represents the first hard disk drive

D: Often represents a CD-ROM drive, but can represent an additional hard disk drive or other removable drive

E:–Z:
      Represent additional hard disk drives or removable cartridges such as Zip or Jaz drives

In addition, drives on other networked systems can be mapped to drive letters, so that they appear as local drives when using this syntax. See "Network Neighborhood" in Chapter 3 for details. Networked drive letters aren't always consecutive.

Pathnames

Files are stored hierarchically on a disk, in folders (directories) that can be nested to any arbitrary level.

The file system on any disk begins with the root (top-level) directory, represented as a backslash. Thus C:\ represents the root directory on the C: drive. Each additional nested directory can be represented as another element in the path, with a backslash used to separate each one. *C:\Windows\System\Color* means that the *Color* folder is in the *System* folder in the *Windows* folder on the C: drive.

Each running program has its own current drive and current directory. Pathnames can be absolute (starting with the root) or relative (starting with the current directory). For example, if the focus is on the Desktop and you create a new directory (using the Desktop context menu → New → Folder), the pathname to that directory will be something like *\Windows\Desktop\New Folder*.

In many places in Windows 95 (including—but not limited to—the command line in Start → Run or the MS-DOS prompt), the special names . and .. refer to the current directory and the parent of that directory, respectively (the parent is the directory one up from the current directory); the directory name ... refers to the grandparent (two levels up), ... the great-grandparent, and so on.

The Explorer gives a tree-structured view of the file system. See Chapter 3 for details. In addition, any time an application asks you to open, save, or find a file, you will see a Browse button, which typically leads to a mini-Explorer view of the file system. All the icons in this view are active: for example, you can right-click on them. You can also right-click on the open area, for example, to create new folders on the fly. Figure 1-10 shows a Browse dialog box.

Network Pathnames

Files on another machine can be referred to via a UNC (Universal Naming Convention) pathname. The first element of a UNC pathname is a system name, prefixed

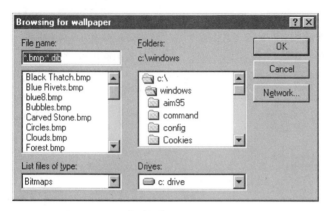

Figure 1-10: A Browse dialog box

by a double backslash. The second element is the remote file, folder or device's share name. A remote system that makes a resource available for sharing will define this name as well as any password required to access it.

For example, the UNC path *printsrv1**othello* refers to a printer named *othello* attached to a machine named *printsrv1*, and the UNC path *troy**nutshell**win95* refers to the *win95* folder in the *nutshell* folder on a machine named *troy*.

For more information on UNC pathnames, see "Network Neighborhood" in Chapter 3.

Short Names and Long Names

DOS and Windows 3.1 supported filenames with a maximum of eight characters, plus a three-character file type extension separated from the name by a period (e.g., *myfile.txt*). The maximum length of a pathname was 80 characters.

Legal characters included any combination of letters and numbers, extended ASCII characters with values greater than 127, and the following punctuation characters:

    $ % ^ ' ` - _ @ ~ ! ( ) # &

Windows 95 supports long filenames (up to 260 characters), which can include the additional punctuation characters:

    + , ; = [ ] .

(Appendix D, *Special/Reserved Characters*, lists the characters you can't use, and explains their special meaning to the system.)

For example, a file could be named *Sales Report 3-5-97*. Extensions are no longer limited to 3 characters; for example, *.html* is perfectly valid (and separate from *.htm*). Note, however, that *really* long filenames are impractical, since the maximum length of a pathname is 260 characters, including backslashes, depending on the application and file system you are using (see note).

Windows 95 supports pathnames up to MAX_PATH characters long. The MAX_PATH value can vary depending on the file system (e.g., FAT is 255 and VFAT is 260 characters). Even if the MAX_PATH value is 255 characters, an individual application may have restrictions that prevent the pathname from reaching the 255 character mark. This is the reason why you can't necessarily create a filename in the Explorer that is 255 characters long.

You can use embedded spaces in names, but since whitespace is often used to separate arguments to commands, you must place quotes around any name that includes spaces when using the DOS command line.

Windows 95's file system is case-preserving, but also case-insensitive. For example, "FooBar" will be preserved with the capital F and B. However, searches for "foobar", "FOOBAR", and so on, would all find this same file, and attempting to create a file named "FOOBAR" will fail if "FooBar" already exists.

Long filenames can be used in the version of DOS that comes with Windows 95. However, some of the older utilities that come with the system don't recognize long filenames, or use an old-style filename and extension to recognize the file type.

As a result, Windows 95 always keeps two names for each file: its long name (if one exists) and its short name and extension. The short name consists of the first six letters of the long name, a tilde, a number from 1 to 9 (the number is incremented for each long filename that would otherwise map to the same short name—after ~9, those six characters are reduced to five), and the file type extension, if any. (If an extension is longer than three characters, the first three characters will be used as the DOS extension.) Any spaces in the first six characters are removed.

For example, use the DOS *dir* command on the directory *C:\Windows\Desktop*, and you'll see that *My Briefcase* has become *MYBRIE~1*. (See Figure 1-11.) As another example, *\Program Files* becomes *\PROGRA~1*.

WARNING

Using older DOS disk utilities (such as backup programs, defragmenters, etc.) that don't understand long filenames could result in the loss of long filename information and file corruption.

File Types and Extensions

The extension of a DOS-style filename represents the type of the file, and is used by Windows 95 and many Windows applications to identify the application that will be used to open that file. Even though file extensions are not a reliable guide to a file's type, Windows 95 relies heavily on them.

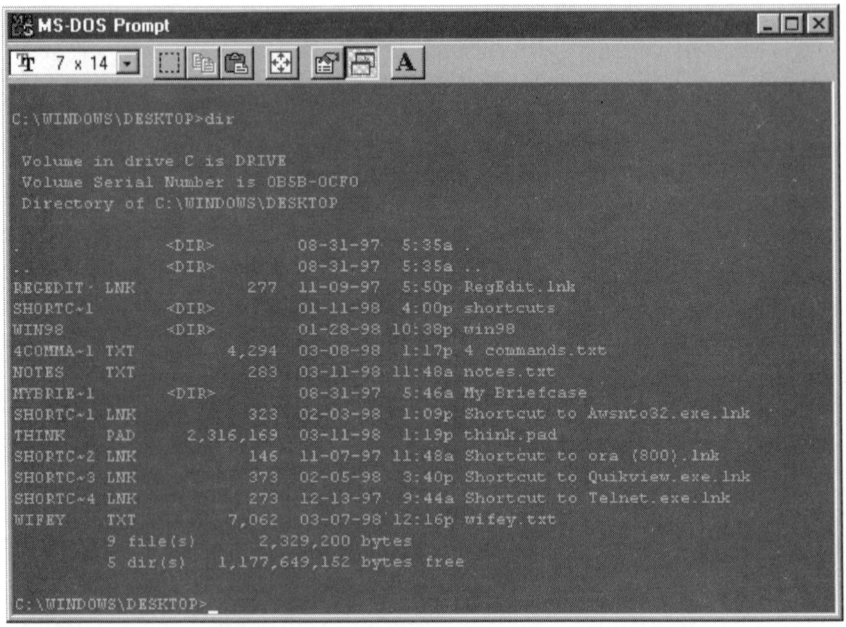

Figure 1-11: The dir command in a DOS box

Some filename extensions and their application associations are:

.doc
> A Word document

.xls
> An Excel spreadsheet

.txt
> A text file, to be opened with Notepad

Appendix B, *Filename Extensions*, gives a list of the most common extensions and their associated applications. If you click on a file of an unknown type, the Open With dialog will pop up. See "File Types" in Chapter 3 for details.

Extensions are hidden by Windows 95 by default. This is a very bad idea, since extensions are still used by the system to identify file types. Change this in the Explorer by selecting View → Options → View and unchecking "Hide MS-DOS file extensions for file types that are registered."

Online Help

Most windows have a Help menu, which you can pull down with the mouse or by typing Alt-H. In addition, press F1 at almost any time to launch an online index to help topics or context help for the current dialog box. The Index tab is often the most useful. Just type a few words that relate to what you're interested in, and if they match a help topic heading, you'll go right to the appropriate point in the index. Try to use keywords like sound, taskbar, or modem. (See *winhlp32* in Chapter 5 for more information.)

In addition, some applications (and many system property sheets and dialog boxes) include a question mark icon on the titlebar. Click on the question mark; the cursor will change to a question mark and an arrow. Move it to some item in the window that you're confused about and click. A small window that explains the purpose of the button or other user interface element will pop up. This is one of the nicest features of Windows 95: don't miss it. (The question mark help is often better than the F1 help, and there's no searching involved.) However, both forms of help are unreliable—sometimes they'll tell you just what you need to know, but more often they'll simply repeat the obvious.

Furthermore, if you hold the pointer over many screen objects (such as items on the Taskbar or a window's toolbar), additional information will pop up in a little "tooltips" bubble that stays up until you move the pointer. This feature is usually limited to toolbars and other main controls—you'll rarely see tooltips in dialogs. In most cases, this will give a phrase describing the operation of the object. In others, it might provide additional functionality. For example, placing the pointer on the system clock pops up the date.

In many applications, even those without the question mark icon on the titlebar, right-clicking a user interface item will pop up a little "What's This?" tooltips bubble. Click on the bubble for an expanded explanation.

At the command line, you can get help on the available command-line options by typing:

```
commandname /?
```

Finally, Windows 95 includes a number of "readme" files, which typically contain "release notes"—information about special handling required for specific applications or hardware devices. The file *C:\Windows\readme.txt* contains a list of all the other "readme" files on the system. Or you can just look in the *Windows* directory for any file with the extension *.txt*. Use Notepad or any other ASCII text editor or word processor to read them.

Shutting Down

You shouldn't just turn off the power to a Windows 95 machine, since it caches a lot of data in memory and needs to write it out before shutting down. See "Shut Down" in Chapter 3 for additional details.

CHAPTER 2

Versions of Windows 95

One of the difficulties in writing about Windows 95 is that there are several different versions available.

The original release of Windows 95 was on 9/24/95.

Immediately thereafter, Microsoft started making patches available on their web site (fixes for Exchange, Dial-Up Networking, etc.). A few months later, they consolidated all the patches into "Service Pack 1" (a.k.a. SP1, Service Release 1, or SR1) and made that available as a single download. More information is available at the following URL:

http://www.microsoft.com/windows95/info/service-packs.htm

After the release of SR1, Microsoft came out with additional updates, available at:

http://www.microsoft.com/windows95/info/system-updates.htm

The second set of updates was incorporated into a new service release called OSR2, along with some new system-level features, such as FAT32 (a new, more efficient file system), a DriveSpace update, MMX support, and other new additions. This release is called OSR2 instead of SR2 because it was available only to OEM vendors—those vendors who preinstalled Win95 on new machines. (This means that previous users of Windows 95 can't get FAT32—legally—until Windows 98.) More information on OSR2, including a listing of all the improvements, and links to the ones that can be downloaded, is available at:

http://www.microsoft.com/windows/pr/win95osr.htm

Soon after OSR2, Microsoft came out with OSR2.1. OSR2.1 adds support for USB (Universal Serial Bus) devices. Other than that, it is exactly the same as OSR2. The 2.0 to 2.1 update is available for download on some Internet sites, but Microsoft doesn't offer it.

Lastly, there's OSR2.5. Released in February 1998, it contains even more updates, but it's not as significant as the jump from the original release to OSR2. The most significant change is that it incorporates IE4 (Internet Explorer 4) rather than IE 3.02, as in OSR2. Again, this is an OEM release, which means that only OEM vendors can get it, but OEMs still have the option of installing OSR2, OSR2.1, or OSR2.5. Some OEMs still preinstall the original release, even though the machines have USB, MMX, and large hard disks (>2GB)—perhaps they need to use up their old licenses. More information on OSR2.5 is available at:

http://www.microsoft.com/windows95/info/osr25.htm

How can you tell which version you have? Right-click on the My Computer icon on the desktop and choose Properties from the context menu that appears. (You can get to the same screen by clicking Control Panel → System.) The revision code will be displayed to the right of the Windows logo. If it says Windows 95 4.00.950, you have the original Windows 95 release; if it says:

> Windows 95 4.00.950 A, you have SR1
> Windows 95 4.00.950 B, you have OSR2
> Windows 95 4.00.950 C, you have OSR2.5

But you can't take these codes as gospel. Control Panel → System takes this information from the Registry values `Version`, `VersionNumber`, and `SubVersionNumber` in the Registry, at the key `HKLM\SOFTWARE\Microsoft\Windows\CurrentVersion`. These values could easily be modified by an OEM, an application, or even a user, and you'd never know the difference. See Chapter 10, *The Registry*, for more information.

The *ver* command (see Chapter 5, *Commands and Applications*) gives a slightly less fragile report. Unfortunately, it uses slightly different codes. For example, you'll see:

```
C:\>ver
Windows 95 [Version 4.00.950]
```

for the original version of Windows 95, which matches the codes from Control Panel → System, but:

```
C:\>ver
Windows 95 [Version 4.00.1111]
```

for OSR2.

If you have the original version of Windows 95, you may or may not have the patches installed, depending on your vendor, or, if you're at a corporate site, on your system administrator.

Add to all this confusion the fact that individual hardware vendors may add components of their own, from custom screen savers and backgrounds to various preinstalled programs, and it's quite likely that your software may differ from that described in this book.

In general, we describe the OSR2 release, but if something is available only in the original release, or in SR1, we try to point that out. We also do describe some of the features available in Microsoft's optional Plus! pack, tools that are available in the Microsoft Windows 95 Resource Kit, and some tools that are available only by downloading them from the Microsoft web site.

Another point that is very important to understand when trying to match up what's documented in this book with your own system is that even for a given release of Windows 95, it's rare that everything on the CD-ROM gets installed. Using the Control Panel applet Add/Remove Programs (see Chapter 5), you can see what components have been installed and add or remove components fairly painlessly. However, there are some optional (one might even say "hidden") programs that can't be installed from the control panel. You need to actually browse the contents of the CD-ROM and copy the necessary files yourself.

> In some (but not all) recent OEM versions of Windows 95, the components installable from the CD-ROM via Add/Remove Programs are actually already loaded on your hard disk, in a compressed form (so called "Cabinet files") in the directory \ *Windows\Options*. However, the components that you must install manually do still require that you have the actual Windows 95 CD-ROM.

If you don't have a program or a feature we describe, you can just grin and bear it, but you can generally find just about anything, either on your CD-ROM, on Microsoft's site, or on some other software archives available over the Internet.

PART II

Alphabetical Reference

CHAPTER 3

The Windows 95 User Interface

This chapter provides an alphabetical reference to many of the major user interface elements in the Windows 95 Desktop.

The Control Panel and Remote Network Access (used by facilities such as the Microsoft Network, Internet Explorer, and Dial-Up Networking) are covered in separate chapters, since they are complex environments in their own right. Many of the utilities and accessories on the Start menu are covered in Chapter 5, *Commands and Applications*, since they are also accessible from the command line.

The alphabetical reference entries are as follows:

> Briefcase
> Clipboard
> Context Menus
> Desktop
> Dial-Up Networking
> The Explorer
> File Types
> Find Files and Folders
> Icons
> Inbox
> Internet
> Login
> My Computer
> Network Neighborhood
> Office Shortcut Bar
> Printers
> Properties
> Recycle Bin
> Run
> Send To
> Shortcuts

> Shut Down
> Start Menu
> Startup Folder
> System Tray
> Taskbar

Note that because of the variety of Windows 95 installation options, not every system will have each of these features on its Desktop. Note also that while most of these items are visible on the Desktop, some are contained within folders or menus. In addition, a few (context menus, File Types, and Properties) refer to context-specific menus or dialogs that can be popped up from many different objects, and will be different for each object.

Each entry contains a brief description, a shorthand "path" showing how to get to the item, a figure (if some aspect of the user interface is sufficiently complex to require it), and a set of notes focusing on features that are buried in the user interface, not obvious, or undocumented.

Almost all of these user-interface elements are provided by the Windows 95 Explorer. If a user interface element has a corresponding file or folder (as well as being an element of the Explorer), it is shown on the title line for the entry:

Entry Name *\pathname*

Brief description.

The path notation we use to show how to reach each user interface element is described in the Preface. If there is more than one way to reach a given user interface element, multiple paths are shown. For example:

> My Computer → Printers
> Start → Settings → Printers

Briefcase *\Windows\Desktop\My Briefcase*

Synchronize files between two computers.

> Desktop → My Briefcase
> Desktop → context menu → New → Briefcase

Description

Before going on a trip, you might want to copy a set of files on your Desktop to the Briefcase, then move the Briefcase to the laptop (or to a floppy disk). You can edit either the original files or the ones in the Briefcase. Then, when you return, copy the Briefcase back to the original machine and use its Briefcase menu → Update to synchronize the Briefcase and original copies of the files. If the machines are networked, you can synchronize files without having to copy the Briefcase back and forth. Synchronization will work with UNC paths to networked files or folders.

To put a file in the Briefcase, you can drag its icon to the Briefcase folder, or can use the Send To menu, which lists My Briefcase as an option. See Figure 3-1.

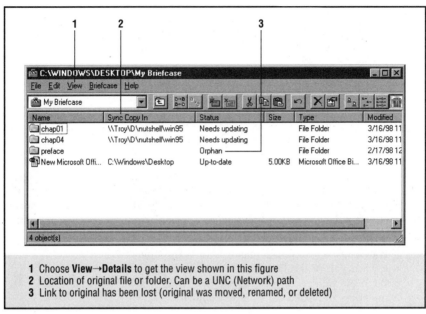

Figure 3-1: My Briefcase

Notes

- You can initiate an update from either the Briefcase menu or the File menu. The Briefcase menu gives you an Update All option, and the File menu allows the update of only selected files (though you can of course Select All).

- When you update the contents of the Briefcase, Windows displays several details, including the modification date of each file, and the direction in which the Briefcase intends to make the update. You can right-click on the directional arrow to change the direction or skip the update.

- The Briefcase mechanism uses the date and time of update to determine which of the two copies of the file is the most up-to-date, so be sure that the clocks on both machines are synchronized.

- My Briefcase is automatically created on the Desktop if you choose Portable setup when installing Windows 95, or if you choose it as part of a Custom installation. To install it later, use:

  Control Panel → Add/Remove Programs → Windows Setup → Accessories → Details → Briefcase

- Create a Briefcase on a floppy if you frequently work on the same set of files at work and at home. You can then synchronize (Briefcase → Update All) at the beginning and end of each day to make sure you have the latest copy on both machines.

- You can create multiple Briefcases by right-clicking on the Desktop and choosing New → Briefcase, or use the following command line:

```
rundll32 syncui.dll,Briefcase.Create
```

(Send To is probably the easiest way to populate a Briefcase, but the command line could be useful if, for instance, you wanted to create a batch file that created a new Briefcase and then copied the contents of the current folder to it.)

You will need multiple Briefcases if you are using floppy disks for the transport mechanism and you have more files than will fit on a single disk. By default, Send To will recognize only My Briefcase, but you can drag and drop to any Briefcase. (See Send To for a discussion of how to add additional items—such as other Briefcases—to the Send To menu.)

- Properties → Update Status for any file in the Briefcase will give details about which version is considered more up to date, and gives options for changing the order of update. (For example, if you'd made changes in the Briefcase, but wanted to revert to the original copy of the file, you could so choose. You can also unlink the Briefcase and original copy by selecting Split from original.)

- If you screw up and make changes to both copies of the file, the Briefcase will warn you of the fact. Some applications are smart enough to walk you through the process of merging the files, but for most, you'll have to look at both copies and make the changes manually.

Visto Corp (*http://www.visto.com*) has a new twist on the Briefcase. For $9.95 a month, you can keep a Visto Briefcase on their web site, and have access to it from wherever you are. The Visto Assistant synchronizes the web-based Briefcase with the one on your disk. It also synchronizes with contact managers including Microsoft Outlook, Lotus Organizer, and Starfish Sidekick.

Clipboard

A shared, system-wide storage area for holding and moving data.

Edit → Cut (Ctrl-X)
Edit → Copy (Ctrl-C)
Edit → Paste (Ctrl-V)

Description

The Clipboard is an invisible storage area, unless you've installed the Clipboard or Clipbook viewer. Data can be cut or copied to the Clipboard, then pasted in a new location, in either the same application or a different application. You must first select the data to be cut or copied. Data in the Clipboard can be pasted again and again, until it is replaced by new data.

Notes

- The Clipboard holds only one item at a time. Cutting or copying something to the Clipboard replaces its previous contents.

- You can paste only data that an application is prepared to receive. For example, you cannot paste an image into an application (such as DOS) that recognizes only text. (DOS can't *really* even paste text, but Windows simulates it by typing out the contents of the Clipboard.) Note that applications like Photoshop have their own non-Windows clipboards, and export the data *sometimes* when you switch applications.

- The Clipboard and Clipbook programs display the otherwise-invisible Clipboard. In other words, these programs are Clipboard "viewers." The Clipboard itself is an area of memory. See *clipbrd and clipbook* in Chapter 5.

- In a DOS window, you must use the buttons on the taskbar to make selections, copy, and paste.

- Some older (Windows 3.0) applications instead recognize the keyboard accelerators `Ctrl-Insert` for copy and `Shift-Insert` for Paste.

See Also

clipbrd and clipbook in Chapter 5

Context Menus

Right-clicking on many windows, icons, or user interface items will pop up a menu with various special operations. The menu's contents will vary depending on which item you've right-clicked, so it is normally called the context menu.

To view the context menu for an object:

Right-click
`Shift-F10` when the object is selected

Description

Figure 3-2 shows the context menu for a folder. Context menus for other types of objects are discussed in the entry for each object.

Notes

- Context menus exist for all of the major interface elements—files, folders (including system folders like My Computer, Network Neighborhood, Recycle Bin, and My Briefcase), the Desktop, the Taskbar, the System Tray, and so on—but they often also exist for elements within an application window or dialog.

  At the least, individual buttons or other user interface elements often have a context menu consisting of the single entry What's This?, which gives a short description of what that element is used for. However, in some cases, the context menu is more extensive. For example, right-clicking in the results window of a Find search yields a View menu that allows you to customize the way the results are displayed.

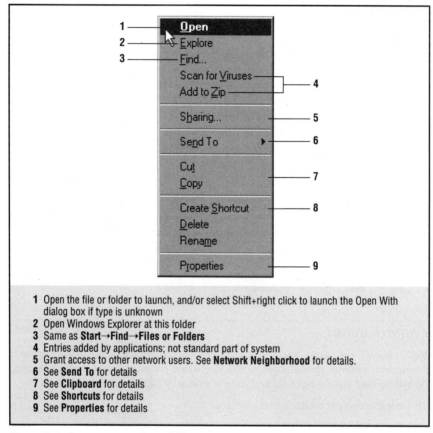

Figure 1 — context menu callouts and legend:

1 — **Open**
2 — Explore
3 — Find...
4 — Scan for Viruses / Add to Zip
5 — Sharing...
6 — Send To ▶
7 — Cut / Copy
8 — Create Shortcut / Delete / Rename
9 — Properties

1 Open the file or folder to launch, and/or select Shift+right click to launch the Open With dialog box if type is unknown
2 Open Windows Explorer at this folder
3 Same as **Start→Find→Files or Folders**
4 Entries added by applications; not standard part of system
5 Grant access to other network users. See **Network Neighborhood** for details.
6 See **Send To** for details
7 See **Clipboard** for details
8 See **Shortcuts** for details
9 See **Properties** for details

Figure 3-2: Context menu for a folder

If you're ever stuck, try right-clicking on a user-interface element and see if anything helpful pops up.

- Right-clicking on the titlebar of a window gives you the context menu for the window. (This is typically the same system menu that you will get by clicking on the icon in the leftmost corner of the titlebar.) Right-clicking in the body of the window gives you the context menu for the application, or the selected element within the application, if one exists. Note that this is different from the context menu that you get by clicking on the program's icon when it is not running.

- The context menu for the Desktop includes a New entry, which allows you to create a new Folder, Shortcut, or empty file.

- The bold item (usually, but not always, at the top) is the default action, carried out when you double-click. View → Options → File Types → Edit lets you change the default action as well as letting you add new actions.

Any program or command line on the system can be made into a new "verb" on a context menu using View → Options → File Types → Edit from any folder or Explorer window. See "File Types" later in this chapter. (To create new verbs directly in the Registry, see Chapter 4, "Customizing Context Menus," in *Windows Annoyances*, by David Karp, O'Reilly & Associates. Note that customizing the context menu for HKEY_CLASSES_ROOT*\shell lets you create verbs for all files; normally they'll apply to particular file types, based in turn on file extensions; objects—drive, folder, unknown, etc.; or URL prefixes—http, ftp, etc.).

Desktop

\Windows\Desktop
\Windows\Profiles\<username>\Desktop

The most visible element of the Explorer user interface. Supports icons, windows, and drag-and-drop functionality.

An overview of the Desktop is provided in Chapter 1, *Using Windows 95*. This section mainly consists of a few implementation notes and useful tips.

Notes

- The Desktop is a folder, and can contain files and other folders. When you put something on the Desktop, you are really putting it in the folder *\Windows\Desktop* (or *\Windows\Profiles\<username>\Desktop* if multiple user profiles are in use). Similarly, any changes you make to that folder—even from the DOS prompt—will result in immediate changes on the Desktop. Rename, copy, or delete files in *\Windows\Desktop* using the command line or the Explorer and the Desktop will change accordingly.

- The Desktop is created and maintained by the Explorer (*explorer.exe*). The Explorer creates the Desktop only when it is run during startup, using the shell= setting in the file *\Windows\system.ini*. Subsequent invocations of the Explorer present the normal paned view. If shell= is given some other command (e.g., *command.com*), the Desktop, the Start menu, and the Taskbar may not be shown.

- Some icons on the Desktop (such as My Computer, Recycle Bin, and Network Neighborhood) aren't files or folders, but system objects. They act like folders but have some special characteristics—including additional menus.

- Context menu → New allows you to create a new Folder, Shortcut, or empty file of various types.

- Desktop Properties (also on the context menu) is the same as Start → Settings → Control Panel → Display.

- Icons can be arranged on the Desktop by type (system facilities, folders, and files, in that order), alphabetically by name, by date (with the most recent first), and by size (with the smallest first). Select AutoArrange if you want the icons in neat rows; unselect it if you want to be able to drag them anywhere on the Desktop. When the Desktop gets full, autoarrange stops working.

- With Microsoft Internet Explorer 4 or Windows 98, you can choose that the "Active Desktop" be viewed as a Web page, thereby making it customizable with HTML, JavaScript, animated GIF files, and so on. See the forthcoming *Windows 98 in a Nutshell*.

Dial-Up Networking

Establish a network connection over a modem.

> My Computer → Dial-Up Networking → *connection*
> Launch any Internet-aware application (Internet Explorer, telnet, ftp, etc.)

Description

Dial-Up Networking provides a collection of facilities for connecting to remote computers over a phone line, most commonly using the Point to Point Protocol (PPP). Dial-Up Networking also supports other protocols, including the Serial Line Internet Protocol (SLIP), Novell NRN Network Connect, Windows for Workgroups, X.25, and ISDN. SLIP is available only with an add-on, unless you're using OSR2 or later.

Before you can use Dial-Up Networking, you must first define a new connection. This consists of:

- A location, which defines the characteristics of the place from which you will be dialing. This includes information such as whether you need to dial a prefix to get an outside line, whether you are using a calling card, whether you need to disable call waiting, and whether the location uses tone or pulse dialing.

- Information about the connection itself, such as the phone number to be dialed, the protocol to be used, the login script, and so on. The protocol can be changed only after the connection has been created, using the properties sheet. The script requires OSR2 or an add-in you can download from Microsoft.

- Dial-Up Networking configuration can be fairly straightforward, but it can also get extremely complex. For that reason, the details of how to set up connections are given in Chapter 7, *Dial-Up Networking*. The remainder of this entry gives a few tips for using existing connections.

Notes

- To start up an existing connection, simply start any Internet-aware application that requires a connection, such as Internet Explorer, Netscape Navigator, *telnet*, or *ftp*. The connection last used by that application will be started up again.

- To start up a connection explicitly, simply double-click on its icon (sometimes called a "connectoid"). A Connect To dialog will give you a chance to change some (but not all) of the dialing parameters before initiating the connection. (For example, you can type in a different phone number, but you can't cause the connection to remember that number.) You can change the username and password, select among available Locations, and create new locations. In OSR2, this box can be turned off.

- The Dial Properties button on the Connect To dialog allows you to define new locations, but not new phone numbers to be dialed. To change the phone number, you need to open the Properties of the connection itself.

- The name you give to the connection appears as a file in the Dial-Up Networking folder. If you will be using the connection often, you may want to make a shortcut and put it on the Desktop. Connections can be renamed just like files.

- Logging in to remote computers can be tricky, since you are establishing a dialog between two computers. If you are having trouble, it often helps to log in manually, so you can see exactly what is happening. To do this, you need to click *connection* → Properties → General → Configure → Options → Bring Up Terminal Window Before Dialing. See Chapter 7 for additional details.

- The Connections menu on the Dial-Up Networking folder has a settings item that pops up a property sheet with a number of useful overall options, including:

  - Whether or not to show an icon on the Taskbar after you've connected (OSR2 only).

  - Whether or not to put up the confirmation dialog before dialing (OSR2 only).

  - Whether to redial a failed connection, how many times, and how often.

  - Whether to prompt before auto-dialing whenever you start up a network application. This option is enabled only if you've checked "Connect to the Internet as needed" on Control Panel → Internet → Connection. Note that if autodialing is enabled, applications like Internet Explorer, telnet, and FTP will start up Dial-Up Networking even if you already are connected via a direct Internet connection. You'll have to click Cancel to continue, using the direct connection.

- The command line for launching an existing "connectoid" is:

```
rundll32 rnaui.dll,RnaDial connectoid-name
```

  where *connectoid-name* is the name of the connectoid. This is useful if the Explorer is not your shell.

The Explorer

\Windows\Explorer.exe

View all the folders and files on your computer.

  Start → Run → **explorer**
  Start → Programs → Windows Explorer
  Context menu → Explore
  Shift-double-click on any folder

Most users think of the Desktop interface as "Windows 95" and the Explorer as an application within it, but in fact, the Explorer is the program that creates and maintains the Desktop and many of the other visible features of Windows 95. However, when you run the Explorer as a separate application, it provides a useful two-pane view of files and folders that allows you to navigate the file system easily. (See Figure 3-3.) It is that view of the Explorer that is discussed here.

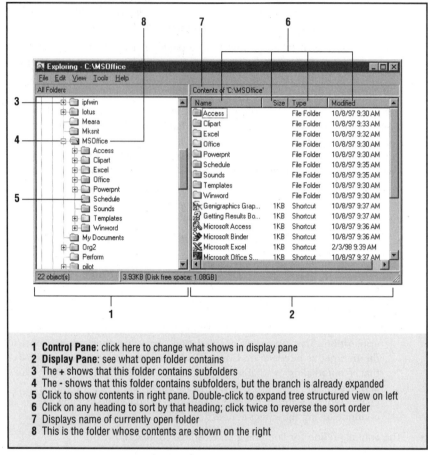

1 **Control Pane**: click here to change what shows in display pane
2 **Display Pane**: see what open folder contains
3 The **+** shows that this folder contains subfolders
4 The **-** shows that this folder contains subfolders, but the branch is already expanded
5 Click to show contents in right pane. Double-click to expand tree structured view on left
6 Click on any heading to sort by that heading; click twice to reverse the sort order
7 Displays name of currently open folder
8 This is the folder whose contents are shown on the right

Figure 3-3: The double-pane Explorer window

Unlike the Windows 3.1 interface, in which you end up with dozens of open windows if you want to navigate somewhere deep in the file system, the Explorer maintains a tree-structured view of the file system in the left pane and opens only a single target folder in the right pane. This behavior applies only to folders, however. If you double-click on a file or program icon in the right pane, a separate application window will open, just as it does on the Desktop.

It may help to think of the left pane as the "navigation pane"—actions here control what will be displayed on the right pane. The right, or display pane, shows the results. Think of this pane as equivalent to any other window, such as a folder open on the Desktop. (This will become very clear to you if you select an alternative view such as View → Large Icons. The right pane will then resemble a normal folder view.)

- Click on any folder in the left pane to show its contents in the pane on the right.

- A plus sign (+) by any folder indicates that it contains subfolders. Click on the plus sign (or double-click on the folder itself) to show the subfolders as part of the tree-structured view in the left pane. The plus sign will change to a minus sign. Click on the minus sign (or double click on the open folder) to collapse that branch of the filesystem tree.

- You can perform the same actions on folders or files shown in either the Explorer pane that you can perform on them in any open window:

  - Double-click on any file or folder in the right pane to open it. A folder will open in the Explorer pane; a file will open its associated application.

  - Drag a file or folder from the Explorer pane onto the Desktop or into any other folder.

  - Pop up the context menu for any file or folder and use it to create Short-cuts, Send To, Rename, Delete, or any other operation that you can perform on files.

Everything that works on the Desktop works in the Explorer, because the Desktop is just part of the Explorer. Each additional instance of the Explorer that you start up is actually just a separate thread of execution in the same program that also creates and maintains the Desktop.

Quick Navigation Tips

Scrolling around full Explorer windows can take a long time. Typing the first letter of any file or folder will jump right to the first matching file or folder. Press the letter again to go to the next matching file or folder. This behavior applies only to folders that are already expanded (i.e., visible in the left pane).

Backspace will take you back up one level in the folder hierarchy. When the focus is in the left pane, the left arrow will do the same, but will also close the open branch. The right arrow will expand branches (any folder with a + next to it); the up and down arrows will move through the expanded branches in a linear fashion, but will not expand any branch that is not already open. Press Enter to expand or open the currently selected folder.

Cut, copy, and paste keys (Ctrl-X, Ctrl-C, and Ctrl-V) can be used in the right pane to move or copy files from one location to another. Much easier than drag and drop! Ctrl-A selects all.

To get a two-pane Explorer view of any folder, press Shift while you click on the folder to open it.

Notes

- The portion of the file system that is initially displayed in the Explorer depends on how you invoke the program.

  Start → Programs → Windows Explorer
  > Starts at C:\

  any folder → context menu → Explore
  > Starts at selected folder

> Start → Run → `explorer` *pathname*
> Give *pathname* as argument, or *C:* by default

- The Explorer has many command-line options. See *explorer* in Chapter 5 for details.

- The amount of free space left on your disk is shown in the Explorer status bar when you select a disk icon.

- If your prefer the Windows 3.1 File Manager, use Start → Run → `winfile`. You can start the Windows 3.1 Program Manager with Start → Run → `prog-man`. Keep in mind that you can't view long filenames in *winfile*.

The Explorer is smart enough to figure out when a floppy disk is full. So you can safely go to a large folder, Select All, copy, and paste to a floppy. When the disk is full, you'll be prompted to insert a new disk.

File Types

Open a file of an unknown type, or associate file types with a different application.

> *any folder* → View → Options → File Types

If you try to open a file of an unknown type (by double-clicking or using context menu → Open, or using the File → Open command from within an application), you will get a dialog that asks you to identify which program you want to use to open the file (see Figure 3-4).

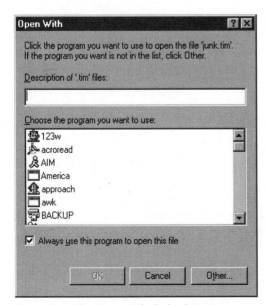

Figure 3-4: The Open With dialog box

If you want to force a new association (for example, because you want *.htm* and *.html* files to be opened by Netscape rather than by Internet Explorer), or just want to open a file with another application than the one that opens it by default, select the file (click once), then hold the Shift key down and right-click on the file, choosing Open With from the context menu.

Or go to View → Options → File Types in any folder Explorer window. Scroll through the list of file types, then click Edit to change any particular association. You can also change associations for objects such as drive, folder, and unknown— see "Context Menus" earlier in this chapter. Click New to create a new file/program association. Figure 3-5 shows a sample Edit dialog box for the Text Document (*.txt*) file type.

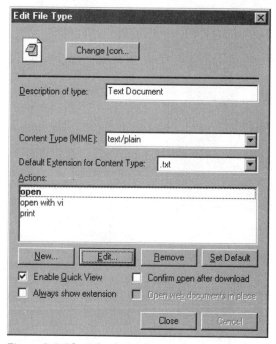

Figure 3-5: The Edit dialog box

For an existing file type, you will typically see one or two actions, such as Open or Print. The one that is in bold type is the default action—the one that will be invoked when you double-click on a file of the specified type.

Other actions will be placed on the file's context menu. Note that you can have more than one open action (although only one can be the default). For example, a text file could have an Open with Notepad action and an Open with Word action or any other program that allows you to edit text files (such as the DOS *edit* command, or a third-party editor such as emacs or vi from the MKS Toolkit).

Click New or Edit to create a new action or edit an existing one. The resulting dialog lets you specify the command line to be used. For example, to print using Notepad, use the command C:\Windows\notepad.exe /p. (Command-line options for all standard Windows 95 commands are given in Chapter 5. For third-party applications, these may be hard to find.)

Not all programs give access to their internal functions via command line options, though. For example, look at the open action for the content type *.gif* image in Figure 3-6.

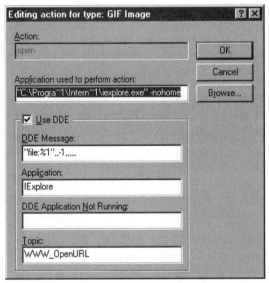

Figure 3-6: Dynamic Data Exchange in an open action dialog box

Sure enough, there's a command line. But "Use DDE" is also checked. DDE stands for Dynamic Data Exchange; it is an ostensibly defunct technology (supposedly replaced by OLE, COM, ActiveX, and who knows what else) that actually plays an important part in Windows 95. For example, both the Explorer and Netscape Navigator can be "driven" with DDE. While command lines specify options given to a program just before it starts, DDE commands can be sent to an already running program. If you're interested in one widely used DDE interface (it's supported by Microsoft as well as Netscape), see "Netscape's DDE Implementation" at either of the following locations:

> *http://developer.netscape.com/docs/manuals/communicator/DDE/abtdde.htm*
> *http://www.spyglass.com/products/smosaic/sdi/sdi_spec.html*

See also:

> *http://www.creativelement.com/software/delegate.html*

Note that you can have more than one extension for a content type. For example, if you've got Netscape Navigator installed, the type Netscape Hypertext Document corresponds to the extensions *.htm*, *.html*, *.xbm*, and *.shtml*. Files with any of these extensions will be opened by Netscape Navigator. See Chapter 10, *The Registry*, for an explanation of this behavior.

Notes

- Clicking "Always use this program to open this file" on the Open With dialog box will create a permanent association between the file type (as defined by its extension), rather than performing one-time transient operations for this specific file.

- The list of file type-program associations is kept in the Registry at `HKEY_CLASSES_ROOT`. See Chapter 10 for a detailed explanation.

- Sometimes you want to get the Open With dialog for a file whose type is already registered, so that you can use a different application to open it. As noted previously, select the file, then `Shift`-right-click on it to get a context menu including Open With.

- Alternatively, you can create a batch file (and then put a shortcut to it on the Desktop, the Start menu, or the Send To folder) containing the following command line:

```
rundll32 shell32.dll,OpenAs_RunDLL %1
```

Find Files and Folders

Quickly locate any file on the system, using either the filename, the date and time the file was created or modified, text contained in the file, or some combination of these criteria. A list of files matching the criteria will appear in the lower window.

> Start → Find → Files or Folders
> Explorer → Tools → Find → Files or Folders
> *any folder* → context menu → Find
> F3 while focus is on the Desktop
> Right-click in Explorer left pane

Search Criteria

Information entered on all three tabs works together to define the criteria for the search. For example, you can search for a file with a specific name, or leave the filename blank and search for all files created since a specific date, or construct a complex search using multiple criteria. Find remembers search criteria, so you can refine a search by defining additional criteria and repeating the search. See Figure 3-7.

Find → Name & Location → Named

Enter any part of the desired filename(s). Find does a substring search—unless you're used to wildcards, you don't have to use them. For example, the string "exec" would return autoexec.dos, autoexec.bat, and jobexec.dll. However, *find* does also recognize the standard file naming wildcards (? and *). For more information on the rules of using these wildcards, see "Wildcards, Pipes, and Redirection" in Chapter 5. You can enter multiple filenames by separating them with a comma (e.g., *.txt, *.bat).

Find also keeps a history of previous filename searches, which you can view by clicking on the down arrow to the right of the field. (This history is preserved even when you clear the previous search using New Search.)

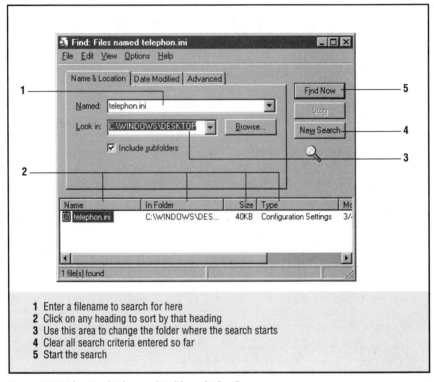

Figure 3-7: *The Find Files and Folders dialog box*

Because the search results area in Find is "active," you can perform any action you like on the files or folders that appear there. You can copy them, rename them, move them, make shortcuts to them—even delete them. This makes Find a workable alternative to the Desktop or the two-paned Explorer view as a primary interface for working with files and folders. One particularly powerful feature is that once you've found a group of files with some common characteristics (such as file type/extension, modification date, or contents), you select all and then act on them as a group.

Find → Name & Location → Look in

Can be given a drive (and optional folder) in which to make the search. You can specify multiple drives or folders by separating their names with a semi-colon (and optional space). For example: *C:*; *D:* will search both the *C:* and *D:* drives. By checking the "include subfolders" box, Windows will search all subdirectories within the main directory you are searching.

Find → Date Modified

Lets you specify a range of dates during which the desired files were last changed.

Find → Advanced → Of type

Lets you specify whether to search for files of only a given type. Obviously, you could do the same by specifying a given filename extension in Find → Name & Location → Named.

Find → Advanced → Containing text

Lets you enter a string of up to 128 characters to search for. Carriage returns are not allowed—they will start the search. $ matches the end of a line in text files, and can be used to "anchor" a search, to find text that ends a line. Find will locate ASCII strings in non-text (binary) files, but it will not locate Unicode (two-byte) strings. Cut and paste accelerators are supported.

Find → Advanced → Size is

Lets you specify a specific size for a file or a minimum (At least) or maximum (At most) size.

If you're like me, you may find yourself leaving files of a particular type (e.g., Excel worksheets or Word files) strewn all over your file system. A good way to "gather them up into one place" is to search for all files of a given extension (e.g., *.xls*), then Select All in the Find Results window, and then Shift-right-click. Choose Create Shortcut from the context menu, and put the shortcuts into a single folder. This way, you can organize your files both by type and by project or other subject-oriented category. Rebuild your "file type" folders periodically using the Date Modified tab of Find → Files & Folders to find your latest work.

Find Dialog Menus

- File menu → Open Containing Folder: opens not the file that has been selected in the Find results window, but the folder that contains it. This can be handy if you want to work on a set of related files. Find one, and go to the folder that contains them all.

- File menu → Save Search: saves the search criteria in a file on the Desktop. If Options → Save Results is checked, the results of the search (and not just the criteria) is saved in the file. Unfortunately, the results can't be read in another application, only read back into the Find window.

    The save filename depends on the search criteria. If the search was for a named file, the name searched for will be part of the saved filename. Otherwise, it will be called All Files (with a number in parentheses if you save multiple searches).

Notes

- Start → Find → Computer is a separate Find function that looks for a named computer on your network. This is handy if you have a very large Network Neighborhood. Enter any character(s) contained in the destination computer name to get a list of UNC pathnames containing those characters. Case is not significant. The list in the output window is active, so once you've found your target computer, you can click on its icon to open a window onto its contents, just like in Network Neighborhood.

See Also

dir and *find* in Chapter 5

Icons

It's easy to take icons for granted. They are a ubiquitous and seemingly immutable feature of the Windows 95 interface, but in fact, you have a degree of control over what icons are used for various types of files. In particular, you can use any icon you like for any shortcuts you create, using Properties → Shortcut → Change Icon.

By default, the Change Icon dialog box for a shortcut usually points to \ *Windows*\ *System*\ *shell32.dll*, which contains about 70 different icons, including the standard icons for folders, disks and so on. A browse button lets you search for other sources of icons. But where do you look?

- \ *Windows*\ *System*\ *pifmgr.dll* contains almost 40 additional icons. Except for the MS-DOS prompt icon, you've probably never seen many of these icons. A lot of them are fun and original.

- \ *Windows*\ *moricons.dll* contains about 100 icons, including icons for many non-Microsoft applications.

- \ *Windows*\ *System*\ *rnaui.dll* contains seven icons with telephone imagery. (This is the default icon set for Dial-Up Networking shortcuts.)

- \ *Windows*\ *Progman.exe* contains about 40 icons, including pointing hands, arrows, a safe, a mailbox, doors, interoffice mail envelopes, and many more.

- \ *Windows*\ *System*\ *user.exe* contains the MS Windows icon, a triangular warning icon, a question mark bubble icon, and so forth.

- Any file on your disk with the *.ico* extension is fair game. Unfortunately, the browse button doesn't make them easy to find. Use Find → Files or Folders and look for **.ico*; a small copy of each icon will appear in the Find display next to its name and location. If you see something you like, navigate to it with Change Icon → Browse. (Unfortunately, you can't just copy the path from the Find dialog box and paste it in.)

- Any executable (*.exe*) file with a unique icon may contain its icon (or icons) within it. For example, *drivespace.exe* contains eight icons, most with a disk or hardware theme, plus one incongruous yellow smiley face; \ *Windows*\ *mplayer.exe* has multimedia-related icons; and \ *Windows*\ *regedit.exe*

---

has a number of building-block–type icons. Pick any *.exe* file from the Browse dialog box; if it contains no icon, you'll get a message to that effect, but otherwise, the icon will be extracted and can be applied to your shortcut.

- Any bitmap (*.bmp*) file can serve as an icon, although most large bitmap files will lose too much detail at icon size. Simply copy the *.bmp* file, and change the *.bmp* extension to *.ico* (again, use Find → Files or Folders to search for *.bmp* files on your disk—or look at the many graphics file archives on the Net). To see what the icon looks like, you can just copy or move it to the Desktop. Any file with the *.ico* extension will appear there with itself as the icon.

Inbox

Double-click the Inbox icon on the Desktop to launch Windows Messaging (email and fax). Whether this is what you want will depend on your version of Windows 95. The original release used Microsoft Exchange for email; OSR2 uses the same program (with only slight revisions), but it's called Windows Messaging.

Notes

- If the Inbox icon isn't on your Desktop, then Windows Messaging has probably not been installed. You can install it using Control Panel → Add/Remove Programs → Windows Setup → Windows Messaging.

- Fax messages appear in Microsoft Exchange, but you must install both Windows Messaging and Microsoft Fax to send and receive fax messages. Without the Inbox icon on the Desktop, you won't be able to use Windows Messaging or Microsoft Fax services.

See Also

exchng32 and *fax* in Chapter 5

Internet

Start Internet Explorer to browse the World Wide Web.

Desktop → Internet
Start → Programs → Internet Explorer
Start → Run → `iexplore`

Internet Explorer is a complex program that is not strictly part of Windows 95, although it most likely will be fully integrated in Windows 98. For more information on IE see *Internet in a Nutshell*, by Valerie Quercia (O'Reilly & Associates).

Notes

Internet → Properties is the same as Control Panel → Internet. This property sheet controls Internet settings that affect any Internet applications that use Microsoft's wininet API (including third-party applications). See Chapter 4, *The Control Panel*, for details.

Login

Depending on your configuration, you may be asked to log on when your system boots up. There are three reasons you may need a login name and password:

- Unlike previous versions of Windows, Windows 95 is multiuser—that is, more than one person can use the same machine, with a somewhat separate Desktop layout, Start menu, and so on. See "Passwords" in Chapter 4 for more information.

- If your machine is connected to a local area network, your login name and password are required to access any network services.

- If you want the system to be able to remember passwords automatically for applications like Dial-Up Networking or Internet access, you must have initial login passwords enabled.

In any of these cases, you should choose a password when you receive your system. You can later change this (using Control Panel → Passwords). See Chapter 4 for additional information.

My Computer

In addition to the Explorer view and the DOS view, you can still use the hierarchical folder-in-folder view of the Desktop by clicking My Computer → Drive (C:).

Notes

- My Computer also gives you access to all drives on the system (fixed, removable, CD, network, etc.), as well as the Control Panel, Printers, and Dial-Up Networking.

- Shift-double-click on My Computer to start up the double-pane Explorer window view, with the same starting point.

- In the Explorer, My Computer contains all other files and folders, except for the Network Neighborhood and Desktop folders.

- My Computer → Properties is the same as Control Panel → System.

- My Computer → Drive (C:) → Properties gives useful statistics on the amount of disk space used and free, access to disk utilities, and to sharing. This is true for additional disks on your system as well.

Network Neighborhood

Access the local network.

    Desktop → Network Neighborhood
    Explorer → Network Neighborhood

Description

The Network Neighborhood (Figure 3-8) provides a quick way to reach other systems on a local or wide area network. When the system is connected, other systems on the same network are displayed as icons in the Network Neighborhood folder on the Desktop. Click on any icon to connect to that system.

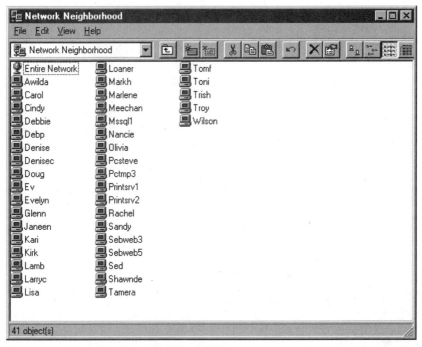

Figure 3-8: The Network Neighborhood folder

Other systems might include print or file servers or other user's client machines. Often a network is divided into workgroups. If so, only the local workgroup will be shown. Click on Entire Network to step up a level and see the other workgroups.

> If you are connected to a local area network and the Network Neighborhood icon is not displayed, go to Control Panel → Network → Configuration → Add → Client → Client for Microsoft Networks.

Any user can designate folders on his or her machine for sharing with other users. You will usually be asked for a password before you can access Shared resources.

Notes

• If you have access to a file or folder on a remote machine, you can create a shortcut to it on your own Desktop or in your own folders, just as you can with a local file.

- On the command line or in the Explorer, you can refer to a resource on a remote system by a UNC (Universal Naming Convention) pathname. A UNC path consists of the name of the remote system followed by the name of the shared resource. For example, the UNC path *tim**c**inanut* refers to the folder called *inanut* on the shared C drive on a machine called *tim*.

- To view or change the name of your own system, as shown in the Network Neighborhood, use Control Panel → Network → Identification.

- Network Neighborhood → Properties is the same as Control Panel → Network.

- To share a folder on your machine, go to the folder's context menu → Sharing. If Sharing... does not appear on the context menu, sharing is not enabled. Go to Control Panel → Network → Configuration → File and Print sharing and click on "I want to be able to give others access to my files."

The Sharing dialog box (Figure 3-9) lets you specify the name and access permissions for a shared folder or printer.

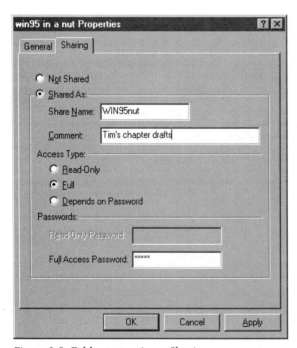

Figure 3-9: Folder properties → Sharing

By default, the folder or printer will be set to Not Shared. Click Shared As if you want it to be shared. By default, the Share Name will be the same as the name of the folder.

You can grant read-only access (the default), which will allow others to view or copy the contents of any files in the folder. Full access will allow them to read and write any files. Click Read-Only or Full and specify the password that will be required to access the folder. If you want some users to have read-only access and others full access, Click Depends on Password and specify two different passwords.

For a printer, full access will allow others to delete jobs from the print queue. You may want to grant full access to printers only to the system or network administrator.

If you leave the password field blank, no password will be required.

The icon for any folder that is shared will change from the standard folder icon to one of a hand holding a folder.

WARNING

If you are using TCP/IP on both your local area network and the Internet, you need to be careful with File and Printer Sharing. You should either make sure that all your shares are password-protected or make sure that the binding for file and printer sharing is disabled. Otherwise, your shared folders will be accessible to anyone out there on the Net.

You can check whether your shares are password-protected using Net Watcher (*netwatch.exe*). Use View → By Shared Folder, then use Administer → Shared Folder Properties for each share.

- You can map a networked disk or folder to a drive letter using the Map Network Drive button on a folder toolbar or in the Explorer at Tools → Map Network Drive. This corresponds to the net use command, and is especially useful for making network access easily available to older DOS-based programs. You can similarly map network printers to local printer ports (LPT1 and so on) by selecting the printer in the Network Neighborhood window and then using File → Capture Printer Port.

- If you experience network problems, an application that attempts to access the network may appear to freeze your system. Wait 20 or 30 seconds and the system will respond again. Most network programs have a built-in timeout, and will give up after that timeout period.

- Network Neighborhood works only with other Microsoft systems. For example, even though you might be using a TCP/IP network (either on a LAN or via Dial-Up Networking), any Unix systems on the network won't show up in the Network Neighborhood. To transfer files to or from a Unix system on the network, use the *ftp* command; use *telnet* for "terminal" access to such a system. A very cool program called Samba can be used to mount a TCP/IP system on Network Neighborhood. See *Windows Annoyances* for details.

See Also

ftp, net, and *telnet* in Chapter 5

Office Shortcut Bar

If you install Microsoft Office on your machine, it will place a toolbar consisting of a series of icons at the top of your screen. This toolbar can be set to occupy the full screen width (Figure 3-10), working much the same way as the Taskbar (and like it, auto-hideable and draggable to any edge of the Desktop), or occupying only the amount of space needed to show the icons it contains (Figure 3-11).

Figure 3-10: A full screen-width Office Shortcut Bar

Figure 3-11: A standard-size Office Shortcut Bar with small icons

The Office Shortcut Bar is not, strictly speaking, part of Windows 95, but it is worth documenting, since it is available on so many systems, and can be used for quick access to any application, not just Microsoft Office.

In addition to the installed Microsoft Office components, this toolbar can display icons for other frequently accessed programs. You can also request additional toolbars (with icons for switching between them) for the Desktop, IE's Favorites, MSN, and the Start menu Programs and Accessories.

To select which toolbars will be displayed, right click on the Office Shortcut Bar. The context menu will list available toolbars.

To customize the Office Shortcut Bar:

> system menu → Customize
> context menu → Customize

The following tabs appear under Customize → View:

Color
> Applies only to the full size toolbar.

Always on Top
> A handy setting, although if you also set Auto Fit, it can get in the way of the minimize and close buttons on a maximized window. (If not set to Auto Fit, a maximized window will place its titlebar below the Office Shortcut Bar.)

Auto Hide between uses
> As with the Taskbar, makes the Shortcut Bar invisible until you move the pointer to the edge of the screen that hides it, at which point it slides into view.

Auto Fit into Titlebar area
> Makes a small toolbar that fits into the upper-right corner of the Desktop (in the titlebar area of a maximized window). If you choose this option, you can neither auto-hide nor drag the toolbar to another location.

Show Tooltips

Tooltips are little information balloons that pop up when you move the pointer over an object: always a handy feature, but especially important if you choose Auto Fit, since the small icons can be hard to distinguish for some tools. (Alternatively, you could choose Large Buttons, but that means losing a lot more screen real estate.)

> Our preferred options are Show Tooltips, Always on Top, and Auto Fit.

Customize → Buttons

You can add other icons besides MS Office to the Shortcut Bar—anything you use often. A standard checkoff list of icons appears. Check any that you want shown, and uncheck any that you want to remove. Select an entry and use the Move buttons to move it up or down in the list. (Icons will be shown in the order in which they appear in this list.) Even better, the Add File and Add Folder buttons let you add any file or folder on the system to the list.

Customize → Toolbars

Lets you choose additional toolbars to display. This list is also available on the context menu, although you get more control via the Customize dialog. You can also create additional custom toolbars containing whatever you like using Add Toolbar. If multiple toolbars are selected, you can customize each of their buttons separately on Customize → Buttons.

Customize → Settings

Specifies the location of MS Office templates.

Printers

The Printers folder contains an Add Printer icon plus icons for any installed printers. Drag items to the printer icons to print them, or click on the printer icon to see or change the status of current print jobs.

Start → Settings → Printers
Control Panel → Printers
My Computer → Printers

Like Fonts (see Chapter 4), Printers is a "virtual folder" rather than a normal Control Panel entry. The folder should include an icon for each printer that is installed on your system.

Add Printer is a wizard that helps you select the appropriate printer driver for a local or network printer. See "Printers" in Chapter 4 for details.

The context menu for any printer allows you to select that printer as the default printer and specify whether print spooling ("offline printing") should be enabled for it. Note that if offline printing is selected, you can print to a network printer even when you aren't connected, or to a local printer when it is turned off; when the printer becomes available, you will be asked whether to print any files in the queue. See "Printers" in Chapter 4 for a description of printer properties.

File → Print is the standard way to print for most applications. Context menu → Print allows you to send a file to the printer without opening it first. You can also create a shortcut to a printer on the Desktop and then drag and drop a file on the printer icon.

WARNING

If you drag more than one file to a printer icon, the system will open a separate copy of the application for each file. This may be okay for text files and a small application like Notepad, but drag a group of Word or Excel files to the printer and you'll bring the system to its knees.

Double-click on any printer icon for a view of the printer's job queue. You'll see the document name, status (printing, paused, and so on), the owner of the job, progress (in number of pages printed), and when the job was started. You can drag your own jobs up and down to change their priority. Use the Printer menu to pause the printer or purge all print jobs. Use the Document menu to pause or cancel printing for any selected document(s). For a network printer, you can only pause, change the priority of, or delete your own jobs.

Properties

Right-click on many objects, then select Properties from the context menu for information about the object and configuration controls.

> *many objects* → context menu → Properties
> Alt-double-click
> Alt-Enter if the item is already selected

Description

Almost every context menu includes a Properties entry. These vary greatly depending on what kind of item has been selected. For example, some of the Control Panel functions such as Display and Date/Time are also available via Properties.

This section describes the features of file and folder properties. Other types of property sheets are described as appropriate elsewhere in the book.

At minimum, a property sheet for a file, folder, or shortcut will have a General tab (see Figure 3-12).

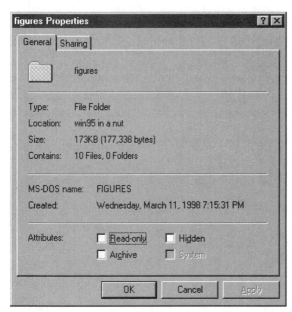

Figure 3-12: A property sheet for a folder

Most of the information on the first page is fairly self-explanatory. A few things need a bit of explanation:

MS-DOS name

The eight-character "short filename" plus three-character extension. If the file has only a short name, this will be the same name that shows up in the Explorer. But if the file has a long name, you will see only the first six characters of the long name, followed by a tilde (~), a digit, and the extension.

Attributes

Check Read-only to prevent a file from being modified by yourself or others. (Obviously, someone else could pop up the property sheet and change the attribute, but it prevents inadvertent modification.)

Check Archive if you want the file to be backed up when a backup program is next run. This attribute is automatically set whenever you modify a file, and is cleared by the same backup programs when the file is copied. By default, hidden files do not show up in the Explorer or via the DOS *dir* command. See *attrib* in Chapter 5 for more information about file attributes.

Notes

- Folders, printers, and disk drives have a second property tab called Sharing. See "Network Neighborhood" earlier in this chapter for details. Shortcuts to MS-DOS programs have five separate property tabs. See "Shortcuts" later in this chapter for details.

- To see the amount of disk space used by a group of files, select them, then view the Properties entry for the selected list. On the first tab, you'll see the size of the whole group. Change any of the attributes, and the change will be applied to all of the files in the selected group. (Unfortunately, if any of the files in the selected group has a different attribute from other files in the group, the checkbox for that attribute will be grayed out, so this does not work in all cases. This seems like rather poor user interface design.)

Recycle Bin   *\Recycled*

Move files to temporary storage, pending true deletion.

    Recycle Bin
    File → Delete
    Del key

Description

Drag any item from the Desktop to the Recycle Bin icon to delete it. File → Delete on the menubar of a folder also moves items to the Recycle Bin, as does selecting the item and then pressing the Delete key. By default, files are not deleted immediately, but are stored until the Recycle Bin runs out of space, at which point they are deleted, oldest first, to make space. Until that time, they can be retrieved by clicking on the Recycle Bin icon, browsing through the contents of the Recycle Bin window, and dragging or sending the file elsewhere.

WARNING

Files dragged to the Recycle Bin (or otherwise deleted) from floppies, network drives, or other external drives such as Zip drives will not be stored in the Recycle Bin. They are simply deleted.

Properties

- A slider allows you to specify how much of each drive can be allocated to the Recycle Bin. The default is 10%. You can specify the same value for all drives or set a separate value for each drive. Keep in mind that on today's huge drives, 10% can be a lot: 10% of a 1 gigabyte disk is 100 megabytes of stored junk. The amount of space actually used by the files in the Recycle Bin is displayed in the Bin's status bar when you open it.

- A checkbox allows you to specify that deleted files are not to be stored in the Recycle Bin but removed immediately from the disk. Check this box only if you want to live dangerously.

- A checkbox asks if you want to display a delete confirmation dialog. This delete confirmation will appear when you select Delete from the File or context menu, but not when you drag an item to the Recycle Bin.

> To delete a file without sending it to the Recycle Bin, use Shift+Delete or the *del* command on the command line.
>
> Another way to send files to the Recycle Bin without confirmation is to add a Recycle Bin shortcut to the Send To folder. Then you can send something out for recycling by clicking Send To → Recycle Bin.

Notes

- With the Details view (the default), you can sort the contents of the Recycle Bin by name, by original location (useful in case you want to put something back where it was!), by Date deleted, by type, or by size. Click on any of the headings to sort contents by that heading. Click again on the same heading to reverse the order of the sort.

- You can delete the entire contents of a floppy disk by dragging the disk icon to the Recycle Bin. You will be prompted for confirmation. You cannot drag the image of a hard disk (such as *C:*) to the Recycle Bin (since the Recycle Bin itself is contained on that disk), nor drag key components of the user interface, such as the My Computer, Network Neighborhood, Control Panel, Dial-Up Networking, Printers, and Fonts folders to the Recycle Bin. (Well, you can drag them there, but they won't go in!)

- Some of these Desktop items can be deleted by right-clicking and selecting delete. So if something won't go, try again this way. If it still won't go, see *Windows Annoyances* (O'Reilly & Associates).

- You can also manipulate the contents of the Recycle Bin from the command line or the Explorer by working in the folder *\Recycled*.

Run

Start programs by typing in a command line.

Start → Run

The Start menu lists many common Windows 95 applications and accessories plus any third-party applications you've installed, but it is far from complete, and navigating to the program you want is often fairly tedious.

Ironically, the increasing complexity of the system pushes even the most graphically oriented user back in the direction of the command line. Just about the quickest way to run any program that isn't already on your Desktop is to choose Run... from the Start menu and type the name of the program, or keep a DOS command-line window open.

The Run... prompt has the advantage of being one of the first items on the Start menu. In addition, it keeps a command history, so you can click on the little down arrow to the right of the text entry area (or use the up and down arrow keys) and re-execute previous commands. Finally (and this is a big advantage), you can type

The Win95 User Interface

the name of a file, folder, URL, or UNC path at the Run prompt and it will be automatically opened by the appropriate application (if one is registered). Doing this at the DOS prompt will get you the message "Bad command or file name." (However, see *start* in Chapter 5 for an easy way to run filenames, URLs, and so on from the DOS prompt or a batch file.)

Some Useful Run Prompt Tricks

Type in a URL (a line starting with any prefix acceptable in your web browser, including *http://, ftp://,* or even *file://* to point to a file on your local disk) and you'll open your default web browser (probably Internet Explorer or Netscape) to the specified web location. If your browser is already running, it will load the specified page in the existing browser window. You can even leave off the *http://* prefix, as long as the web address you're looking for begins with *www.* or *ftp.*

Type in a UNC pathname to open a shared folder on another computer.

Drag a file icon onto the Run Prompt dialog. Its complete path will be displayed on the Run command line. This is great for building a command line, but is also useful even if all you want to do is find out a file's extension.

With the focus on the Desktop, type a period at the Run prompt to pop up a folder window showing the contents of the Desktop. This can be handy if you have a cluttered Desktop and don't want to minimize all windows in order to see what's underneath. Of course, if you're smart, you'll close the window when you're done or you'll just add to the clutter! (If the focus is not on the Desktop or the Taskbar, this command will open another copy of whatever folder has the focus.)

A DOS window has an advantage in that it can always be left open and that it provides familiar commands (internal to *command.com*) such as *dir, del, copy,* and so on. To open a DOS window:

       Start → Programs → MS-DOS Prompt

or:

       Start → Run → command

A more important difference, though, is the context in which commands issued from either of these prompts run. A command interpreter, or shell, always has a particular context, or environment, in which it runs. This "environment" can create significant differences in the results when you type a command name.

A significant example of this is the search path, the sequence of directories that will be searched to find an executable file with a name matching the command you type. In DOS, the search path is stored in a variable called PATH, which is typically set in the file *C:\autoexec.bat*, a startup file that is automatically executed

---

(if present) when the system is booted. (See *path* and *set* in Chapter 5 for more information on the content on the search path; see Chapter 9 for more information on *autoexec.bat.*) A typical PATH setting might look like this:

```
set PATH=C:\;C:\WINDOWS;C:\WINDOWS\COMMAND
```

which says to look in the three directories *C:*, *C:\Windows*, and *C:\Windows\Command.* If there is a file with the same name in any of these directories, the one that is found first (i.e., in the directory that occurs earlier in the search path) will be executed first.

The search path followed by the Run prompt is:

1. *\Windows\Desktop*

2. *\Windows\System*

3. *\Windows*

4. The contents of the variable PATH, if found. (It's a good idea to put *\Windows\Command* in your path.)

When you install applications, they sometimes (but not always) update the search path setting in *autoexec.bat* or the Registry settings that control the Run prompt path. Many more recent applications (including those in Office 97) don't rely on the directory search path at all, but instead store the individual application's path in the Registry, under the key `HKLM\SOFTWARE\Microsoft\Windows\Current-Version\App Paths`. So, for example, if you've installed Microsoft Office and you type `winword` at the Run prompt, Word will quite predictably execute. But type it at the DOS prompt, and you'll get the message "Bad command or file name." If you want to be able to run Word from the DOS prompt, you need to add the directory *C:\Program Files\Microsoft Office\winword* to your search path, or type the complete pathname of the command. Neither of these options may be acceptable, especially if you use a lot of applications with this behavior. Fortunately, the start program (see Chapter 5) is aware of the `App Paths` Registry key. So the surest way to run *winword* or any similar application from the DOS prompt is simply to type `start winword`. You can also give start the name of any file and it will open the file using the associated application.

A further consequence of the environment concept is that commands typed into a DOS window or the Run prompt sometimes have a scope that is local only to that window. For example, the DOS *break* command, which controls the frequency with which the system checks for `Ctrl-C` interrupting a program, sets that condition for only the window from which it was issued. It therefore doesn't make any sense to type that command at the Run prompt. If you do, it creates what you can think of as a tiny bubble of execution context in which it holds true, and then exits without a trace.

In addition, there are a number of commands that you can issue at the DOS prompt that are "built in" to the DOS command interpreter, *command.com.* These built-in commands are labeled as such in Chapter 5. They cannot be issued from the Run prompt.

For the most part, though, you can use the two command lines interchangeably. If you type the name of a Windows GUI application, it will launch in its own window. If you type the name of a text-based program (for example, *ping*) it will display its output in the current DOS window, or, if issued from the Run prompt, will launch its own DOS window, which will last only as long as the command itself is executing.

See Also

For more information on the DOS command interpreter, see *command* in Chapter 5.

Send To

Send a selected item to a program, disk drive, or folder.

> context menu → Send To

Right-click on any file or folder and select Send To to copy quickly to My Brief-case, a floppy disk in the *A:* drive, an Internet mail client, or any other application or folder that shows up in Send To menu. The result is the same as if the file was dragged into that program: if it's sent to an Explorer component (such as My Brief-case or drive *A:*), it might be moved or copied—otherwise, it's opened.

Notes

- The options that appear in the Send To menu are determined by the contents of the *\Windows\SendTo* folder. To add another Send To recipient, place a shortcut to the desired program into that folder. For example, if you put a shortcut to *winword.exe* into that folder, you could "send" a text file to Word to open it there rather than using Notepad (which would normally be used to open a file with a *.txt* extension).

  Or add a shortcut to Notepad if you want to be able to easily open text files that don't have the right extension (**.txt*) for Notepad to recognize them auto-matically. That way you can just select Send To Notepad.

  > If you place a shortcut to the Send To folder itself in *\Windows\SendTo*, you can create new Send To destinations simply by sending them to the Send To folder!

- Place shortcuts to folders in Send To for an easy way to organize your files. You can work on files on the Desktop then use Send To to move them to their storage location when you're done. You can even create shortcuts to shared folders on other machines.

- If you want to have a lot of Send To locations, you can create subfolders in *\Windows\SendTo*. They will show up as cascading submenus on the Send To menu.

WARNING

Send To works a bit differently depending on the destination. Sending to a folder (including the Recycle Bin) actually moves the file there; sending to a program simply opens the file. You can use Send To on shortcuts with impunity, but when you use it on an original file, remember that you may actually be moving the file.

Shortcuts

A link to a program, file, or part of a document.

> *any file or folder* → context menu → Create Shortcut
> Desktop → context menu → New → Shortcut

You'll notice that some of the items on the Desktop may be labeled "Shortcut to...". A shortcut is also sometimes called a *link*. It is a small file (with the extension *.lnk*) that points to another file, and, if it is a shortcut to a program, contains instructions for executing it. The icon for a shortcut has a small arrow in its lower-left corner, by default.

When you create a new shortcut, it will always have the filename "Shortcut to..." plus whatever the original filename was. You can "train" Windows 95 to change this default behavior by creating and renaming three shortcuts in a row. Do this by right-dragging a file from an Explorer two-pane window onto the Desktop and immediately renaming it to remove the "Shortcut to..." prefix; repeat twice for a total of three times. This trick works only for shortcuts dragged from an Explorer window, not those created in a normal folder view. If you have TweakUI (see *powertoy* in Chapter 5), you can toggle this behavior with Control Panel → TweakUI → Explorer.

Shortcuts to Programs

While you can start a program by double-clicking on its icon on the Desktop, very few programs *have* icons on the Desktop, unless you yourself put them there.

If you find that there's a program you use often, and you want it on the Desktop, use the Explorer to navigate to the directory where the program's executable is stored. (The location is given along with the description of each program in the alphabetical program listings in Chapter 5.) You could move the original program icon to the Desktop, but that's often not wise, since the program may have various supporting files that belong with it in the directory in which it was originally installed. Instead, create a shortcut. When you drag an *.exe* file, it automatically makes a shortcut, unless you have other types of files selected as well when you drag.

The best way to create a program shortcut is to right-drag an item and select "Create Shortcut(s) Here."

You can also put shortcuts in the Start menu folder, the Send To folder, or many other locations. Many system menus such as these are built dynamically from shortcuts stored in a particular folder, so to add a new menu item, all you need to do is put a shortcut in the right place.

You can also create shortcuts to DOS programs. This is a handy alternative to typing at the command line, and lets you put the DOS programs on the Desktop, the Start menu, and the Office Shortcut Bar. See "Shortcut Properties of DOS Programs" later in this section for more information.

Shortcut Properties

To get more information about a shortcut, go to its property sheet. Figure 3-13 shows an example of the second page of a shortcut's properties.

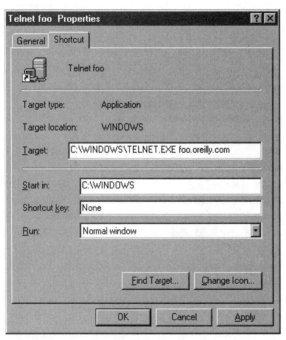

Figure 3-13: Shortcut properties

Target

If the shortcut is to a command with a command-line equivalent (including, but by no means limited to, DOS programs), you can specify any command-line options or arguments here. For example, if I want a shortcut to telnet to a Unix system, *foo.oreilly.com*, I would change the target from *C:\Windows\telnet.exe* to *C:\Windows\telnet.exe foo.oreilly.com*. Note that if you type the name of a shortcut at the Run or command prompt, any parameters or options supplied there will override options set on the Target line.

Start in

> If the shortcut is to a program, this option specifies the folder in which the program will run, and where, by default, it will look for files to open or save.

Shortcut key

> You can map a key sequence to open or execute the shortcut. Press any key on the keyboard and you will see CTRL+ALT+*key* appear as the shortcut key sequence. Type that sequence to launch the shortcut without clicking on it. You should check Appendix A, *Keyboard Accelerators*, to make sure that you aren't creating conflicts with any existing keyboard accelerator.

WARNING

If you delete a shortcut with a keyboard accelerator configured, Windows *won't* release it. It will warn you when you try to create another accelerator that duplicates a previous one, whether or not it's been deleted. If you've defined a keyboard accelerator, clear it before deleting the shortcut.

Run

> A drop-down list allows you to specify whether the target application should run in its normal window, maximized, or minimized.

Find Target

> Click this button to open the folder containing the original file to which this shortcut is a link. The original file will be selected in the folder window.

Change Icon

> You can select from hundreds of available icons. See "Icons" earlier in this chapter for details.

Shortcut Properties of DOS Programs

Since DOS programs weren't originally designed to function in a Windows environment, they've been retrofitted using a construct called Program Information Files (*.pif* files). Notice that the MS-DOS name on the General tab for any shortcut to a DOS program ends with the *.pif* extension. (Actually, these *.pif* files apply not so much to DOS programs as to character-mode programs. Besides DOS programs, Windows 95 also supports character-mode 32-bit Windows programs, called "console" applications, such as *xcopy32.exe*, *start.exe*, and *rundll32.exe*.)

The *.pif* file contains the information required for the character-mode program to function in the Windows environment. The property sheet is the interface for editing the *.pif* file.

A *.pif* file's properties have the following five tabs in addition to the General tab: Program, Font, Memory, Screen, and Misc.

Program

> This tab is similar to the Shortcut tab of a normal shortcut (as shown in Figure 3-13). It lists the command line associated with the shortcut, with information such as the working directory, a keyboard accelerator, if one exists

---

(the Shortcut key), and whether the program should run in a normal window, iconified, or maximized. There's a "close on exit" checkbox; removing the check is useful for programs whose output you need to see after the program has exited (*mem.exe*, for example).

The Advanced button lets you specify how the program will interact with Windows. Some older programs (especially games and other programs that are accustomed to having full control over the hardware) have difficulty cooperating with Windows. There are two workarounds: prevent Windows from answering "yes" to any "is Windows running?" calls the program might make (this is similar to faking the DOS version number with *setver.exe*; see Chapter 9, *Windows Startup*), and closing Windows before running the program (MS-DOS mode). The default is "Suggest MS-DOS mode as necessary." If this box is checked, when you click on the shortcut, Windows does its best to determine whether the program needs MS-DOS mode and puts up a dialog asking if you want to enter MS-DOS mode. See Figure 3-14.

Figure 3-14: Advanced program settings

If you check MS-DOS mode, clicking on the shortcut will close all Windows programs and shut down Windows before running, and will restart Windows when it is done. You can then choose from two radio buttons: "Use current MS-DOS configuration" and "Specify a new MS-DOS configuration." If you choose the former, MS-DOS mode will use your existing *config.sys* and *autoexec.bat* files (if present). If you choose the latter, MS-DOS mode will construct temporary versions of those files containing the commands listed on the dialog box shown in Figure 3-15. Type in additional commands or click Configuration for a wizard that will help you build additional entries for these files.

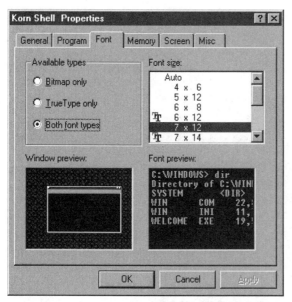

Figure 3-15: The Font tab

Font

Lets you choose the display font size for the DOS window (see Figure 3-15). Fonts are identified by a width and height in pixels (e.g., 7×12).

Memory

Lets you specify any specific memory or extended memory settings required by the program. In particular, you can set the size of the DOS environment.

Screen

This tab has several useful options. You can specify whether the program will run full size or in a window, and the initial size of the window in lines.

If you choose "Display toolbar," the DOS window will include a useful toolbar that gives you access to the Clipboard, the properties, the font, and a button to switch into full-screen mode. (To return from full-screen mode to window mode, press Alt-Enter.)

"Restore settings on startup" means that if you change the font or size, they will be remembered the next time you start up this program.

Misc

The Misc tab is shown in Figure 3-16.

Allow screen saver

Unless this box is checked, an open DOS program window will not give up control of the screen to a screen saver, effectively disabling the screen saver. However, if it is checked, performance may suffer, so you may not want to choose this setting while running games or other performance-intensive programs.

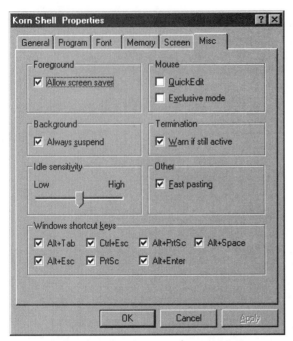

Figure 3-16: The Misc tab

Always suspend

Keeps the program from using any system resources when it is invisible. Select this for programs that don't do anything useful when running in the "background." (Communications programs should never leave "Always suspend" checked, or they will likely hang up if you switch to another window.) The Idle sensitivity slider controls how long the program will need to go without any keyboard input before it is considered inactive, and has its CPU utilization reduced.

QuickEdit

Enable the mouse for selections and cut and paste in the DOS window if this is checked. Otherwise, you must click the Mark button on the toolbar before you can make selections. Note that QuickEdit will not work with all programs (which is why the Mark button is provided on the toolbar).

Exclusive mode

Reserve the mouse for use by this program. It can't be used outside this program's window. Set this only if the program absolutely requires it.

Warn if still active

Many DOS programs don't have the nice Windows feature of asking you to save your files if you haven't done so when you exit. Checking this box tells Windows to warn you if you try to close this program's window while it is still running.

Windows shortcut keys

If the program uses some of the keyboard accelerators that are normally used by Windows, you can disable them here. Clear the checkbox for a key sequence if you want Windows to ignore it when the program is in use.

Shut Down

Shut down the system.

Start → Shut Down
`Ctrl-Alt-Del` → Shut Down

A Windows 95 machine should never be simply turned off, because the system caches data in memory and needs time to write it out to disk before it is turned off. Use Shut Down before you turn off the power.

Notes

- Start → Shut Down pops up a dialog box from which you can choose to shut down, reboot, reboot in DOS mode, or simply close all programs and login as another user. The old `Ctrl-Alt-Del` "three-finger salute" is no longer a system-wide "Vulcan nerve pinch." Instead, it brings up a Close Program dialog box from which you can end a specific task or shut down the system. If you choose Shut Down, shutdown will begin immediately. You don't have the same options as you get with Start → Shut Down.

- Some programs cannot be closed automatically by the shutdown process. If one of these programs is running, you will be given an opportunity to close the program and continue with shutdown (click OK) or to cancel (click Cancel) the shutdown operation.

- To restart Windows without rebooting the computer, hold down the `Shift` key while clicking OK in the Shut Down dialog box.

- Choose "Close all programs and log on as a different user," but then log back on as yourself for a quick reboot. This is usually sufficient to unwedge any stuck programs. It's also a great way to force Win95 to save any Explorer settings, such as the positions of the icons on the Desktop.

See Chapter 9 for a more detailed description of system startup and shutdown.

Start Menu

A quick way to get to many of the most common system functions.

Desktop → Start
`Ctrl-Esc`
Press the Windows logo key on Win95 keyboards

The Start menu is one of Windows 95's answers to the growing size and complexity of the operating system. There's just not enough room on the Desktop for every program or file that a user wants to keep handy.

The Start menu includes a few important system commands, followed by cascading menus labeled Settings, Documents, and Programs (see Figure 3-17).

Figure 3-17: The Start menu

One of the fastest ways to use the Start menu is to press Ctrl-Esc, then use underlined letters or arrow keys to pick items from the menu. For example, Ctrl-Esc R will pop up the Run prompt.

Notes

- Any file or folder stored in the folder \ *Windows\Start Menu* will show up on the Start menu. Not all the entries are created this way, however. Some of the menu items are built into the Explorer, and others are stored in other folders.

- To add a program to Start → Programs, just put a shortcut to the program into \ *Windows\Start Menu\Programs*. You could add any other frequently used folder as well. Folders can be nested; each level of nesting will result in another level of cascading menu. Feel free to reorganize Start → Programs any way you like.

  Since everything in that directory is a shortcut, you can delete things without fear. You can also rename them or put them in subdirectories so that they appear in a different order. And of course, you can make new programs appear on the Start menu by putting shortcuts to them into that directory.

  Start → Programs can also be customized using Taskbar → Properties → Start menu Programs. The Advanced button launches an Explorer window with its root at the \ *Windows\Start Menu\Programs* folder; you can reorganize using the Explorer. You can also right-click on the Start menu button and select Explore or Open.

- You can also add programs to the top level of the Start menu by dragging and dropping their icons onto the Start button. This will place a shortcut directly into the \ *Windows\Start Menu* folder rather than \ *Windows\Start Menu\Programs;* the icon for the program will appear in alphabetical order in a section at the top of the Start menu. You should do this only for programs that you use fairly often. Good programs to add there might be the Explorer and DOS.

Start Menu Customization Tips

- If you customize your Start menu frequently, create a shortcut called *Customize,* and put it in the Start menu folder. Specify the following command line as the target for the shortcut:

  ```
  C:\WINDOWS\EXPLORER.EXE /e, /n, /root,c:\windows\start menu
  ```

  Now clicking on your Customize button will open an Explorer view of the Start menu folder, and you can add, delete, rename, and reorganize shortcuts there to your heart's delight.

- If you like keyboard accelerators, you might consider adding some numbered items to the top of your Start menu. Pick your nine favorite programs, and create shortcuts whose names begin with a number. For example 1 Solitaire, 2 Hover... :) Then you only have to type Ctrl-Esc 1 to start the first program, Ctrl-Esc 2 for the second , and so on.

- Start → Programs can get fairly cluttered, since most programs add shortcuts to this menu as part of their installation process. As a result, you might not notice a couple of important subfolders:

  - Start → Programs → StartUp contains shortcuts to any programs that should be started automatically when the system boots up. Put shortcuts to programs into the folder *C:\Windows\Start Menu\Programs\StartUp* to have them run automatically. See "Startup Folder" later in this chapter for additional details.

  - Start → Programs → Accessories contains many of the bundled Windows 95 utilities, including system tools and games.

- Start → Documents contains a cache of shortcuts to any recently opened files. The cascading menu off this item reflects the contents of the folder \ *Windows\Recent,* and any file operations performed on that folder will be reflected in this menu. You can also clear the cache (i.e., remove all the shortcuts from this folder) using Taskbar → Properties → Start Menu Programs → Documents Menu → Clear. But if you want to clear some of the entries but not others, you need to go to the folder with the Explorer or the DOS prompt and do the dirty work there.

See Also

Chapter 5 for a discussion of Start → Settings
Other entries in this chapter for a discussion of other menu items

---

Startup Folder   *\ Windows\Start Menu\Programs\StartUp*

If you want a program to start up automatically when you reboot the system, put a
shortcut to it into the directory *C:\ Windows\Start Menu\Programs\Start Up*. If you
want it to start up minimized (in which case it will simply appear in the Taskbar),
set the shortcut's Properties → Program → Run to Minimized.

Notes

- If you want programs in the Startup folder to run in a particular order, instead
  of putting in shortcuts to each program, create a single DOS batch file, containing lines of the form:

  start *programname*

  The programs will start in the order in which they are listed in the batch file.
  If you want a program to complete before the next one starts, use *start /w*.

- To bypass the programs in the Startup folder, hold down the Shift key while
  the system is booting. Keep holding it down until the Desktop is complete
  with pointer. Obviously, this won't work if you have to log in as part of the
  startup process.

- In addition to the startup folder contents, the Registry settings HKEY_LOCAL_
  MACHINE\Microsoft\Windows\CurrentVersion\Run and \CurrentVer-
  sion\RunServices specify a list of programs to run, as does the Run= entry
  in the *win.ini* file. (See Chapter 9 for details.) See also \Current Version
  \RunOnce, \CurrentVersion\RunOnceEx, and \CurrentVersion\RunSer-
  vicesOnce.

System Tray

A part of the Taskbar is used for displaying various system status indicators,
including the system clock. If no status indicators have been selected, the System
Tray will not be displayed. The clock is displayed by default on most systems.
Some of these icons are "active"—but they are extremely inconsistent in this
behavior: some respond to a right-click, some to a left-click, some to a double-
click, and some don't respond at all.

Table 3-1 summarizes the indicators that can be put into the System Tray with the
location of the checkbox that controls whether the item is to be displayed.

Table 3-1: System Tray Indicators

Item	Control Location
Audio volume	Control Panel → Multimedia → Audio → Show volume control
Clock	Taskbar → Properties → Taskbar Options → Show Clock

Table 3-1: System Tray Indicators (continued)

Item	Control Location
Desktop color palette, resolution and font size	Control Panel → Display → Settings → Show settings
Dial-Up connection	Dial-Up Networking → Connections menu → Settings → Show an icon on Taskbar after connected
FilterKeys	Control Panel → Accessibility Options → Keyboard → Filter Keys → Settings
Language	Control Panel → Keyboard → Language
MouseKeys	Control Panel → Accessibility Options → Mouse
Power status	Control Panel → Power → Show Battery Meter
PCMCIA card	Control Panel → PC Card → Socket Status → Show Control
StickyKeys	Control Panel → Accessibility Options → Keyboard → Sticky Keys → Settings

Notes

- Leave the pointer over the clock for a few seconds to display the date in a Tooltips bubble.

  Right-click on the clock when it is displayed to adjust the system date or time. (You can also do this with the Date and Time commands or Control Panel → Date/Time.) The tabbed dialog that appears also allows you to set the time zone and have the system automatically adjust the clock for daylight savings time changes.

- The System Tray is available to any application that chooses to use it—or misuse it. For example, AOL 4.0 installs a startup icon in the System Tray (as well as just about anywhere else it can put one)—a clear abuse of the intended purpose.

- On OSR2 systems, Dial-Up Networking places a network icon (two connected computers) in the System Tray while a network connection is active. On earlier systems, the connection status dialog appears as a regular button on the Taskbar, and a modem icon is shown in the System Tray. Click on the icon to display current connection status, including the amount of time online and the number of bytes transferred. A button on the status dialog box also allows you to terminate the connection.

- The language indicator is useful only if multiple keyboard layouts are enabled. Click on the indicator to display a popup menu that lets you switch between available keyboard layouts.

- The power status indicator is generally useful only on laptops. It shows a plug when the system is connected to AC power, and a battery when the system is running on the battery. The height of the color in the battery gives a rough idea of how much power is left; to get a more precise estimate, hold the pointer over the indicator until a Tooltips bubble pops up showing the percentage charge remaining.

- The PC card indicator gives you a quick way to get to the Control Panel → PC Card property sheet. This is useful if you are going to be taking PC cards in and out of your system frequently, since the system prefers to be notified before you do so.

Taskbar

The Taskbar contains buttons for each open window on the Desktop (see Figure 3-18). The button corresponding to the window that has the focus appears depressed. To bring a window to the front, click on its Taskbar button. When a window is minimized, its icon appears on the Taskbar rather than on the Desktop itself (as in Windows 3.1).

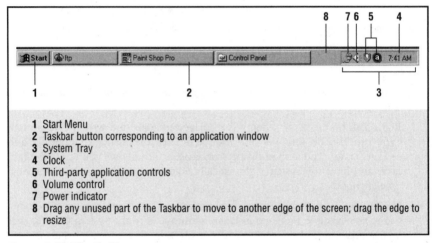

1 Start Menu
2 Taskbar button corresponding to an application window
3 System Tray
4 Clock
5 Third-party application controls
6 Volume control
7 Power indicator
8 Drag any unused part of the Taskbar to move to another edge of the screen; drag the edge to resize

Figure 3-18: The Taskbar

Notes

- By default, the Explorer displays the Taskbar at the bottom of the screen. You can drag it to the top or either side using any empty space on the bar as the drag handle.

- As you open more windows, the Taskbar buttons become smaller, displaying less and less text. If you have so many open windows that only the 16×16 icon for each one is showing on the Taskbar, no more will be displayed. A small "spin control" will be displayed so that you can rotate which icons are visible.

  However, you may want to modify the size of the Taskbar by dragging the edge up or down (or sideways, if you've moved it to the right or left side of the screen).

- If the focus is on the Taskbar, you can use the arrow keys to move between the buttons for open programs. Ctrl-Esc will open the Start menu.

- By default, windows are scattered around the Desktop as left by the user. The context menu for the Taskbar lets you cascade all open windows or tile them horizontally or vertically. You can also use the context menu to minimize all windows at once (reduce them to the Taskbar) or to move them to the Desktop.

Properties

- Enable Taskbar → Properties → Taskbar Options → Always on top (see Figure 3-19) to specify that the Taskbar can't be covered by open windows as you move them around the Desktop. Note that the working Desktop space is decreased with this option—maximized windows stop above the Taskbar.

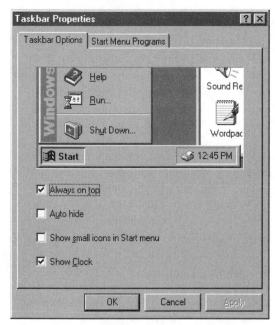

Figure 3-19: The Taskbar Options tab

- If Taskbar → Properties → Taskbar Options → Auto Hide is enabled, the Taskbar will be invisible until you move the pointer to the edge of the screen where it is hidden. It will then slide up into view. This gives you a bit more Desktop real estate, but can be a little disconcerting. Even if Auto Hide is on, if you give the Taskbar the focus, it will stay visible until you give the focus to another window.

- Enable Taskbar → Properties → Taskbar Options → Show Clock to display the time in the System Tray if it's not already visible.

- Taskbar → Properties → Start menu can be used to add or remove programs from the Start menu. The Add... button prompts you for the name of a program command line; a wizard will add a shortcut to the \Windows\Start Menu\Programs folder. The Advanced... button launches an Explorer view of the Start menu folder hierarchy. See "Start Menu" earlier in this chapter for an easier way to customize the Start menu.

- Another button on the same property sheet lets you clear the contents of the Documents menu. (You can do the same thing from the command line or the Explorer by deleting all the shortcuts from the folder *Windows**Recent.*)

CHAPTER 4

The Control Panel

The Control Panel provides a point-and-click environment for configuration of many Windows 95 features. The Control Panel also demonstrates just how inconsistent the Windows 95 interface can be.

When you choose Start → Settings → Control Panel, you get to a folder containing various icons (or control panel applets) representing system features. (See Figure 4-1.)

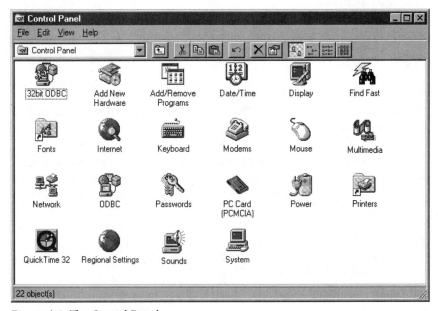

Figure 4-1: The Control Panel

Clicking on most of these icons pops up a tabbed property sheet controlling the associated system features (such as Date/Time, Display, and so on.) These are often the same property sheets that you can get to by right-clicking on some other item on the Desktop and then choosing Properties. (For example, Control Panel → Display is the same as Desktop → Properties, and Control Panel → Date/Time is the same as the Property sheet you get when you right-click or double-click on the clock in the System Tray.)

However, other icons (such as Add New Hardware) spawn a wizard that walks you through the process of configuring a new device.

Still others, such as Fonts, are shortcuts to folders. Inside the Control Panel → Fonts folder, which is just a shortcut to \Windows\Fonts, you'll find all of the font files used on the system. Clicking on any one of the font files will launch a program (*fontview.exe*) that allows you to see what that font looks like. But if you want to add a new font, for instance, use the File menu of the Fonts folder window, or just drag-drop a font file into the folder: hardly what you'd expect, given the user interface to the rest of the Control Panel icons.

Even the majority of the Control Panel icons, which use the property sheet approach, can be confusing, since what appears to be the same property sheet shows up at several points in the system. For example, when you click on the Properties button on a Dial-Up Networking connection, you get a property sheet that looks very like one reached from Control Panel → Modem. It's only later that you realize that the Control Panel sets the defaults, and the connection properties override them on a per-connection basis, except for the "Extra Settings" in the Advanced Connection Settings window. Even though the interface is the same, the effect is very different.

Command-Line Access to Control Panel Applets

As it turns out, you can also access the property sheet style control panel applets (and some of the wizards) from the command line, using the *control.exe* program. This is really just a shell for *rundll.exe*, but it has a much simpler syntax. With *control.exe*, you can create batch files or shortcuts that pop up the relevant control panel applet, in some cases even opening the control panel applet to a specific tab.

Most of the control panel applets are stored in files with the extension *.cpl*. When you start up the Control Panel, it populates its window by searching \Windows\System for any files with this extension. (Some others are incorporated into software and hardware drivers.) This allows third-party application developers to add control panel applets.

The command-line syntax (hardly something that you'd want to type on a regular basis, but good for embedding in batch files, or shortcuts on the Desktop or in the Start menu) is as follows:

```
control filename.cpl {,applet_name} {,property_tab}
```

For example:

```
control timedate.cpl ,Date/Time ,1
```

Note the placement of the commas. This is not accidental. The comma immediately precedes the command-line argument (with no space), rather than following the preceding argument, as you might expect. Get the commas wrong, and the command line won't work at all.

In practice, you don't usually need to include the applet name, and can just specify the property tab. For example:

```
control sysdm.cpl ,1
```

will pop up the Device Manager. If you regularly add or configure devices, embedding this command line in a shortcut is a lot easier than going to Control Panel → System and then clicking on the second tab.

In documenting each of the control panel applets in this chapter, we've generally omitted the applet name, choosing the shorter format except in those cases (such as Add New Hardware and Keyboard) where the applet name must be specified, because more than one control panel applet shares a single *.cpl* file. Keep in mind that every applet on a user's system may not be documented here, since they're extensible and defined by an open specification. For example, if you've installed TweakUI on your system, you will have a TweakUI applet in your Control Panel.

Finally, to cement the "quirky syntax" prize, not all tabbed control panel applets recognize the property tab arguments from the command line. It's not up to *control.exe* to recognize this syntax, but rather the *.cpl* applet itself, and not all do.

Control panel applets sometimes reside within *.dll* files; these can be loaded via the [MMCPL] section of \ *Windows\control.ini*, with a statement such as "ScanSet=Lpsc-nmgr.dll". The [don't load] section of *control.ini excludes cpls* that would otherwise normally be loaded. For example, the setting "sticpl.cpl=no" excludes the Scanners and Cameras applet, and "joystick.cpl=no" excludes the Joystick applet. Also, TweakUI can be used to exclude any control panel applet. See *powertoy* in Chapter 5, *Commands and Applications*, for more information about TweakUI.

If a third-party application has added a control panel applet and you want to temporarily keep it from appearing in the Control Panel, simply give the *.cpl* file another extension or move it to another folder than \ *Windows\System*.

Control Panel

Accessibility Options   \ *Windows\System\access.cpl*

Manage features to make Windows 95 more usable by people with disabilities.

To Launch

Control Panel → Accessibility Options

Command Line

```
control access.cpl [,property-tab]
```

Property Tabs

,0 Keyboard

,1 Keyboard

,2 Sound

,3 Display

,4 Mouse

,5 General

Each Accessibility Options property tab consists of a series of checkboxes to enable various options, along with a settings button to configure that option. The following sections outline the options and associated settings for each tab. Many of the accessibility options also have an associated keyboard accelerator (a bit of a misnomer, since most are quite complex!) that allows you to toggle it on and off. The accelerator is not enabled by default.

Keyboard

StickyKeys lets you type the individual keys that make up keyboard accelerators one after another rather than all together. For example, with StickyKeys enabled, typing Ctrl, then Alt, then Del one after another would have the effect of Ctrl-Alt-Del. StickyKeys are useful if you have trouble holding down multiple keys at once. Keyboard accelerator: press Shift five times.

FilterKeys lets you configure Windows 95's behavior when a key is held down. FilterKeys → Settings lets you control how long a key must be held down before it starts to repeat and how fast it repeats once it starts. Similar functions are available at Control Panel → Keyboard → Speed. However, FilterKeys also lets you disable keyboard repeat completely. Keyboard accelerator: hold down the right Shift key for eight seconds.

ToggleKeys causes the keyboard to beep whenever you press Caps Lock, Num Lock, or Scroll Lock. Keyboard accelerator: hold down Num Lock for five seconds.

Sounds

SoundSentry lets you substitute visual warnings (e.g., flashing the titlebar or the entire screen) for sounds normally made for the system. Keyboard accelerator: none.

ShowSounds lets you substitute captions for sounds in programs that support this feature. Not many do. Keyboard accelerator: none.

Display

High Contrast lets you pick white on black, black on white, or a custom Desktop scheme (this is the same list as available at Control Panel → Display; look for schemes with large or extra large in the scheme name for appropriate entries). To create your own scheme (and add it to the Custom list), go to Control Panel → Display. Keyboard accelerator: left Alt+left Shift+Print Screen.

If you have trouble seeing the display, you may also want to use large pointers or enable Mouse Trails (which leaves a ghost track when you move the pointer). These are settable at Control Panel → Mouse → Pointers and Control Panel → Mouse → Motion, respectively.

Mouse

MouseKeys lets you use keys on the numeric keypad to move the pointer around the screen (see Figure 4-2).

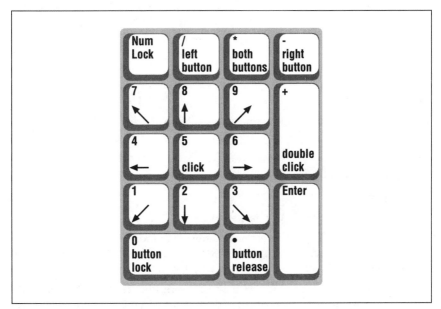

Figure 4-2: The numeric keypad with MouseKeys

Move the pointer to an object and press Ins to start dragging. Press Del to end the drag.

Press – to switch "clicking" to the right button. That is – then 5 to right-click or – then + to right–double-click. "Right-click" mode remains enabled until you press / to switch back to left-clicking.

Hold down Shift while using the arrow keys to move the pointer pixel by pixel; hold down Ctrl to move in big jumps.

The Settings dialog box lets you control how fast the pointer moves and how quickly it speeds up when you hold down a key:

Top speed
> We recommend a high speed, but try different settings for yourself.

Acceleration
> For maximum control, we recommend a slow acceleration.

Use MouseKeys when Num Lock is [on/off]
> Toggle this checkbox if you plan to use the numeric keypad for numbers as well as MouseKeys. Show MouseKey status on screen. We like having the icon in the System Tray, especially since MouseKeys occasionally turns itself off for no obvious reason. Keyboard accelerator: left Alt+left Shift+Num Lock.

General
> Automatic Reset lets you choose whether to apply the chosen Accessibility Options to the current session only rather than leaving them in place, and also lets you set a timeout to turn them off after the system has been idle for a set number of minutes.

Notification lets you specify whether messages or sounds should be used to let you know when an accessibility option is turned on or off.

SerialKey devices enables the use of special alternative input devices attached to a serial port.

Add New Hardware   *\Windows\System\sysdm.cpl*

Run a wizard that will autodetect newly installed hardware and install the appropriate drivers.

To Launch

Control Panel → Add New Hardware

Command Line

```
control sysdm.cpl Add New Hardware
```

Generally, Windows 95 will detect new hardware and use the appropriate drivers automatically (this is called "Plug and Play"). However, you may sometimes need to intervene manually (this is called "Plug and Pray").

If you ask the wizard to autodetect new hardware (the Yes radio button on the first page), it will look for any hardware devices for which it does not have associated drivers and ask you for configuration only for that device. If you want to add a specific device by name, specify No on the first page, and step through the wizard to pick the general type of the device, then the specific manufacturer and model. If your model is not listed or you have a specific driver installation disk you want to load, click the "Have Disk..." button. The disk must include an *.inf* file provided by the manufacturer.

Notes

- The "Add New Hardware" argument is necessary on the command line because *sysdm.cpl* contains multiple control panel dialog boxes. Running `control sysdm.cpl` by itself launches the System Properties dialog box (Control Panel → System).

- You should have the Windows 95 CD-ROM handy when using this wizard, or the wizard will eventually stall. Fortunately, it recovers more gracefully than many Windows programs.

- You can modify information for existing hardware devices using Control Panel → System → Device Manager.

Add/Remove Programs   *\Windows\System\appwiz.cpl*

Add or remove programs from the system, set up various system options, and create startup disks.

To Launch

Control Panel → Add/Remove Programs

Command Line

```
control appwiz.cpl [,property-tab]
```

Property Tabs

,0   Install/Uninstall

,1   Install/Uninstall

,2   Windows Setup

,3   Startup Disk

Install/Uninstall

Lets you install a new program from a floppy disk or CD ROM, and offers a scrollable list of all programs that can be uninstalled by Windows. This list includes Microsoft applications and all well-behaved third-party applications, but in most cases does not include system components. (That's the next tab.)

Windows Setup

Lets you install various Windows 95 system features, including Accessibility Options, Accessories, Communications, Disk Tools, Microsoft Fax, Multilanguage Support, Multimedia, The Microsoft Network, and Windows Messaging. Components that have already been installed will be checked.

Note that the first-level dialog box is usually only the top level, and each component may have additional subcomponents visible via the Details button. At the bottom of the Description area, you will see a message like "4 of 5 components selected." This refers to the subcomponents that are available by clicking on the Details button. Figure 4-3 shows the Communications component, and the five sub-components can be seen in Figure 4-4. In other words, if you're trying to figure out what's installed, don't look at just the first dialog box.

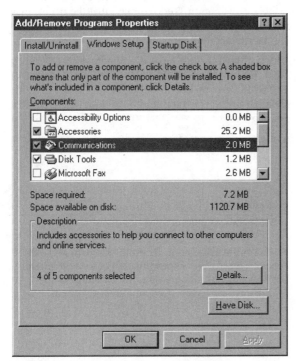

Figure 4-3: The Communications component

Figure 4-4: Details of the Communications component

Table 4-1 lists the components found on the Windows Setup tab, and the various details for each component, which can be viewed by selecting the component and pressing the Details button. Keep in mind that the details may vary slightly depending on what version of Windows 95 you're running, the hardware you're running it on, and other factors.

On older versions of Windows 95, you must have the Windows 95 CD handy to install any element that hasn't been installed. Some recent versions of Windows 95 include most of the contents of the distribution CD-ROM in the directory *Windows**Options*. If you have this setup, you don't need the CD-ROM to add components.

Select any item to see a brief explanation of its contents and how much disk space it takes up.

Table 4-1: The Windows Setup Components

Components	Details
Accessibility Options	Accessibility Options
Accessories	Calculator, Character Map, Clipboard Viewer, Desktop Management, Desktop Wallpaper, Document Templates, Games, Imaging, Mouse Pointers, Net Watcher, Online User's Guide, Paint, Quick View, Screen Savers, System Monitor, System Resource Meter, Windows 95 Tour, WinPopup, WordPad

Table 4-1: The Windows Setup Components (continued)

Components	Details
Communications	Dial-Up Networking, Direct Cable Connection, HyperTerminal, Microsoft NetMeeting, Phone Dialer
Disk Tools	Backup
Microsoft Fax	Microsoft Fax Services, Microsoft Fax Viewer
Multilanguage Support	Baltic Language Support, Central European, Cyrillic, Greek, Turkish
Multimedia	Audio Compression, CD Player, Media Player, Multimedia Sound Schemes, Sample Sounds, Sound Recorder, Video Compression, Volume Control
The Microsoft Network	The Microsoft Network
Windows Messaging	Microsoft Mail Services, Windows Messaging

Startup Disk

Lets you store essential system files onto a floppy. This startup disk can be used to boot your system if you are having problems booting. Surprisingly, it doesn't make a fully bootable Windows 95 disk. To boot the full Win95 with a GUI from a floppy, the floppy must include *io.sys*, *msdos.sys*, and a *config.sys* file. The *config.sys* should look something like the following:

```
shell=c:\command.com /p /e:1024
device=c:\windows\himem.sys
device=c:\windows\ifshlp.sys
device=c:\windows\setver.exe
dos=high
```

If you want to boot automatically into the Win95 GUI, then you also need an *autoexec.bat* with at least one line:

```
c:\windows\win.com
```

See Chapter 9, *Windows Startup*, for more information on each of these files.

Notes

- Add/Remove Programs → Windows Setup installs everything that has been checked in the Components list, but it also removes everything that has been unchecked, so be careful not to remove some existing component when installing something new.

- If your system doesn't match the contents of this book (e.g., if you can't find a program we describe), look in Add/Remove Programs to see if a relevant component is installed. (It could also be something that Microsoft added in a later version.)

- TweakUI can be used to add, remove, or edit items in the Add/Remove Programs list. After all, once you've removed a program, you may never want to see it again! See *powertoy* in Chapter 5.

Date/Time   *\Windows\System\timedate.cpl*

Set the date, time, or time zone.

To Launch

Control Panel → Date/Time
Double-click on clock in System Tray

Command Line

```
control timedate.cpl [,property-tab]
```

Property Tabs

,0   Date & Time

,1   Time Zone

Date & Time

Gives you a graphical, self-explanatory control panel for setting the system date and time. Since this is the only built-in calendar in the system, it's also useful if you want to figure out if a date next March is a Tuesday or a Wednesday—as long as you remember to set the calendar back to the current date before you exit, or choose Cancel rather than OK when closing the control panel.

Time Zone

In the original version of Windows 95, shows a nifty world map on which you can click to select the appropriate time zone. (For example, try clicking directly on Newfoundland.) In OSR2, however, the map is inactive, and you must instead use the list box at the top, which contains a complete listing of the world's time zones. Pick the appropriate zone for where you are located. Each zone is accompanied by the number of hours it varies (+ or -) from Greenwich Mean Time (GMT). (If anyone knows why the later release took such an obvious step backwards in functionality, please let us know.)

A checkbox on this tab also allows you to specify whether the system should adjust automatically for daylight savings changes.

Notes

- Even if you don't need to change the time zone, the Time Zone tab can be very handy, since it lists the variance from GMT for most major locations worldwide. If you need to figure out what time it is in Tokyo, you can do so, using your system clock and some simple addition or subtraction.

- Time Zone names and other data are stored in the Registry. To add new Zone names, use *tzedit*.

See Also

date, *time*, and *tzedit* in Chapter 5

Desktop Themes

Personalize your Desktop with additional wallpapers, screen savers, sounds, and pointers. (Requires Microsoft Plus!.)

Command Line

```
control themes.cpl
```

Choose a theme from the drop-down box (see Figure 4-5) and a sample will be displayed. Although these settings can be configured from individual tabs in the Display, Mouse, and Sounds applets in the Control Panel, Desktop Themes combines all of the options into one place, allowing you to easily pick and choose a screen saver, sound event, pointer, wallpaper, and so on, in coordinated "themes."

Another nice thing about Desktop themes is that you can sample different themes and options without committing to any changes on your system. This is similar to the ability to view different screen savers in the Display applet before you commit them

Plus! contains many, many more wallpapers, cursors and screen savers than the standard distribution.

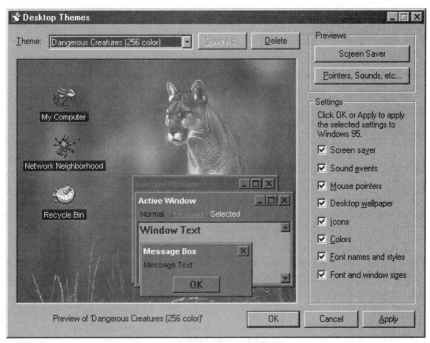

Figure 4-5: The Desktop Themes dialog box

Display   \ *Windows\System\desk.cpl*

View or modify settings for video adapter and monitor, and for Windows 95 background, screen saver, and general appearance.

To Launch

> Control Panel → Display
> Desktop → context menu → Properties

Command Line

> ```
> control desk.cpl [,property-tab]
> ```

Property Tabs

,0 Background

,1 Screen Saver

,2 Appearance

,3 Settings (Video adapter and monitor)

The optional Plus! and Web property tabs (from Windows 95 Plus! and Microsoft Internet Explorer 4, respectively) are accessible from the command line using even more obscure syntax than normal:

```
control desk.cpl,,@Web
control desk.cpl,,@Plus!
```

(Yes, the ! is part of the command line.)

Most modern video adapters will add additional tabs for special features and settings.

Background

> Select the Desktop background pattern. There are two types of background, Pattern and Wallpaper. Patterns are small bitmaps that will be repeated ("tiled") across the entire screen. Patterns can be edited using the popup pattern editor. They can also be deleted from the system this way. Any bitmap (*.bmp*) file can be used as wallpaper; a large bitmap can be centered, while a small one with a repeating pattern is better tiled. The default list of bitmaps shows *.bmp* files stored in the \ *Windows* directory, but a Browse button lets you look for other bitmaps on the disk or on the network.

> The Microsoft Windows 95 Plus! pack includes additional patterns and wallpapers, and many more are available over the Net. (Using Internet Explorer or Netscape Navigator, right-click on any graphic displayed on a web page, and select Set As Wallpaper from the context menu.)

> In addition to *.bmp* files, you can use *.rle* (Run Length Encoded) files. These are bitmap files that have been compressed by encoding repeating pixel values into a more compact format. Bitmaps can be saved in *.rle* format by many graphics programs. If you want to use one of these, just type **.rle* in the browse dialog box and navigate to the folder where the file is stored.

Screen Saver

Specify whether a screen saver will become active if you leave your machine unattended. In addition to choosing a screen saver, you can specify whether a password is required to regain access to the screen. If you don't click the Change button to set a screen saver–specific password, your password will be the same as the one you use to log on to Windows 95.

Many individual screen savers have their own control panel dialog boxes, accessible by selecting the screen saver and clicking Settings.

Figure 4-6 shows the controls for the Mystify Your Mind screen saver.

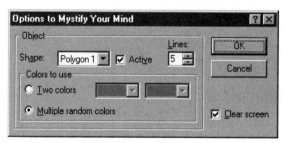

Figure 4-6: Screen saver controls

Screen saver *.scr* files (usually stored in \ *Windows\System*) are really just Windows executables with a different file extension. They can even be executed from the command line.

The Screen Saver tab in Control Panel → Display also controls energy-saving features of the monitor, including timers for low-power standby and shutting off the monitor automatically.

Appearance

Offers a large selection of "schemes" that govern the appearance of Windows 95 GUI elements: the size and color of titlebars, windows, menus, icons, and so on. Among the most useful schemes are Windows Standard, Windows Standard (Large), and Windows Standard (Extra Large). You can also set the size and color of about 20 different user-interface elements individually.

If you decide to modify the individual elements, you should save them as a new scheme using the Save As... button. The scheme is saved in the Registry. If you don't save your changes as a named scheme, they will be lost when you switch to another scheme.

Windows 95 Plus! offers an expanded version of schemes referred to as Desktop Themes, which combine schemes with sounds, wallpapers, and so on. For more information, see Desktop Themes.

If you click the down arrow by Display Properties → Appearance → Color, you get a palette of available colors. Clicking the Other... button at the bottom of the Palette gets you into a wonderful little color editor. Dragging the mouse pointer through a rainbow-hued color space lets you explore the full range of possible colors on your monitor and save any you like to a custom color palette. As an added "geek thrill," you can see the Hue and Saturation values (as well as the RGB color values) change as you move through the color space. A slider on the left controls the luminosity. You can see how, regardless of the hue, as the luminosity goes up, the color washes out to white, and as the luminosity goes down, it fades into black. A neat, hands-on exposure to color theory at work.

(Actually, this dialog box is a standard part of Windows, not tied in particular to the Display control panel applet. For example, in MS Paint, see Colors → Edit Colors → Define Custom Colors.)

Figure 4-7 shows this hidden gem. The black-and-white figure doesn't do it justice. It's fun to play with even if all you want to do is understand how colors work.

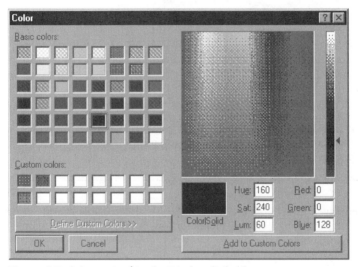

Figure 4-7: Color options in the Display dialog box

Settings

Controls the Windows 95 color palette, Desktop resolution, and the size of the font in the Windows 95 user interface. Also lets you choose your monitor and associated device drivers. See Figure 4-8.

Show settings icon on taskbar

Puts a control into the System Tray that brings up the Display Properties tab. This might be handy if you use different monitors, or even if you just like to change your screen saver regularly.

Color palette

Lets you choose between three color settings: 256 color (8-bit), High Color (16-bit), and True Color (24-bit). The 256 color setting is generally adequate for the standard Windows 95 Desktop and applications, but higher resolution is necessary if you want to display photographs or other images with lots of color gradations.

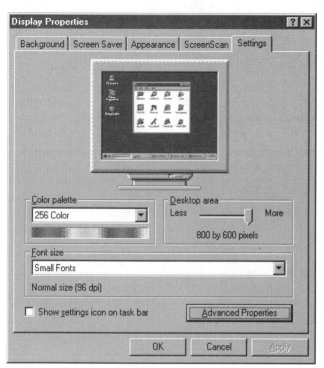

Figure 4-8: Settings

One thing many users find confusing is the way that the number of colors seems linked to the resolution: you can't always have lots of colors and a high resolution at the same time. The color depth and resolution are in fact closely related to the amount of video RAM. This isn't the amount of system RAM, but the memory installed on your video card.

Here's how it works. A system looks up colors from a color table using a value for each individual pixel on the screen. An 8-bit value for each pixel can point to 2^8, or 256 colors. A 16-bit value can point to 2^{16}, or 65,536 colors, and a 24-bit value can point to 16 million unique colors. If you use a larger number of bits per pixel, you need more video RAM. Similarly, you need more RAM for higher resolution, because higher resolution means that the screen display is made up of more pixels.

The horizontal and vertical dimensions (in pixels) are multiplied to find the total number of pixels on the screen. Then that number is multiplied by the amount of memory required by each pixel to get the total memory required by a particular setting. For example, to find out how much video RAM is required by 1024×768 in RGB mode (24-bit, or 16 million colors):

$$\frac{1024 \text{ pixels} \times 768 \text{ pixels} \times 24 \text{ bits/pixel}}{8 \text{ bits/byte}} = 2,359,296 \text{ bytes } (2.4 \text{ MB})$$

If you have only 2 MB of video RAM (a common amount), you won't be able to set your display to this mode. However, you'll be able to use a resolution of 800×600 with this color depth, since that will require only 1.4 MB of video RAM. To use a higher resolution, you'd have to drop your color depth to 16-bit mode (64,000 colors), which would require only 1.6 MB.

Advanced Properties

Leads to a separate dialog box with three tabs: Adapter, Monitor, and Performance.

The Adapter tab allows you to change the current video driver (although the manufacturer of your video hardware may require a different method), and to change the refresh rate of the display (OSR2 only). Set the refresh rate to Optimal, unless you encounter a problem—in that case, set it to the highest setting that will work with your hardware.

The Monitor tab lets you specify your monitor—a good idea if Windows can't do it automatically. Windows uses this setting to determine the maximum resolution, color depth, and refresh rate of your monitor, which are all reflected in the settings. If you know that your monitor (or video card) supports something that Windows isn't letting you do (such as a higher refresh rate or resolution), odds are that it's not configured properly.

Check the "Monitor is Energy Star compliant" option to allow Windows to shut it off after a period of inactivity (further settings are inconveniently located in the Screen Saver tab of Display Properties).

The Performance tab lets you control hardware graphics acceleration. It also lets you configure Windows to apply changes (most commonly made in the Settings tab of Display Properties) *without* having to restart Windows. Ironically, this setting won't take effect until you restart Windows.

Notes

- If Microsoft Internet Explorer 4 is installed (and in the forthcoming Windows 98), Display also provides a Web property tab that controls the Active Desktop, allowing the user to select whether the Windows Desktop is an HTML page, for example.

- There may be additional system-specific tabs, especially on laptop machines, as well as tabs added by applications. For example, McAfee VShield (virus-detection software) installs a ScreenScan tab.

Fonts   *\Windows\Fonts*

View available fonts on the system, and install new fonts.

To Launch

Control Panel → Fonts
Start → Run → `\windows\fonts`

Unlike most of the other items in the Control Panel window, Fonts is not a control panel applet (*.cpl* file) but a shortcut to a folder.

The folder contains a file for each font available on the system. Double-click on any font to view it using the *fontview* program, or right-click on any font and select Properties to see more information about the font.

Menus

All of the control panel–like functionality is provided by the menubar of the font folder:

File → Install New Font...

Allows you to copy a new font from another folder, disk, or network drive to the Fonts directory. You can also drag and drop a font file from the Explorer.

View → List Fonts by Similarity

Lets you choose a font and then list other fonts by their relationship to the selected font. (The relationship is based on the PANOSE type-matching system; see *http://www.fonts.com/hp/panose.*) This can be handy if you're trying to find a replacement font that is close to one you're currently using.

View → Details

Gives filenames and sizes for each font.

View → Hide Variations

Shortens the list of fonts by eliminating bold and italic forms of each font from the listing.

Notes

- Fonts can be either bitmapped (many screen fonts, which have the *.fon* extension) or scalable (used in word processors and graphics applications). True-Type fonts are the most common scalable fonts on Windows machines, and have the *.ttf* extension. TrueType fonts often emulate equivalent Adobe Post-Script fonts, although not exactly (since Microsoft didn't want to license the original font designs). New Times Roman is roughly equivalent to Times Roman, and Arial is roughly equivalent to Helvetica. Small differences between the fonts can make major differences in printing, so if absolute fidelity is required, you should install additional fonts to match those stored in your output device.

    You can use Adobe Type 1 fonts with Windows 95, but you need Adobe Type Manager. See *http://www.adobe.com.*

- The *charmap* program (Start → Programs → Accessories → Character Map) is perhaps more useful than *fontview.* You can't get as good a look at what the font looks like, but you can see what characters are contained in it and what key will generate each character. (This is especially useful with symbol fonts.) You can select non-printing characters for pasting into other applications. Figure 4-9 shows the Wingdings font as it appears in *charmap.* See *charmap* in Chapter 5 for further details.

- There is not always a one-to-one mapping between font name (e.g., in a drop-down list for font selection) and font file. For example, the *Vgasys.fon* and *Vgaoem.fon* files contain several of the fonts used in DOS windows. Still others are found in the *Dosapp.fon* and *8514oem.fon* files.

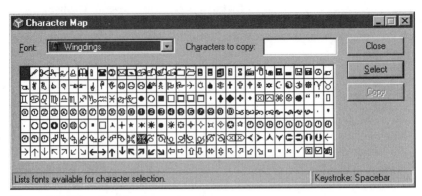

Figure 4-9: Wingdings in charmap

- The *Marlett.ttf* font is used for constructing user interface elements such as the minimize, maximize, and close buttons on the Windows titlebar, the checkmark that appears when you click on a checkbox, the arrows that appear in scrollbars and drop-down lists, and so on. As a kind of security measure, this file actually doesn't show up in the Control Panel; if you were to delete it, Windows 95 wouldn't work properly, so it's marked as a hidden file. It won't show up in the Explorer either, even if you tell the Explorer to display hidden files! However, you can view it from the command line (`fontview \Windows\Fonts\marlett.ttf`), or from the drop-down font list in Character Map (*charmap*).

- Other useful special-purpose fonts that feature symbols (often called dingbats by typesetters) include *Wingdings.ttf, Mapsym.ttf* (map symbols), Symbol (*symbol.ttf* and *symbole.fon*), and the various math fonts.

- See *http://www.oreilly.com/homepages/comp.fonts/ifa* (the Internet Font Archives) for more information about fonts.

- *Windows**Fonts* is a "special" folder that can sometimes lose its "magic." In other words, it's possible for the fonts folder to stop working and just display the files normally. This can be fixed with TweakUI.

WARNING

Since the Fonts folder is special, it's possible to lose files there. Sometimes a non-font file is copied into the Fonts folder, and won't be visible, even to the Explorer or Start → Find → Files or Folders. The only way to see it and get it out is from the DOS prompt (using *dir* and *move*) or the old Windows 3.1 File Manager (*winfile*).

Internet   \ *Windows*\ *System*\ *inetcpl.cpl*

Configure Internet settings used by Internet Explorer (IE) and any other applications that use Microsoft's WinInet API.

To Launch

> Control Panel → Internet
> Internet → View → Options...

Command Line

```
control inetcpl.cpl
```

The property tabs are not addressable from the command line for this control panel. There are six tabs:

> General
> Connection
> Navigation
> Programs
> Security
> Advanced

(The description in this section is based on IE version 3.02, the version installed with most current versions of Windows 95. If you have upgraded to IE 4.0, some of the information here may be incorrect. See the forthcoming *Windows 98 in a Nutshell*.)

General

Lets you specify whether IE should display graphics, play sounds or videos, as well as what colors to use for text, background, and links (see Figure 4-10). It also lets you customize the layout and contents of the IE toolbar. Note that these Internet settings are just for IE; Netscape Navigator and Communicator don't use them.

Connection

Describes your connection to the Internet (see Figure 4-11). If you use a dial-up connection, check Connect to the Internet as Needed if you want IE to fire up a Dial-Up Networking connection when you start it. (If you enable this option, other Internet applications such as *telnet* will inherit the same behavior.) Note that even if you don't check this option, you can still use IE over a Dial-Up Networking connection; you will simply have to make the connection manually.

Auto-connect doesn't always work properly—it can sometimes have trouble connecting, even when manual connections work fine. Also, it can connect for no apparent reason and stay on for hours. See Chapter 7, *Dial-Up Networking*, for more information on manual versus automatic connection.

If you are sometimes connected to a local area network that is gatewayed to the Internet, and sometimes use dial-up, you may still want to check "Connect...As Needed." IE is not smart enough to detect the existing network connection, and will bring up the dial-up connection request even when you are already connected. Simply click Cancel, though, and IE (or any other Internet-enabled application) will then use your existing network connection. (However, network routing problems may occur if you switch between a dedicated and dial-up connection without rebooting. See Chapter 7 for details.)

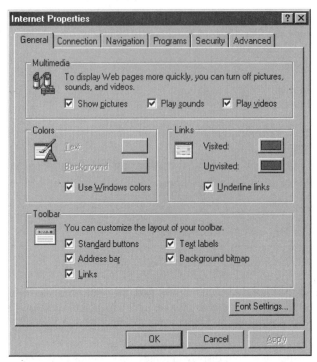

Figure 4-10: The General tab for IE configuration

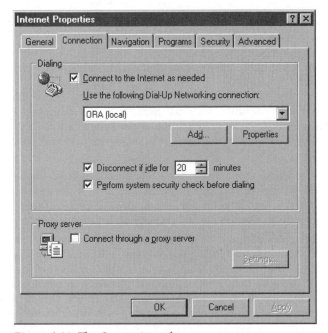

Figure 4-11: The Connection tab

You can select from existing connections or add a new one. Add... starts up the Make New Connection wizard from Dial-Up Networking. Properties... opens the Property tab for the selected connection.

WARNING

It's a bit dangerous to check "Disconnect if idle" if you are using other Internet applications than IE, since it doesn't recognize activity in other applications (such as *telnet*), causing unexpected hangups.

"Perform system security check before dialing" can disable file and printer sharing. This is highly recommended before connecting to the Internet.

Click "Connect through a proxy server" if your site uses a firewall or a proxy server for caching frequently accessed data. The Settings dialog box is shown in Figure 4-12.

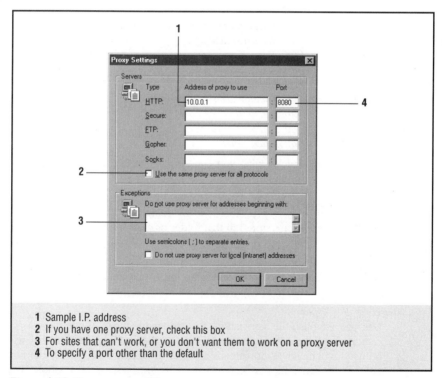

1 Sample I.P. address
2 If you have one proxy server, check this box
3 For sites that can't work, or you don't want them to work on a proxy server
4 To specify a port other than the default

Figure 4-12: Proxy server settings

You can specify a separate proxy server for each Internet application. The address should be specified as the DNS hostname or IP address of the machine that will act as the proxy server for each server. HTTP is the web proxy; FTP and gopher are proxies for their eponymous applications. Secure and Socks are security proxies. The port number is an optional designator that is used if the server is not found at the standard port for that service. Contact your network administrator for details.

Exceptions lets you specify individual site addresses that are allowed to bypass the proxy server. The exception list can contain hostnames, domain names, or port numbers. Port numbers should be preceded by a colon. Each entry is separated by a semicolon. For example, the following exception would allow direct connections to any host within the *foo.com* domain, to the specific host *magic.foobar.com*, and to port 80 on any other host:

```
foo.com;magic.foobar.com;:80
```

Navigation

Customize lets you select which web address should be displayed when the browser starts up. You can also specify the web page that should be used for IE's search button, and what five pages should appear on its Quick Links toolbar.

Addresses of some well-known search engines that you might want to use include:

AltaVista:	*http://www.altavista.digital.com*
Excite:	*http://www.excite.com*
Hotbot:	*http://www.hotbot.com*
Infoseek:	*http://www.infoseek.com*
Lycos:	*http://www.lycos.com*
MetaCrawler:	*http://metacrawler.cs.washington.edu*
Northern Light:	*http://www.nlsearch.com*
WebCrawler:	*http://www.webcrawler.com*
Yahoo!:	*http://www.yahoo.com*

When customizing Quick Links, you can also customize the names that will be given to each of the links.

History lets you specify how many days to keep a history of which sites you've visited. (The history is stored in the folder *Windows**History.*) You can also view the files are stored in that folder or clear it out.

Programs

Mail and news

Lets you choose which mail and news programs you want to use along with IE.

Viewers → File Types

Lets you establish file associations for various file types. While these associations are primarily meant for identifying "helper" applications that will be used whenever IE downloads a file of a specific type, you are in fact editing the same file associations used by the system as a whole. For more information, see "File Types" in Chapter 3, *The Windows 95 User Interface.*

IE should check to see if it is the default browser

This setting is a shot in the Netscape-Microsoft browser wars. If you check this, any time you start up Internet Explorer (as long as it isn't already your default browser, of course), it will ask you if you want to make it your default browser, supplanting Netscape or whatever is currently configured as the default browser. (The default browser is the one that you'll get if you click on *.htm* or *.html* files. So this is really just a shortcut to change a bunch of file/program associations; see the Explorer View → Options → File Types. For a utility that makes this process a little easier, see *http://www.creativelement.com/software/delegate.html.*) Unless you're fond of what has come to be called "nagware," we recommend leaving this box unchecked.

Security

Contains a number of functions that allow you to control what can and can't be viewed by IE. (See Figure 4-13.) Many of the features here are not widely used and still have a few kinks to be worked out.

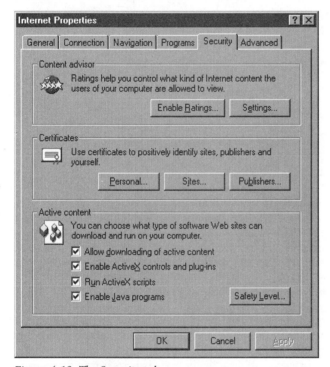

Figure 4-13: The Security tab

Content Advisor

Lets you use an Internet ratings service to screen out potentially offensive content. The first time you use this function, you will be asked to define a supervisor password. You will thereafter need to enter this password to change any of the content ratings.

By default, the only content advisor installed is RSACi (the Recreational Software Advisory Council internet advisor; see Figure 4-14). RSACi depends on voluntary ratings by sites as to the amount of violence, sex, and profanity they contain. While this may seem silly, sites with potentially objectionable content (such as porn sites) are embracing such "self-regulation" to forestall more stringent government regulation.

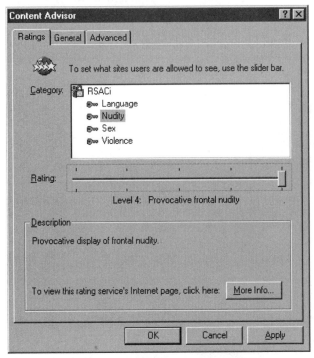

Figure 4-14: RSACi, the default IE content advisor

The rating system is fairly self-explanatory—you choose one of four levels for each of four types of "objectionable" content (Language, Nudity, Sex, Violence); by default, every slider is set to the lowest level. Raise it to block out sites that announce that they carry, for instance, full frontal nudity. In practice, though, ratings are far from clear-cut. See *http://public.antipope.org/charlie/nonfiction/rant/rsaci.html* for a critique. See *http://www.rsac.org* for the official explanation of the rating methodology. In addition to the philosophical problems explored at the *antipope.org* site, there is a practical problem: the browser expects a rating from every site and requires a password to access it if it has none. Since few sites have RSACi ratings, you're greatly limiting your Internet access by using this feature.

Ratings services publish their ratings in files of type *.rat.* A source for additional rating service files is *http://www.classify.org/pics.htm.* Download the *.rat* file for a given service, save it in \ *Windows\System*, then go to the Advanced tab → Ratings Systems button to add the ratings file to the Content Advisor → Ratings page.

Certificates

It's fairly easy for one site to masquerade as another. Digital Certificates, which use cryptography to create unique identifiers that can't be forged, can be used by sites that want to prove their identity to you. Here, you can identify which certification authorities (certificate issuers) you want to trust. Unfortunately, you can't add new certification authorities, and if IE receives a certificate issued by an authority it doesn't know about, it will not display the associated web page. Especially in an intranet context, companies sometimes self-certify their pages. You can view pages that have no certificate at all, but an unknown certificate will block display of the page: hardly a desired feature.

Active Content

Some web pages include active content with Java applets or ActiveX controls: these are actually programs that execute on your system. Potentially hostile applets could destroy data, copy information from your system, or do other harm. Here, you can select which types of active content to allow, and, via the Safety Level button, decide what happens when each of these types is encountered. Checking any type of active content and then selecting Safety Levels → High is the same as unchecking that content type. Safety Levels → Medium warns you whenever any type of active content is downloaded to your machine, and lets you choose whether to execute it. Safety Levels → None turns off safety checking for active content.

Advanced

Contains additional security settings as well as a grab bag of other configuration settings (see Figure 4-15):

Warn before sending over an open connection

Web sites can use either an *http* (hypertext transfer protocol) server or an *https* (secure *http*) server. Secure servers make up a very small fraction of all web servers, but many of those accept credit cards or other financial information. Check here if you want to be warned whenever you are asked to fill out a form or otherwise send data to an ordinary *http* server rather than a secure *https* server. "Warn if changing between secure and insecure mode" will issue a warning whenever you switch from *http* to *https*.

Warn about invalid site certificates

If someone gets a certificate for their site, but then changes a URL in the certificate, you'll get a warning.

Warn before accepting cookies

Cookies are small data records that a site can store on your machine to help them track repeat visits and (theoretically) serve you better. Most cookies are harmless, but there is some fear that the technology could be misused. Click here to be warned any time a site tries to store a cookie on your disk. IE stores cookies in \ *Windows*\ *Cookies*. (Netscape uses its own *cookies.txt* file.)

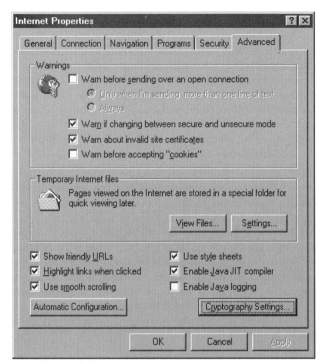

Figure 4-15: The Advanced tab

Temporary Internet Files

> Internet sites don't necessarily change all that often. Since an *.html* file must be downloaded temporarily to your machine in order for you to view it, it's possible to keep these downloaded files around in case you want to go back to the same page again. Settings controls how much of your disk can be used for these temporary (cached) files and how often IE should check to make sure it has the most current version of the page.

Show Friendly URLs

> A bogus setting that changes the URL shown in the status bar from the full http address, such as *http://www.oreilly.com/windows.html,* to a meaningless message like "shortcut to windows." You're better off with the full URL.

Enable Java JIT compiler

> Checking this option enables Microsoft's "Just In Time" (JIT) on-the-fly compiler for Java, which can speed up execution of any downloaded Java content.

Enable Java Logging

> For security reasons, you may want IE to keep a log of any Java program's actions. This log is stored in *\Windows\Java\javalog.txt.*

Automatic Configuration

You can supposedly set up IE to update itself over the web automatically whenever Microsoft issues new versions. Unfortunately, we've never found the URL that you need to specify to make this work. (Finding anything on the Microsoft site is a nightmare.)

Cryptography Settings

You can set the level of SSL (Secure Sockets Layer) that you will accept. Given the current fragmentary state of Internet security, you probably want to accept any of the security protocols, unless you have reason to do otherwise.

Joystick

Select the model of joystick connected to your system, and optionally calibrate it.

To Launch

Control Panel → Joystick

Command Line

```
control joy.cpl
```

There is only one tab for this applet—the Joystick tab—and it contains the following properties:

Current Joystick

The drop-down list contains generically numbered joysticks (e.g., Joystick 1, Joystick 2, etc.); you can associate these with specific joystick configurations. For example, you can set up Joystick 1 as a two-button gamepad.

Joystick Selection

Lists the types of joysticks you can choose from. If you've selected Joystick 2, for instance, from the Current Joystick box, then this is the box where you want to select the type of joystick (e.g., CH Virtual Pilot). If the type isn't listed, then select Custom and a dialog box will pop up allowing you to choose the types you have, i.e., three axes, four buttons, etc.

Calibrate button

Click this button to calibrate your joystick. This sets the range of motion for your joystick. If your joystick has a throttle, point-of-view (POV) hat, or rudder controls, you can also calibrate these features.

Test button

Click this to test your joystick's calibration.

Rudder checkbox

Enables you to use rudder controls. If this checkbox is unavailable, either you don't have a rudder control, or you specified a four-axis joystick in the Custom Joystick dialog box.

Reset button

Resets your joystick to the default value range. This can be helpful, since some games reset your joystick's value range, causing it to function incorrectly with other games.

Keyboard   *Windows\System\main.cpl*

Control the speed of key repetition, the cursor blink rate, the keyboard language and layout, and the keyboard hardware that is attached to the system.

To Launch

Control Panel → Keyboard

Command Line

```
control main.cpl Keyboard [,property tab]
```

(You must specify "Keyboard," because by default, *main.cpl* launches the Mouse control panel applet.)

Property Tabs

,0 Speed

,1 Language

,2 General

Speed

Controls the speed of character repeat and cursor blinking. Sliders allow you to specify how long a key must be held down before it starts to repeat, and how fast it will repeat once it starts. A test box lets you check out your settings before you OK them. Another slider lets you set the blink rate of the text cursor.

Language

Lets you specify the keyboard layout. Use Language → Properties to switch to a foreign language keyboard layout or an alternative English language layout such as Dvorak.

If multiple languages are enabled, you can also choose the keyboard accelerator that will be used to switch between languages (left Alt+Shift or Ctrl+Shift).

The Enable indicator on Taskbar checkbox has meaning only if multiple languages are enabled. If the indicator is displayed, you can click on it to display a popup menu of available keyboard layouts.

General

Lets you install additional keyboard drivers.

Modems   *Windows\System\modem.cpl*

Configure any modems used with your system.

To Launch

Control Panel → Modems

Command Line

```
control modem.cpl
```

If you have not already installed a modem, this command will run the Install New Modems wizard; otherwise, it will bring up Modems Properties with a list of available modems.

This configuration involves a fairly complicated tree of interconnected dialog boxes and property sheets, many of them with very similar names. This maze is further complicated by the fact that applications that use the modem, like Dial-Up Networking, HyperTerminal, and others, create individual connection setup records called *connectoids*, which use many of the same dialog boxes.

The settings made in Properties and Dialing Properties for any modem are the global defaults; they can be changed in any specific connectoid. What's more, changes here will not propagate to any existing connectoids. Furthermore, the property sheet for a given connectoid (e.g., a connection in Dial-Up Networking) has a Configure button that gives additional options not available in Control Panel → Modems. See Chapter 7, *Dial-Up Networking*, for additional details.

The hierarchy of property tabs, buttons, and dialog boxes under Control Panel → Modem looks like this:

```
General → Add
        → Remove
        → any modem → Properties → General
                    → Properties → Connection
                    → Properties → Connection → Port Settings
                    → Properties → Connection → Advanced → Dialing
                          Properties → My Locations
Diagnostics → Driver
Diagnostics → More Info
```

General → Add

An entry point to the Install New Modems wizard. General → Remove lets you remove an installed modem from the list.

General → <any modem> → Properties → General

Set the speaker volume and a maximum speed for the connection. This maximum speed may be greater than the actual line speed of your connection, since your modem may do data compression, and, if so, will be able to accept data from the system faster than it actually sends it over the phone. If your communications applications are experiencing errors, you may want to reduce the maximum value.

Modems normally try to connect first at their highest rated speed. If the remote modem cannot match that speed, or the line quality is poor, they cycle down to the next available speed. Check "Only connect at this speed" if you don't want to use a lower speed when the connection is poor.

General → <any modem> → Properties → Connection → Connection preferences

Set the number of data bits, the parity, and the number of stop bits. These days, the correct answers are almost always 8, none, and 1. Serial connections send each byte of data in a frame consisting of a start bit, 7 or 8 data bits, an optional parity (error checking) bit, and one or two stop bits. In the past, various operating systems used different combinations of data, parity, and stop bits; nowadays, you shouldn't need to change the defaults unless you're communicating with an older system or online service.

General → <any modem> → Properties → Connection → Call preferences
If you travel internationally, you need to uncheck "Wait for dial tone before dialing," since Windows 95 won't recognize the dial tone offered by most foreign phone networks. You can also set the timeout for how long to wait before hanging up if a connection is not completed (i.e., when you hear the modems screaming at each other, but not finding a mutually satisfactory tone). You can also set how long a connection should be left idle before hanging up.

General → <any modem> → Properties → Connection → Port Settings
Set the sizes of the data buffers in the modem. You shouldn't need to change this unless you're having problems.

General → <any modem> → Properties → Connection → Advanced

"Use error control" and "Compress data" will be appropriate for only certain combinations of modem and online service. The compression specified here is hardware compression. If you are using a compressed protocol, the two may conflict, and you should disable hardware compression.

"Extra settings" are Hayes-compatible modem command strings to be sent to the modem on initialization. (Don't type the AT prefix to get the modem's attention, since the extra settings will be tagged on to the end of the existing initialization string. For example, for dial-pulse, whose Hayes command is ATDP, you would just put DP.) A list of these AT commands is available at: *http://www.compaq.com/athome/presariohelp/us/modems/modatcr.html.*

The option to "Record a log file" logs debugging information in the file \ *Windows\modemlog.txt.*

General → Dialing Properties
Provides access to the My Locations dialog box. See Chapter 7 for details. Locations are stored in the file \ *Windows\telephon.ini.*

Diagnostics
Provides information about the modem installed on each COM port. More Info actually sends various information requests to the modem and returns the result. You can interrogate the modem directly if you set Connection → Properties → Configure → Options → Bring up terminal window before dialing.

Notes

- Additional information about the modem can be found via the Device Manager (Control Panel → System → Device Manager).

- For more information on Dial-Up Networking connections, see Chapter 7.

Mouse

Control pointer cursors and mouse movement parameters.

To Launch

Control Panel → Mouse

Command Line

```
control main.cpl
```

There are four property tabs, but the [,**property-tab**] syntax does not work for this control panel. The tabs are as follows:

Buttons

> Specify a right- or left-handed mouse. If you select left-handed, the meaning of click and right-click are reversed from the standard usage specified in this book. You can also specify how close together two clicks must occur to be considered a double-click.

Pointers

> Pick from several schemes, each of which determines the shape and size of pointer icons (arrow, hourglass, text insert, and so on). Click Browse to look at possible cursor icons in *Windows**Cursors* to substitute another cursor for any of those shown. Plus! includes many additional schemes and individual cursors.

Motion

> Specify the speed with which the pointer moves in response to mouse movements, and whether the pointer should leave a "ghost trail" showing its path (useful for laptops or where the visibility of the mouse is problematic).

General

> Change the pointing device attached to your system.

Control Panel

Multimedia

Control sound volume, video playback, and other multimedia features.

To Launch

> Control Panel → Multimedia

Command Line

```
control mmsys.cpl [,property-tab]
```

Property Tab

See Figure 4-16 for a display of the Property tab.

,0 Audio

,1 Video

,2 MIDI

,3 CD Music

,4 Advanced

Audio

> Gives access to the volume control for playback of *.wav* files (such as those used for system sounds), and the recording volume for applications such as Sound Recorder (*sndrec32.exe*). More importantly, a checkbox allows you to put a Volume Control icon on the Taskbar. The volume control program that icon invokes is much more powerful. See *sndvol32* in Chapter 5 for details.

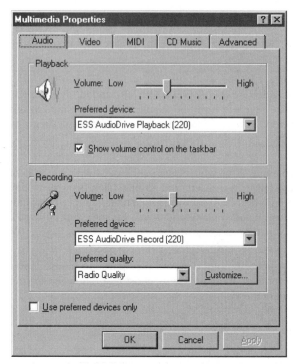

Figure 4-16: Multimedia Properties dialog box

The Playback volume control corresponds to the Wave control in *sndrec32*; and the Recording volume control corresponds to the Volume Control → Recording → Recording Volume control in *sndrec32*. (If you run both Control Panel → Multimedia → Audio and *sndrec32*, you can see how moving the slider in either application affects the other.)

The Preferred quality listbox lets you choose how much data should be saved when you record sounds. CD Quality requires 172 KB/second; Radio quality requires 22 KB/second for mono and 43 KB/second for stereo; Telephone quality requires 11 KB/second for mono and 22 KB/second for stereo. The Customize button lets you match up preferred quality names with the amount of data to be sampled and the type of sound file to be created.

Video

Choose whether a video file will be displayed in a window or on the full screen. The window can be the original size (as defined in the video source file), scaled to double the original size, to 1/16, 1/4, or 1/2 of the screen size, or in a maximized window.

MIDI

Configure MIDI output from the PC. MIDI is the Musical Instrument Digital Interface, a standard for mixing computers and musical instruments (usually synthesizers). See *http://www.midi.com*.

CD Music

Select the drive to be used for CD music applications like *cdplayer.exe* and control the volume.

Advanced

Lets you browse an Explorer-like expandable/collapsible tree view of available multimedia devices (audio devices, MIDI instruments, mixers, line input devices, video and audio compression codecs, and so on), and display or change properties for each one.

Notes

- Multimedia → Audio → Playback volume controls the volume of system sounds and alerts; of all the various sound controls, this is the one you will really make use of!

- Control Panel → System → Device Manager may be helpful for reconfiguring multimedia hardware.

See Also

cdplayer, sndrec32, and *sndvol32* in Chapter 5

Network

To Launch

Control Panel → Network
Network Neighborhood → Properties

Command Line

```
control netcpl.cpl
```

The Network control panel lets you configure both Microsoft and non-Microsoft networks, assuming you have the appropriate network devices and drivers installed. There are three property tabs: Configuration, Identification, and Access Control. They are not individually addressable from the command line.

You will usually have to reboot your system after changing any of the settings in this control panel.

Configuration

This tab (Figure 4-17) leads to a complex maze of dialog boxes. You must first select a network component, then view or modify its properties.

There are four types of network components: clients, adapters, protocols, and services. Each has a distinctive icon. (Click Add for a description of each icon if they are not immediately obvious to you.)

A *client* is the software that allows your computer to connect to other computers. Clients might include client software from Banyan (VINES), Novell (Netware), Sunsoft (PC NFS), Microsoft, or third-party TCP/IP vendors such as FTP Software. In the detailed descriptions that follow, we provide information for Microsoft's Client for Microsoft Networks. For other network clients, see the vendor's documentation.

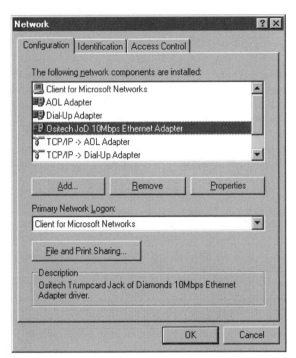

Figure 4-17: The Network Configuration tab

An *adapter* is the hardware device that makes the physical connection, such as a modem or Ethernet adapter. To add a new adapter, click Add → Adapter, select the appropriate adapter from the manufacturer/model list, and be prepared to load the disk containing the necessary drivers. The Properties page for each adapter generally contains hardware-specific settings, which are not discussed here.

A *protocol* is the language that computers use to communicate over a given network. Protocols always show up in the component list as "bound" to an adapter. For example, you might see TCP/IP → Dial-Up Adapter for TCP/IP over a modem, or TCP/IP → 10 Mbps Ethernet Adapter for TCP/IP over an Ethernet network. The Properties page for the supported protocols contains information that you may need to view or modify. In the detailed descriptions that follow, we provide information for the TCP/IP protocol, the native protocol of the Internet, and, increasingly, the default protocol for Microsoft networks.

A *service* is the program that allows your system to provide services (such as file or print sharing) to other systems. In the detailed descriptions that follow, we provide information only on Microsoft's file and printer sharing for Microsoft networks.

Client for Microsoft Networks → Properties

Specify whether your system should automatically log on to a Windows NT domain. A *domain* is a group of computers sharing a common security policy and account database. The combination of domain name and computer name uniquely identify the computer on the network. The NT domain name has nothing to do with the DNS domain name used by TCP/IP networks.

Choose whether to reconnect all network drives whenever you log on, or wait until you actually use them. The "Quick logon" option will decrease the time it takes to log on, but will increase the time it takes the first time you try to access a given network drive.

TCP/IP Properties

This is a seven-tabbed dialog box: IP Address, WINS Configuration, Gateway, DNS Configuration, NetBIOS, Advanced, and Bindings. Note that you can have different settings for each adapter to which the protocol is bound (e.g., for both a modem and a LAN adapter).

IP Address

Uniquely identifies your computer to other computers on the network (see Figure 4-18).

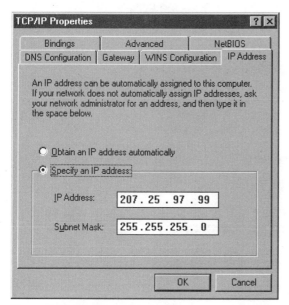

Figure 4-18: The IP Address tab

An IP address is a 32-bit number, typically written as four decimal numbers from 0 to 255, separated by dots. For example, the IP address of the machine that hosts *www.oreilly.com* is 204.148.40.9.

Some TCP/IP networks support a protocol called DHCP (Dynamic Host Configuration Protocol), which automatically assigns IP addresses from an available pool. You will almost always choose "Obtain an IP address automatically" when dialing in to an Internet service provider, although this option is also used with many local area networks. If DHCP is used, all of the address fields will be filled in automatically.

If you explicitly specify the IP address, you must get the correct address for your machine and any DNS or WINS servers from your network administrator.

The subnet mask is used to tell the system which part of the IP address is the network address and which part is the host address. The subnet mask to be used depends on the size of your network, and whether the network administrator has divided it up into subnetworks. A common subnet mask is 255.255.255.0; however, this is not something you can guess. Ask your network administrator or ISP for the correct value.

WINS Configuration

WINS (Windows Internet Naming Service) allows you to use programs that require Microsoft's older NetBIOS protocol over a TCP/IP network. See Figure 4-19. Your network administrator will let you know if you need to configure this protocol. The WINS server is the TCP/IP-based computer that will perform the mapping between the two protocols.

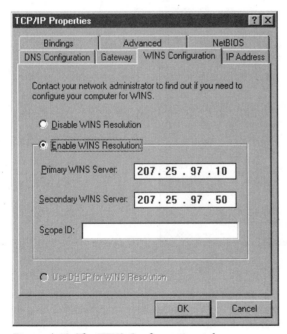

Figure 4-19: The WINS Configuration tab

Gateway

A *gateway* is a router or other device that connects two otherwise incompatible networks. Check with your network administrator about whether you need to fill in this tab.

DNS Configuration

DNS (Domain Naming System) is the Internet facility for mapping IP addresses like 204.148.40.24 into names like *windows.oreilly.com*. You must specify your computer's name and the DNS domain to which it belongs, as well as the IP addresses of two or more computers that will act as domain name servers for your system. (See Figure 4-20.)

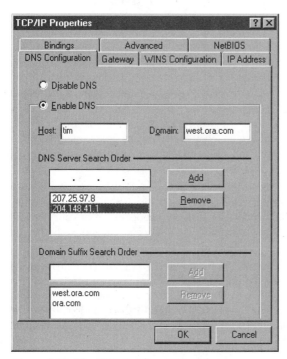

Figure 4-20: The DNS Configuration tab

Your network administrator or Internet service provider will give you the appropriate IP addresses to enter here. Type the IP address in the data entry area containing four subfields separated by dots, then click Add. The servers will be searched in the order in which you add them. If you want to change the search order, you must remove existing addresses and add them back in the correct order. The dialog box does not support drag or move operations.

Note that if you are in a large network, there may be multiple subdomains. The Domain suffix search order specifies whether the top level domain or subdomain will be contacted first. As with DNS server search order, you must enter them in the right order, and re-enter them to change the order.

NetBIOS

Lets you enable NetBIOS over TCP/IP.

Advanced

This tab is empty on the systems we've examined.

Bindings

Lets you specify which services will communicate using this protocol. The components on the available list will depend on what network services are installed on your system.

File and Printer Sharing for Microsoft Networks → Properties

Allows you to specify your system as the Browse Master or LM announce for a network. This means that your system will maintain the list of available resources (folders and printers) for the network or workgroup. On most local area networks, an NT server will provide these functions.

Identification

In order to participate in a network, each computer must have a name that is unique on its segment of the network. The name can have up to fifteen characters, and cannot include spaces. It will be the first component of any UNC pathname referring to files on your computer. For example, entering *bob* as the name of your computer will mean that any shared resources on your computer, such as *printer1*, will be known as *bob\printer1*.

Computers can be organized into workgroups for purposes of resource sharing. You can enter a new name of up to fifteen characters into the workgroup field, but you shouldn't do so without the cooperation of your network administrator, since workgroup naming must be coordinated with that on other computers.

The description field is optional, but it's wise to put in a comment giving more information about the computer, such as the name of the user or the resources that are available for sharing on that computer. Two or more computers must have the same workgroup name to show up side-by-side in Network Neighborhood. Otherwise, connected machines will show up in "Entire Network" in the Network Neighborhood.

Access Control

There are two options for access control: share-level, and user-level. Share-level access means that any time you designate a resource for sharing (*folder* → Properties → Sharing or Printers → *selected printer* → File → Sharing), you must specify a password that other users must type in before they can access the shared folder or printer. User-level access control allows a master list of users and/or workgroups to be granted access to shared resources without having to supply a password. The master list is kept not on your computer, but on the network server, so you shouldn't specify user-level access control without the cooperation of your network administrator.

ODBC/32-bit ODBC

To Launch

Control Panel → ODBC

Command Line

```
control odbccp32.cpl
```

ODBC (Open Database Connectivity) is a standard for connecting applications to compliant databases. The ODBC control panel lets you associate an ODBC driver with a data source name. These are closely tied to any MS Office applications that are installed. When Access is installed, for example, it installs several database drivers, all of which are shown here. This applet is useful primarily to people developing database applications.

Passwords

Change passwords, and enable remote administration or user profiles.

To Launch

Control Panel → Passwords

Command Line

```
control password.cpl
```

The Passwords control panel has three tabs: Change Passwords, Remote Administration, and User Profiles. They are not individually addressable from the command line.

Change Passwords
Changes the Windows password as well as passwords for other password-protected devices. (For example, if you've enabled a screen saver with a password, you can change that password here.)

Remote Administration
Allows your system to be administered from a remote computer. It includes remote Registry administration, remote policy administration (System Policy Editor), and possibly other settings.

User Profiles
Specify whether user profiles are enabled, or whether all users of the machine use the same settings. Profiles allow users to customize the Desktop and other preferences.

Notes

- If user profiles are enabled at Control Panel → Passwords → User Profiles, two things happen:

  1. The user branch of the Registry (*user.dat*) will keep track of all information that is different from user to user. The user branch of the Registry is stored in two files: the system default *user.dat* and the individual user's *user.dat*.

  2. If individual Desktops and Start menus are enabled via checkboxes on Control Panel → Passwords → User Profiles, the system folders \ *Windows\Desktop* and \ *Windows\Start Menu* will be replaced by \ *Windows\Profiles\ <username>\ Desktop* and \ *Windows\Profiles\ <username>\ Start Menu*.

- A good way to pick a password that is easy for you to remember but hard for others to guess is to use the initials of a phrase that is meaningful to you. For example, "I Like My Dog Spot Quite A Lot!" might become ILMDSQAL! While the character sequence might not stick in your mind, you can always remember the phrase to reconstruct it, and over time it will become easy to use. A minimum of six characters, with punctuation, numbers, and a combination of upper- and lowercase characters makes for a password that is harder to crack.

- The exact password requirements for your system may be set by a system administrator using the System Policy Editor. The administrator can set the minimum password length, whether or not a password must include numbers as well as letters, and whether passwords can be cached (remembered) by applications. It is even possible to disable the Password control panel so that users can't change the passwords that are assigned to them. System policies are typically implemented only on corporate networks, and are set on a logon server, not on the Windows 95 client.

WARNING

The use of passwords can lead you to believe that Windows 95 provides some level of security for user files. In fact, any user can gain access to your machine at the initial login prompt without knowing your password. All they have to do is hit Esc to log in as the "default" user. Or they can type in a new login name (and optional password). This will create a new user profile with the same settings as those of the default user. As one wag put it, Microsoft offers two security options: Windows NT wears a chastity belt, and Windows 95 a fig leaf.

- Many users on single-user machines don't like being asked for a login name and password when they boot up, so they leave the password field blank. On subsequent reboots, you will not be prompted for a password. However, this can cause problems for subsystems such as Dial-Up Networking. Even though Dial-Up Networking uses a different password than the initial login, the system's ability to remember passwords is enabled only if you have a login password to begin with.

- Use Control Panel → Display → Screen Saver → Password protected to require a password to regain access to the system after a screen saver has kicked in.

PC Card (PCMCIA)

Stop a PCMCIA card before removing it from its slot. This is visible only if the computer has a PCMCIA slot.

To Launch
Control Panel → PC Card (PCMCIA)

Command Line
```
control main.cpl,PC Card (PCMCIA)
```

There are two tabs: Socket Status and Global Settings. They are not individually addressable from the command line.

Socket Status

Select a PC card from the list, and click Stop before removing it from the slot. If you swap PC cards often, specify a Stop control for each specific PC card on the Taskbar. "Display warning if card is removed before it is stopped" can be unchecked only if a control is displayed on the Taskbar.

Global Settings

Specifies memory allocation for the selected card. Use Automatic selection unless you know what you're doing. You can also disable PC card sound effects here.

Notes

If you omit the comma and the "PC Card (PCMCIA)" argument on the command line, you will get the Mouse control panel instead. There are several control panels within *main.cpl*, and Mouse happens to be the first.

Power

Control power management features of the computer.

To Launch

Control Panel → Power

Command Line

```
control main.cpl,Power
```

Power management refers to the ability of a computer to step down its power usage gradually when left unattended, eventually going all the way to shutdown.

Windows 95 will give you access to power management features only if your computer supports them and they are enabled in the computer's BIOS (Basic Input/Output System). To enter your computer's BIOS setup screen, see your user's manual. (That being said, it's usually accessible by pressing the DEL key just after your computer is first turned on.) Look for a setting called APM (for advanced power management), and make sure that power management is enabled.

There are three tabs: Power, Disk Drives, and PC-Card Modems. They are not individually addressable from the command line.

Power

Displays the power source (AC or battery) and the amount of battery life remaining (if present). Allows you to display a battery indicator on the Taskbar, and to enable automatic Windows power management.

Power → Advanced

Enable the Suspend command on the Start menu. (This is really useful only on laptops.) Also lets you specify whether an incoming phone call should wake up the system.

Disk Drives

Allows you to specify how long Windows should wait before switching disk drives to low power when the system is inactive. Separate time limits can be set for AC and battery power.

PC-Card Modems

Allows you to turn off power to PC card modems when they are not in use.

Notes

• Most laptops have power management subsystems of their own, which are usually more sophisticated than the generic Windows power management features.

• If you omit the ,Power argument on the command line, you will get the Mouse control panel instead. There are several control panels within *main.cpl*, and Mouse happens to be the first.

Printers

Add a new printer, or get and set information about existing printers.

To Launch

> Control Panel → Printers
> Start → Settings → Printers
> My Computer → Printers

Command Line

> control main.cpl,Printers

The Control Panel proper, as launched from the command line or Control Panel → Printers → Add Printer, is a wizard that steps you through the process of configuring a new printer. If you choose Add Printer → Next → Local, you will see a list of printer manufacturers and models to choose from. If your printer is not listed, and you have an installation disk containing drivers for your printer, click "Have Disk...".

LPT1: is the standard parallel printer port for the PC, but a printer can also be connected to either of the two standard serial ports, COM1: or COM2:. Choose FILE: to create a pseudo-printer that will copy the output destined for a printer to a disk file instead. This is useful if you want to save the PostScript that would be generated for printing into a file, or if you don't have a printer attached to your system, but have access to one in some form.

By default, the name given to the printer will be its model name, but you can give it any name you like. In an installation with multiple printers, it's often nice to come up with a suite of related names—constellations, Shakespearean characters, or what have you.

If you choose Add Printer → Network, the system will look through the Network Neighborhood for existing printers. What you are really doing is creating a shortcut to that existing printer. If you already know the printer name, type its UNC pathname (see "Network" earlier in this chapter) or browse until you find it. You need not give it the same name as it has at its destination, but it would probably be wise.

Printer Properties

Use the Properties sheet for any selected printer to get detailed configuration information about the printer and change any of its settings. With the exception of Properties → Paper, you probably don't need to change any of the settings, and it is better to set this in your applications.

Properties → Details → Capture Printer Port can be used to link a network printer to a logical printer port name. This can be useful for older DOS programs that require a DOS-style printer port name such as LPT1:.

Regional Settings

Control the display of country-specific information such as numbers, currency, time, or dates in Windows and in applications (such as MS Office) that support regional settings.

To Launch

Control Panel → Regional Settings

Command Line

```
control intl.cpl [, property-tab]
```

Property Tabs

,0 Regional Settings

,1 Number

,2 Currency

,3 Time

,4 Date

Regional Settings

This is the master tab. Select a location here, and the other tabs will show the standard representation for numbers, currency, and so forth in that location.

Number

Shows the default treatment of numbers in that region. This includes things like the decimal point, the number of digits shown after a decimal, how digits are grouped and how the groups are separated, and so on. For example, the number represented in the U.S. as 123,456,789.00 will be represented as 123 456 789,00 in France.

Currency

Shows the default representation of currency, including the currency symbol for the region and its placement before or after the numbers.

Time

Shows the treatment of time, as demonstrated by the system clock in the System Tray. While there is less variation in time representation than in the other categories, there are variations in whether A.M./P.M. indicators are used, whether leading zeros are shown for hours before 10, and whether a 12- or 24-hour clock is used.

Date

Shows the treatment of dates, in both short form (12/24/98) and long form (December 24, 1998).

Notes

* After changing the location and either clicking Apply or trying to switch to another tab, you will be told that the settings will not take effect until you restart the machine. This does not appear to be the case. For instance, if you have a clock displayed in the System Tray, you can see it change to the new format as soon as you click Apply or go to another tab. Excel and Word also appear to recognize the new regional setting immediately.

* Even if you are not changing regions, this control panel can be a useful resource for finding out the standard representations in other countries.

* Although you can modify any of the settings without changing the region itself, there really isn't a good reason to do this, since they accurately reflect local custom.

Sounds

Control the sound schemes used by Windows and Windows applications to signal various system events.

To Launch

Control Panel → Sounds

Command Line

```
control mmsys.cpl,Sounds
```

The Sounds control panel (Figure 4-21) lets you associate specific sounds with various Windows events. Additional sound associations can be installed by various applications. This is the place to change or remove all those annoying noises that Windows makes when it starts up, shuts down, or wants to let you know that you've made a mistake.

Under each application, you'll see a list of events (such as Exit Windows or Maximize). Any event that has an associated sound will be accompanied by a speaker icon. Select the event, and see the name of the associated sound file. Use the drop-down list under Sound Name to change the sound associated with the selected event. Change the sound to "(None)" if you don't want to hear a sound for that event. To hear a preview of a given sound, click the arrow in the Preview box.

Sounds are stored as *.wav* files in the *Windows**Media* directory. You can use the Browse button to add sound files stored elsewhere on your disk. See *http:// www.yahoo.com/Computers_and_Internet/Multimedia/Sound/Archives/WAV* for more sounds available from the Net.

Sounds are grouped into Schemes, just like Desktop patterns and window borders. Change the scheme, and all of the sound associations change. Try some of the different schemes, and preview the various sounds until you find one you like.

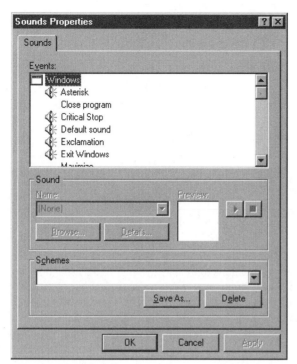

Figure 4-21: The Sounds control panel applet

If your system has a microphone, you can use the Sound Recorder (*sndrec32*) to record your own sounds and attach them to Windows events. You can also use *sndrec32* to "edit" the existing sound files—creating various special effects, or just changing the volume.

Notes

- If you omit ,**Sounds** on the command line, you will get the Multimedia control panel instead. Sounds is really the sixth tab of the Multimedia control panel.

- If you change any of the specific sound/event associations, use the Save As button to save them as a new scheme. (You can also modify the existing schemes by saving your custom scheme with one of the existing names.) Note that you don't need to save a scheme for any individual changes to be remembered when you exit the control, but be aware that they will be lost if you ever switch to another scheme.

- The sound volume is controlled by Multimedia → Audio → Volume (*sndvol32.exe*). You'd expect to find it here, but you'd be wrong.

- The only way to disable the system beep is with TweakUI. If you remove the sound event for errors, the built-in computer speaker will still beep.

System

Manage hardware and device drivers.

To Launch

> Control Panel → System
> My Computer → Properties

Command Line

```
control sysdm.cpl [,property-tab]
```

Property Tabs

,0 General

,1 Device Manager

,2 Hardware Profiles

,3 Performance

General

Gives information about the manufacturer and the registered user: not very useful, except to learn which build of Windows you're running (950, 950B, 1111, etc.).

Device Manager

Gives you an Explorer-like expandable/collapsible tree view of the hardware devices known to your system. Select a device and click Properties to get information about the device. (Double-clicking on the device name will also open the Property sheet.) Note that the properties for generic device types (like Keyboard or Modem) won't contain much information. You have to expand the view to see and select specific devices first.

The data available here is not the same as the properties available from the Control Panel. For example, Device Manager → Modems → *any modem* will not give you the same properties as Control Panel → Modems. The information here is of a lower level; you should not change these settings manually, since it will interfere with your system's automatic plug and play configuration. You can get a hard copy printout of a lot of this information with *hwdiag.exe* (see Chapter 5). Discussion of this material is beyond the scope of this book.

Possibly more interesting than specific devices are the properties under the first heading, Computer (see Figure 4-22). You can use this dialog box to view information such as the IRQ (Interrupt Request) for each device, I/O addresses, and reserved memory. Using this summary view is easier than going to the properties for each individual device.

Use the Print... button to print out and store a complete record of settings. This is especially useful if you plan to make any changes.

If you actually want to change the resource for any device, you must go back to the main Device Manager list, and open the Property sheet for the desired device.

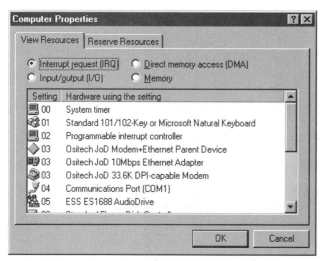

Figure 4-22: Computer Properties in the Device Manager tab

Hardware Profiles

Hardware profiles provide a way of optimizing the drivers that are loaded for a computer that can be used in more than one configuration. For example, you might have different profiles for a portable computer when it is docked and undocked.

Performance

Contains some useful information about your system, such as the amount of memory and whether disk compression is installed. Advanced settings should be modified only by system administrators or knowledgeable users.

Users

Add, configure and delete multiple users.

To Launch

Control Panel → Users

Command Line

```
control inetcpl.cpl,Users
```

This applet is present only if your system is configured for multiple users (see Figure 4-23).

This control panel contains only one property tab: User List.

Use the New User button to add a new username. An applet will pop up and walk you through lists of dialog boxes with checkboxes to enable or disable options on the Desktop, the Start menu, the Favorites folder, and so on.

The Delete button deletes the selected user. Interestingly enough, you don't need a password to delete a user.

Figure 4-23: The Users applet

To change the password of a user, select a user and click Set Password.

To change individual settings of a user (the same settings that are available when pressing the New User button) select a user and click Change Settings.

CHAPTER 5

Commands and Applications

Windows 95 ships with over 150 separate utilities and other add-on programs. Some of these are an intrinsic part of the system, and are always installed. Others are optional, and can be installed or removed via Control Panel → Add/Remove Programs → Windows Setup.

The optional programs (once installed) are listed on the Start menu under Programs → Accessories. They are also accessible from the command line, although without a book such as this one, it might take you a while to figure out just what the command name might be.

Ironically, it is the programs that are built in that are least visible in the user interface. These include commands such as *copy* and *rename* that are built into the DOS command interpreter, as well as external DOS commands like *deltree* and *sort*, system administration programs like the Registry Editor (*regedit*), or networking commands like *netstat, ping,* and *tracert.* You can explore the \ *Windows,* \ *Windows\ Command,* or \ *Windows\ System* directories looking for files with *.exe* or *.com* extensions, but, in an effort to convince the world that Windows 95 was no longer based on DOS, Microsoft has made it quite difficult to find many extraordinarily useful programs.

Finally, even well-known programs such as the Explorer and Control Panel have command-line equivalents, which can often be surprisingly useful.

Unfortunately, because all of these programs are provided with little or no documentation, figuring out just how they work once you get them to run is often a process of trial and error.

This chapter is designed to let you know just what you've got. It documents virtually every accessory, DOS command, and other utility. We've listed each program alphabetically by its actual DOS filename (*explorer.exe* rather than the Windows Explorer, or *sndvol32.exe* rather than Volume Control), since many of these programs have no other, more descriptive name in the Windows 95 interface. Even for those that do, you'll find that using the short name on the command line is often much easier than selecting the program from a long series of cascading menus. (We do actually list accessories by both their Start menu name and their canonical executable filename, but the Start menu name merely provides a cross reference to the executable name, which hosts the complete entry.)

Run Prompt Versus MS-DOS Command Window

Windows 95 provides two different command lines: the Run prompt (Start → Run), and a DOS, or "command" window. An easy way to open a DOS window is to use:

> Start → Run → `command`

However, a DOS window is sufficiently useful that you may want to put a shortcut to *command.com* into *Windows\Start Menu\Programs\StartUp*, so that a DOS window will be opened up whenever you boot your machine. You can open multiple DOS windows at the same time.

> With IE4 installed, one of the Taskbar toolbars, the address bar, can also be used as a command line—it's always at the bottom of the screen. (See the forthcoming *Windows 98 in a Nutshell* for details.)

There are a few significant differences between the Run command line and the DOS command line. The most important are:

- Some commands (such as *cd, dir, copy, rename*, and so forth) are internal to *command.com*. They can be invoked from the Run prompt only by a syntax too complex to be worthwhile. These internal commands are so noted in their reference entries.

- Each instance of the command interpreter runs in its own virtual machine, each with its own "environment." The environment includes such information as the current directory, the search path (the directories in which the command interpreter looks for the commands whose names you type), and the format of the prompt. Some commands, once issued, change the environment for subsequent commands. The most obvious example of this is when you type commands at the DOS prompt such as:

```
C:>cd \windows\desktop
C:\Windows\Desktop>notepad myfile.txt
```

This example illustrates one of the limitations of the Run prompt. Since it executes only one command at a time and then exits, concepts such as "the current directory" have little meaning for it. As a result, you must always specify complete pathnames for any filenames you want to edit.

Commands such as *cd, break, path, prompt, set*, and others whose principal function is to affect the command environment thus have no effect at the Run prompt.

- On the other hand, the Run prompt keeps a history of recent commands in a drop-down list. This makes commands easy to re-execute. (However, you can get an even more powerful command history function in a DOS window using the *doskey* command.)

   In addition, the Run prompt allows you to type the pathname of a file to launch the associated application. Typing the name of a disk or folder will open a folder window to display its contents. Doing the same thing at a DOS prompt will earn you an error message. (However, you can run the application associated with a file, or even open a folder or drive window even if you don't know the application, using the *start* command at the DOS prompt.)

- The search path for the Run prompt comes from the global settings made in the \ *autoexec.bat* file when the system is started. You can't change the path without changing *autoexec.bat* and then rebooting. In a DOS window, you can change the path with either the *path* or *set* commands.

- You must enclose long filenames in quotes to use them in a DOS window, since the command interpreter uses spaces to separate command-line arguments.

For more information on the Run prompt, see Chapter 4, *The Control Panel*; for more information on the DOS command interpreter, see the entries for *command* and *set* in this chapter, as well as Chapter 6, *The Batch Language*, which describes the Windows batch language.

Wildcards, Pipes, and Redirection

Special symbols that can be used on the command line are listed in Table 5-1.

Table 5-1: Wildcards, Pipes, and Redirection Symbols

Symbol	Description
*	Refers to multiple characters in a file or directory name.
?	Refers to a single character in a file or directory name.
>	Redirects a command's output to a standard device (e.g., the monitor) or a file.
>>	Appends the output from a command to the specified file.
<	Directs input to a command from a nonstandard source.
|	Redirects the output of a program or command to a second program or command. (This is called a "pipe.")

Examples

The following examples demonstrate some uses of wildcards, pipes, and redirection:

.

   All files with all extensions.

professor.*

   All files with "professor" anywhere in the name, with any extension.

bonelli.

All files with names ending with "bonelli" (or "Bonelli"), with any extension

chap?.doc

All files named "chap" plus one character and with doc extensions (e.g., *chap1.doc*, but not *chap-1.doc* or *chap.doc*).

Keep in mind that not all commands handle wildcards in exactly the same way. For example, *dir ** and *dir *.** list the same thing, but *del ** will delete only files without an extension.

dir c:\windows /o/a > c:\data\windows.txt

List all files ordered alphabetically in the *Windows* directory, and create a file of this listing called *windows.txt*. If the file already exists, it will be overwritten.

Instead of directing to a file, you can direct to a device, such as NUL (an electronic void): useful if you want a command to run without sending output to the screen.

dir c:\windows\system /o/a >> c:\data\windows.txt

Add the directory listing of the files in the *C:\Windows\System* directory to the end of the file *windows.txt*.

If the specified file doesn't exist, one is created. If one does exist, the output from the command is added to it, unlike with the > key, where the original contents are overwritten.

sort /+12 < c:\nutshell\mylist.txt

To sort the lines in a text file (*c:\nutshell\mylist.txt*) on the twelfth character, the *sort* command is fed input from the file.

echo y | del *.*

If you try to delete all the files in a directory, *del* will prompt you for confirmation. Piping a "y" to the program using *echo* supplies the required answer automatically.

What Commands Are Available?

The following lists give you a quick overview of all of the available programs, organized into functional groups.

Command Interpreters and Program Control

command	DOS 7 command interpreter
doskey	Edit and recall command lines and create macros for DOS commands
exit	Quit the *command.com* program
for	Run a specified command for each instance in a list
more	Read one screen of text at a time
path	Set or display the command search path

progman	The Windows 3.1 Program Manager, replaced by the Explorer in Win95
prompt	Change the Windows command prompt
set	Display, set, or remove MS-DOS environment variables
taskman	Display currently running programs
win	Bootstrap loader for Windows 95 (see Chapter 9, *Windows Startup*)
winset	Set or remove global Windows environment variables

Communications and User Networking

awsnto32	Windows 95 fax server
dialer	Dial voice telephone calls
directcc	Establish a direct serial/parallel cable connection between two computers
exchng 32	The Windows 95 e-mail program.
faxcover	Add graphic elements to fax cover pages
faxview	View *.dcx* and *.awd* files in the original Windows 95 release
ftp	Transfer files between a host and a remote computer over the Internet
hypertrm	Terminal access to remote computers
iexplore	The Microsoft browser (3.02) used to access resources on the Web
netdde	Network Dynamic Data Exchange program
scanpst	The Inbox Repair Tool
sysagent	System Agent for scheduling programs (Microsoft Plus!)
telnet	Create an interactive session on a remote computer using TCP/IP
winchat	Conduct "chat" sessions with other Windows 95 users
winpopup	Send pop-up messages to other Windows 95 computers on your network

Editing Tools

edit	A DOS-based full-screen ASCII text editor
notepad	Edit ASCII text files
sort	Sort text input in alphanumeric order
type	Display the contents of a text file
wordpad	A simple word processor that comes with Windows 95

Commands & Applications

File Management

attrib	Display, set, or remove current file and directory attributes
backup	Copy (back up) files from your hard drive to a floppy disk or tape
cd or *chdir*	Display the name of or change the current directory
cls	Clear the DOS window, leaving only the command prompt and cursor
copy	Copy one or more files to another location
del or erase	Delete one or more files
deltree	Delete a directory and all the subdirectories and files in it
dir	Display a list of files and subdirectories in a directory
explorer	The 32-bit interface shell that allows you to view files and directories in a tree-like structure
fc	Compare two files (or sets of files) and display the differences between them
find	Search one or more files for a specified text string
label	Create, change, or delete the volume label of a disk
lfnbk	A long filename backup utility used in MS-DOS
lfnfor	Enable/disable long filenames when processing *for* commands
md or *mkdir*	Create a new directory
more	Read one screen of text at a time
move	Move files and directories from one location to another
rd or *rmdir*	Remove (delete) a directory
ren or *rename*	Rename a file or directory
winfile	The Windows 3.1–style File Manager
xcopy32	Copy files and directories, including subdirectories

Games

freecell	A solitaire card game
hover	A game in which you steer a hovercraft through the world of Hover
mshearts	Card game that can be played over the network with other Windows 95 users
pinball	3D Space Cadet Pinball game
sol	The popular Microsoft Solitaire game
winmine	Minesweeper game

Miscellaneous

batch	Set up batch files for installing Windows 95 on multiple computers
calc	The Windows 95 calculator
charmap	Display symbols and special characters from specified fonts
clipbrd and *clipbook*	
	View the contents of the Clipboard
jview	Start the Microsoft command-line loader for Java ·
powertoy	A collection of "powertoys" or extra utilities for Windows 95
qbasic	Microsoft Quick Basic programming environment
quikview	View the contents of a file without launching the application
ver	Display the Windows 95 build number
winhlp32	WinHelp engine and viewer

Multimedia

aniedit	Create and edit animated cursors and icons
cdplayer	Play audio CDs in the CD-ROM drive
imagedit	Create or modify bitmap, cursor, or icon files
mplayer	The default Windows 95 video player
mspaint	Create, modify, or view image files
raplayer	Real-time audio delivery system for the Web
sndrec32	Record and play sound files with a *.wav* extension
sndvol32	Control volume and balance of the system's sound devices
wangimg	Read or import different types of image file formats

Network Administration

arp	Display or modify the IP-to-physical address translation tables
nbtstat	Display protocol statistics and current TCP/IP connections using NetBIOS over TCP/IP
net config	Display your current workgroup settings
net diag	Run the Microsoft Network Diagnostics program
net help	Display information about *net* commands and error messages
net init	Load protocol and network adapter drivers
net logoff	Break a network connection
net logon	Identify a computer as a member of a workgroup
net password	Change your logon password
net print	Display information about the print queue on a shared printer
net start	Start Windows 95 networking services

net stop	Stop Windows 95 networking services
net time	Synchronize a computer's clock with a shared clock on a server
net use	Connect or disconnect a computer from a shared resource
net ver	Display the type and version number of the workgroup redirector
net view	Display a list of computers in a specified workgroup
netstat	Display protocol statistics and current TCP/IP network connections to and from the local computer
netwatch	View users connected to your shared directories
ping	Verify connection to a remote TCP/IP host
route	Manipulate the TCP/IP routing table for the local computer
tracert	Internet trace route utility
winipcfg	Display the current TCP/IP settings on your computer

System Tools

cfgback	Configuration Backup Tool for backing up the Windows 95 Registry
cmpagent	Compress drives (comes with Microsoft Plus!)
control	Display the Control Panel, which contains the configuration applets for Windows 95
date	Display or set the system date
debug	Test and edit files and system memory in real-mode MS-DOS
defrag	Reorganize the files on a disk to optimize disk performance
diskcopy	Copy the contents (files and directories) of one floppy disk to another
drvspace	Compress and uncompress data on floppy disks or hard disk drives
drwatson	Provides system error information when a GPF (General Protection Fault) occurs
eru	Windows 95 Emergency Recovery Utility
extract	Extract files and lists from a Windows cabinet (*.cab*) file
fdisk	Configure a fixed disk for use with DOS or another operating system
fontview	View TrueType fonts
format	Format a disk for use
hwdiag	A very useful report tool for hardware, available only on the OSR2 CD
infinst	Integrate *.inf* files from the Windows 95 CD-ROM

krnltoys	A collection of useful tools ("kernel toys") assembled by Microsoft
logview	View and edit the most recent copies of log files
mem	Display the amount of real-mode memory available on your system
mkcompat	Change settings to make a Windows 3.1 program compatible with Windows 95
packager	Create "packages" for insertion into documents via OLE
poledit	Standardize Windows 95 for a group of users
pwledit	Delete passwords from a stored password list
qfecheck	Check versions of system files
quickres	Change monitor resolution and color depth without restarting Windows
regclean	Clean up the Registry
regedit	View and modify the contents of the Registry
rsrcmtr	Monitor the system resources programs are using
rundll32	Provide "string invocation," command-line-based run-time dynamic linking
scandisk	Check the disk surface for errors
setup	Set options to customize and control a Windows 95 installation
shortcut	Command-line tool for creating and maintaining Windows 95 shortcuts
start	Start applications in a new window
sys	Create a bootable MS-DOS disk
sysedit	Edit system initialization files
sysmon	Monitor memory functions and disk cache settings
time	Display or set the system time
tzedit	Time Zone Editor
wintop	A daemon that tracks all running Windows 95 applications

The Resource Kit help file is located on the CD-ROM, and the Resource Kit tools referred to later can be downloaded from:

http://www.microsoft.com/windows95/info/win95reskit.htm

If you are running the initial or SR1 version of Windows 95, and you'd like to find out about or download available OSR2 components:

http://www.microsoft.com/windows95/info/updates.htm

Table 5-2 lists the applications in this chapter that don't exist in the typical Win95 installation (CD-ROM, downloadable from the Web, SR1, OSR2, Plus!, and the Resource Kit) and where they can be found.

Table 5-2: Application List by Category

Category	Application
CD-ROM (OSR2)	batch (also Resource Kit), cfgback, eru, hover, lfnbk, logview, poledit, pwledit, qbasic, rsrcmtr, shortcut, winchat, winset
Download	drwatson, krnltoys, powertoy, raplayer, regclean
OSR1-specific	faxview
OSR2-specific	hwdiag, wangimg
Plus	cmpagent, pinball, sage
Resource Kit	aniedit, batch (also CD-ROM), imagedit, infinst, quickres

Table 5-3 lists the applications that must be installed from the CD-ROM, and the locations of the executables (when applicable) on the OSR2 CD-ROM.

Table 5-3: Application List by CD-ROM Location

Application	OSR2 CD-ROM Location
batch (also Resource Kit)	\Admin\NetTools\Bsetup
cfgback	\Other\Misc\Cfgback
eru	\Other\Misc\ERU
hover	\FunStuff\Hover
lfnbk	\Admin\AppTools\lfnback
logview	\Other\Misc\Logview
poledit	\Admin\AppTools\poledit
pwledit	\Admin\AppTools\pwledit
qbasic	\Other\OldMSDOS
rsrcmtr	Control Panel → Add/Remove Programs (with CD)
shortcut	\Admin\AppTools\Envvars
winchat	\Other\Chat
winset	\Admin\AppTools\Envvars

Format of Each Entry

Each entry starts with the name, the location of the executable file, and a brief description. For instance:

---

sol   *\Windows\sol.exe*

The popular Microsoft Solitaire game that comes free with Windows 95.

If the executable file must be installed from the Win95 CD-ROM, or downloaded from the Web, a "To Install" section follows the location of the file. In this section, we provide the location of the installation file on the Win95 OSR2 CD-ROM.

This is followed by instructions on how to launch the program. If there is more than one way to do it, we generally list the most convenient one first. For example:

> Start → Run → `sol`
> Start → Programs → Accessories → Games → Solitaire

For programs with command-line options, this "To Launch" section contains a description of the command-line syntax. For example:

> ftp [options] [host] [-s: filename]

Command-line arguments shown in brackets are optional. If options must occur in a specific order, they are listed in that order on the syntax line. A vertical bar between two options means you can use one or the other, but not both.

If there are multiple option/argument combinations, or multiple names for a command, we list several syntax lines with the options and arguments that must be used together. Otherwise, we just use the dummy argument [options] and list the options later. For example:

> [+ | –]

means you can use a plus sign (+) *or* a minus sign (–).

Example text in *italic* should be replaced by user-specific information, whereas `constant width` text should be typed literally "as is." **Constant width bold** is used in examples to distinguish text that should be typed by the user from text output by the system.

Unless specified otherwise, filename arguments can be any combination of drive letter, directory path, and filename. The directory path can be absolute (starting with \), relative to the current directory, or a UNC path (including the name of another host in the network). The filename can include wildcards (* and ?).

We then give a brief description of the program. We don't document every obvious feature of the graphical user interface (if one exists), but we do highlight important features.

Where appropriate, we also provide interesting side notes, the names of configuration files or other associated files, and any additional commands internal to the program, as well as references to sources of additional information, including useful web sites. For administration programs not normally installed on the disk, and programs from Microsoft Plus! and the Resource Kit, we give brief instructions on how to install them if they are not already installed.

Commands & Applications

---

aniedit   *\Program Files\Resource Kit\aniedit.exe*

Create and edit animated cursors and icons.

To Install

> Control Panel → Add/Remove Programs → Windows Setup → Have Disk → *Resource Kit directory* → OK → check Animated Cursor Editor and Image Editor → Install

---

To Launch

Start → Programs → Resource Kit → Animated Cursor Editor

Description

aniedit allows you to create and edit animated cursors and icons, and arrange and animate frames produced with the Image Editor. It creates animated cursors by defining a sequence of image frames and the speed with which they will be played. *aniedit* can edit cursors and icons in color or monochrome, including small Windows 95–style icons (16 colors, 16×16 pixels). *aniedit* saves files with an *.ani* extension; you can either open an existing *.ani* file on your computer or create your own animated cursors and icons by using the File → Import Frame option and saving the file. When using the Import Frame option, you can open any cursor (*.cur*) or icon (*.ico*) file on your computer. You can also use the Image Editor to create your own cursors and icons, which you can then import to your *aniedit* file.

To create your animated cursor or icon, import *.cur* or *.ico* files as frames into *aniedit*. As soon as you add frames into the editor, *aniedit* will begin playing the frames in the order created. You then select a Jiffy (1/60th of a second) number for each frame to adjust the length of time each frame is played. An example that comes with Windows 95 is the *hourglas.ani* file, which contains a spinning hourglass (see Figure 5-1).

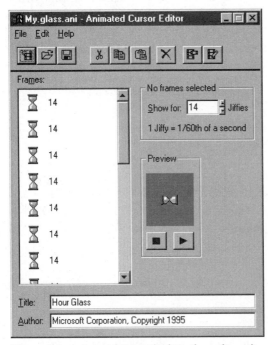

Figure 5-1: Animated Cursor Editor (aniedit.exe)

An important feature in *aniedit* is the toolbar button, which automatically launches a selected frame into the Image Editor, allowing you to make modifications to the image. Then save the image and close the Image Editor, which automatically replaces the original frame image with the modified one.

See Also

> *imagedit*

---

arp

Display or modify the IP-to-physical address translation tables.

To Launch

> arp -s inet_addr eth_addr [if_addr]
> arp -d inet_addr [if_addr]
> arp -a [inet_addr] [-N if_addr]

Description

arp compares the destination IP address to a hardware address. If there is a matching entry, then the hardware address is retrieved from the cache. If not, *arp* broadcasts an ARP Request Packet onto the local subnet, requesting that the owner (machine) of the IP address in question reply with its address. When an *arp* reply is received, the *arp* cache is updated with the new information, and it is used to address the packet at the link layer. Entries in the *arp* cache may be viewed, added and deleted using *arp.exe*.

arp accepts the following options:

-a	Displays current *arp* entries by displaying the cache contents. If *inet_addr* is specified, the IP and physical addresses for only the specified computer are displayed. If more than one network interface uses *arp*, entries for each *arp* table are displayed.
-d	Deletes the host specified by *inet_addr*.
eth_addr	Specifies a physical address as six hexadecimal bytes separated by hyphens, such as 08-00-20-77-2B-87.
-g	Same as -a.
if_addr	If present, this specifies the Internet address of the interface whose address translation table should be modified. If not present, the first applicable interface will be used.
inet_addr	Specifies an Internet address, such as 10.25.99.3.
-N *if_addr*	Displays the *arp* entries for the network interface specified by *if_addr* (used with -a).
-s	Adds the host and associates *inet_addr* with the *eth_addr*. The entry is permanent (i.e., across reboots, normal behavior is to lose cache as entries time out).

Commands & Applications

Examples

From the command line:

```
C:\>ping whitehouse.gov
C:\>arp -a
```

The host will return a reply from the Internet address, indicating that the address has been set and the communication is established. Output similar to the following is displayed:

```
Interface: 10.26.45.123
Internet Address        Physical Address        Type
198.137.241.30          20-53-52-43-00-00       dynamic
10.26.97.8              20-53-52-43-00-00       dynamic
10.26.97.50             20-53-52-43-00-00       dynamic
```

Notes

- *arp* tables don't normally require any manual intervention. They are built automatically. *arp* might be useful, for instance, if two systems were mistakenly set up to use the same IP address. You could use *arp* to discover the host that was misconfigured.

- Normally, cached entries will time out in a matter of minutes. Entries created with the -s option are always available.

- If you have an empty *arp* table (seen with **arp -a**), you must first *ping* an existing unit on your network (see previous example).

See Also

ping
TCP/IP Network Administration, by Craig Hunt (O'Reilly & Associates)

---

attrib   *Windows\Command\attrib.exe*

Display, set, or remove current file and directory attributes.

To Launch

attrib [+ | - attributes] [filename] [/s]

Description

Under DOS and Windows 95, each file has four attributes: read-only, archive, system, and hidden. These attributes are normally set and cleared by Windows or DOS applications, or on the property sheet for a file, but they can also be set or cleared manually with the *attrib* command. *attrib* is particularly useful if you want to change the attributes for several files at once, since it's much easier to do this with *attrib* than by opening the property sheet for each file in turn.

attrib with no arguments displays the attributes of all files in the current directory (including hidden files). Specify a file path to see or set the attributes of the file. You can even use wildcards with *attrib* to help automate tasks (see examples).

attrib accepts the following attributes:

+	Sets an attribute.
–	Clears an attribute.
a	Archive file attributes set by applications whenever they create or modify a file, and cleared by backup programs such as *xcopy* when they make an archive copy of the file.
h	Hidden file attribute. If set, the file will not show up in normal *dir* listing (use dir /ah). The Explorer can be set to show or not show hidden files. For this reason, hidden files are much less "secret" then they were in older versions of DOS and Windows.
r	Read-only file attribute. If set, the file can't be modified.
s	System file attribute. If set, the file is used by DOS or Windows as part of its operation. The file should then not be deleted, moved or renamed.

The following option, if specified, must follow the filename:

/s	Process files in all subdirectories in the specified path.

Examples

Set the file *readme.txt* to read-only:

```
C:\>attrib +r readme.txt
```

Set the file *readme.txt* to read/write, but make it hidden:

```
C:\>attrib -r +h readme.txt
```

Make all files in the root directory (including *msdos.sys*, etc.) unhidden and writable:

```
C:\>attrib -s -h -r \*.*
```

If you just want to see these files use dir /a or dir /ah.

Unmark archive checkbox on all backup files created by applications before doing backup with *backup* or *xcopy* (first, change directory to the top of the directory hierarchy you plan to back up):

```
C:\>attrib -a *.bak /s
```

Notes

- Hidden files can still be opened by DOS programs; they just won't show up in *dir* listings. They will show up in the Explorer and in the open dialog box of Windows applications, unless you select Explorer → View → Options → View → Hide Files of these types.

- Multiple attributes can be set or cleared by combining options (separated by a space), but system and hidden attributes must be cleared before read-only and archive attributes can be cleared. For example:

```
C:\>attrib -s -h -r \msdos.sys
```

Old DOS hands will say that *attrib* is the only way to clear the archive bit from a group of files. But in fact, you can do this via the GUI, too. When you select a group of files, changes to Properties → Attributes will affect all selected files. This is particularly handy when combined with Start → Find → Files or Folders. Unfortunately, there is a flaw in the GUI design. If all the selected files don't have the same attributes, the checkboxes to change attributes will be grayed out (inactive), so in many cases, you'll need *attrib* after all.

- Setting a file's system, hidden, or read-only attribute will prevent the file from being deleted or moved by using the *del, erase,* or *move* commands, but it will not protect the file from the *deltree* or *format* commands.

- In the Explorer, you can view and change file/directory attributes in the File → Properties menu when a file/directory is selected.

- In the Explorer, an extra warning message is given when attempting to move or delete a directory or file with the read-only attribute set (see Figure 5-2).

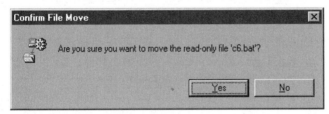

Figure 5-2: Warning when moving a read-only file

- You can also view file attribute settings with `dir /v`.

- In some instances, trying to change certain attributes without first clearing other attributes will cause it to fail. For example, the following won't work (assuming *filename* has +h and +s set):

```
attrib -h filename
attrib -s filename
```

But this does work:

```
attrib -s -h filename
```

See Also

backup, del, deltree, dir, erase, format, move, xcopy

---

awsnto32   *\Windows\System\awsnto32.exe*

Windows 95 fax server.

To Install

Control Panel → Add/Remove Programs → Windows Setup → Microsoft Fax

---

To Launch

Start → Run → `awsnto32`

Start → Programs → Accessories → Fax → Compose New Fax

In Windows Messaging/Exchange: Compose → New Fax

awsnto32 is also used to request a fax:

Start → Run → `awsnto32 -p`

Start → Programs → Accessories → Fax → Request a Fax

In Windows Messaging/Exchange: Tools → Microsoft Fax Tools → Request a Fax

Description

In order to use *awsnto32* to fax documents from Windows 95, you need the Inbox icon on your Desktop, and you need to set up the Inbox by using the setup wizard.

You can send or request a fax by launching *awsnto32* from the command line or from the Start menu, but you can also send or request a fax from within Windows Messaging/Exchange. If you drag a shortcut of *awsnto32* to your Desktop, you can simply drag a document you want for fax right onto the shortcut.

The following are the six steps (different dialogs—use the Back and Next buttons to navigate between them) to sending a fax in Windows 95:

1. Dialing Properties (to access an outside line, tone dialing, and so on).

2. The recipient of the fax. (The Address Book button accesses your Personal Address Book if you have Windows Messaging/Exchange installed, and retrieves the fax number, etc.)

3. Cover Page. (Choose a default one such as Generic, Urgent!, etc., or if you've created your own with *faxcover*, select it here—see Figure 5-3.)

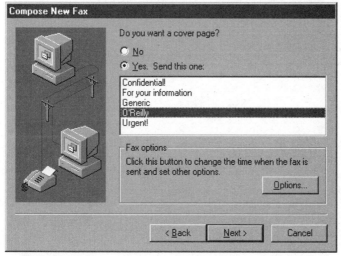

Figure 5-3: Selecting a fax cover page (awsnto32.exe)

4. Choose a Subject and Note.

5. Add a file (select the Add File button and the Windows open dialog box appears).

6. Click the Finish button to send the fax.

Notes

* In Windows Messaging/Exchange you can set passwords on your faxes (Tools → Microsoft Fax Tools → Advanced Security).

* You can access the fax properties (Tools → Microsoft Fax Tools → Options). This is the same dialog that is available from: Control Panel → Mail and Fax → Services → Microsoft Fax → Properties. See Figure 5-4.

Figure 5-4: Fax properties

See Also

faxcover

---

backup
\Program Files\Accessories\backup.exe

Copy (back up) files from your hard drive to a floppy disk or tape.

To Launch

Start → Programs → Accessories → System Tools → Backup
Start → Run → **backup**

Description

Backup (Figure 5-5) works by creating a special file called a backup set, which lists all the files to be backed up. By default, the file has the *.set* extension and is stored in the directory *\Program Files\Accessories*. Create the backup set using an Explorer-like two-pane view to select the files you want backed up. Click on any folder icon to open it and navigate through the file system. Click on the checkbox next to a file or folder to select it for backup.

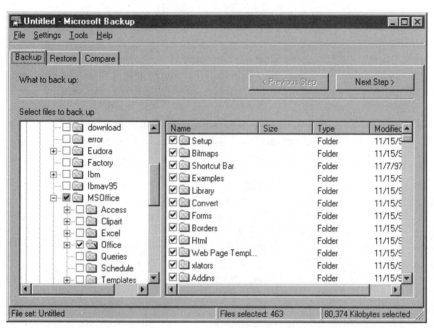

Figure 5-5: The Backup utility dialog box (backup.exe)

The first time you run *backup*, it creates a backup set called *Full System Backup.set*, which includes every file in the system. If you have a tape drive, Jaz drive, Zip drive, or other high volume backup medium, you might actually want to back up this set. If you have only floppies, you probably want to navigate to a particular folder or folders and define a smaller backup set! To define a new backup set, select some particular set of files and folders to be backed up, plus a destination for the backup (a disk or tape drive), and then choose Edit → Save As. This will create a backup set, by default in *\Program Files\Accessories*, although you can save it in any other location.

To restore files, use File → Open File Set to load a particular backup set, and then go to the Restore tab to select the specific files to be restored. You can also compare the files currently on the disk with those in the backup set using the Compare tab.

> **WARNING**
>
> Backup doesn't check the archive file attribute (see *attrib*), but instead relies on its own internal records in the backup set. You must load a specific backup set to do an incremental backup of files that have changed since that backup set was last run.

Notes

- To do another backup of the same set of files, load the desired backup set, click Next Step, and follow the prompts. Obviously, if you want to create a new backup set, it may be easier to open an existing backup set and modify it than to start from scratch. Be sure to save the new backup set if you want to use it again.

- Settings → Options → Backup lets you select a full backup (all files in the set are backed up) or an incremental backup (only files in the set that have changed are backed up). You can also specify whether to verify the backup, whether to use compression, and whether to erase the current contents of the backup medium before copying the new files onto it. Verification does a compare operation between the backup and the original when the backup is finished. It's always wise to be safe and use this option. Compression, on the other hand, is strongly discouraged. Because of the way compression is done, the data on a disk is much more fragile; a single bad bit can make a compressed file unreadable.

- Settings → Options → Restore lets you choose whether to restore files to their original locations, to a new location (maintaining the hierarchical relationships in the original files and folders), or to a single directory. You can also choose whether the restored file will overwrite an existing file, overwrite an existing file only if it's older than the backed up file, or prompt you before overwriting.

- Settings → File Filtering lets you choose files to be backed up by modification date, and lets you exclude files with certain extensions.

- If you receive an "operation complete" message when doing a compare, then you know the files are identical. If, however, you receive the "errors occurred during this operation" message, you know the files aren't identical. You'll be given the choice to view the *error.log* file, which will explain how the files in the backup set and the source are different.

- You can download an updated version called *backupd2.exe*, which has no additional features, but has several fixes for bugs that exist in *backup.exe*:

  http://premium.microsoft.com/support/downloads/dp2076.asp

- You can also do backups with *xcopy32*, or even (for smaller filesets) with the Explorer. For example, use Find → Files or Folders to select files by name or date, then Select All, copy, and drop onto a floppy disk. The Explorer is smart enough to ask for another floppy if needed. What you lose is the fine-grained control that backup gives you over exactly which files to restore and how. You have to keep track of that manually. But there are certainly cases where that is entirely adequate.

See Also

xcopy32

---

batch   *\Program Files\Resource Kit\batch.exe*

Set up batch files for installing Windows 95 on multiple computers (Batch Setup).

To Install

From the OSR2 Win95 CD-ROM:

> Navigate to *\ADMIN\NETTOOLS\BSETUP*
> Run *setup.exe.*

From the Resource Kit:

> Download *rktools.exe* and run it to extract the files.

To Launch

> Start → Run → `batch`

Description

The OSR2 Win95 CD-ROM contains a newer 32-bit version (2.4) of Batch Setup than the version (1.0) in the Resource Kit or OSR1.

You can use the setup script created by Batch Setup to automate the Windows 95 Setup process. By using Batch Setup, you won't have to provide additional information such as the installation type or target folder during Setup. Batch Setup is also useful for standardizing settings such as protocols, disk tools, services. This is useful for installing the same configuration of Windows 95 on several computers. See Figure 5-6.

Batch Setup doesn't run Windows 95 Setup; it only prepares the *.inf* file for use with it. After running Batch Setup, *bsetup.inf* is created, which serves as a script during Windows 95 installation. Windows 95Setup then consults this file instead of prompting for each piece of information. This means that you can install Windows 95 unattended and at full speed. In order to use the script, use the *setup* command followed by the path and filename for the *.inf* file:

```
setup c:\bsetup.inf
```

The *bsetup.inf* file will be renamed *msbatch.inf* after it has been used by Setup.

See Also

> *setup*

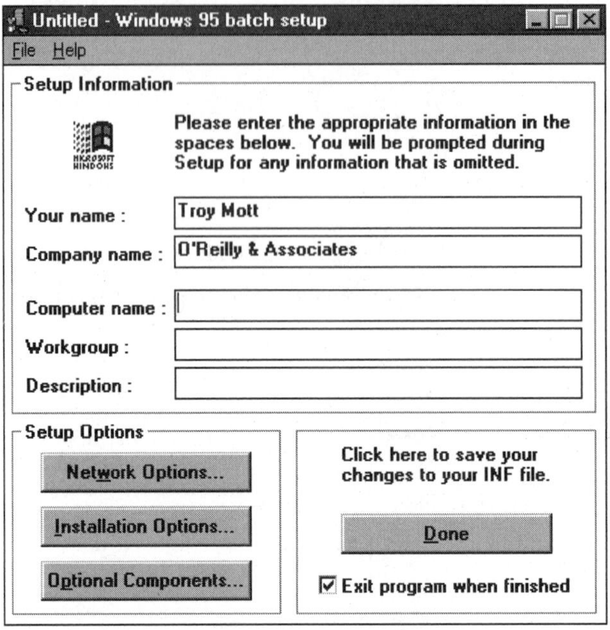

Figure 5-6: Batch Setup window (batch.exe)

---

calc

\Windows\calc.exe

Windows 95 calculator.

To Launch

Start → Run → calc
Start → Programs → Accessories → Calculator

Description

By default, the Calculator starts in standard mode, but a scientific mode is also available (View → Scientific) for performing complicated calculations (see Figure 5-7).

The following description focuses on the more complex scientific calculator; those functions that are available in the standard calculator are identical there.

Entering Data and Performing Calculations

Data can be entered by clicking the buttons, or from the keyboard. All keys have keyboard equivalents. Non-obvious equivalents are documented as appropriate in the following sections. The +/- key changes the sign of the entered number (keyboard equivalent = F9). The Int key displays only the integer part of a decimal number. To see only the fractional part, use Inv + Int (keyboard equivalent = ;).

Check MS to store a number in memory. To recall it, click MR. To clear the memory, click MC. To add the displayed number to the number already in memory,

---

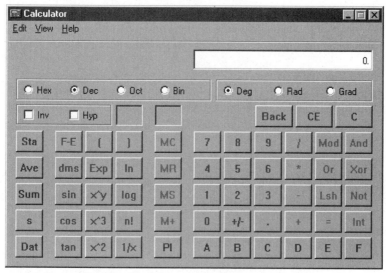

Figure 5-7: Calculator in scientific mode (calc.exe)

click M+. When a number is stored in memory, an M appears in the box above the memory buttons. Only one number can be stored in memory at a time. The keyboard equivalents are listed in Table 5-4.

Table 5-4: Calculations and Keyboard Equivalents

Calc Button	Keyboard Key	Action
C	Esc	Clear all calculations
CE	Del	Clear last entry
Back	Backspace	Clear last digit
MC	Ctrl-L	Memory clear
MR	Ctrl-R	Memory recall
MS	Ctrl-M	Memory store
M+	Ctrl-P	Memory add

Number System

By default, the number system is decimal. Click the radio buttons to switch. Or use keyboard equivalents (see Table 5-5).

Table 5-5: Number Systems and Keyboard Equivalents

Keyboard Key	Action
F5	Hexadecimal
F6	Decimal
F7	Octal
F8	Binary

Hexadecimal values A–F can be entered from the keyboard or using the A–F buttons on the calculator. When in binary mode, selecting Dword, Word, or Byte will display 32-, 16-, or 8-bit values, respectively. 16- or 8-bit values are the low order bits of a 32-bit number (see Table 5-6 for keyboard equivalents).

Table 5-6: Binary Mode Keyboard Equivalents

Keyboard Key	Action
F2	Dword
F3	Word
F4	Byte

Bitwise operations buttons and keyboard equivalents are listed in Table 5-7.

Table 5-7: Bitwise Buttons and Keyboard Equivalents

Calc Button	Keyboard Key	Action
Mod	%	Modulus
And	&	Bitwise AND
Or	|	Bitwise OR
Xor	^	Bitwise exclusive OR
Lsh	<	Left shift (right shift via Inv + Lsh, or >)
Not	~	Bitwise inverse

If you convert a fractional decimal number to another number system, only the integer part will be used.

When in Decimal mode, the Deg, Rad, and Grad radio buttons switch between degrees, radians, and gradients (see Table 5-8).

Table 5-8: Decimal Mode Keyboard Equivalents

Keyboard Key	Action
F2	Deg
F3	Rad
F4	Grad

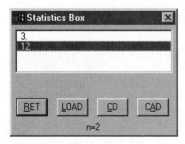

Figure 5-8: The Statistics Box

Statistical Functions

To perform a statistical calculation, you must enter the first data, then click the Sta button (this opens the Statistics Box; see Figure 5-8), click the Dat button (displays the data in the Statistics Box), and then continue entering the data, clicking Dat after each entry. When you've finished entering all the numbers, click the statistical button you want to use (Ave, Sum, or S). The buttons available in the Statistics Box are listed in Table 5-9.

Table 5-9: Statistics Box Buttons

Calc Button	Action
RET	Returns the focus to the calculator
LOAD	Displays the selected number in the Statistics Box in the Calculator display area
CD	Clears the selected number (data)
CAD	Clears all numbers (data) in the Statistics Box

Scientific Calculations

The Inv and Hyp checkboxes modify the function keys listed in Table 5-10.

Table 5-10: Scientific Calculations Buttons and Keyboard Equivalents

Calc Button	Keyboard Key	Action
Inv	i	Sets the inverse function for sin, cos, tan, Pl, x^y, x^2, x^3, Ln, log, sum, and s.
Hyp	h	Sets the hyperbolic function for sin, cos, and tan.
F-E	v	Turn scientific notation on and off. Can only be used with decimal numbers. Numbers larger than 10^{15} are always displayed with exponents.
( )	( )	Start and end a new level of parentheses. The maximum number of nested parentheses is 25. The current number of levels appears in the box above the) button.
dms	m	If the displayed number is in degrees, convert to degree-minute-second format. Use Inv + dms to reverse the operation.
Exp	x	The next digit(s) entered constitute the exponent. The exponent cannot be larger than 289. Decimal only.
Ln	n	Natural (base e) logarithm. Inv + Ln calculates e raised to the *n*th power, where *n* is the current number.
sin	s	Sine of the displayed number. Inv + sin gives arc sine. Hyp + sin gives hyperbolic sine. Inv + Hyp + sin gives arc hyperbolic sine.
x^y	y	*x* to the *y*th power. Inv + x^y calculates the *y*th root of *x*.

Table 5-10: Scientific Calculations Buttons and Keyboard Equivalents (continued)

Calc Button	Keyboard Key	Action
Log	l	The common (base 10) logarithm. `Inv + log` yields 10 to the xth power, where x is the displayed number.
Cos	o	Cosine of the displayed number. `Inv + cosin` gives arc cosine. `Hyp + cosin` gives hyperbolic cosine. `Inv + Hyp + cosin` gives arc hyperbolic cosine.
x^3	#	Cubes the displayed number. `Inv + x^3` gives the cube root.
n!	!	Factorial of the displayed number.
tan	t	Tan of the displayed number. `Inv + tan` gives arc tan. `Hyp + tan` gives hyperbolic tan. `Inv + Hyp + tan` gives arc hyperbolic tan.
x^2	@	Squares the displayed number. `Inv + x^2` gives the square root.
1/x	r	Reciprocal of displayed number.
Pi	p	The value of pi (3.1415...). `Inv + Pi` gives 2×pi.

Notes

By right-clicking on any button on the calculator, you can choose the "What's This?" option for information about the selected button.

See Also

There are many different types of calculators available on the Web. For an extensive list:

> *http://www-sci.lib.uci.edu/HSG/RefCalculators.html*

For a good example of a calculator created with JavaScript:

> *http://www.sonic.net/~undoc/WebCalc.html*

---

cd or chdir   Internal to: \ *Windows*\ *command.com*

Display the name of or change the current directory.

To Launch

> cd [filename]
> chdir [filename]

Description

With no arguments, *cd* displays the full pathname of the current directory. Given the pathname of another directory, it changes the current directory to the specified directory. Given only a drive letter, it changes to the same directory (if present) on the other drive.

Pathnames can be absolute (including the full path starting with the root) or relative to the current directory. A path can be optionally prefixed with a drive letter. The special paths .. and ... (and so on) refer respectively to the parent and grandparent of the current directory.

The *chdir* and *cd* commands are functionally identical.

Examples

If the current drive is *C:*, make *C:\temp\wild* the current directory:

```
C:\>cd \temp\wild
```

If the current directory is *C:\temp* all that is necessary is:

```
C:\temp>cd wild
```

Change the current directory *C:\more\docs\misc* to the directory *C:\more*:

```
C:\more\docs\misc>cd ...
```

Move to the root directory of the current drive:

```
C:\Windows\Desktop\>cd \
C:\>
```

Notes

- The directory change affects only the DOS window and any programs subsequently launched from that window.

- To change to the current directory on a different drive, enter the drive letter followed by a colon (i.e., **a:**).

---

cdplayer   \Windows\cdplayer.exe

Play audio CDs in the CD-ROM drive.

To Launch

Start → Run → cdplayer
Start → Programs → Accessories → Multimedia → CD Player

Description

By default, *cdplayer* should start automatically once an audio CD is inserted into the CD-ROM drive, but it can also be run from the DOS prompt, the Run prompt, or the Start menu.

You can control the volume in several ways. From the *cdplayer* interface (see Figure 5-9), choose View → Volume Control. You can also click or double-click the volume icon on the Taskbar, if you have checked the "Show Volume Control on the Taskbar" box in the Multimedia control panel applet (Control Panel → Multimedia → Audio). Another option is to type *sndvol32* at the Run prompt.

Configurable playlists (Disk → Edit Play List) store information from CDs, including the name of a CD, the artist, and the names of each track on the CD. With *cdplayer*, you can select individual tracks, and even skip to locations within a track.

Figure 5-9: CD Player in action (cdplayer.exe)

cdplayer stores several hundred bytes of information about each CD in *cdplayer.ini*, and *.ini* files (including *cdplayer.ini*) are limited to 64K in size, so if you have a substantial collection of CDs, 64K may not be enough space.

It is possible to create a batch file to run *cdplayer* and maintain multiple play lists in *.ini* files. The batch file temporarily copies one of the *.ini* files over *cdplayer.ini*, and then copies any changes back to the source file. You will need to insert **start /w** in front of the batch line that launches *cdplayer.exe* to prevent the batch file from continuing on to the next instruction in the batch file. See Chapter 6, *The Batch Language*, for an example.

Associated Files

> *cdplayer.ini*
> *sndvol32.exe*

Notes

- Insert an audio CD, select your CD drive in the Explorer, and find the tracks (*.cda* files). Here are some things to try:

  - Right-click on a track and choose "Play" from the Quick menu to play it. If you double-click on a track, it will play automatically.

  - Drag a track onto your Desktop. Create a shortcut, and rename the shortcut after the song. Whenever you have the CD in the drive, you can double-click on the shortcut to play the song. You can drag tracks to your hard drive and put them in your Start menu, or create a directory with CD tracks in it.

- To disable AutoPlay temporarily, press the **Shift** key when inserting an audio CD.

- You can turn off the AutoPlay feature off by doing the following:

  1. Right-click on the My Computer icon.

  2. Choose the Device Manager tab.

  3. Open the CD-ROM branch, and select the entry for your CD-ROM drive.

  4. Click Properties, and then choose the Settings tab.

5. Turn off the "Auto insert notification" option.

6. Click OK, and then OK again.

See Also

Download Pro Audio CD Player, which provides more options than *cdplayer.exe*:

http://www.aldridge.com/cdplayer.html

For detailed information on the format of *cdplayer.ini*, *.cda* files, and so on:

http://www.binzen.de/cdplayer

---

cfgback   \ *Windows\cfgback.exe*

Configuration Backup Tool for backing up the Windows 95 Registry.

To Launch

Start → Run → cfgback

Description

You can run *cfgback* (Configuration Backup; see Figure 5-10) directly from the Win95 CD-ROM (\ *Other\Misc\Cfgback*), or you can copy *cfgback.exe* to a directory on your hard drive. If you do copy it to your hard drive, be sure also to copy the *cfgback.hlp* file to the *Windows\Help* directory on the hard drive if you want to access Help when using *cfgback*.

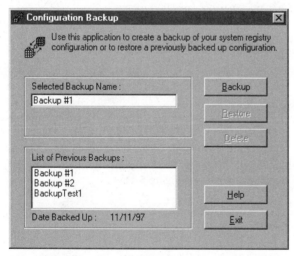

Figure 5-10: Configuration Backup Tool (cfgback.exe)

Associated Files

cfgback.hlp
regbackX.rbk
regback.ini

Notes

- If you select the "Do not display this page in the future" checkbox on the first dialog box that pops up when running *cfgback*, and you later decide you want this screen back, you can edit the *regback.ini* file from:

```
[StartWizard]
Show=0
```

to:

```
[StartWizard]
Show=1
```

- *cfgback* allows you to save up to nine backups of the Registry. *cfgback* backs up the information stored in the HKEY_LOCAL_MACHINE and HKEY_USERS trees of the Registry. The other root keys are not backed up because they are dynamic and can change during a single session.

- The backed up information is stored in files in the *Windows* directory. The files are named *regbackX.rbk*, where *X* is a number between 1 and 9. To see which file is associated with a particular backup name, look in the *regback.ini* file, which can also be found in the *Windows* directory.

See Also

regedit

---

charmap   *Windows**charmap.exe*

Displays symbols and special characters from specified fonts.

To Install

Control Panel → Add/Remove Programs → Windows Setup → Accessories → Character Map

To Launch

Start → Run → charmap
Start → Programs → Accessories → Character Map

Description

charmap lets you copy symbols and characters from specified fonts to the Clipboard for pasting into Windows documents (see Figure 5-11).

To use Character Map:

1. Select a font from the Font drop-down list.

2. Double-click each character you want (or click once and then click the Select button). Each character will appear in the "Characters to copy" box. (To magnify a character, click it and hold down the mouse button.)

3. Click Copy to copy the character(s) to the Windows clipboard.

4. Switch to your other application, click where you want the character(s) to appear, and paste (using either the Edit menu or Ctrl-V).

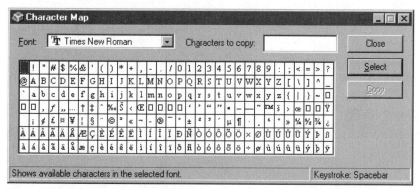

Figure 5-11: Character Map (charmap.exe)

5. Select the newly inserted character(s), and then change them to the same font you used in Character Map. (This step is crucial!)

Notes

*   Although Microsoft's documentation says that *charmap* works only with Windows-based programs, this isn't necessarily true. It is true, however, that *charmap* usually won't work with programs such as Notepad where fonts can't be specified. The key is that except for the more common "special" characters, the target program should be able to select fonts.

*   *charmap* is helpful not only for selecting non-English characters, but also for "dingbats" (see the two "Wingdings" fonts); Greek characters (see the "Symbol" font); fractions (see the "MS Reference" font); and so on.

*   *charmap* is useful for finding out what key combination will produce a nonstandard character in any given font. Select a character in any cell, and see the corresponding keystrokes on the status bar. Many characters can generated by the Alt-key combinations.

---

chat

See *winchat*.

---

clipbrd and clipbook   \ *Windows*\ *clipbrd.exe*

View the contents of the Clipboard.

To Install

To install *clipbrd* (preview contents of the Clipboard):

> Start → Settings → Control Panel → Add/Remove Programs → Windows Setup → Accessories → Clipboard Viewer

To install *clipbook* (for Clipboard access on networked machines):

Start → Settings → Control Panel → Add/Remove Programs → Windows Setup
→ Have Disk → (Win95 CD) *Other\Clipbook\clipbook.inf*

To Launch

Start → Run → `clipbrd`
Start → Programs → Accessories → ClipBook Viewer
Start → Programs → Accessories → Clipboard Viewer

Associated Files

clipbrd.ini

Description

clipbrd and *clipbook* are Clipboard viewers. Typically, the Clipboard is accessed
with the Cut, Copy, and Paste commands available in most programs, but *clipbrd*
lets you preview the contents of the Windows Clipboard and save it to a file. *clipbook* is a superset of *clipbrd*, providing multiple named clipboard items; these can
also be accessed from other machines on a network. Either *clipbrd* or *clipbook*,
once installed, will be present on your machine as *clipbrd.exe* (even though *clipbook* is *clipbook.exe* on the Win95 CD-ROM). See Figure 5-12.

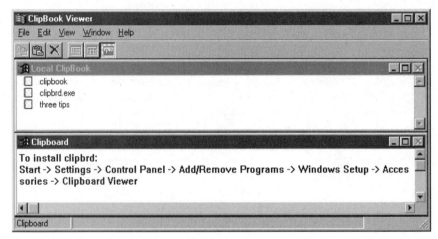

Figure 5-12: The Clipboard Viewer (clipbrd.exe)

Notes

- Supported Clipboard formats include text, bitmap, DIB bitmap, picture, SYLK,
  TIFF, OEM text, palette, Pen Data, RIFF, and Wave Audio. Applications may
  also provide their own clipboard viewers so they can display some custom
  format. This is called "owner display."

- *clipbrd*'s File → Save menu item saves the Clipboard contents as a *.clp* file; it
  can then be restored at a later time with File → Open.

- To save the current Windows Clipboard contents as a named item in the *clipbook*, switch to the "Local ClipBook" window and paste (`Ctrl-V`); you will
  be prompted for a name for the new item.

- To move a *clipbook* item to the Windows Clipboard, select it in the "Local ClipBook" window and copy (Ctrl-C).

- To see both the *clipbrd* and local *clipbook* windows at the same time, see the Window → Tile options.

- To view all your local *clipbook* items at the same time, see the View → Table of Contents and View → Thumbnails menu items.

- With network access, a user on one machine can, for example, do a PrtSc or Alt-PrtSc screen dump, and a different user can then paste the screen dump into a document on another machine. For network access, you must first run *netdde*.

- To connect to the Clipboard on other machines, use the File → Connect menu item in *clipbook*. The machine you want to connect to must also be running *clipbook*, *clipsrv*, and *netdde*.

- If the File → Connect menu item does not appear, exit *clipbook*, run *netdde*, and restart *clipbook*.

- Starting *clipbook* will also automatically start *clipsrv*, which acts as the server for *clipbook* accesses from other machines. (In other words, *clipbook* is the client, *clipsrv* is the server, and *netdde* provides the underlying transport.)

See Also

netdde

For a good description of how to use the networking features of *clipbook*:

http://www.winmag.com/library/1996/0796/07b01001.btm

ClipMate 4.2 provides Clipboard "history"; the ability to cut/paste a series of items, etc.:

http://www.thornsoft.com

---

cls   Internal to: \ *Windows**command.com*

Clear the DOS window, leaving only the command prompt and cursor.

Description

If you have information in your DOS box that you'd rather keep to yourself, just use the *cls* command and the window will be cleared instantly.

cls is also useful in complex batch files, for clearing the screen after one set of interactions or command output. The name *cls* (Clear Screen) refers to the old days when DOS owned the whole screen.

---

cmpagent   *Program Files**Plus!**cmpagent.exe*

Compress drives (Microsoft Plus!).

To Launch

Start → Program → Accessories → System Tools → Compression Agent

---

Description

The Compression Agent (*cmpagent.exe*) comes with Microsoft Plus and is an application for compressing drives. Compression runs only on DriveSpace 3 compressed drives. You can run *drvspace* if you don't have a DriveSpace 3 compressed drive.

The Compression Agent supports additional compression types, which deliver up to 50% more compression than standard compression. You can yield substantial additional disk space with this feature at no sacrifice to performance. Once a disk has been compressed, you should run the Compression Agent regularly to free up additional space.

See Also

drvspace

---

command
\ *Windows\command.com*

DOS 7 command interpreter.

To Launch

command [path] [device] [options]
Start → Programs → MS-DOS Prompt

Description

command starts a new copy of the Windows command interpreter, *command.com*. If entered from the Run prompt in the Start menu, it also opens a new command interpreter window.

The command interpreter allows you to perform many operations much more quickly than with the corresponding point-and-click programs.

The entire Windows 95 interface created by the Explorer runs in an invisible "system" DOS box that is created when the system boots. Each new instance of *command* inherits the environment created with that initial invocation of DOS. The *autoexec.bat* file (which DOS users will recognize as containing commands to be executed when DOS first starts up) is not reread for each new instance of command unless you use the /p option.

command accepts the following parameters and options:

/c command	Executes the specified command and returns. This must be the last option on the command line. Note that the command doesn't normally wait for user input, so if you use this option from the Run prompt, the window will flash on the screen and disappear. Use /k if you want the window to stick around.
device	Specifies the device to use for command input and output.
[drive:]path	Specifies the directory containing *command.com*.
/e:*nnnnn*	Sets the initial environment size to *nnnnn* bytes. The value of *nnnnn* should be between 256 and 32,768. See *set* for more information.

/f	Forces a "Fail" response to the command interpreter's error handling routine query: "Abort, Retry, Fail?".
/k *command*	Executes the specified command and continues running. This must be the last option on the command line.
/l:*nnnn*	Specifies internal buffer length (requires the /p option). The value of *nnnn* should be between 128 and 1,024.
/low	Forces *command* to keep its resident data in low memory.
/msg	Stores all error messages in memory (requires the /p option).
/p	Makes the new command interpreter permanent (can't use exit; will load *autoexec.bat*). You can still terminate the *command* window using the window's "Close" control or File → Close.
/u:*nnn*	Specifies the input buffer length (requires the /p option). The value of *nnn* should be between 128 and 255.
/y	Steps through the batch program specified by /c or /k.
/z	Causes the ERRORLEVEL number returned by external DOS commands to be displayed as follows: "Return code (ERROR-LEVEL): *n*", where *n* is the ERRORLEVEL returned by the last executed external command. If this option is used with a nonresident *command* (i.e., no /p), the following message is displayed: "WARNING: Reloaded COMMAND.COM transient".

Examples

Create a new instance of the DOS command interpreter from the Run prompt:

> Start → Run → command

Start an instance of the command interpreter to give a single directory listing and then quit:

> Start → Run → command /c dir c:\ /p

(The /p is necessary to display the listing long enough for you to read it.)

Run *command.com* and set the environment to 1024 bytes:

> `C:\>command /e:1024`

Notes

- The *exit* command is used to quit any nonpermanent instances of *command*. In Windows 95, the "permanent" instances can actually be terminated with the close box, System Menu → Close (Alt-space C), or with a local reboot (Ctrl-Alt-Del).

- When a DOS window is opened from the Run... prompt or the Start menu, a new instance of the command interpreter is run in a separate window; thus, several instances of *command.com* can be running independently at the same time. However, you may even want to run an instance of *command.com* from within another existing DOS window. This could useful if, for example, you wanted to set special environment variables or other options for that instance of *command*. If you type command at the DOS prompt, the new instance of

Commands & Applications

command overlays the previous one, in the same window, rather than creating a new window.

- You can store a sequence of commands in any file with the .bat extension, and execute the file simply by typing its name. See Chapter 6 for details.

See Also

Chapter 6

---

control   *\Windows\control.exe*

Display the Control Panel, which contains the configuration applets for Windows 95.

To Launch

control [filename.cpl] [applet_name] [,property_tab]

Description

control launches the Control Panel folder, which contains many applets used to configure everything from Accessibility Options to Sounds. Many of the applets in *control* are also accessed from a context menu (e.g., right-click on the Desktop for the Display applet) or the System Tray (e.g., double-click on the time for the Date/Time applet). Chances are, if you need to configure something in Windows 95, this is the place to look. See Figure 5-13.

Figure 5-13: The Control Panel (control.exe)

---

control accepts the following parameters:

`applet_name` The name of the applet you want to launch. It must be spelled and capitalized exactly. Unless there's more than one applet within a *.cpl* file, you can omit the `applet_name`.

`filename.cpl` The filename of the applet in the Control Panel (found in \ *Windows\System*) that you want to launch. If there's more than one control panel applet within the *.cpl* file, you also need to specify the `applet_name`. For example:

control sysdm.cpl Add New Hardware
Launches the Add New Hardware wizard

control sysdm.cpl
Launches the System Properties dialog

`,property_tab` The number (e.g., `,0`—the comma is required) that launches an individual tab of a control panel applet. Not all tabbed control panel applets recognize the property tab arguments from the command line, since it's up to the applet to recognize this syntax, and not all do. For details on all the control panel applets, as well as the applicable `property_tab`s, see Chapter 4.

Examples

Launch the Date/Time applet, with the Time Zone tab selected:

```
C:\>control timedate.cpl ,1
```

Launch the Add/Remove Program applet, with the Windows Setup tab selected:

```
C:\>control appwiz.cpl ,2
```

Notes

- Although some of the *control* command lines may seem a bit unwieldy, you can embed them in the Target lines in shortcuts on the Desktop or in the Start menu. This can be especially helpful if you have a certain tab in an applet that you acess frequently.

See Also

rundll32

---

copy   Internal to: \ *Windows\command.com*

Copy one or more files to another location.

To Launch

copy source destination
copy [/a | /b] source [/a | /b] [+ source [/a | /b] [+ ...]] [destination [/a | /b]] [/v] [/y | /-y]

Description

copy makes a complete copy of an existing file. If the destination filename already exists, you will be asked if you want to overwrite it.

It is also possible to use the *copy* command to concatenate (combine) files. To concatenate files, specify a single file for the destination, but multiple files for the source (using wildcards or *file1+file2+file3* format). You can specify a relative or absolute path (including disk names and/or UNC paths), or use a simple filename. When attempting to concatenate files, *copy* expects ASCII files by default, so in order to concatenate binary files, you need to use the /b option. The reason for this is that binary files contain one or more bytes outside the normal ASCII printable range (i.e., 32 through 127).

If the file (or files) to be copied is in a different directory or on a different disk, you can omit the destination filename. The resulting copy or copies will have the same name as the original.

You can use the special device name con (or con:) in place of either the source or destination filename to copy from the keyboard to a file, or from a file to the screen.

copy accepts the following parameters and options:

/a	Specifies that the file to copy is in ASCII format
/b	Specifies that the file to copy is a binary file
/v	Verifies that new files are written
/y	Suppresses prompting to confirm you want to overwrite an existing destination file
/-y	Enables prompting to confirm you want to overwrite an existing destination file with the same name (default)

Examples

Copy the file *temp.txt* from *C:* to *D:\files* (both examples do the same thing):

```
C:\>copy c:\temp.txt d:\files\temp.txt
C:\>copy c:\temp.txt d:\files\
```

Copy all the files from the directory *D:\FunStuff\Hover* to the current directory, giving the copies the same names as the originals:

```
C:\>copy d:\funstuff\hover\*.*
```

Copy the file *words.txt* in the current directory to *D:\files*, renaming it to *morewords.txt*:

```
C:\>copy words.txt d:\files\morewords.txt
```

Create a text file by typing its contents directly, first enter:

```
C:\>copy con mystuff.txt
```

then type the text for the file followed by Ctrl-Z and Enter. The text typed from the keyboard in this example is saved as *mystuff.txt*.

Copy the contents of the file *mystuff.txt* to the screen:

```
C:\>copy mystuff.txt con
```

Concatenate *mon.txt*, *tue.txt*, and *wed.txt* into one file named *report.txt*:

```
C:\>copy mon.txt+tue.txt+wed.txt report.txt
```

Notes

- The *copy* command is internal and easy to use, but *xcopy* is more powerful and flexible.

- Binary file copy is assumed for normal copying, but the /b option should be used when appending one binary file to another, as in:

  `C:\>copy newfile file1+file2 /b`

  By default, when concatenating, both source and destination files are assumed to be ASCII format, since binary files can seldom be usefully concatenated due to internal formatting.

- You can substitute a device (e.g., COM1) for either the source or the destination. The data is copied in ASCII by default.

- *copy* doesn't copy files that are 0 bytes long; use *xcopy* to copy these files.

- When concatenating, if no destination is specified, the combined files are saved under the name of the first specified file.

See Also

set, xcopy

---

cover page editor

See *faxcover.*

---

date

Internal to: \ *Windows\command.com*

Display or set the system date.

To Launch

date [date]

Description

On most systems, a long-life battery retains the date information in memory, so the date doesn't need to be set every time the computer is started. If you type **date** on the command line without an option, the current date setting is displayed, and you are prompted for a new one. Press **Enter** to keep the same date.

date accepts the following options:

date   Specifies the date. Use *mm-dd-*[*yy*]*yy* format. Values for *yy* can be from 80 through 99; values for *yyyy* can be from 1980 through 2099. Separate month, day, and year with periods, hyphens, or slashes.

Notes

- The date format depends on the **country** setting you are using in your *config.sys* file. To display the date in other format besides *mm-dd-yy*, add the **country** command to your *config.sys* file. You can change the date format to the European standard format (*dd-mm-yy*) or to the Scientific International

(Metric) format (*yy-mm-dd*). You can also make these changes via Control Panel → Regional Settings (see Figure 5-14).

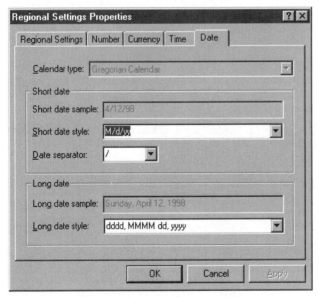

Figure 5-14: Setting the system date

- MS-DOS records the current date for each file you create or change. This date is listed next to the filename in the directory listing.

See Also

config.sys in Chapter 9

---

debug   \ *Windows\Command\debug.exe*

Test and edit files and system memory in real-mode MS-DOS.

To Launch

debug [filename] [testfile-parameters]

Description

debug is limited to the first megabyte of memory, but it is useful for examining boot sectors and for determining the MS-DOS version on your system. Refer to an advanced-level book on MS-DOS programming for more information on how to use the *debug* commands.

The *debug* options are:

`filename`   Specifies the file to test.

`testfile-parameters`
              Specifies the command-line information required by the file you want to test.

After *debug* starts, type ? to display the following list of debugging commands:

a [address]	Assemble
c range address	Compare
d [range]	Dump
e address [list]	Enter
f range list	Fill
g [=address] [addresses]	
	Go
h value1 value2	Hex
i port	Input
l [address] [drive] [firstsector] [number]	
	Load
m range address	Move
n [pathname] [arglist]	
	Name
o port byte	Output
p [=address] [number]	
	Proceed
q	Quit
r [register]	Register
s range list	Search
t [=address] [value]	
	Trace
u [range]	Unassemble
w [address] [drive] [firstsector] [number]	
	Write
xa [#pages]	Allocate expanded memory
xd [handle]	Deallocate expanded memory
xm [lpage] [ppage] [handle]	
	Map expanded memory pages
xs	Display expanded memory status (for example: use *debug* to view boot sector, or assemble a call to get version number).

Examples

Examine the boot sector (0) on drive C: (2), load data from the sector into address 100, then dump contents of memory at address 100:

```
C:\>debug

-L 100 2 0 1
-d 100 300
```

```
117A:0100 EB 3E 90 4D 53 57 49 4E-34 2E 30 00 02 20 01 00 > .MSWIN4.0.. ..
117A:0110 02 00 02 00 00 F8 C2 00-3F 00 20 00 3F 00 00 00 .....?. ?...
117A:0120 41 3D 18 00 80 00 29 E4-18 69 30 20 20 20 20 20 A=..)..i0
117A:0130 20 20 20 20 20 20 46 41-54 31 36 20 20 20 F1 7D FAT16 .}
........
117A:02E0 53 59 53 4D 53 44 4F 53-20 20 20 53 59 53 80 01 SYSMSDOS SYS..
117A:02F0 00 57 49 4E 42 4F 4F 54-20 53 59 53 00 00 55 AA WINBOOT SYS.U.
```

To check the MS-DOS version number by calling INT 21h Function 3306h, create the following script with a text editor such as *edit* or *notepad*. (In the example, we assume the script has already been created and saved in the file *dosver.dbg*. We use the *type* command to show the contents of the file.)

```
C:\>type dosver.dbg
a
mov ax,3306
int 21
ret

g 105
r bx

q
C:\>debug < dosver.dbg
....
BX 0007
```

The number in BX at the end is the hexadecimal DOS version number: 0007 for MS-DOS 7.0, 0A07 for MS-DOS 7.10.

This example also shows how to write *debug* "scripts." Note that all blank lines are essential (for example, the first blank line exits from "A" mode).

You can also check the Windows version number with INT 2Fh function 160Ah: create a *winver.dbg* like *dosver.dbg* in the previous example, but change 3306 to 160A, and 21 to 2F. Windows 4.0 (Windows 95) is 0400, Windows 4.10 (Windows 98) is 040A.

See Also

For information on a genuine Windows debugger (Soft-Ice/Windows):

http://www.numega.com

---

defrag *\Windows\defrag.exe*

Reorganize the files on a disk to optimize disk performance.

To Launch

Start → Programs → Accessories → System Tools → Disk Defragmenter
defrag [drive: | /all] [options] [/concise] [/detailed] [/f] [/noprompt] [/q] [/u]

Description

A heavily fragmented disk (one in which files are no longer stored contiguously on the disk) affects machine performance, because it takes longer to find and

---

piece together fragmented files. Running *defrag* makes it easy to monitor and maintain system performance so that you can identify problem issues and remove them. If system performance starts to drop off, run *defrag* to see if it helps.

defrag includes a user interface and can be run from Windows or MS-DOS. If you use *defrag* from the command line, you can use options to control the behavior of the program without having to configure settings in the user interface. If you type *defrag* at the command line without options, you will launch the *defrag* dialog, which contains the user interface for configuring settings. That being said, defragging a large disk can take the better part of an hour, so ideally you should do this sometime when you have the time or can walk away!

defrag accepts the following options:

/all   Defragment all local, nonremovable drives.

/concise   Display the Hide Details view (default).

/detailed   Display the Show Details view. The detailed view (accessible
                using the /detailed command-line option or the Show Details
                button (once *defrag* is running) gives a fascinating view of the
                state of your disk (see Figure 5-15).

                Click the Legend button for an explanation of what all the little
                colored boxes mean (see Figure 5-16).

drive: Drive letter of the disk to be optimized.

/f   Defragment files and free space.

/noprompt   Do not stop and display confirmation messages.

/q   Defragment free space only.

/u   Defragment files only.

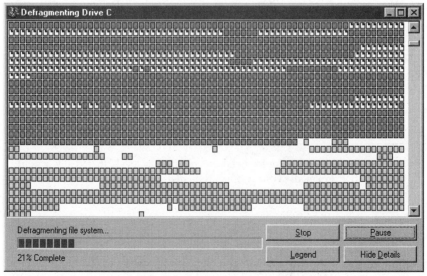

Figure 5-15: defrag in action—the Details view (defrag.exe)

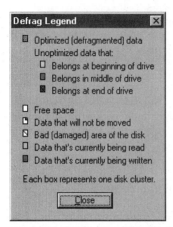

Figure 5-16: Meaning of the defrag Details view

Examples

Defragment files only (don't attempt to consolidate free space):

```
C:\>defrag c: /u
```

Defragment all non-removable drives (i.e., hard drives):

```
C:\>defrag /all
```

Defragment *E:* drive and show details:

```
C:\>defrag e: /detailed
```

Notes

- My Computer → *disk drive* → Properties → Tools → Defragmentation status tells you how long it has been since *defrag* was used on the drive, and gives you the option to Defragment Now.

- When running *defrag* from the Explorer, or when typing `defrag` from the command line without parameters or options, *defrag* checks the drive for fragmentation, reports the amount of fragmentation (e.g., Drive C is 6% fragmented), and suggests whether you should defragment now (Start) or wait (Exit).

> Defrag will suggest you don't need to continue at levels that really would improve performance. You should run *defrag* regularly, and tell it to continue whenever fragmentation is over 2 or 3%.

- You can run other programs while *defrag* runs in the background, but it can cause other programs and *defrag* to run slowly: *defrag* has to restart as other programs touch the disk. Keep in mind that even a screen saver is a running program that will slow down *defrag*. Turn off any screen savers for best per-formance. Also, be sure to turn off the System Agent and even the Office Shortcut Bar, if you have that running.

- With Microsoft Plus!, you can set System Agent to run *defrag* when you're away from your system (for example, on Sunday nights). Note that *defrag* will stop if it finds disk or file errors, so it's a good idea to run *scandisk* just before *defrag*, either from a batch file or by setting the agent to run these programs in sequence.

- Defragmentation is typically used with hard disk drives. *defrag* is unable to defragment a CD-ROM, a network drive, or a *subst*ed drive.

See Also

scandisk

---

del or erase   Internal to: \ *Windows\command.com*

Delete one or more files.

To Launch

del filename [/p]
erase filename [/p]

Description

The *del* and *erase* commands are functionally identical; they can both delete one or more files from the command line.

The *del* options are:

filename   Specifies the file(s) to delete. If you do not specify the drive or path, the file is assumed to be in the current directory. You can use standard * and ? wildcards to specify the files to delete.

/p   Prompts for confirmation before deleting each file.

Examples

Delete the file *myfile.txt* in the *C:\files* directory:

```
C:\>del c:\files\myfile.txt
```

Delete all files with the pattern *myfile.** (*myfile.doc*, *myfile.txt*, etc.) in the current directory, but prompt for each deletion:

```
C:\>del c:\files\myfile.* /p
```

Notes

- Using the *del* command to delete a file does not move it to the Recycle Bin. In other words, you can't get a file back once you use the *del* command, unless you have disk recovery utilities to do so.

- Although *del* only accepts one parameter (**filename**), which specifies what is to be deleted, you can delete multiple files using wildcards (* and ?). For example: *del *.txt*. If more than one parameter is specified explicitly (e.g., *del c:\files.txt d:\myfile.doc*) the command aborts and an error message is displayed. Since *del* interprets long filenames with spaces as multiple options, you must enclose long filenames with spaces in quotes to delete the file.

- Files having read-only, hidden, and/or system attributes set can't be deleted with the *del* command. Use *deltree* or modify the file with *attrib* in order to delete these files.

See Also

attrib, deltree

---

deltree \Windows\Command\deltree.exe

Delete a directory and all the subdirectories and files in it.

To Launch

deltree [/y] directory

Description

deltree will delete a directory (and all its subdirectories), regardless of whether they are marked as hidden, system, or read-only.

The *deltree* options are:

directory   Specifies the name of the directory you want to delete.

/y   Suppresses prompting to confirm that you want to delete any subdirectories.

Examples

Delete the *C:\myfiles* directory and all subdirectories and files contained within it:

```
C:\>deltree c:\myfiles
```

Delete all the files and subdirectories but leave the directory itself:

```
C:\>deltree [/y] directory\*.*
```

Notes

- Use *deltree* with caution. To avoid mistakes, provide full and absolute paths when using the *deltree* command. This will help avoid deleting subdirectories you want to keep.
- Unlike the typical syntax order for most DOS commands, the /y option must precede the directory name.
- The *deltree* command supports wildcards, but if you specify a wildcard that matches both directory names and filenames, both will be deleted. Use the dir /a command to view files and directories you want to delete, to avoid deleting incorrect files or directories.

dialer ⸻ \Windows\dialer.exe

Dial voice telephone calls.

To Install

> Control Panel → Add/Remove Programs → Windows Setup →
> Communications → Details → Dialer → OK → OK

If your *.cab* files are in \Windows\Options\CAB then it should install—if not, insert the Win95 CD-ROM.

To Launch

> Start → Run → dialer
>
> Start → Programs → Accessories → Phone Dialer

Description

Dials voice telephone calls, acts as a proxy for applications making simple voice telephony requests, and maintains a phone-call log (see Figure 5-17).

Figure 5-17: Using Phone Dialer (dialer.exe)

Associated Files

> \Windows\dialer.ini, \Windows\calllog.txt

Notes

- *dialer* can log incoming as well as outgoing calls.

- Even though there is no option to save the call log to a file, it is automatically saved as \Windows\calllog.txt. The call log window can also be cut and pasted to a different file.

- "Speed dial" numbers and the last twenty dialed numbers are kept in *dialer.ini.*

- *dialer* has about twenty built-in calling-card options (AT&T, British Telecom, MCI, US Sprint, etc.), and the ability to add new calling cards.

- To use *dialer* to handle voice-call requests from other programs, see the "Connect Using..." menu.

See Also

"Modems" in Chapter 4

Chapter 7, *Dial-Up Networking*

---

dir   Internal to: \ *Windows\command.com*

Display a list of files and subdirectories in a directory.

To Launch

dir filename [/p] [/w] [/a[[:]attributes]] [/o[[:]sortorder]] [/s] [/b] [/l] [/v]

Description

Without any options, *dir* displays the disk's volume label and serial number, a list of all files and subdirectories (except hidden and system files) in the current directory in the order in which they are listed in the FAT, file/directory size, date/time of last modification, long filename, the total number of files listed, their cumulative size, and the free space (in bytes) remaining on the disk.

If you specify one or more file or directory names (optionally including drive and path, or full UNC path to a shared directory), information only for those files or directories will be listed.

Wildcards (* and ?) can be used to display a subset listing of files and subdirectories. * and *.* are equivalent.

dir accepts the following options:

/a [attributes]

     Display only files with/without specified attributes (using – as a prefix specifies "not," and a colon between the option and attribute is optional). If no file(s) with the specified attribute is found, you will get the message "File not found." That is, /a lists only files with the attribute. To see all files, including those with hidden attributes, use *dir* /a (without specifying any attributes). If you specify multiple attributes (separated by spaces), only those files with all of the specified attributes will be displayed. Attributes are:

     a Files ready for archiving

     d Directories

     h Hidden files

     r Read-only files

     s System files

/b	Use bare format (no heading information or summary). Use with /s to find a filename.
/c	Display compression ratio of files on Dblspace or DrvSpace drives, assuming 16 sectors/cluster.
/ch	Same as /c, but more accurate: uses actual sectors/clusters of host drive.
/l	Use lowercase.
/o [sortorder]	List files in sorted order (using – as a prefix reverses the order, and a colon between the option and attribute is optional):

> a   By Last Access Date (earliest first)
>
> d   By date and time (earliest first)
>
> e   By extension (sorted alphabetically)
>
> g   Group directories first
>
> n   By name (sorted alphabetically)
>
> s   By size (smallest first)

/p	Pause after each screenful of information. Press any key to continue.
/s	Display files in specified directory and all subdirectories.
/v	Verbose mode. Display attributes, date last accessed, and disk space allocated for each file in addition to the standard information.
/w	Wide list format. File and directory names are listed in five columns.

Examples

Display all files in the current directory that end with *.txt* extension:

```
C:\>dir *.txt
```

Display all files, pausing for each screenful:

```
C:\>dir /p
```

Display all files, sorted by date and time, latest first:

```
C:\>dir /o-d
```

Display only directories:

```
C:\>dir /ad
```

List all files on disk, sorted by size, and store in the file *allfiles .txt*:

```
C:\>dir \ /s /os > allfiles.txt
```

List the contents of the shared folder *cdrom* on machine *larryc*:

```
C:\>dir \\larryc\cdrom
```

Notes

- You can preset *dir* parameters and switches by including the *set* command with the `dircmd` environment variable in your *autoexec.bat* file. For example:

  ```
  set dircmd= /p /o:gne
  ```

  presets *dir* to pause if the display gets too long to fit on a single screen, and to list subdirectories first, followed by files in alphabetical order, with files with the same name but different extensions alphabatized by extension.

- *dir filename* /b /s acts as a kind of "find" command, looking in all subdirectories of the current directory. For example:

  ```
  C:\>dir telephon.ini /b /s
  C:\Windows\telephon.ini
  C:\Windows\Desktop\Win95\Misc\faq\telephon.ini
  ```

  Unfortunately, you must specify an actual filename (not a wildcard) for this to work. For example, *dir* `*.ini` /b will not work.

- One of the Explorer's weaknesses is that it doesn't enable either of these very useful operations:

  - To print out a sorted directory listing of all files in the Windows directory:

    ```
    C:\>dir c:\windows /oa > lpt1
    ```

  - To create a file containing the directory listing of the same directory:

    ```
    C:\>dir c:\windows /oa > c:\myfiles\windows.txt
    ```

    Actually, *dir* can be used to fix this weakness of the Explorer. See *Windows Annoyances* for details on how to give the Explorer a Print-Dir facility.

- When using a redirection symbol (>) to send *dir* output to a file or a pipe (I) or to send *dir* output to another command, you may want to use /b to eliminate heading and summary information.

- If a directory is hidden but specified as an option, *dir* displays everything in the directory.

- The /s, /v, and /c options are not supported for UNC pathnames. In addition, when specifying a UNC path, you must specify the path to the actual shared folder. For example, even if folder *larryc**cdrom* is shared, typing *larryc* will give you the message: "The share name was not found. Be sure you typed it correctly."

See Also

attrib

set

directcc \hfill \Windows\directcc.exe

Establish a direct serial/parallel cable connection between two computers.

To Install

> Control Panel → Add/Remove Programs → Windows Setup →
> Communications → Details → Direct Cable Connection

To Launch

> Start → Run → `directcc`
> Start → Programs → Accessories → Direct Cable Connection

Description

By running *directcc*, you can establish a direct serial or parallel cable connection between two computers in order to share the resources of the computer designated as the host. *directcc* must be running on both computers, since it requires a client and a server. If the host is connected to a network, the guest computer can also access the network. For example, if you have a portable computer, you can use a cable to connect it to your work computer and network. To establish a local connection between two computers, you need a compatible serial or null-modem parallel cable. Parallel cables transmit data simultaneously over multiple lines, making it the faster of the two connection methods. Serial cables transmit data sequentially over one pair of wires, and are slower than parallel cables. Use a serial cable only if a parallel port is unavailable.

The first time you run *directcc*, you will be asked if the computer you are using will act as the host or the guest. The host listens on the designated port for contact from the guest. On subsequent invocations, you will be asked on the host to check your settings, then click Listen to start up the connection.

Notes

- To have the guest connect automatically upon startup, change the shortcut in the Start menu to: "directcc.exe connect". To do this, use the Explorer to navigate to the shortcut (\Windows\Start menu\Programs\Accessories). Right-click on the Direct Cable Connection shortcut, choose Properties, click the Shortcut tab and add `connect` in the Target line after . . . *directcc.exe*. (See Figure 5-18.)

- You can also have the guest connect automatically by typing `directcc connect` from the DOS or Run prompt.

- Both the guest and host computer must be running *directcc*, and must use the same type of port. You should start *directcc* on the host first.

- Direct Cable Connect and Dial-Up Networking can operate at the same time.

See Also

For detailed information on using *directcc.exe*:

> *http://www.tecno.demon.co.uk/dcc.html*

For information on *directcc* troubleshooting:

> *http://www.cs.purdue.edu/homes/kime/directcc/faq95.htm*

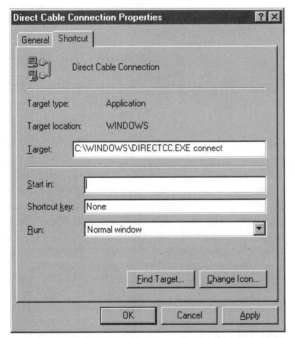

Figure 5-18: Automatically connecting to Direct Cable Connection (directcc.exe)

---

diskcopy \Windows\Command\diskcopy.com

Copy the contents (files and directories) of one floppy disk to another.

To Launch

diskcopy [source [destination]] [/l] [/v] [/m]

Description

When using *diskcopy* to copy contents of a floppy disk onto another disk, keep in mind that any data on the destination disk will be overwritten. Both *source* and *destination* must be valid floppy drive designations, such as *A:* and *B:*.

/l   Copies only the first side of the disk (seldom used).

/m   Force multipass copy using memory only.

/v   Verifies that the information is copied correctly.

Examples

Copy *A:* drive to *B:* drive:

```
C:\>diskcopy a: b:
```

Copy *A:* drive to another diskette using *A:* drive (*diskcopy* will prompt you to insert and remove the appropriate floppy):

```
C:\>diskcopy a: a:
```

Notes

- The two floppy disks must be the same type. That is, if the source drive is a 1.44MB floppy, the destination drive must be as well. If they are not, the error message "Drive and/or diskette types not compatible" is displayed.

- You may specify the same drive for source and destination. The system will prompt you to swap the diskettes as needed.

- *diskcopy* will not work with a hard disk or a network drive.

- Prompts to insert source and destination disks are displayed once *diskcopy* is running.

- The Explorer has a GUI diskcopy facility: Context Menu → Copy Disk → rundll32.exe diskcopy.dll, DiskCopyRunDll.

disk defragmenter

See *defrag*.

doskey   \ *Windows\ Command\ doskey.com*

Edit and recall command lines and create macros for DOS commands.

Syntax

doskey [options] [macroname=[text]]

Description

doskey is an essential aid for anyone using the DOS command line regularly; so much so that you should normally load it into memory from *autoexec.bat*. Once it is loaded, you can use the function key on the keyboard to recall and edit previous commands before reissuing them. You can also define macros for commonly used commands.

doskey supports a number of command-line options. These options fall into two groups: those that affect the copy of *doskey* already running, and those that must be used the first time *doskey* is run. These are listed below as install options and runtime options. All options can be specified as a full word, or using only the first letter. To change an install option once doskey is running, use the `/reinstall` option.

doskey is a little unusual in that you issue the *doskey* command again, with any of the runtime options, to change its operation.

The install options are:

`/bufsize:size` Sets the size of shortcut macro and command buffer (default is 512 bytes).

`/keysize:size` Sets the size of keyboard type-ahead buffer (default is 15 bytes).

`/line:size` Sets the maximum size of line edit buffer (default is 128).

The runtime options are:

/echo:on |off	Enables or disables echo of shortkey macro expansions (default is on).
/file:*file*	Specifies a file containing a list of shortcut macros. Each macro should be on a separate line and should be of the form:

macroname = text of macro

Macros can contain a number of special characters as defined later in this section.

/history	Displays all commands stored in memory.
/insert	Inserts new characters into line when typing. This makes it difficult to edit an existing command!
/macros	Displays all *doskey* shortcut macros. Can be used with redirection to save existing macros to a file.
/overstrike	Overwrites new characters onto line when typing (this is the default).
/reinstall	Installs a new copy of *doskey*.

doskey Commands

The last command entered is referred to as the template. Function keys and other keyboard accelerators are used to recall a different command into the template, where it can be edited. Among the most useful keys are F7, which displays a numbered history of stored commands; F9, which lets you pick a numbered line from that history; and F8, which lets you pick a command beginning with a specified character or characters. The complete list of keyboard commands is as follows:

Left/Right arrow	Moves the cursor back/forward one character.
Ctrl + L/R arrow	Moves the cursor back/forward one word.
Home/End	Moves the cursor to beginning/end of line.
Up/Down arrow	Scroll up (and down) through the list of stored commands. Each press of the up arrow recalls the previous command and displays it on the command line.
Page Up/Down	Recalls the oldest/most recent command in the buffer.
Insert	Insert text at the cursor.
Delete	Delete text at the cursor.
F1	Copies the next character from the template to the command line. This works with and without *doskey*.
F2 + *key*	Copies text from the template up to (but not including) *key*.

F3	Copies the template from the present character position to the command line. This works with and without *doskey*.
F4 + *key*	Deletes the characters from the present character position up to (but not including) *key*.
F5	Copies the current command to the template and clears the command line.
F6	Places an end-of-file character (^Z) at the current position on the command line.
F7	Displays a numbered list of the command history.
Alt-F7	Deletes all commands stored in the buffer.
chars + F8	Entering one or more characters followed by F8 will display the most recent command beginning with *chars*. Pressing F8 again will display the next most recent command beginning with *chars*, and so on. If no characters are specified, F8 cycles through the existing commands in the buffer.
F9 + *command#*	Displays the designated command on the command line.
Alt-F10	Deletes all macro definitions.

doskey Macros

You can define macros on the *doskey* command line, but you will probably want to save them in a file to be reloaded using the /f option. Each macro should be on a separate line. Macros have the following form:

> *macroname* = *text*

The text of a macro can include spaces and tabs, and any of the following special codes:

$G	Redirects output—equivalent to the redirection symbol >.
GG	Appends output to the end of a file—equivalent to the append symbol >>.
$L	Redirects input—equivalent to the symbol <.
$B	Sends macro output to a command—equivalent to the pipe symbol |.
$T	Separates commands when creating macros.
$$	Use for the $ sign.
$1 to $9	Represents any command-line parameters that can be specified when the macro is run. Comparable with the %1 to %9 characters in batch programs.
$*	Represents command-line information that can be specified when *macroname* is written. $* is similar to the replaceable parameters $1 through $9, except that everything typed on the command line after *macroname* is substituted for the $* in the macro.

Commands & Applications

Examples

Load *doskey* into memory:

```
C:\>doskey
```

Create a *doskey* macro called *win95* to change to a frequently used directory:

```
C:\>doskey win95 = cd "C:\Windows\Desktop\win95\tim's draft"
```

Play the macro:

```
C:\>win95
```

Delete the macro:

```
C:\>doskey win95=
```

Display all current *doskey* macros:

```
C:\>doskey /macros
```

Notes

- To automatically run *doskey* in every DOS command window, you can either:
  - Open MS-DOS Prompt → Properties and enter *Windows**Commands* *doskey.com* as the batch file.
  - Specify an actual batch file at that same location, including *doskey* as well as any other commands.
  - Run doskey from *autoexec.bat*. This uses extra memory and can increase boot time, but it means that you can have a global command memory no matter how many DOS prompts you open. To open a new copy of *doskey* automatically when you open a DOS prompt, see *Windows Annoyances*.

- Because macros are stored in the buffer, they are lost when a DOS session is ended or if *doskey* is reloaded with doskey /r. To save macros across sessions:

```
C:\>doskey /m > macros.txt
```

These macros can be retrieved in a later session by using:

```
C:\>doskey /f:macros.txt
```

Of course, you need to be in the same directory where you stored *macros.txt*, or provide the full path.

---

drvspace   *Windows**drvspace.exe*

Compress and uncompress data on floppy disks or hard disk drives.

To Launch

```
drvspace /compress d: [/size=n| /reserve=n] [/new=e:]
drvspace /create d: [/size=n | /reserve=n] [/new=e:] [/cvf=nnn]
drvspace /delete d:\d??space.nnn
drvspace /format d:\d??space.nnn
drvspace /host=e: d:
```

---

drvspace [/info] d:
drvspace /mount [=nnn] d: | d:\d??space.nnn] [/new=e:]
drvspace /move d: /new=e:
drvspace /ratio[=n] d:
drvspace /settings
drvspace /size[=n | /reserve=n] d:
drvspace /uncompress d:
drvspace /unmount d:

Description

DriveSpace can compress and uncompress data on floppy disks, removable media, or hard disk drives, and can be used from the command line or from its graphical interface. The first time you use DriveSpace to compress data or space on a drive, the disk will have 50 to 100 percent more free space than it did before. You can use a compressed drive just as before compressing it. When you run DriveSpace without command-line arguments, the DriveSpace Manager appears, with menu commands for selecting the operations to perform.

DriveSpace creates a new uncompressed drive, called the host drive, where it stores the compressed volume file (*.cvf*). If the host drive contains any free space in addition to the *.cvf*, you can also use it to store files that must remain uncompressed.

drvspace accepts the following options:

/compress	Compress a hard disk drive or floppy disk.
/create	Create a new compressed drive in the free space on an existing drive.
/cvf=*nnn*	Reports extension of the compressed volume file (*.cvf*) file.
d:	The first drive.
d??space.*nnn*	The filename of the hidden compressed volume file on the host drive, which can be either **drvspace.*nnn*** or **dblspace.*nnn***, where *nnn* represents the actual filename extension.
/delete	Delete a compressed drive.
e:	The second drive.
/format	Format a compressed drive.
/info	Display information about a compressed drive.
/interactive	Can be added to any command line to have DriveSpace ask for any missing parameters.
/mount	Mount a compressed volume file (*.cvf*). When DriveSpace mounts a *.cvf*, it assigns it a drive letter; you can then use the files that *.cvf* contains.
/new=e:	Specifies the drive letter for the new compressed drive. The /new option is optional; if you omit it, DriveSpace assigns the next available drive letter to the new drive.

/noprompt	Can be added to any syntax except the /info option. The /noprompt option prevents any confirmation dialog boxes from appearing (except for error messages).
/ratio	Change estimated compression ratio of a compressed drive.
/reserve=n	Specifies how many megabytes of free space DriveSpace should leave on the uncompressed drive. To make the compressed drive as large as possible, specify a size of 0.
/size	Change the size of a compressed drive.
/size=n	Specifies the total size, in megabytes, of the compressed volume file. (This is the amount of space on the uncompressed drive that you want to allocate to the compressed drive.) You can include either the /reserve switch or the /size switch, but not both.
/uncompress	Uncompress a compressed drive.
/unmount	Unmount a compressed drive.

Associated Files

drvspace.inf
drvspace.sys

Examples

All of the following examples use the command line, but you can do all of the same things using the graphical interface.

Compress drive *E:*

```
C:\>drvspace /compress d:
```

Create a new compressed drive that uses all available space on uncompressed drive *E:*

```
C:\>drvspace /create e: /reserve=0
```

Delete the compressed volume for drive *C:*

```
C:\>drvspace /delete h:\dblspace.###
```

Change the size of drive *C:* so that it is as large as possible:

```
C:\>drvspace /size /reserve=0 c:
```

Notes

- You can include either the /reserve option or the /size option, but not both. If you omit both options, *drvspace* uses all but 2 MB of free space. The /reserve option can be abbreviated as /reser.

- Before you use DriveSpace to compress a drive, you should back up the files the drive contains.

- To compress the startup hard disk drive, a drive must contain at least 2 MB of free space. Other hard disk drives and floppy disks must have at least 768K of free space.

- If a drive-letter conflict occurs, DriveSpace resolves the conflict by reassigning its drive letters.

- The original Windows 95 DriveSpace version can create a compressed drive of up to 512 MB. The Microsoft Plus! version of DriveSpace can create a compressed drive of up to 2 GB.

- When mounting a compressed drive, you must assign a drive letter to the compressed volume file.

- To mount a compressed disk that wasn't present when you started your computer (for example, a floppy disk), you need to mount it. Use *drvspace* /mount from the command line or Advanced → Mount from the GUI. To delete a compressed drive, the /delete option must specify the complete pathname of the compressed volume file (e.g., *d:\drvspace.002*).

- If any files on the drive are open, DriveSpace will prompt you to close them before it compresses the drive. For drives that always have files opened (such as the drive containing Windows 95), DriveSpace will restart the computer and use a limited version of Windows in place of Windows 95 while it compresses the drive. To do this, a directory named *failsave.drv* is created that contains the system files required for this operation. After compression, your computer will restart again, this time with Windows 95. When the compression is completed, DriveSpace shows how much free space is available on the drive.

- For compression ratios of files, use *dir* /c and *dir* /ch.

See Also

dblspace, scandisk

---

drwatson   \ *Windows\drwatson.exe*

Provides system error information when a GPF occurs.

To Install

Download *drwatson.exe* from the following location:

> *http://www.pointcast.com/support/pcn/pcn20/20faqs/drwatson.html*

and place the executable in your \ *Windows* directory.

To Launch

drwatson should be started whenever Windows is started. One way to do this is to edit the [windows] section of the *wini.ini* file as follows:

```
load=drwatson.exe
```

drwatson will then be launched every time Windows is started.

Another way to start *drwatson* automatically is to create a shortcut for the utility and place it in the \ *Windows\Start Menu\Programs\StartUp* directory.

Description

Dr. Watson is a diagnostic tool that provides information on the internal state of Windows when a system error (General Protection Fault, or GPF) occurs. This utility must be downloaded; it doesn't come with Windows 95.

Dr. Watson remains inactive until a GPF error occurs. When this happens, a dialog box will appear asking for comments on the activities prior to the error. The comments you input will be added to a file called *drwatson.log*. You can use Notepad to view *.log* files.

Sometimes Dr. Watson detects a fault that might not be fatal, and you have the opportunity to ignore the fault or close the application. If you choose to ignore the fault, Windows continues without performing the faulting instruction. You might be able to save your work in a new file at this point, but you should then restart Windows.

See Also

For more information about *drwatson.exe*:

> *http://premium.microsoft.com/msdn/library/techart/msdn_drwatson.htm*

---

edit   \ *Windows\Command\edit.com*

A DOS-based full-screen ASCII text editor.

To Launch

> edit [/b] [/h] [/r] [/s] [/<nnn>] [file(s)]

Description

edit is very useful when working with ASCII files (e.g., batch files) from the command line. It supports the standard cut, copy, and paste commands and their shortcuts, Find, Repeat Last Find, and Replace commands, and it allows you to split the window and resize it, and even to change the color settings for the program (see Figure 5-19). Of course the standard File menu commands are also present (Save, Save As, Close, Print, and so forth).

The *edit* options are:

/*nnn*	Loads binary file(s), wrapping lines to *nnn* characters wide.
/b	Forces monochrome mode.
file(s)	Specifies the initial file(s) to edit. You may use wildcards and multiple filenames.
/h	Displays the maximum number of lines possible for your hardware.
/r	Loads file(s) in read-only mode.
/s	Forces the use of short filenames.

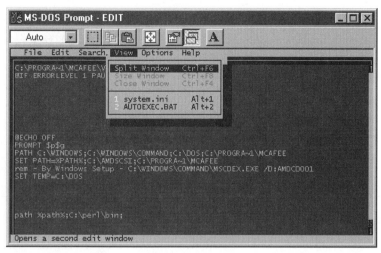

Figure 5-19: Using edit.com, the text editor

Examples

View a binary file (for example, you can search for "MS-DOS Version 7", but be careful not to make any changes—do not save the file on exit):

```
C:\>edit /70 c:\command.com
```

Edit *autoexec.bat* file:

```
C:\>edit c:\autoexec.bat
```

Edit all of the text files on your Desktop:

```
C:\Windows\Desktop>edit *.txt
```

Notes

- *edit.com* loads much faster than Notepad, WordPad, or Word.

- You can cut and paste between multiple files by switching windows. Edit's clipboard is not the same as Window's.

See Also

notepad, wordpad

---

eru   *\Emergency Recovery Utility (ERU)\eru.exe*

Windows 95 Emergency Recovery Utility.

To Install

Control Panel → Add/Remove Programs → Windows Setup → Have Disk →
\Other\Misc\ERU on Win95 CD-ROM → OK → OK

To Launch

You must put an *eru* shortcut somewhere in your Start Menu directory (or anyplace else such as the Desktop) or include the directory in the PATH line of *autoexec.bat* to run *eru* from the Run prompt.

Description

eru is designed to provide a backup of your system configuration files in case a problem occurs. The program will back up the following files along with the restore program (*erd.exe*): *config.sys, autoexec.bat, win.ini, system.ini, protocol.ini, user.dat, system.dat, io.sys, command.com*, and *msdos.sys*.

Notes

- To restore your configuration files, use *erd.exe* (*Emergency Recovery Utility (ERU)\erd.exe*). First, you need to boot your machine to the command prompt (real mode) in order to execute the restoration utility (*erd.exe*). To do this, reboot your machine and press the **F8** key when you see the "Starting Windows 95" message on the screen. You then need to choose the "Safe Mode Command Prompt Only" option, change to your backup directory, and run the *erd.exe* utility. If you don't want to restore all of the files listed, simply use the spacebar to untoggle them, and then start the restoration process.

- You need to choose a location to store your backup information. A floppy in drive *A:* is typically used, but you can store it on any drive, including a network drive.

- Be sure to make a fresh copy of your backup disk any time you install new hardware or software to keep it current.

- *eru* will arbitrarily drop files from the backup set if there isn't room on the destination medium. There is no warning or notification given.

- To back up only certain files, click the Custom button at the file list screen.

---

exchng32   OSR2: *Program Files\Windows Messaging\exchng32.exe*

The Windows 95 email program.

If you have the original version of Windows 95, you will find *exchng32* at the following location: *Program Files\Exchange\exchng32.exe*.

To Launch

    Double-click the Inbox icon on the Desktop
    Start → Run → exchng32
    Start → Programs → Windows Messaging (OSR2)
    Start → Programs → Exchange (OSR1)

Description

Since it would require a small book to explain Windows Messaging/Exchange in detail, this section touches on the non-obvious highlights that a user may find helpful when using the email program. For this discussion we will use the OSR2 name, Windows Messaging.

There are a couple of useful command-line options that can be used if Windows Messaging isn't running, with the following syntax:

exchng32 [/a] [/n]

Options include:

/a   Opens the address book without launching *exchng32*.

/n   Activates the New Message option without launching *exchng32*.
                The message won't be sent until *exchng32* is running.

Both of these command-line options can be used with a shortcut as well. Just point to the location of *exchng32* in the Target field under Properties, and provide a space and then list the option.

Figure 5-20 shows Windows Messaging running with the two-pane display, which can easily be toggled to one pane with the Show/Hide Folder List button.

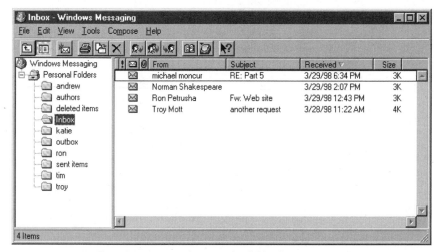

Figure 5-20: Windows Messaging, showing the folder list

Here is a short list of some non-obvious features:

Tools → Remote Mail

Lets you see mail headers without downloading the messages themselves. With this option, you can mark messages for download, delete messages without download, and so forth. It is very handy for reading mail from a dial-up connection.

Tools → Options → Services or Tools → Services

This is the same thing as Control Panel → Mail and Fax, where you configure server, connnection, general, and other options.

Tools → Address Book

The Address Book is great for storing names and information for those people you send email to on a regular basis. You can create aliases, store phone numbers in the Business tab so they can be viewed from the Address Book list, and, when creating a new message, you can select the To, Cc, or Bc button to launch the Address Book.

View → Personal View

With this option, you can sort your mail in the Windows Messaging Folder list by From, Subject, or Conversation Topic. So, for instance, if you have a lot of email from several different people, you might want to sort by From, since this lists the names of the people only in the Inbox. Each name becomes a folder with all of the messages from that person nested within it.

Notes

- Windows Messaging can't use the signature feature available on most email programs. A third-party add-on located at *http://www.angrygraycat.com/goetter /widgets.htm* allows you to use signatures with Windows Messaging.

- You might want to run the Inbox Repair Tool (*scanpst*) once in a while to prevent lockups and problems in Windows Messaging. If you have a large number of stored messages, it will take a while to scan and repair them.

- To preview your messages before you open them, select View → Columns → Item Text → Add → OK. This will give you a small portion of the first line of the message in the Inbox.

- You can quickly add an address to the Address Book in Exchange by right-clicking on the address in the From field and selecting Add to Personal Address Book on a message you've received.

- Windows 98 will come with Outlook Express instead of Windows Messaging.

See Also

scanpst

---

exit   Internal to: \ *Windows\command.com*

Quit the *command.com* program.

Description

exit is used without parameters or options, and is also used to get back into Windows after you choose "Restart windows in MS-DOS mode" on startup.

---

explorer   \ *Windows\explorer.exe*

The 32-bit user interface shell that allows you to view files and directories in a tree-like structure.

To Launch

Start → Run → **explorer**
Start → Right-click → Explore
Start → Programs → Windows Explorer
explorer [/n] [/e][,/root,object][[,/select],subobject]

Description

The Explorer is the default Windows shell. It creates the Desktop and all of the standard icons, folders, and menus (including the Taskbar and the Start menu) the first time it is run. Running it thereafter will create a two-paned window in which you can navigate through all of the files, folders, and other resources on your computer. See "The Explorer" in Chapter 3, *The Windows 95 User Interface*, for a description of the user interface. On the command line, *explorer* supports the following options (note that if you specify more than one option, including /e and /n, they must be separated by commas—this is different from most Windows 95 programs):

/e	Use the Windows Explorer view. The default is Open view (a one-pane folder) if you specify a folder or other object on the command line.
/n	Always open a new window when starting the Explorer (even if the specified folder is already open).
/root,*object*	Specify the object (directory) that will be used as the root of this Windows Explorer Folder. The default is to use the Desktop. The Explorer can go anywhere inside the root, but not outside or "above" it. The root can be a disk, UNC pathname, or folder name.
/select	Specifies that the parent folder is opened and the specified object is selected.
subobject	Specify the folder to receive the initial focus, unless /select is used. The default is the root.

Examples

Open a window rooted at *nut* so you can easily browse the whole server, but nothing else:

```
C:\>explorer /e,/root,\\nut
```

Open a folder window on *C:\Windows* (or make an open window active) and select *sol.exe*:

```
C:\>explorer /select,c:\windows\sol.exe
```

Notes

- You can use the command-line switches for the Windows Explorer in short-cut links (Figure 5-21) or batch files; for example, you can run the Explorer with a specified file selected.

- The Target line accepts all of the command options mentioned. Note that the "Start in:" line can be used instead of the /root,*object* option.

- The shell= setting in *system.ini* accepts Explorer command-line options. After changing the shell= line in *system.ini*, loading a new shell requires only a logoff/logon; a full reboot is not necessary.

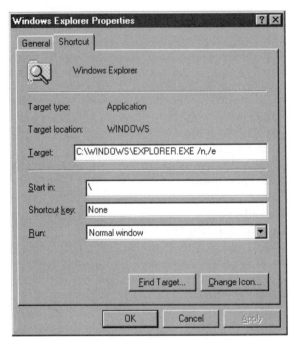

Figure 5-21: The standard Explorer configuration as seen in an Explorer shortcut

---

extract

\ *Windows*\ *Command*\ *extract.exe*

Extract files and lists from a Windows cabinet (*.cab*) file.

To Launch

> extract [/y] [/a] [/d | /e] [/l dir] cabinet [filename ...]
> extract [/y] source [newname]
> extract [/y] /c source destination

Description

This utility is provided to extract one or more files from the cabinet archives on the Win95 CD-ROM, generally only done if it is suspected that an installed file was corrupted in some way. (To install optional pieces of Windows 95, it is best to use Control Panel → Add/Remove Programs → Windows Setup.)

The Windows 95 CD-ROM contains a cabinet "set" starting at *win95_02.cab*. If you don't know the exact location of a file, use the /a option to "walk" the entire set, starting at *win95_02.cab*. Note, however, that there are three other *.cab* files not in the set: *mini.cab*, *precopy1.cab*, and *precopy2.cab*.

extract accepts the following options:

/a	Process *all* cabinets. Follows cabinet chain starting in first cabinet mentioned.
/c	Copy source file to destination (to copy from DMF disks).

---

cabinet	Cabinet file (contains two or more files).
/d	Display cabinet contents; do not extract files.
/e	Extract (use instead of *.* to extract all files).
filename	Name of the file to extract from the cabinet. Wildcards and multiple filenames (separated by blanks) may be used.
/l *dir*	Location to place extracted files (default is current directory).
newname	New filename to give the extracted file. If not supplied, the original name is used.
source	Compressed file (a cabinet with only one file).
/y	Do not prompt before overwriting an existing file.

> Cabview, a utility available with PowerToys, lets you browse *.cab* files and extract files using drap and drop and other standard GUI file manipulation operations. See *powertoy*, later in this chapter, for details on how to get this utility.

Examples

Display the contents of a *.cab* file called *win95_13.cab* in the current directory:

```
C:\>extract /d win95_13.cab
```

Extract the file *canyon.mid* from the entire set of Windows 95 *.cab* files; in the current directory, and place the extracted file in *C:\Windows*:

```
C:\>extract /a win95_02.cab /l c:\windows\ canyon.mid
```

fax

See *awsnto32*.

faxcover   *Windows\faxcover.exe*

Add graphic elements to fax cover pages.

To Launch

Start → Run → faxcover
Start → Programs → Accessories → Fax → Cover Page Editor

Description

You can add logos or other graphic elements to your fax cover pages using the application's built-in tools or by inserting bitmap (*.bmp*) files. If a desired graphic isn't in *.bmp* format, you can copy it to the Clipboard and then paste it in the cover page editor. When you have finished with a fax cover page, save it as a *.cpe* file, so you can attach it when sending a Microsoft fax. See Figure 5-22.

Figure 5-22: Fax Cover Page Editor (faxcover.exe)

Notes

- *faxcover.exe* stores several icons that can be assigned to fax cover pages, but you can easily add your own icons.

- There are several *.cpe* files that act as fax cover page templates, which you can modify, or you can create your own *.cpe* files that contain customized cover pages.

- In OSR1, there was a bug with fax cover pages, but the following lines added to *autoexec.bat* provide a fix:

```
rem for fax cover pages to appear
c:\windows\command\attrib +a c:\windows\*.cpe
```

  This problem was fixed in OSR2.

See Also

You can download the OSR2 *faxcover* component (if you have OSR1) as well as other OSR2 components from:

> *http://www.microsoft.com/windows95/info/updates.htm*

---

faxview   \ *Windows\faxview.exe*

View *.dcx* and *.awd* files in the original Windows 95 release.

To Launch

> Double-click on a *.dcx* or *.awd* file
> Start → Run → faxview *filename*

Description

View *.dcx* and *.awd* files, which are fax viewer documents.

Notes

With the release of OSR2, *faxview* was replaced with *wangimg*. You can use *wangimg* at the command line in the same way that *faxview* is used. You can also view *.tif* files with *wangimg*.

See Also

> *wangimg*

---

fc   *Windows\Command\fc.exe*

Compare two files (or sets of files) and display the differences between them.

Syntax

> fc file1 file2
> fc [/a] [/b] [/c] [/l] [/lb*n*] [/n] [/t] [/w] [/*nnnn*]

Description

fc is most useful if you can't quite remember the difference between two ASCII files that you'd like to run. For example, if you have two batch files named *foobar.bat* and *bar.bat*, you can run *fc* to see the differences quickly.

The *fc* options are:

/*nnnn*	Specifies the number of consecutive lines that must match after a mismatch (default value of *nnnn*: 2).
/a	Display only first and last lines for each set of differences, as opposed to the default of every different line.
/b	Perform a binary comparison.
/c	Disregard the case of letters.
/l	Compare files as ASCII text.
/lb*n*	Set the maximum consecutive mismatches to the specified number of lines (default value of *n*: 100).
/n	Display the line numbers on an ASCII comparison.
/t	Do not expand tabs to spaces. By default, tabs are treated as spaces with 1 tab = 8 spaces.
/w	Compress whitespace (tabs and spaces) to a single space for comparison.

Examples

Compare *autoexec.bat* with *autoexec.old*:

> `C:\>fc autoexec.bat autoexec.dos`

Make a binary comparison of two files named *term.exe* and *year.exe*:

> `C:\>fc /b term.exe year.exe`

Notes

- If *filename1* includes a wildcard, all applicable files are compared to *filename2*. If *filename2* also includes a wildcard, each file is compared with the corresponding *filename1*.

---

fdisk \ *Windows* \ *Command* \ *fdisk.exe*

Configure a fixed disk for use with DOS or another operating system.

To Launch

```
C:\>fdisk
```

Description

fdisk is a menu driven utility used to configure and/or display information about the partitions on a hard disk. You can control the operation of *fdisk* with command-line options, or from a menu that is displayed by typing *fdisk* without any options (see Figure 5-23).

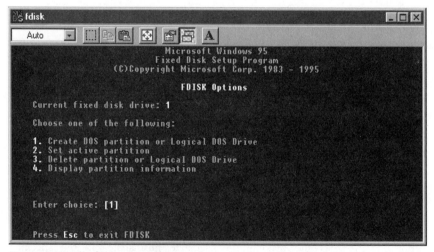

Figure 5-23: The fdisk menu (fdisk.exe)

The following tasks can be performed by *fdisk*:

- Switching between FAT16 and FAT32 "large disk support" (MS-DOS 7.10, OSR only)

- Creating a DOS partition or Logical DOS Drive

- Setting an active partition

- Deleting a partition or a Logical DOS Drive

- Displaying partition information

If you want to repartition a hard disk from multiple partitions into a single drive, you must first use *fdisk* to delete all existing partitions and logical drives, and then create a new primary partition and make it active.

WARNING

Using *fdisk* to create, modify, or delete partitions on a hard drive deletes all the data stored on that disk.

---

fdisk accepts the following options:

/ext	Creates extended partition.
/log	Creates logical DOS volume in the extended partition.
/mbr	Writes the Master Boot Record without altering the partition table information. This switch can be used to repair a Master Boot Record that has been corrupted or damaged by a boot sector virus.
/pri	Creates a primary partition.
/prmt	Prompts for action.
/q	Quiet—no messages displayed during processing.
/status	Displays partition information.
/x	Ignores extended disk-access support. Use this switch if you receive disk access or stack overflow messages.

Examples

To display an overview of partition information, use the /status option:

```
C:\>fdisk /status
```

Notes

- If the /status option doesn't provide enough detail about your hard disk (such as the drive type of system), then start the *fdisk* program without the /status option and choose option 4 (Display partition information) from the GUI.

- In MS-DOS 7.0, the maximum partition size is 2 GB. FAT32 (OSR2, MS-DOS 7.10) supports drives over 2 GB. To change the size of a partition, it is necessary to delete the partition and create a new one of the required different size.

- *fdisk* works only on hard disks physically installed on your computer. *fdisk* does not work on a drive formed by using the *subst* command, nor does it work on a network or an Interlink drive.

- *fdisk* doesn't display information about compressed drives, since they are hidden, read-only system files.

See Also

For a better disk utility, try PowerQuest's Partition Magic:

http://www.powerquest.com/product/pm

Commands & Applications

---

find

Search one or more files for a specified text string.

To Launch

find [/v] [/c] [/n] [/i] "string" [filename[...]]

Description

After searching the specified files, *find* displays any lines of text that contain the string you've specified for your search. *find* is useful for searching for specific words (strings) in files, but don't get it confused with the Find → Files or Folders that is available in the Explorer (available from context menus, the Start menu, and elsewhere). Find → Files and Folders can search for text, files, directories, etc., and has many other capabilities that the *find* command doesn't have. See "Find Files and Folders" in Chapter 3.

The *find* options are:

/c	Displays only the count of lines containing the string
/i	Ignores the case of characters when searching for the string
/n	Displays line numbers with the displayed lines
/v	Displays all lines *not* containing the specified string

Examples

Search for "set" in *autoexec.bat*:

```
C:\>find "set" autoexec.bat
```

Search for "set" in *autoexec.bat* and *autoexec.dos*:

```
C:\>find "set" autoexec.bat, autoexec.dos
```

Count occurrences of "put" in *autoexec.bat*:

```
C:\>find /c "put" autoexec.bat
```

Search the current directory for the string "cls" in all *.bat* files and store the result in the file *cls.txt* (note that >> rather than > is necessary when redirecting the output of a *for* loop):

```
C:\>for %f in (*.bat) do find "cls" %f >> cls.txt
```

Notes

- You can search through multiple files by specifying each file to search on the command line, but unfortunately, wildcards (* and ?) are not accepted in the filename. To search for a string in a set of files, however, it's often possible to use the *find* command within a *for* loop structure. If redirecting *for* to a file, use >> rather than >.

- If a filename is not specified, *find* searches the text input from the "standard" source (usually the keyboard), a pipe, or a redirected file.

You might be tempted to try something like:

```
dir c:\ /s /b | find "chap"
```

to search the contents of all files with "chap" in their names, but in fact, all you'd be doing is running *find* on the list of filenames, not on their contents.

• *find* won't recognize a string that has a carriage return embedded in it. For example, if "chapter" is at the end of the line, and "05" on the next, find won't report a match on "chapter 05".

---

fontview   \ *Windows\fontview.exe*

View TrueType fonts.

To Launch

Start → Settings → Control Panel → Fonts
fontview [/p] <filename.extension>

Description

fontview is normally invoked automatically by double-clicking on a font file. If run from the command line, the complete filename of the font, including its extension (such as *.fon* or *.ttf*) must be typed. To print the font information, use the /p option.

Examples

View the Times New Roman font (see Figure 5-24):

```
C:\>fontview \windows\fonts\times.ttf
```

Figure 5-24: TrueType font viewer (fontview.exe)

Notes

- Windows 95 keeps most font files in \ *Windows\Fonts*.

- *fontview* does not display every character in the font, it only shows some basic information such as the font's copyright notice and "The quick brown fox jumps over the lazy dog. 1234567890" in sizes from 12 to 72 points.

- *fontview* is not helpful for special characters. See *charmap* for a full display of all characters.

- FontViewer97 is a better Windows font-viewer utility:

  http://pw2.netcom.com/~andrepm/prod03.html

See Also

Control Panel → Fonts

---

for   Internal to: \ *Windows\command.com*

Run a specified command for each instance in a list.

To Launch

for %variable in (set) do command [command-options] [%variable]

Description

A *for* loop is a programming construct that allows you to repeat a command for a list of items (such as filenames). You specify an arbitrary variable name and a set of values to be iterated through. For each value in the set, the command is repeated.

The values in the set are enclosed in parentheses, and should be separated by spaces. Wildcards can be used to supply a list of filenames.

Examples

Display the contents of all the files in the current directory that have the extension *.txt*:

```
C:\>for %f in (*.txt) do type %f
```

Redirect the output of the previous example to LPT1 (a printer port):

```
C:\>for %f in (*.txt) do type %f > lpt1:
```

Create a set of numbered directories (such as for chapters in a book):

```
C:\>for %x in (1 2 3 4 5) do md ch0%x
```

Notes

- in and do are not options, but a required part of the *for* command. If you omit either of these keywords, MS-DOS displays an error message.

- When redirecting the output of a for loop to a file, you must use >> (append to a file) rather than >, or else you will save only the last iteration of the loop. (The previous LPT1 reduction example is an exception, since LPT1 isn't a file, but a device, which will spool the output of each successive redirection in the loop.)

- When using the *for* command in a batch program, specify `%%variable` instead of `%variable`.

- You need not actually use the variable a second time as an argument to the command. You could, for instance, simply use the variable list to repeat a command some number of times.

See Also

lfnfor

---

format   *Windows**Command**format.com*

Format a disk for use.

To Launch

format drive: [/v[:label]] [/q] [/f:size] [/b | /s] [/c]
format drive: [/v[:label]] [/q] [/t:tracks /n:sectors] [/b | /s] [/c]
format drive: [/v[:label]] [/q] [/1] [/4] [/b | /s] [/c]
format drive: [/q] [/1] [/4] [/8] [/b | /s] [/c]

Description

Before data can be stored on a disk, the disk must be formatted. This process creates various low-level data structures on the disk, such as the File Allocation Table. It also tests the disk surface for errors and stores bad sectors in a table that will keep them from being used.

The *format* options are:

/b	Allocates space on the formatted disk for system files.
/c	Tests clusters that are currently marked "bad."
drive:	Specifies the drive that contains the disk to format.
/f:*size*	Specifies the size of the floppy disk to format (such as 160, 180, 320, 360, 720, 1.2, 1.44, 2.88).
/n:*sectors*	Specifies the number of sectors per track.
/q	Performs a quick format, which means that the top-level file-system information will be wiped out without actually erasing the data. After a quick format, data previously stored on the disk could possibly be recovered with an "unerase" or "unformat" utiltiy.
/s	Copies DOS system files to the formatted disk. This will be a DOS system disk only.
/t:*tracks*	Specifies the number of tracks per disk side.
/v[:*label*]	Specifies the volume label. This is an arbitrary title you give the disk. It can be up to 11 characters and can include spaces. The volume label will show up at the top of *dir* listings for the disk. See *label* for more information. If the /v option is omitted, or

Commands & Applications

the label isn't specified, a prompt for a volume label is displayed after the formatting is completed. If a label is specified with /v and more than one disk is formatted in a session, all of the disks will be given the same volume label.

/1   Formats a single side of a floppy disk.

/4   Formats a 5.25-inch 360K floppy disk in a high-density drive.

/8   Formats eight sectors per track.

Examples

Format floppy in drive *A:* using default settings:

    C:\>**format a:**

Format floppy in drive *A:* specifying 720K capacity:

    C:\>**format a: /f:720**

Format floppy in drive *A:* specifying a label:

    C:\>**format a: /v:mydisk**

Notes

- *format* size (specified with the /f option) must be equal to or less than the capacity of the disk drive containing the disk to be formatted. For example: a 1.44 MB capacity drive will format a 720K disk, but a 720K drive will not format a 1.44MB disk.

- *format* assumes that a floppy disk in a 3.5" drive will be formatted as 1.44MB, unless the /q option is used.

- A disk created with **format** /s won't boot into the Windows 95 GUI. Neither will a disk created with Emergency Recovery Utility (ERU). The Windows 95 GUI requires the loading of *himem.sys* and *ifshlp.sys*. To boot the full Win95 with a GUI from the floppy, you need *io.sys*, *msdos.sys*, and a *config.sys* that looks something like the following:

```
shell=c:\command.com /p /e:1024
device=c:\windows\himem.sys
device=c:\windows\ifshlp.sys
device=c:\windows\server.exe
DOS=high
```

and the following line in *autoexec.bat*:

```
c:\windows\win.com
```

- By default, each sector on the disk is checked during formatting, so data can be sorted properly (unless /q is used). Bad sectors are marked and not used.

- *format* can't be used on network or *subst*ed drives.

- To format compressed disks, see **drvspace /format**.

- To format a disk from the Explorer, use Drive → Context Menu → Format.

freecell \ *Windows\freecell.exe*

A solitaire card game.

To Launch

Start → Run → `freecell`

Start → Programs → Accessories → Games → FreeCell

Description

freecell is a Windows 95 solitaire card game (see Figure 5-25). The object of the game is to move all the cards to the home cells, using the free cells. It feels like a cross between Solitaire and the Towers of Hanoi computer science problem.

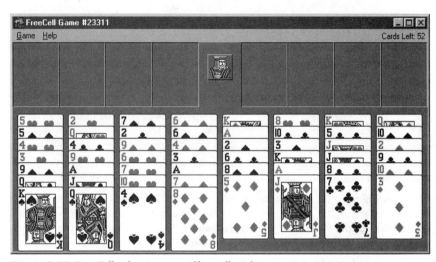

Figure 5-25: FreeCell solitaire game (freecell.exe)

Notes

- In *freecell*, there are 32,000 different instances of the game. *freecell* is unlike *sol* in that, according to the help, "It is believed (although not proven) that every game is winnable." In fact, it has been proven that one game, #11982, is not winnable.

- Another variation of *freecell* is Spider, a classic solitaire game played with two decks of cards.

See also

sol

There is an incredibly active FreeCell community on the Web at:

*http://msn.yahoo.com/Recreation/Games/Computer_ Games/Titles/
Strategy/Freecell/*

For a catalog of *freecell* solutions:

http://www.capecod.net/~wcallan/freecell.htm

For the "Internet FreeCell Project," which has a list of "hard" games:

http://physics.tamu.edu/~Cdude/freecell.html

For FreeCell Plus, which has many more options than *freecell*:

http://www.goodsol.com/freeplus.html

FreeCell Pro (including a solver):

http://www.capecod.net/~wcallan/freecell/fcpro.htm

For a Web version of FreeCell written in Java:

http://www.freecell.minivend.com

---

ftp   \ *Windows\ftp.exe*

Transfer files between a host computer and a remote computer over the Internet (File Transfer Protocol).

To Launch

ftp [-v] [-n] [-i] [-d] [-g] [host] [-s: filename]

Description

Like many Internet programs, *ftp* is a client-server application. Your local ftp client connects to a remote Internet server and issues commands to the server to upload or download files, display data, and so on.

You must log in to the remote server; however, there are many public servers that allow anonymous ftp. Enter the login name *anonymous*, and enter your email address (or, frankly, any text) as the password. The complete list of commands you can issue once you are connected is documented later in this section.

You must specify the hostname or IP address of the remote computer. Most public ftp servers have a hostname beginning with "ftp" such as *ftp://ftp.uu.net*, but any remote host might be running an ftp server. Any files will be transferred to and from the current directory, by default. Wildcards are supported for specifying the filenames in commands like *dir, ls, mget,* and *mput,* unless turned off with the *glob* command.

ftp options are:

-d	Enables debugging, displaying all *ftp* commands passed between the client and server.
-g	Disables filename globbing, which permits the use of wildcard characters in local file and path names. (See the *ftp* glob command.)
-i	Turns off interactive prompting during multiple file transfers.
-n	Suppresses autologon upon initial connection.
-s: *filename*	Specifies a text file containing *ftp* commands; the commands will automatically run after *ftp* starts. Use this option instead of redirection (>).
-v	Suppresses display of remote server responses.

Figure 5-26 shows a sample ftp session.

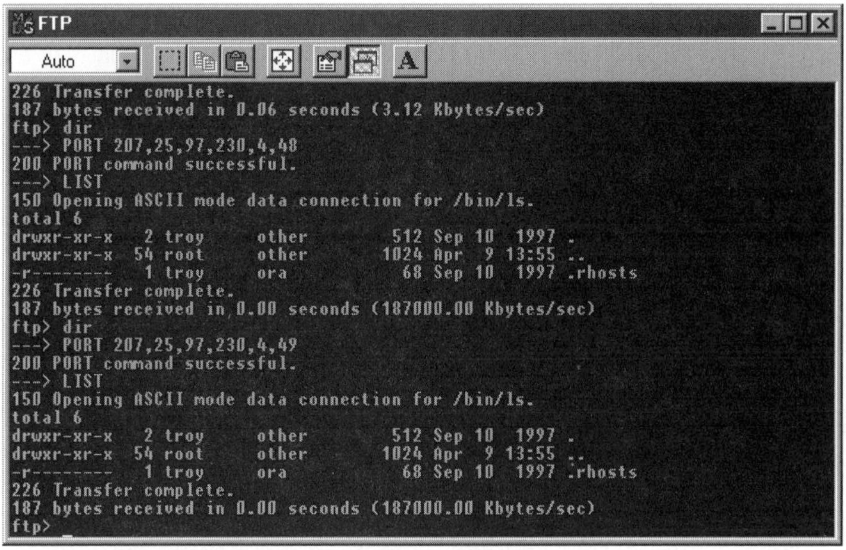

```
226 Transfer complete.
187 bytes received in 0.06 seconds (3.12 Kbytes/sec)
ftp> dir
---> PORT 207,25,97,230,4,48
200 PORT command successful.
---> LIST
150 Opening ASCII mode data connection for /bin/ls.
total 6
drwxr-xr-x   2 troy      other         512 Sep 10  1997 .
drwxr-xr-x  54 root      other        1024 Apr  9 13:55 ..
-r--------   1 troy      ora            68 Sep 10  1997 .rhosts
226 Transfer complete.
187 bytes received in 0.00 seconds (187000.00 Kbytes/sec)
ftp> dir
---> PORT 207,25,97,230,4,49
200 PORT command successful.
---> LIST
150 Opening ASCII mode data connection for /bin/ls.
total 6
drwxr-xr-x   2 troy      other         512 Sep 10  1997 .
drwxr-xr-x  54 root      other        1024 Apr  9 13:55 ..
-r--------   1 troy      ora            68 Sep 10  1997 .rhosts
226 Transfer complete.
187 bytes received in 0.00 seconds (187000.00 Kbytes/sec)
ftp>
```

Figure 5-26: An ftp session

FTP Commands

The following list shows the commands available once *ftp* is running. Not all commands may be effective for every server. For example, you may not be able to upload files to some servers, or delete files that are there. For most purposes, the most important commands to know are put, get, mput, mget, cd, lcd, and dir. If you are transferring binary files, be sure to use the binary command first, or the files will be damaged in transit.

!   Runs the specified command (e.g., cd) on the local computer. ! allows you to issue local (DOS) commands. For example, you can use it to rename, copy, or delete files on the local disk, or to change the local working directory.

? [command]   Displays descriptions for *ftp* commands. Identical to help. ? by itself gives a list of available commands. ? command gives a brief description of each command.

append   Appends a local file to a file on the remote computer.

ASCII   Sets the file transfer type to ASCII, the default.

bell   Toggles a bell to ring after each file transfer command is completed. By default, the bell is off.

binary   Sets the file transfer type to binary (crucial for *.zip*, *.gif*, and other binary file formats).

bye   Ends the *ftp* session with the remote computer and exits *ftp*. Keep in mind that the standard DOS *exit* and *quit* commands won't work here.

cd [*directory*] Changes the working directory on the remote computer (to *cd* locally, use ! cd or lcd).

close   Ends the *ftp* session with the remote server and returns to the *ftp* command interpreter. Use **open** to connect to a different ftp server.

debug   Toggles debugging. When debugging is on, each command sent to the remote computer is printed, preceded by the string --->. By default, debugging is off.

delete *remote_file*
      Deletes a file on the remote computer. Only a single file can be deleted.

dir   Displays a list of a remote directory's files and subdirectories.

disconnect   Disconnects from the remote computer, retaining the *ftp* prompt.

get *remote_file* [*local_file*]
      Copies a remote file to the local computer. If *local_file* is not specified, the copy will be given the same name as the original.

glob   Toggles filename "globbing." Globbing permits use of wildcard characters in local file or pathnames. By default, globbing is on.

hash   Toggles hash-mark (#) printing for each 2048-byte data block transferred. This is a crude status indicator. By default, hash-mark printing is off.

help [*command*]
      Displays the description for each command (e.g., **help get**). For a list of the available commands just type **help** or ? at the ftp prompt.

lcd [*directory*]
      Changes the working directory on the local computer. By default, the current directory on the local computer is used.

literal [*command_line*]
      Sends arguments, verbatim, to the remote *ftp* server. A single *ftp* reply code is expected in return. Allows you to send arbitrary command lines to the remote server. (Whether they can be executed depends on your login privileges at the remote server.) Spaces are allowed.

ls   Displays an abbreviated list of a remote directory's files and subdirectories. This is useful when a directory contains a lot of files. Occasionally, anonymous users may not be able to use *ls*; in this case, you need to know the filename you're looking for.

mdelete [*files*]
      Deletes multiple files on remote computers. Wildcards are supported.

mdirep [*remote_files*][*local_file*]

> Stores a directory listing of a remote directory's files and subdirectories, including file size and modification date. remote_files can be a list of file or directory names, and can include wildcards.

mget [*remote_files*]

> Copies multiple remote files to the local computer using the current file transfer type. Wildcards (* and ?) can be used. You will be asked to confirm each transfer unless you turn off prompting with the **prompt** command. Local files will be given the same name as remote files.

mkdir [*directory*]

> Creates a remote directory.

mls [*remote_dir*][*local_file*]

> Stores a list of a remote directory's files and subdirectories in *local_file*.

mput [*local_files*]

> Copies multiple local files to the remote computer, using the current file transfer type.

open [*hostname or IP address*]

> Connects to the specified *ftp* server. If no host is specified, you will be prompted for one.

prompt

> Toggles prompting. During multiple file transfers (mget and mput), *ftp* provides prompts to allow you to retrieve or store files selectively; mget and mput transfer all files if prompting is turned off. By default, prompting is on.

put [*local_file*][*remote_file*]

> Copies a local file to the remote computer, using the current file transfer type (ASCII or binary). If no local filename is specified, you will be prompted for one. If no remote filename is specified, the local filename will be used.

pwd
> Prints the current directory on the remote computer.

quit
> Ends the *ftp* session with the remote computer and exits *ftp*.

quote [*command_line*]

> Sends arguments, verbatim, to the remote *ftp* server. A single *ftp* reply code is expected in return. Identical to **literal**. Spaces are allowed.

recv [*remote_file*][*local_file*]

> Copies a remote file to the local computer. Identical to **get**.

remotehelp [*command*]

> Displays help for remote commands supported by the server. This is probably similar to the commands available on the client, but may not be identical. As with ? and **help**, supplying no arguments returns a list of command names. Use remotehelp *command* to get more info on each command. Figure 5-27 shows the output of remotehelp.

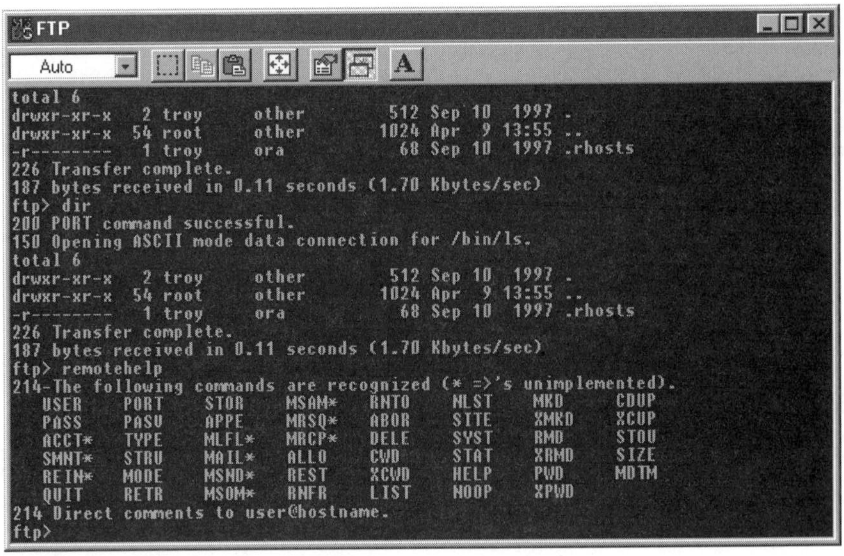

```
FTP                                                      _ □ ×
Auto    ▼  [::] 🗐 🗐  🗐  🗐🗐  A
total 6
drwxr-xr-x   2 troy      other        512 Sep 10  1997 .
drwxr-xr-x  54 root      other       1024 Apr  9 13:55 ..
-r--------   1 troy      ora           68 Sep 10  1997 .rhosts
226 Transfer complete.
187 bytes received in 0.11 seconds (1.70 Kbytes/sec)
ftp> dir
200 PORT command successful.
150 Opening ASCII mode data connection for /bin/ls.
total 6
drwxr-xr-x   2 troy      other        512 Sep 10  1997 .
drwxr-xr-x  54 root      other       1024 Apr  9 13:55 ..
-r--------   1 troy      ora           68 Sep 10  1997 .rhosts
226 Transfer complete.
187 bytes received in 0.11 seconds (1.70 Kbytes/sec)
ftp> remotehelp
214-The following commands are recognized (* =>'s unimplemented).
    USER    PORT    STOR    MSAM*   RNTO    NLST    MKD     CDUP
    PASS    PASV    APPE    MRSQ*   ABOR    SITE    XMKD    XCUP
    ACCT*   TYPE    MLFL*   MRCP*   DELE    SYST    RMD     STOU
    SMNT*   STRU    MAIL*   ALLO    CWD     STAT    XRMD    SIZE
    REIN*   MODE    MSND*   REST    XCWD    HELP    PWD     MDTM
    QUIT    RETR    MSOM*   RNFR    LIST    NOOP    XPWD
214 Direct comments to user@hostname.
ftp>
```

Figure 5-27: The output of remotehelp

rename [*from_name*] [*to_name*]
>   Renames a remote file.

rmdir [*remote_directory*]
>   Deletes a remote directory.

send [*local_file*] [*remote_file*]
>   Copies a local file to the remote computer, using the current file transfer type. Identical to put.

status
>   Displays the current status of *ftp* connections and toggles.

trace
>   Toggles packet tracing; displays the route of each packet when running an *ftp* command.

type
>   Sets or displays the file transfer type.

user *username* [*password*]
>   Specifies a user to the remote computer. If no password is specified, you will be prompted for one. If no username is specified, you'll be prompted for one of those, too. This is great for a second attempt at logging on to a machine that kicked you off for mistyping your password, without having to exit and start over.

verbose
>   Toggles verbose mode. If on, all *ftp* responses are displayed; when a file transfer completes, statistics regarding the efficiency of the transfer are also displayed. By default, verbose is on.

Examples

To copy the file *preface.doc* from the directory */pub/nutshell* on a remote computer to *\temp\docs* on your local computer, once you're logged on to a server, you would perform the following from the DOS prompt (note that cd within *ftp* is for the remote computer):

```
C:\>cd \temp\docs
C:\temp\docs>ftp remote_computer
username
password
ftp>binary
ftp>cd /pub/nutshell
ftp>get preface.doc
```

Run a script containing *ftp* commands:

```
C:\>ftp -s:myfile.scr
```

This will load *ftp*, and run *myfile.scr*, executing any *ftp* commands in the file.

Notes

- All *ftp* command names can be abbreviated to the first four letters; sometimes fewer.

- If arguments are omitted, you will be prompted for them.

- When using the get or mget commands, the files on the remote computer will be copied to whatever directory you launched *ftp* from, unless specifed otherwise with the lcd command.

- In *ftp* you must use the forward slash "/" instead of the backslash "\" in pathnames; directory and filenames are case-sensitive in most instances, unless you log in to a computer running NT.

- *ftp* is a standard way to transfer files from computer to computer on the Internet, regardless of machine type. You can *ftp* any type of file from a Mac to a PC as easily as from one PC to another PC, or from a Unix workstation to a PC or Mac.

- Use remotehelp to get a command list from the remote server.

- Most web browsers support the *ftp://* protocol, which is equivalent to *ftp* get. See *iexplore*. You can also put files and log in with non-anonymous *ftp* (i.e., *ftp://username@host*), if you have login privileges on a given server.

See Also

To download WS_FTP, a GUI ftp client for Windows 95, for qualified non-commercial use:

http://www.ipswitch.com/downloads/ws_ftp_LE.html

For a long list of alternative *ftp* utilities for Windows:

http://www.theshareware.net/directories/internet/utilities/ftp/windows.htm

---

hearts

See *mshearts*.

Commands & Applications

hover \Hover\hover.exe

A game in which you steer a hovercraft through the world of Hover.

Description

hover is a game included on the Windows 95 CD-ROM. Match your wits with robotic pilots as you steer your hovercraft through the murky realms of Hover. See Figure 5-28.

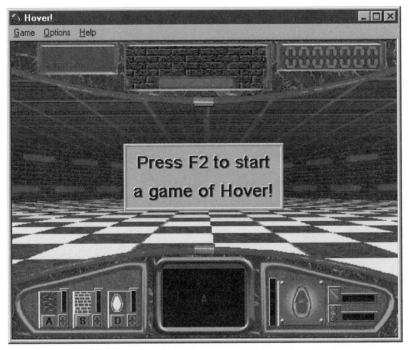

Figure 5-28: Hover! game (hover.exe)

Notes

- You can copy the entire \Hover directory from the CD-ROM at \FunStuff \Hover onto your hard drive. To start the game, double-click on *hover.exe*.

- For tips on playing Hover, be sure to read the *hovrread.txt* file in the \Hover directory.

---

hwdiag \Windows\hwdiag.exe

A very useful report tool for hardware, available only on the OSR2 CD.

To Launch

Copy *hwdieag.exe* from the CD-ROM (\Other\Misc\Hwtrack) to your \Windows directory, and run the executable:

Start → Run → hwdiag

Description

hwdiag (Figure 5-29) is a good alternative to the Device Manager, because it can perform the same functions and more: it can filter information, hunt down problematic devices, present printable resource summaries (for IRQs, addresses, and so forth), display hardware-oriented Registry entries, and save output to a file.

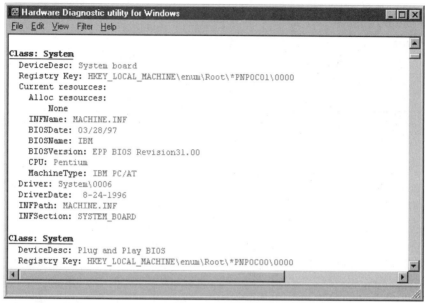

Figure 5-29: Windows hardware diagnostic utility (hwdiag.exe)

Notes

If you have an earlier, non-OEM or floppy disk version of Windows 95, you won't be able to obtain *hwdiag*, since it isn't available from the Microsoft site.

---

hypertrm   \Program Files\Accessories\Hyper Terminal\hypertrm.exe

Terminal access to remote computers.

To Launch

    Start → Run → **hypertrm**
    Start → Programs → Accessories → HyperTerminal

Description

With HyperTerminal and a modem, you can connect to a remote computer that supports terminal access, send and receive files, and so on. This is useful for connecting to computer bulletin boards; however, dial-up terminal access has largely been replaced by the Internet.

HyperTerminal uses connection files and locations similar to those used by Dial-Up Networking. HyperTerminal comes with a number of predefined connections for services such as MCI Mail, CompuServe, and AT&T Mail. You can open one of these existing connections or create a new one. Connections are stored in *.ht* files in the directory *\Program Files\Accessories\HyperTerminal.* HyperTerminal uses the locations and credit card information stored in the *telephon.ini* file, but the actual connections are distinct from those used by Dial-Up Networking. See Chapter 7 for additional details on locations.

Notes

- HyperTerminal replaces Windows Terminal from Windows 3.1. You can get a version of HyperTerminal newer than the default Win95 version from *http://www.hilgraeve.com.*

- Network managers use HyperTerminal frequently for connecting to network devices using VT100 emulation (Unix machines, routers, hubs, switches, CSU/DSUs, etc.).

---

iexplore   *\Program Files\Internet Explorer\iexplore.exe*

The Microsoft browser (3.02) used to access resources on the Web.

To Launch

> Start → Run → `iexplore`
> Start → Programs → Internet Explorer

Description

Internet Explorer (IE) 3.02 is a full-featured browser that can be used to view the Web; it comes with OSR2 or can be downloaded from Microsoft's web site. In addition to recognizing the standard protocol types like *http*, *ftp*, and *telnet*, IE can send Internet email and comes with a news client. Figure 5-30 shows the Internet Explorer window.

In this section, you will find some of the non-obvious highlights about IE 3.02. For in-depth information, see *Internet in a Nutshell*, by Valerie Quercia (O'Reilly & Associates).

The following syntax can be used from the command line:

> iexplore -nohome [url]

-nohome   Starts IE without loading the home page. You can also specify any URL (e.g., *altavista.digital.com*), and it will be loaded instead.

Notes

- View → Options provides a lot of configurable options for IE. See "Internet" in Chapter 4 for details.

- Go → Open History Folder stores URLs for up to 20 days. The number of stored days can be altered in View → Options → Navigation, where you can also view or clear the History Folder.

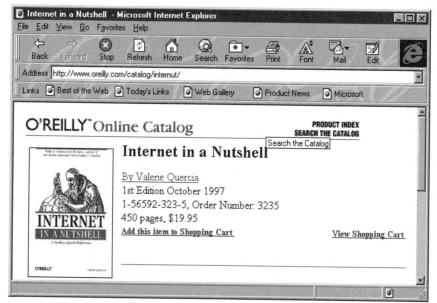

Figure 5-30: Internet Explorer (iexplore.exe)

- The Favorites menu item allows you to store shortcuts, or bookmarks, to your favorite sites.

- IE has an autosearch feature. With autosearch, you can type in the following URL, and Yahoo will return the information you are seeking:

  http://msie.yahoo.com/autosearch?p=<text>

  Where *<text>* is the subject or word you are looking for. All of the standard Yahoo searching variables (+, –, "", etc.) can be used here as well.

- IE has an autocompletion feature, which allows you to leave off *http://* and even *www* in your URLs, and the site will still be found and loaded, as long as the site is in the *.com* domain.

- You can view the contents of your hard drive in the IE window. For instance, if you type in **\windows**, everything in the *\Windows* directory will be shown. IE 3.02 won't be able to run any of your programs, but IE 4 has this capability (see the forthcoming *Windows 98 in a Nutshell*).

- You can even enter UNC network pathnames into the IE Address line and view any shared folders.

See Also

Chapter 4

imagedit \hfill *\Program Files\Resource Kit\imagedit.exe*

Create or modify bitmap, cursor, or icon files.

To Install

After downloading *rktools.exe* to a directory (for instance, *\Program Files\Resource Kit*) and running the executable, *imagedit* will be ready for use.

To Launch

```
C:\>imagedit
```
Start → Run → Programs → Resource Kit → Image Editor

Description

imagedit.exe is a Windows-based utility (the Image Editor) that allows you to create or modify bitmap (*.bmp*), cursor (*.cur*), or icon (*.ico*) files in color or monochrome, and also helps you create animated cursors (*.ani* files) by drawing and editing frames from within the Animated Cursor Editor.

The following options are available by default when creating bitmaps, cursors, or icons in the Image Editor (see "Notes" for ways to make adjustments on icon and cursor options):

Bitmap
> Width and height: adjustable in pixels (the range is 1–256 pixels); 16-color; 2-color (monochrome)

Icon
> EGA/VGA 16-color 32×32; monochrome 2-color 32×32; CGA 2-color 32×16

Cursor
> VGA-mono 2-color 32×32; VGA-color 16-color 32×32

The Image Editor by default will match the color values for the display on which it is running. You can change the selection, by selecting the 2-color option for monochrome displays or the 16-color option for all other displays.

The Image Editor supports standard Windows cut/copy/paste operations. This makes it easy to copy an existing image and paste it into the Image Editor. If the image being pasted is a different size than the currently selected image, the application will ask you to shrink or enlarge the image, or to crop it to fit in the area specified.

You can edit colors in the color palette by using the Edit button in the Color Palette. This enables you to replace existing colors with a selection from the basic colors. If you've created a customized color palette, you can save it in a palette file (*.pal*), and load it at any time by selecting File → Load Colors. See Figure 5-31.

Notes

- By default, the Image Editor allows you to edit images for common display devices such as VGA or monochrome. You can create definitions of image types for other display devices by modifying the *imagedit.ini* file located in your *\Windows* directory.

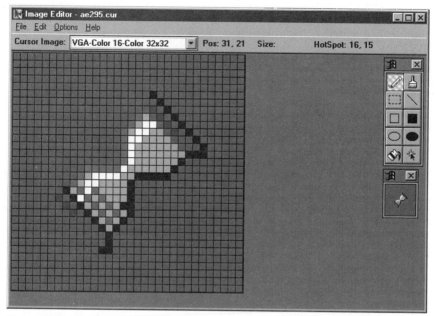

Figure 5-31: The Image Editor (imagedit.exe)

- You can add a string containing four fields to the *imagedit.ini* file:

    1. Name of the display device (up to 12 uppercase and lowercase letters)

    2. Number of colors in the icon or cursor image

    3. Horizontal size of a cursor or icon in pixels

    4. Vertical size of a cursor or icon in pixels

- The following lines show an example specifying information for a Super-VGA device:

```
[ImagEdit.Icon]
SuperVGA=16,64,64
[ImagEdit.Cursor]
SuperVGA=16,32,32
```

    The Image Editor will display this information when you choose a new image, and display the characteristics for the image type after you load the image into the editor.

- Every cursor must have a single pixel designated as the exact location of the cursor. This location is called the *hot spot*. When you click your mouse, the firing will take place at the hot spot. It should be placed at a location where the eye is drawn naturally to it. For example, if your cursor is in the shape of an arrow, the tip of the arrow is a good place for the hot spot.

To mark the hot spot in a cursor:

1. Select the hot spot tool from the Toolbox.

2. Move the tool to the desired location on the cursor image.

3. Click the left mouse button.

The status bar now displays the coordinates of the grid location chosen for the hot spot.

- If you need to know exactly where the pixels are located on an image, you can display a grid over the drawing area (Options → Grid).

See Also

> *aniedit*

---

imaging

See *wangimg*.

---

inbox repair tool

See *scanpst*.

---

infinst   *\Program Files\Resource Kit\infinst.exe*

Integrate *.inf* files from the Win95 CD-ROM.

To Launch

> Start → Run → infinst
> Start → Programs → Resource Kit → INF Installer

Description

The *infinst* tool (shown in Figure 5-32) can be used to integrate *.inf* (and related) files from the Win95 CD-ROM to prepare for installing software and run-once actions in Win95 setup files.

The server-based setup for Windows 95 can't be used to add extra components, such as Resource Kit utilities or applications and services from the *\Admin* directory on the Win95 CD. To add such components or any other software that uses Windows 95 *.inf* files, you must make sure the source files are installed correctly, the *.inf* files used by Windows 95 Setup are modified properly, and correct entries are added to *msbatch.inf*. *infinst.exe* takes these actions automatically for any software that has a Windows 95 *.inf* file.

You can use the INF Installer to add external components, like the SNMP agent (in *\Admin\NetTools\SNMP* on the Win95 CD-ROM), to the *netsetup* tree and (optionally) force installation of the components using a batch script.

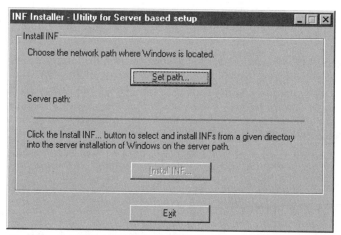

Figure 5-32: INF Installer (infinst.exe)

---

jview

Starts the Microsoft command-line loader for Java.

To Launch

jview [/a] [/cp <classpath>] [/cp:a <path>] [/cp:p <path>] [/d:<name>=<value>]
[/n <namespace>] [/p] [/v] <classname> [arguments]

Description

jview is used to run Java programs that aren't applets (Java programs run within a
browser). *jview* uses Microsoft's version of the Java Virtual Machine (JVM), which
is very fast, since it uses Just-In-Time compiler technology.

/a	Executes AppletViewer
arguments	Command-line arguments to be passed on to the class file
classname	*.class* file to be executed
/cp <classpath>	
	Sets class path
/cp:a <path>	Appends path to class path
/cp:p <path>	Prepends path to class path
/d:<name>=<value>	
	Defines system property
/n <namespace>	
	Namespace in which to run
/p	Pauses before terminating if an error occurs
/v	Verifies all classes

Notes

- Typing *jview* in a command window will display the version of the currently installed JVM.

- In the Microsoft VM for Java that is included with Internet Explorer 3.x, only trusted class files can access resources outside the Java sandbox. Class files from digitally signed *.cab* files are trusted. If the HTML file is run from Microsoft Developer Studio (MSDEV), the class files are also trusted. This can be very helpful during applet development. However, to deliver your applets to other users, you must place them in a signed *.cab* file.

- Unfortunately, there is not an option or Registry setting for *jview* that enables Java logging. However, you can redirect the output when invoking an application, as in the following example:

  ```
  C:\>jview main > javalog.txt
  ```

- When you run a Java Application using *jview* from within the Developer Studio IDE, the MS-DOS command prompt window closes immediately after the Java Application terminates. To prevent the MS-DOS window from closing immediately, you can have an input statement as the last statement in your Java application. For example:

  ```
  system.in.read();
  ```

  A second option is to run your Java application externally (outside the Developer Studio environment).

See Also

For sample utilities written in Java, see JSplit, JZip, and JUnzip:

http://www.compaction-tech.com/jsplit.html

For the Microsoft SDK containing the latest Java compiler and Virtual Machine for using Java with the WIN32 API only:

http://www.microsoft.com/java/download.htm

---

krnltoys   *\Program Files\krnltoys.exe*

A collection of useful tools ("kernel toys") assembled by Microsoft. Install anywhere; for example, *C:\Program Files\Kernel Toys.*

To Install

Download your copy:

http://www.microsoft.com/windows95/info/kerneltoys.htm

Follow the install instructions there.

Description

krnltoys aren't supported or included with Windows 95, but they are very useful tools and are worth installing. You can download individual Kernel Toys or the entire set from the listed URL. The following list provides details the individual Kernel Toys. Most of the Kernel Toys have documentation in a *.txt* file with the same name as the associated *.exe* file.

Conventional Memory Tracker
convmem.vxd

This tool tracks the amount of memory that is allocated by virtual device drivers (VxDs) in conventional memory. On startup, it creates the file *Windows* *convmem.txt* (contains the output) and places the file in the *Windows* directory and writes its output there. View the contents in Notepad or any other text editor (see Figure 5-33). *convmem* gives more detail than *mem* /c, since it shows the memory used by individual VxDs, rather than lumping it all together as used by *vmm32*.

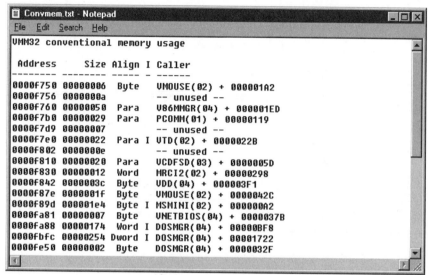

Figure 5-33: Output of conventional memory tracker (convmem.vxd)

To install, copy *convmem.vxd* to your *Windows**System* directory, and add the line device=comvem.vxd to the [386Enh] section of the *system.ini* file. Restart Windows 95. To uninstall, delete the file *convem.vxd*, then remove the previous line from your *system.ini* file.

MS-DOS Mode Configuration Wizard Customization Tool
doswzcfg.exe

This program lets you customize the MS-DOS mode configuration wizard. (This wizard can be found at *any MS-DOS program* → Properties → Program → Advanced → Configure.)

When you run *doswzcfg*, you'll see a dialog box that lets you view the options that are already available in the DOS Configuration Wizard. The drop-down list labeled Option (see Figure 5-34) lists the available wizard options. The Attributes section lists the associated value of that option. You can change the attributes of existing settings, delete settings, or add new ones.

Windows Time Zone Editor
tzedit.exe

Helps you control of the time zone in Windows 95: a Windows 95 version of the Windows NT time zone editor. If your country changes its daylight savings time switchover rules, this is a good tool to use. For additional information, see *tzedit*. To run, double-click the executable (no installation is required).

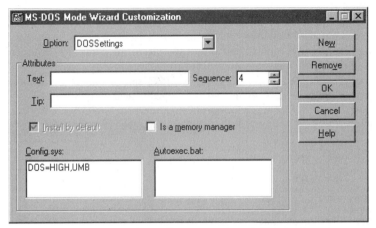

Figure 5-34: MS-DOS mode configuration wizard (doswzcfg.exe)

Windows 95 Keyboard Remap   *keyremap.vxd*

Lets you reprogram the CapsLock, left and right Ctrl, Alt, and Shift keys, as well as the Window and Menu keys. A keyboard control panel extension lets you use the "natural keyboard." After you install it, go to Control Panel → Keyboard → Remap and set up your keyboard the way you like it (see Figure 5-35). Once installed, the *.vxd* will always be running (as long as Windows 95 is running, of course).

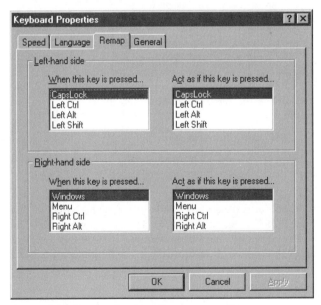

Figure 5-35: Remapping keys (keyremap.vxd)

To install, right-click on *keyremap.inf.* Select Install. Click OK, and when it tells you that you need the disk, browse to the directory where you downloaded the Kernel Toys.

Windows Process Watcher
wintop.exe

This tool lets you view how much of your CPU is being used by specific programs (see Figure 5-36). This is the best of the bunch.

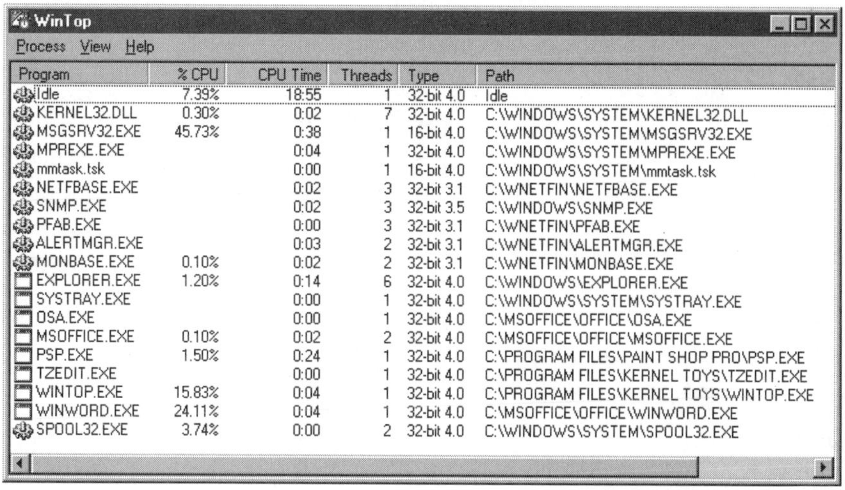

Figure 5-36: Wintop shows what programs are using your CPU (wintop.exe)

To install, right-click the *wintop.inf* file. Select Install. Click OK, and when it tells you that you need the disk, browse to the directory where you downloaded the Kernel Toys. To uninstall, go to Control Panel → Add/Remove Programs → Wintop.

WARNING

Do not uninstall WinTop while it is running!

Windows Logo Key Control for MS-DOS Programs
doswinky.vxd

This tool allows you to disable the Windows logo key in MS-DOS programs. This is useful when you are playing a video game and keep pressing that key by mistake. Once installed, the *.vxd* should always be running.

To install, right-click *doswinky.inf.* Select Install. Click OK, and when it tells you that you need the disk, browse to the directory where you downloaded the Kernel Toys. For the changes to take effect, you must restart the computer.

See Also

powertoy

label \ *Windows\Command\label.exe*

Create, change, or delete the volume label of a disk.

To Launch

label [drive:][label]

Description

The label appears at the top of the listing when you display a directory with the *dir* command, or view the disk with the Explorer.

The *label* options are:

[drive:]	Specifies the drive that contains the disk you wish to label. If you omit the drive option, the current drive is used by default.
[label]	Specifies the label for the disk. If you omit the label the system will prompt you to provide it. The label must be no more than 11 characters in length.

Examples

Create/change the label for the disk in drive *A*:

```
C:\>label a: newlabel
```

Notes

* If label is not specified, the following prompt is displayed:

  ```
  Volume in drive A has no label
  ```

  ```
  Volume label (11 characters, ENTER for none)?
  ```

* A volume label can contain up to 11 characters and can include spaces, but not the following characters:

  ```
  * ? / \ | . , ; : + = [ ] ( ) & ^ < > "
  ```

* Volume labels are displayed in uppercase letters only.

* To display the current disk label, use the *dir* command.

See Also

dir, vol

---

lfnbk \ *Windows\lfnbk.exe*

A long filename (*.lfn*) backup utility used in MS-DOS.

To Install

Copy *lfnbk.exe* from the CD-ROM (\ *Admin\Aapptools\Lfnback*) to your \ *Windows* directory.

lfnbk [/v] [/b] [/r] [/pe] [/nt] [/force] [/p] [<drive>]

Description

If you use an older backup program that has not been designed with Windows 95 in mind (e.g., a DOS or Windows 3.1 program), long filenames will be lost on the backup, and filenames (and possibly data) will be lost on the restore. *lfnbk* can help. Note that some long filename information can be lost even when using *lfnbk*.

Run *lfnbk* with the /b option before using your backup program to convert all long filenames to 8.3 filename aliases, and again, with the /r option, to convert them back after you restore.

WARNING

Do not use *lfnbk* with OSR2 where a FAT32 partition is in use!

---

lfnbk might not be able to rename files with exact matches to long filename aliases (i.e., the associated 8.3 name paired with each long filename), and the related alias is not guaranteed to be the same as before running *lfnbk*.

The *lfnbk* options are:

/b	Backs up and removes long filenames on the disk.
/force	Forces *lfnbk* to run, even in unsafe conditions.
/nt	Does not restore backup dates and times.
/p	Finds long filenames, but does not convert them to 8.3 file-name aliases. This reports the existing long filenames, along with the associated dates for file creation, last access, and last modification of the file.
/pe	Extracts errors from backup database.
/r	Restores previously backed-up long filenames.
/v	Reports actions on the screen.

Notes

- *lfnbk* actually renames each file with a long filename to its associated alias. The filename changes are stored in the *lfnbk.dat* file in the root of the drive where you are running *lfnbk*. *lfnbk.dat* is used to restore long filenames (when you run *lfnbk* with the /r option).

- After you run *lfnbk* and then restart Windows 95, the default Start menu will appear, rather than your custom Start menu. After you run lfnbk /r to restore long filenames, your custom Start menu will also be restored.

---

lfnfor   Internal to: \ *Windows\command.com*

Enable/disable long filenames when processing *for* commands.

To Launch

　　lfnfor [on | off]

Description

If you use the *lfnfor* command without any options, the current *lfnfor* setting (on or off) will be displayed.

The *lfnfor* options are:

off   Disable long filenames

on   Enable long filenames

Examples

Display in a batch file the contents of all the files in the current directory that have the *.txt* extension, and show the long filenames of these files:

```
C:\>lfnfor on
C:\>for %f in (*.txt) do type %f
```

See Also

for

---

logview

View and edit the most recent copies of log files.

To Install

Copy *logview.exe* from the Win95 CD-ROM in the *Other\Misc\Logview* directory to your *Windows* directory.

To Launch

Start → Run → `logview`

Description

logview can be helpful when you're troubleshooting some parts of your system, since it quickly loads the most recent copies of log files created by Windows 95 (see Figure 5-37). These log files frequently contain insightful information about an application. For example, the *scandisk.log* file will tell you when *scandisk* was last run, what options were used, and what type (if any) errors were found. The following log files are normally created by Win95 (others may also be displayed):

bootlog.txt
detlog.txt
netlog.txt
setuplog.txt
scandisk.log
ndislog.txt

Notes

- There is no save option.
- You can use *logview* to open and print ASCII files.
- The standard Window functions such as cut, copy, paste, and delete all work in *logview*.

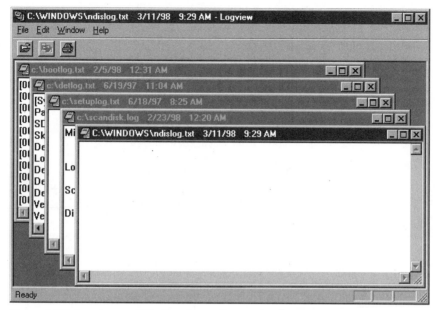

Figure 5-37: Log viewer utility (logview.exe)

md or mkdir

Internal to: \ *Windows\command.com*

Create a new directory.

To Launch

    md [drive:]path
    mkdir [drive:]path

Description

Windows 95, like DOS and Windows 3.1, uses a hierarchical directory structure to organize its file system. On any physical disk, the file system begins with the root directory, signified by a backslash.

You can create additional directories (typically referred to as *folders* in any Windows 95 GUI application) via the New → Folder option in the Explorer File menu or on any context menu, or by using the DOS *mkdir* command. The *md* and *mkdir* commands are functionally identical.

md and *mkdir* accept the following option:

[drive:]path   Specifies the directory to create

Examples

Create a new directory called *newdir* within the current directory:

    C:\>md newdir

Create a new subdirectory called *newdir* under the *c:\olddir* directory:

```
C:\>md c:\olddir\newdir
```

Create a subdirectory named *BASIC*:

```
C:\>md basic
```

If you omit the backslash, *md* creates the new directory under the current directory.

Create a directory at the root called *this is a very long directory name*:

```
C:\>md "\this is a very long directory name"
```

Notes

- In order to create directories or subdirectories with long names including spaces, enclose the name in quotation marks.

- If you do not specify a drive, the current drive is assumed. If your path starts with a backslash (\), DOS starts its directory search with the root directory. If you omit the backslash, DOS uses the current directory.

- You may indicate a absolute or relative path for the path parameter. When absolute, the new directory is created as specified from the root directory. When relative, the directory is created in relation to the current directory.

- The maximum length of any path from the root directory to the new directory is 244 characters, including backslashes. See Chapter 1, *Using Windows 95*.

- When creating a series of directories and subdirectories, you must create them one at a time. For example, to create *MyFiles\January*, you would need to issue two *md* commands:

```
C:\>md \MyFiles
C:\>md \MyFiles\January
```

---

media player

See *mplayer*.

---

mem   *\Windows\Command\mem.exe*

Display the amount of real-mode memory available on your system.

To Launch

mem [options]

Description

The PC was originally designed to store applications in the first 640K bytes of physical memory. This was an unfortunate design decision. With newer processors, larger amounts of memory could be addressed, but the system memory allocated above 640K created a barrier between the "conventional" memory and newer "extended" or "expanded" memory schemes. Most Windows 95 programs

---

simply go right for the expanded memory above it, leaving low memory for any DOS programs that may be running.

While *mem* reports on the total amount of real-mode memory available (in the first megabyte), it provides the greatest amount of detail on the low memory area used by DOS programs. Using *mem* without options will display the available conventional, upper, reserved, and extended memory. If you're interested in viewing dynamic memory data in Windows 95, you can download the Wintop program available in Microsoft's Kernel Toys (see *krnltoys*).

mem accepts the following options:

?	Displays help information.
/a	Also displays available memory in High Memory Area (HMA).
/c *(or* /classify*)*	Classifies programs by memory usage. Lists the size of programs, provides a summary of memory in use, and lists largest memory block available.
/d *(or* /debug *)*	Displays status of all modules in memory, internal drivers, and other information.
/f *(or* /free *)*	Displays information about the amount of free memory left in both conventional and upper memory (but not expanded memory).
/m *(or* /module *)*	Displays a detailed listing of a module's conventional memory use. This option must be followed by the name of a module, optionally separated from /m by a colon. A module is a DOS program, a device, or a TSR (Terminate and Stay Resident program).
/p *(or* /page *)*	Pauses after each screenful of information.

Examples

Display the amount of conventional memory used by *doskey.com*:

```
C:\>mem /m doskey
```

Display the status of the computer's used and free memory:

```
C:\>mem
```

Notes

To display the status of the upper memory area, install a UMB provider such as *emm386* and include the command **dos=umb** in the *config.sys* file.

---

minesweeper

See *winmine*.

---

mkcompat \ *Windows*\ *System*\ *mkcompat.exe*

Change settings to make a Win 3.1 program compatible with Win95.

To Launch

```
C:\>mkcompat
```
Start → Run → mkcompat

Description

mkcompat.exe lets you change settings to try to make a poorly behaving Win 3.1 program compatible with Windows 95.

To use *mkcompat*:

1. Select File → Choose Program

2. Check any of the following options that seem applicable to the Win 3.1 problem you're having:

   − Don't spool to enhanced meta files

   − Give application more stack space

   − Lie about printer device mode size

   − Lie about Windows version number

   − Win 3.1 style controls

3. Select File → Save

4. Try running the modified file. If none of the options seems to work, you can load the application in *mkcompat* again and select File → Advanced Options. This will provide you with a lot more options (see Figure 5-38).

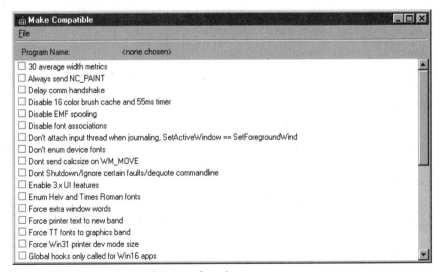

Figure 5-38: Some advanced options for mkcompat.exe

more

Read one screen of text at a time.

To Launch

more [filename]

Description

more displays one screen of text at a time (i.e., to read standard input from a pipe or redirected file). *more* is often used as a filter with other commands that may send a lot of output to the screen. Press any key to see the next screenful of output. Press Ctrl-C to end the output before it is done.

Examples

Display the contents of \Windows\\system.ini and pause for each screenful of text:

```
C:\>more \windows\system.ini
```

Keep the output of *net view* from scrolling off the screen before you can read it:

```
C:\>net view | more
```

Notes

* Some commands (like *dir*) have a /p option that "pages" the output, but many do not. *dir | more* is the same as *dir* /p.

See Also

type

move

\Windows\Command\move.exe

Move files and directories from one location to another.

To Launch

move [/y | /-y] [drive:][path]filename1[,...] destination

Description

To move several files in a directory, you can list the files as the [drive:][path]filename1 option. In other words, you aren't limited to one filename. To move a directory full of files, use the directory name instead.

move can be used to rename directories (and files), but using the enhanced *rename* or *ren* command may be more intuitive.

The *move* options are:

[drive:][path]filename1
Specify the location and name of the file or files you want to move.

destination
Specify the new location of the file. The destination parameter can consist of a drive, a directory name, or a combination of the two. When moving one file, you may include a filename if you want to rename the file when you move it.

| /y | Suppress prompting to confirm creation of a directory or over-writing of the destination. This is the default when *move* is used in a batch file. |
| /-y | Cause prompting to confirm creation of a directory or over-writing of the destination. This is the default when *move* is used from the command line. |

Examples

Move *myfile.txt* from the current directory to *d:\files*:

```
C:\>move myfile.txt d:\files\
```

Same, but rename the file to *newfile.txt*:

```
C:\>move myfile.txt d:\files\newfile.txt
```

Change the name of the directory *d:\files* to *d:\myfiles*:

```
C:\>move d:\files myfiles
```

Notes

- *copy*, *move*, and *xcopy* normally prompt you before overwriting an existing file. To force these commands to overwrite in all cases without prompting you, set the copycmd environment variable to /y. To restore the default behavior, set copycmd to /-y.

- To override all defaults and the setting in the **copycmd** environment variable, use the /y option.

See Also

ren or rename

---

mplayer   *\Windows\mplayer.exe*

Windows 95 video player.

To Launch

Start → Run → mplayer [/play] [/close] [filename]
Start → Programs → Accessories → Multimedia → Media Player

Description

mplayer is the default video player that comes with Windows 95 (see Figure 5-39). With *mplayer* you can play the following types of files: ActiveMovie, *.avi* (Video for Windows), *.wav* (sound), *.mid* or *.rmi* (MIDI, or Musical Instruments Digital Interface), and *.cda* (audio CDs).

When running *mplayer* from the command line, you can use the following options:

| /play | Play the specified file (*filename*). Without this option, the file will be loaded but not played. |
| /close | Close when playing (the default is to remain open). |

Figure 5-39: Default Windows 95 video player (mplayer.exe)

Notes

- Although *mplayer* can play *.avi* files, in OSR2, Windows 95 will invoke the ActiveMovie program if you simply double-click on an *.avi* file. ActiveMovie also comes bundled with Internet Explorer 3.0.

- Any files playable by *mplayer* can be inserted as objects into a WordPad document, and then run from within WordPad.

- All sorts of songs recorded as *.mid* files can be downloaded from the Web and played by *mplayer*.

See Also

actmovie, wordpad

For detailed information about MIDI, and for MIDI freeware and shareware:

http://www.midiweb.com/

---

msbearts   \ *Windows*\ *msbearts.exe*

Card game that can played over the network with other Win95 users.

To Launch

Start → Run → msbearts
Start → Programs → Accessories → Games → Hearts

Description

The object of Hearts (see Figure 5-40) is to have the lowest score at the end of the game. Unlike the other games that come with Windows 95, it is designed to be played with other players on a network (although it can also be played as a solitaire game). The online help tells how to play the game, and provides strategy and tips.

Notes

- To play against the computer (virtual players Pauline, Michele, and Ben), select "I want to be dealer", then press F2 to "begin with current players" rather than "wait for others to join." The game will provide basic directions on how to play.

- Network player versions must be compatible with the dealer's version.

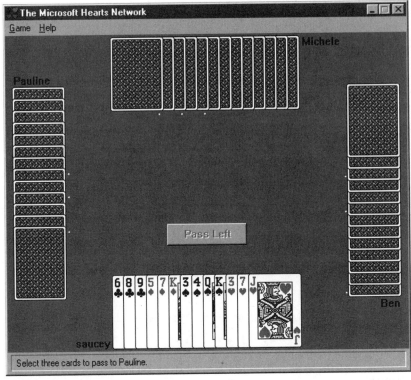

Figure 5-40: Hearts card game (mshearts.exe)

- Microsoft's Internet Gaming Zone web site (*http://www.zone.com*) has ongoing Hearts games. The Zone currently requires MSIE.

See Also

http://www.yahoo.com/Recreation/Games/Card_Games/Hearts/
http://www.ccnet.com/~paulp/software/hearts/hearts.htm

---

mspaint   \Program Files\Accessories\mspaint.exe

· Create, modify, or view image files.

To Launch

Start → Run → mspaint
Start → Programs → Accessories → Paint

Description

mspaint is a graphics program that comes with Windows 95, allowing you to create, modify, or view image files (Figure 5-41). This program replaces Paintbrush from Windows 3.1.

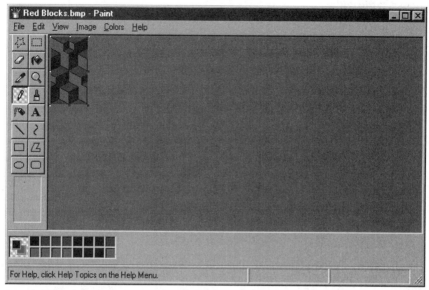

Figure 5-41: Paint graphics program (mspaint.exe)

mspaint deals primarily with bitmap files (*.bmp*). With MSPaint, you can create or open monochrome bitmap files, as well as 16-color, 256-color, and 24-bit *.bmp* files (you can create 256-color icons with *mspaint*, since they're really just 32×32 *.bmp* files). You can also create or open *.pcx* files (PC Paintbrush), which store images from 1 to 24 bits in pixel depth, and are recognized by most still-image graphics programs. Microsoft has developed a new version of MSPaint that can also create and open *.gif* and *jpeg* files.

Some of the tasks you can perform with images in MSPaint are:

File → Set as Wallpaper (Tiled or Centered)
Set *.bmp* files as wallpaper for your Desktop

View → Zoom → Show Grid
Show a grid (Ctrl+G)

View → Zoom → Show Thumbnail
Show a thumbnail

Image → Flip/Rotate
Flip/Rotate (Ctrl+R)

Image → Stretch/Skew
Stretch/Skew (Ctrl+W)

Image → Invert Colors
Invert colors (Ctrl+I)

Colors → Edit Colors
Edit colors

Image → Attributes
> Alter width or height

File → Send
> Send an image by mail or fax

Notes

- If you convert an image to black and white (Image → Attributes → Black and White), you'll lose all of the color information, and the action can't be undone.

- You must save a newly created file before choosing it as wallpaper.

- If you paste an image into MSPaint that is larger than the bitmap you currently have open, you are prompted and can choose to have the bitmap enlarged.

- MSPaint doesn't allow editing of text that's been created, because the text on the screen is actually a graphic. To change the text you must erase it with the Eraser button, and recreate it with the Text button on the toolbar.

- If you'd like the Explorer to show miniature previews (icons) of *.bmp* files in the Explorer, make the following change to the Registry:

  1. Navigate to HKEY_CLASSES_ROOT\Paint.Picture\DefaultIcon

  2. Select the Default value

  3. Modify the value data to %1

  To change it back:

  1. Navigate to HKEY_CLASSES_ROOT\Paint.Picture\DefaultIcon

  2. Select the Default value

  3. Modify the value data to c:\progra~1\access~1\mspaint.exe,1

  These directions assume that your *mspaint.exe* file is in the default directory (*\Program Files\Accessories*).

See Also

To download a free copy of the updated MSPaint (*paint95.exe*), which allows you to create *.gif* and *.jpg* files:

> *http://support.microsoft.com/download/support/mslfiles/Paint95.exe*

For a more advanced image editing tool, download the shareware version of Paint Shop Pro:

> *http://www.jasc.com/*

---

nbtstat

\Windows\nbtstat.exe

Display protocol statistics and current TCP/IP connections using NetBIOS over TCP/IP (NBT).

To Launch

> nbtstat [-a RemoteName] [-A IP address] [-c] [-n] [-r] [-R] [-s] [-S] [interval]

Description

nbtstat can display various statistics about current names, and can also delete names from the NetBIOS name cache. If you are having trouble reaching a remote computer, you can see if the remote computer name is in your name cache.

Type the *nbtstat* command without options to display information about the command (same as `nbtstat /?`).

The *nbtstat* options are:

`-a`	(Adapter status) Lists the remote machine's name table, given its name.
`-A`	(Adapter status) Lists the remote machine's name table, given its IP address.
`-c`	(Cache) Lists the remote name cache including the IP addresses (it's not "remote" unless you use –[aA]).
`interval`	Redisplays selected statistics, pausing `interval` seconds between each display. Press `Ctrl-C` to stop redisplaying statistics.
`IP address`	Dotted decimal representation of the IP address.
`-n`	(Names) Lists local NetBIOS names.
`-r`	(Resolved) Lists names resolved by broadcast and via WINS.
`-R`	(Reload) Purges and reloads the remote cache name table (copying in entries from *lmhosts* with #PRE token).
`remotename`	Remote host machine name.
`-s`	(Sessions) Lists sessions table converting destination IP addresses to host names via the *hosts* file.
`-S`	(Sessions) Lists sessions table with the destination IP addresses.

Examples

Display sessions using NetBIOS names:

```
C:\>nbtstat -s

NetBIOS Connection Table
Local Name State In/Out Remote Host Input Output
----------------------------------------------------
VECTRA2 <03> Listening
VECTRA2 <00> Connected Out ICA <20> 3KB 2KB
Display sessions using IP addresses:
NetBIOS Connection Table
Local Name State In/Out Remote Host Input Output
----------------------------------------------------
VECTRA2 <03> Listening
VECTRA2 <00> Connected Out 10.0.0.1 3KB 2KB
```

If you have an out-of-date or incorrect *lmhosts* file, you can edit it by using *nbtstat*:

```
ping Host Address IP    make sure remote computer is reachable
edit lmhosts            edit lmhosts file
nbtstat -R              rebuild name cache
nbtstat -c              display new cache
net view \\goo          try to view remote computer
```

Notes

Notice the lower- and uppercase a, r, and s characters for the different options.

---

net \ *Windows\net.exe*

Contains all of the *net* commands. The most useful for users are *net print, net use,* and *net view. net init, net logon, net logoff, net password,* and *net stop* can be used only from DOS before Windows is booted (e.g., from *autoexec.bat* or in Safe mode). These latter commands are largely obsolete, but may be useful in some circumstances, such as with a diskless Windows 95 system, or for testing networking before Windows is started. See Chapter 9.

See Also

> *net config, net diag, net help, net init, net logoff, net logon, net password, net print, net start, net stop, net time, net use, net ver, net view*

---

net config Internal to: \ *Windows\net.exe*

Display your current workgroup settings.

To Launch

> net config [/yes]

Description

Control Panel → Network → Identification is the GUI equivalent of *net config*.

net config accepts the following option:

/yes   Carries out the *net config* command without first prompting you to provide information or confirm actions.

Examples

To display your computer's current workgroup settings:

```
C:\>net config

Computer name \\CHARLES
User name CHARLIE
Workgroup WORKGROUP
Workstation root directory C:\Windows
Software version 4.00.950
Redirector version 4.00
The command was completed successfully.
```

---

net diag

Internal to: *Windows**net.exe*

Run the Microsoft Network Diagnostics program.

To Launch

net diag [/names | /status]

Description

Use *net diag* to test the hardware connection between two computers and to display information about a single computer.

net diag can assist you in troubleshooting network connectivity problems by establishing a diagnostic server and then verifying that the local computer can connect to this server.

With no options, *net diag* looks for another computer that is already running *net diag* to act as the diagnostic server. If one is not found, it asks if *net diag* is currently running on any other computer. If you answer N, the current computer will act as the server. Go to the second computer, and run *net diag* there. If the *diag* server is found, the network is running correctly. The /status option gives more detail, and also does not require *net diag* to be already running on another computer.

The *net diag* options are:

/names   Specifies a custom diagnostic session name in order to avoid conflicts when *net diag* is used simultaneously by multiple users. This option works only when the network uses a NetBIOS protocol. You will be prompted for the session name. You then have to use the same name on the other computer.

/status Enables you to specify the computer you want more detailed network diagnostics information from. You will be prompted for the name of the remote computer you want to use to test network connectivity. Use the computer name without the \\ UNC prefix. For example, *troy* would be specified as *troy*. If you don't specify a name, the local computer's interface will be tested.

Examples

Check the status of a remote computer named *troy*:

```
C:\Windows\Desktop>net diag /status

Please enter the remote computer's NetBIOS name, or press ENTER
to examine a local adapter's status.

troy

Remote adapter status:

Permanent node name: 080009B12D81
```

```
Adapter operational for 0 minutes.
0 free NCBs out of 0 with 0 the maximum.
0 sessions in use
0 sessions allocated
0 packets transmitted 0 packets received.
0 retransmissions 0 retries exhausted.
0 crc errors 0 alignment errors
0 collisions 0 interrupted transmissions.
name 1 TROY               status 04
name 2 WORKGROUP          status 84
name 3 TROY               status 04
name 4 WORKGROUP      -   status 84
name 5 TROY           ✿   status 04
The command was completed successfully.
```

net help   Internal to: *Windows**net.exe*

Display information about *net* commands and error messages.

To Launch

> net help [command | errornum]

Description

If you type *net help* at the command line without any options, a brief description of all Microsoft *net* commands will be displayed. Specify a *net* command name for information about that command. Specify an error number for information about that error. This is rather bogus, since it simply repeats the text of the message.

The *net help* options are:

command
: Specifies the *net* command you want information about. One of *config, diag, init, logoff, logon, password, print, start, stop, time, use, ver,* or *view.*

errornum
: Specifies the number of the error message that you want information about.

Examples

Since many of the help messages are longer than a single screen, you can pipe them through the *more* command (the message will pause at each screenful with -- More -- displayed until you press a key:

> `C:\>net help stop | more`

net init   Internal to: *Windows**net.exe*

Load protocol and network-adapter drivers without binding them to Protocol Manager. Cannot be used from within Windows.

To Launch

> net init [/dynamic]

Description

net init may be required if you are using a third-party network adapter driver. You can then bind the drivers to Protocol Manager by typing:

```
C:\>net start netbind
```

net init accepts the following option:

/dynamic   Loads the Protocol Manager dynamically. This is useful with some third-party networks, such as Banyan® VINES®, to resolve memory problems.

Examples

To set up VCSTS with Windows 95, make sure the following line exists in *autoexec.bat*:

```
net init /dynamic
```

See Also

net, net start

---

net logoff   Internal to: \ *Windows\net.exe*

Break the network connection.

To Launch

net logoff [/yes]

Description

If you're using Microsoft Networking in MS-DOS mode, and have logged in with *net login*, you can use *net logoff* to break the network connection between your computer and the shared resources to which it is connected. This command can't be used from within Windows. If you are already logged on as another user, you may need to type *net logoff* to end your current session.

net logoff accepts the following option:

/yes   Carries out the *net logoff* command without first prompting you to provide information or confirm actions.

See Also

net, net init, net logon, net start

To download a freeware screensaver that forces a network logoff when a thirty-second timer expires:

http://www.bayside.net/users/techead/spikesoft/spikesoft.htm

---

net logon   Internal to: \ *Windows\net.exe*

Identify a computer as a member of a workgroup.

To Launch

net logon [user [password | ?]] [/domain:name] [/yes] [/savepw:no]

Description

Normally, if Microsoft Networking is enabled, you will log on to the network when starting Windows. (See "Login" in Chapter 3.) If you're using the system in MS-DOS mode (perhaps because you're debugging a startup problem—see Chapter 9), and you want to use networking, you must log in with *net login*.

If you would rather be prompted to type your username and password instead of specifying them in the *net logon* command line, type *net logon* without options. *net logon* can be used only before Windows is started.

The *net logon* options are:

?	Specifies that you want to be prompted for your password.
/domain	Specifies that you want to log on to a Microsoft Windows NT or LAN Manager domain.
name	Specifies the Windows NT or LAN Manager domain you want to log on to.
password	The unique string of characters that authorizes you to gain access to your password-list file. The password can contain up to 14 characters.
/savepw:no	Carries out the *net logon* command without prompting you to create a password-list file.
user	Specifies the name that identifies you in your workgroup. The name you specify can contain up to 20 characters.
/yes	Carries out the *net logon* command without first prompting you to provide information or confirm actions.

Examples

For a diskless computer that uses Client for Microsoft Networks, *autoexec.bat* might be set up like this:

```
net start basic
net logon /savepw:no /yes
net use x: \\server\share
```

See Also

net start, net use

---

net password   Internal to: \ *Windows*\ *net.exe*

Change your logon password.

To Launch

```
net password [oldpassword [newpassword]]
net password \\computer I /domain:name [user [oldpassword
    [newpassword]]]
```

Description

The first syntax line is for changing the password for your password-list file. The second syntax line is for changing your password on a Windows NT or LAN Manager server or domain. *net password* can't be used from within Windows. Once Windows has been started, use Control Panel → Passwords → Change Windows Password to change passwords.

The *net password* options are:

computer	Specifies the Windows NT or LAN Manager server on which you want to change your password.
/domain	Specifies that you want to change your password in a Windows NT or LAN Manager domain.
name	Specifies the Windows NT or LAN Manager domain in which you want to change your password.
newpassword	Specifies your new password. It can have as many as 14 characters.
oldpassword	Specifies your current password.
user	Specifies your Windows NT or LAN Manager username.

net print

Internal to: \ *Windows\net.exe*

Display information about the print queue on a shared printer.

To Launch

net print \\computer[\printer] | port [/yes]
net print \\computer | port [job# [/pause | /resume | /delete]] [/yes]

Description

You can stop, suspend, or delete a print job on a network computer with *net print*, instead of using the GUI interface at Control Panel → Printers.

When you specify the name of a computer by using the *net print* command, you receive information about the print queues on each of the shared printers that are connected to the computer.

The *net print* options are:

computer	Specifies the name of the computer about whose print queue you want information.
job#	Specifies the number assigned to a queued print job. You can specify the following options:

> /pause   Pauses a print job.
>
> /resume   Restarts a print job that has been paused.
>
> /delete   Cancels a print job.
>
> /yes   Carries out the *net print* command without first prompting you to provide information or confirm actions.

`port`	Specifies the name of the parallel (LPT) port on your computer that is connected to the printer you want information about.
`printer`	Specifies the name of the printer you want information about.

Examples

Examine the print queue DeskJet on a computer named ICA:

```
C:\>net print \\ica\DeskJet

Printers at \\ica
Name Job # Size Status
DeskJet Queue 1 jobs *Printer Active*
Administrator 5 1170041 Printing
```

---

net start   Internal to: \ *Windows\net.exe*

Start Win95 networking services.

To Launch

net start [basic | nwredir | workstation | netbind | netbeui | nwlink] [/list] [/yes] [/verbose]

Description

To start the workgroup redirector you selected during setup, type **net start** without options (in most instances you won't need to use options). *net start* can only be run before Windows itself is started.

The *net start* options are:

`basic`	Starts the basic redirector
`/list`	Displays a list of the services that are running
`netbeui`	Starts the NetBIOS interface
`netbind`	Binds protocols and network-adapter drivers
`nwlink`	Starts the IPX/SPX-compatible interface
`nwredir`	Starts the Microsoft Novell®–compatible redirector
`/verbose`	Displays information about device drivers and services as they are loaded
`workstation`	Starts the default redirector
`/yes`	Carries out the *net start* command without first prompting you to provide information or confirm actions

---

net stop   Internal to: \ *Windows\net.exe*

Stop Win95 networking services.

To Launch

net stop [basic | nwredir | workstation | netbeui | nwlink] [/yes]

Description

To stop the workgroup redirector, type **net stop** without options. Note that this breaks all your connections to shared resources and removes the *net* commands from your computer's memory. *net stop* can only be run before Windows itself is started.

The *net stop* options are:

basic   Stops the basic redirector

netbeui   Stops the NetBIOS protocol

nwlink   Stops the IPX/SPX-compatible interface

nwredir   Stops the Microsoft Novell®–compatible redirector

workstation   Stops the default redirector

/yes   Carries out the *net stop* command without first prompting you to provide information or confirm actions

---

net time   Internal to: \ *Windows**net.exe*

Synchronize a computer's clock with a shared clock on a server.

To Launch

net time [\\computer | /workgroup:wgname] [/set] [/yes]

Description

net time displays the time from or synchronizes your computer's clock with the shared clock on a Microsoft Windows for Workgroups, Windows NT, Windows 95, or NetWare time server.

The *net time* options are:

computer   Specifies the name of the computer (time server) with whose time you want to check or synchronize your computer's clock.

/set   Synchronizes your computer's clock with the clock on the computer or workgroup you specify.

wgname   Specifies the name of the workgroup containing a computer with whose clock you want to check or synchronize your computer's clock. If there are multiple time servers in that workgroup, *net time* uses the first one it finds.

/workgroup   Specifies that you want to use the clock on a computer (time server) in another workgroup.

/yes   Carries out the *net time* command without first prompting you to provide information or confirm actions.

Notes

The */yes* option is helpful when the *net time* command is used within a batch file.

net use   Internal to: \ *Windows*\ *net.exe*

Connect or disconnect a computer from a shared resource.

To Launch

> net use [drive: | *] [\\computer\directory [password | ?]] [/savepw:no] [/yes] [/no]
> net use [port:] [\\computer\printer [password | ?]] [/savepw:no] [/yes] [/no]
> net use drive: | \\computer\directory /delete [/yes]
> net use port: | \\computer\printer /delete [/yes]
> net use * /delete [/yes]
> net use drive: | * /home

Description

In addition to connecting or disconnecting your computer from a shared resource, *net use* also displays information about your connections.

With no options, net use prints a list of the computers with shared resources to which you have made connections and the status of these connections.

The *net use* options are:

*	Specifies the next available drive letter. If used with /delete, closes all of your connections.
?	Specifies that you want to be prompted for the password of the shared resource. You don't need to use this option unless the password is optional.
computer	Specifies the name of the computer sharing the resource.
/delete	Breaks the specified connection to a shared resource.
directory	Specifies the name of the shared directory.
drive	Specifies the drive letter you have assigned to a shared directory.
/home	Makes a connection to your home directory, if one is specified in your LAN Manager or Windows NT user account.
/no	Carries out the *net use* command, responding with no automatically when you are prompted to confirm actions.
password	Specifies the password for the shared resource, if any.
port	Specifies the parallel (LPT) port name you assign to a shared printer.
printer	Specifies the name of the shared printer.
/savepw:no	Specifies that the password you type should not be saved in your password-list file. You must retype the password the next time you connect to this resource.
/yes	Carries out the *net use* command without first prompting you to provide information or confirm actions.

Notes

Be sure to use quotation marks for any computer name or share name that contains spaces.

See Also

Explorer → Tools → Map Network Drive

Examples

Connect the shared printer named *hp* on machine *troy* to port LPT2:

```
net use lpt2: \\troy\hp
```

Connect the shared folder *budgets* on machine *sandy* as drive *F:* with password *secret*:

```
net use F: \\sandy\budgets secret
```

---

net ver   Internal to: *Windows**net.exe*

Display the type and version number of the workgroup redirector.

To Launch

net ver

There are no options for this command.

Examples

```
C:\>net ver
Microsoft Client - Full Redirector. Version 4.00
Copyright (c) Microsoft Corp. 1993-1995. All rights reserved.
```

---

net view   Internal to: *Windows**net.exe*

Display a list of computers in a specified workgroup.

To Launch

net view [\\computer] [/yes]
net view [/workgroup:wgname] [/yes]
net view [/workgroup:wgname] [\\computer]

Description

net view displays the shared resources available on a specified computer (see Figure 5-42). This is often easier than clicking your way through the Network Neighborhood.

To display a list of computers in your workgroup that share resources, type *net view* without options.

The *net view* options are:

computer   Specifies the name of the computer whose shared resources you want to see listed

---

wgname	Specifies the name of the workgroup whose computer names you want to view
/workgroup	Specifies that you want to view the names of the computers in another workgroup that share resources
/yes	Carries out the *net view* command without first prompting you to provide information or confirm actions

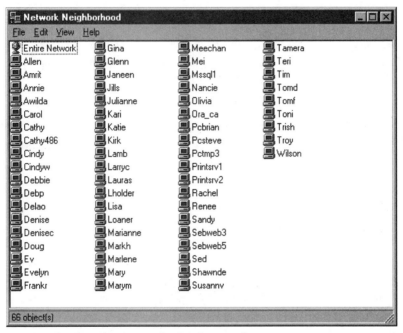

Figure 5-42: Shared resources display (net view)

Examples

net view \\troy, for example, produces the following output:

```
Shared resources at \\TROY

Sharename    Type         Comment
---------------------------------------
D            Disk
WIN95NUT     Disk
WINERROR     Disk
The command was completed successfully.
```

---

netdde   \Windows\netdde.exe

Network Dynamic Data Exchange program.

To Launch

Start → Run → netdde

Under Windows 95, *netdde* is not automatically started. If you use programs that depend on it, you can create a *netdde.exe* shortcut and place it in the *StartUp* directory (\ *Windows\Start Menu\Programs\Startup*) to make Windows 95 start *netdde* every time the system boots.

Description

The Network Dynamic Data Exchange program enables Windows 95 applications that support it (*clipbook, mshearts,* and *winchat*) to share data in memory over a network.

There is no user-accessible GUI for *netdde,* so it's hard to know whether it's running. It is possible, however, to run *wintop* (see *powertoy*) to see whether *netdde* is running. (See HKEY_LOCAL_MACHINE\SOFTWARE\Microsoft\NetDDE \DDE Share in the Registry for a list of the applications dependent on *netdde* that are installed on your machine.)

Notes

- There isn't an error displayed in Clipbook if *netdde* isn't running, but if you click on the File menu and see only Open, Save As, and Exit available to you, then you know that *netdde* isn't running. Exit Clipbook and launch *netdde.* Reopen Clipbook, and now when you select the File menu, you should be able to see Share, Stop Sharing, Connect, and Disconnect options. Now you can share Clipbook information with a separate machine that is also running Clipbook with a running *netdde* file.

- The Microsoft Hearts game and WinChat also use *netdde.* If *netdde* isn't running, an error message should inform you that this is the case. As with Clipbook, you need to exit the program, launch *netdde,* and then reopen the program. If you put the *netdde.exe* shortcut in your startup directory, you shouldn't have this problem.

---

netstat

\ *Windows\netstat.exe*

Display protocol statistics and current TCP/IP network connections to and from the local computer.

To Launch

netstat [-a] [-e] [-n] [-s] [-p proto] [-r] [interval]

Description

netstat can be used to verify which TCP (Transmission Control Protocol) and UDP (User Datagram Protocol) services are being offered to other computers and who is currently using them.

Typing *netstat* without options will show all active TCP connections and their connection status.

The *netstat* options are:

-a   Displays all connections and listening ports. (Server-side connections are normally not shown.)

-e   Displays Ethernet statistics. This may be combined with the -s option.

interval   Redisplays selected statistics, pausing *interval* seconds between each display. Press Ctrl-C to stop redisplaying statistics.

-n   Displays addresses and port numbers in numerical form (useful when DNS is not working or configured).

-p *proto*   Shows connections for the protocol specified by *proto*; *proto* may be tcp or udp. If used with the -s option to display per-protocol statistics, *proto* may be tcp, udp, or ip.

-r   Displays the contents of the routing table. This is the same as *route* print.

-s   Displays per-protocol statistics. By default, statistics are shown for TCP, UDP, and IP; the -p option may be used to specify a subset of the default.

Examples

Show active TCP connections and available UDP ports:

```
C:\>netstat -a

Active Connections
Proto Local Address Foreign Address State
TCP ray:1390 maple.work.net:80 CLOSE_WAIT
TCP ray:1391 maple.work.net:80 CLOSE_WAIT
TCP ray:1392 maple.work.net:80 CLOSE_WAIT
UDP ray:nbname *:*
UDP ray:nbdatagram *:*
UDP ray:nbname *:*
UDP ray:nbdatagram *:*
```

Display the addresses and port numbers in numerical form:

```
C:\>netstat -n

Active Connections
Proto Local Address Foreign Address State
TCP 10.0.0.1:1390 10.0.0.1:80 CLOSE_WAIT
TCP 10.0.0.1:1391 10.0.0.1:80 CLOSE_WAIT
TCP 10.0.0.1:1392 10.0.0.1:80 CLOSE_WAIT
```

Notes

- Table 5-11 lists the possible states that *netstat* can return and their explanations.

- TCP sockets in the listening state aren't shown. This is a limitation of *netstat* in Microsoft's implementation.

- Before data transfer takes place in TCP, a connection must be established. TCP employs a three-way handshake. The *netstat* command can tell you what TCP connections are present between your computer and other computers.

Only the TCP ports that are being used will be shown, but *netstat* does display the UDP ports your computer is listening on.

- It is normal to have a socket in the TIME_WAIT state for a long period of time.

Table 5-11: Possible States Returned by netstat

State	Explanation
SYN_SEND	Indicates active open.
SYN_RECEIVED	Server just received SYN from the client.
ESTABLISHED	Client received server's SYN and session is established.
LISTEN	Server is ready to accept connection.
FIN_WAIT_1	Indicates active close.
TIMED_WAIT	Client enters this state after active close.
CLOSE_WAIT	Indicates passive close. Server just received first FIN from a client.
FIN_WAIT_2	Client just received acknowledgment of its first FIN from the server.
LAST_ACK	Server is in this state when it sends its own FIN.
CLOSED	Server received ACK from client and connection is closed.
Ack flag	If on, indicates that the acknowledgment field is significant.
Syn flag	If on, indicates that the sequence numbers are to be synchronized. This flag is used when a connection is being established.
Fin flag	If on, indicates that the sender has no more data to send. This is the equivalent of an end-of-transmission marker.

netwatch

\ Windows\ netwatch.exe

View users connected to your shared directories.

To Launch

Start → Run → netwatch

Description

netwatch is a very useful tool if you have shared directories that are being accessed. By running Net Watcher, you won't have to guess about who is connected to your shared drives. You will be given this information automatically, along with lots of other details (see Figure 5-43).

There are three different view options in *netwatch*:

1. *By connections*

   Displays the username, computer name, number of shared directories, open files, connected time, and idle time. You can disconnect a user when in this view.

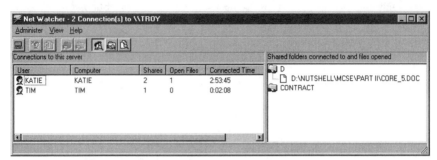

Figure 5-43: Net Watcher list of connected users (netwatch.exe)

2. *By shared folders*

   Displays the folder name, "shared as" name, access type (full, depends on password, etc.), and comment. You can add a shared folder when in this view.

3. *By open files*

   Displays the open filename, the name of the directory being shared, the username that is accessing the file, and the open mode (e.g., Read/Write). You can close a selected file when in this view.

Note

If there is a server to which you have access that you'd like to administer with Net Watcher, select Administer → Select Server, and provide the information.

---

notepad

\ *Windows*\ *notepad.exe*

Edit ASCII text files.

To Launch

    Start → Run → notepad
    Start → Program → Accessories → Notepad
    notepad [/p] [filename]

Description

By default, Win95 is set up so that double-clicking on a *.txt* file runs Notepad (see Figure 5-44). Notepad is also launched by default with other files such as *.bat* and *.inf.*

Notepad handles files only up to 32K. If you try to use it to open a larger file, the following message will appear: "This file is too large for Notepad to open. Would you like to use WordPad to read this file?" Press the Yes button to launch w*ordpad.*

notepad accepts the following option:

/p   Prints the file without opening an editing window. This option is used to create the print action on the context menu for many file types, such as *.txt, .bat*, and *.inf.*

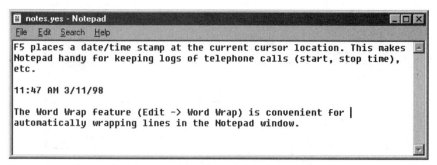

Figure 5-44: Notepad ASCII text editor (notepad.exe)

Notes

- Notepad is a very small program, so it loads faster than WordPad or Word.

- F5 places a date/time stamp at the current cursor location. This makes Notepad handy for keeping logs of telephone calls (start, stop time).

- The Word Wrap feature (Edit → Word Wrap) will reformat long lines so that they are visible in the Notepad window without horizontal scrolling. Unfortunately, this option must be reset each time you use Notepad.

- If you type *.log* as the first line in a text file, Notepad will put the time and date at the bottom of the file (with the cursor right below it) every time you open that file.

See Also

edit, wordpad

For a good third-party editor, try UltraEdit-32:

http://www.ultraedit.com

---

packager

\ *Windows\packager.exe*

Create "packages" for insertion into documents via object linking or embedding (OLE).

To Launch

Start → Run → packager

Description

A package displays as an icon that represents a file, part of a file, or an executable command. This makes it possible to create "executable menu" documents containing icons that, when clicked, run various commands. Most of the functionality provided by Object Packager is available without explicitly running the program. For example, in WordPad, you can insert various types of objects into a document by dragging and dropping or with Insert → Object (see Figure 5-45).

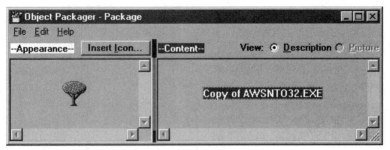

Figure 5-45: OLE package creation (packager.exe)

In particular, you can insert links to executable files into documents, so that when the reader double-clicks on an icon representing the link, Windows 95 runs the executable file. Such executable menu documents can be created from within any OLE-enabled program, including WordPad.

However, some programs allow you to insert a file, but don't provide any place for you to specify a command line to that file. You could insert an object representing *command.com*, for example, but not *command.com* /c dir, or *control.exe* but not *control.exe* timedate.cpl ,1.

This is one area in which *packager* is essential. If you right-click on a newly inserted object and select Package Object → Edit Package from the context menu, Windows 95 will run *packager*. You can then select Object Packager's Edit → Command Line menu item, and give the object a full command line, including options such as /c dir.

Notes

- If you run *packager* explicitly after assembling a package, you can then select Edit → Copy Package to copy the package to the Windows 95 clipboard. You can then switch to another application and insert the package via Paste (Ctrl-V). The Object Packager window is split into two panes: the Appearance window displays the icon that will represent the package you insert, and the Content window displays the name of the document that contains the information you want to insert.

- To create a package, copy the contents of the Appearance and Content windows and paste the information into a document. The package appears in the document as an icon.

- If the package contains a sound or animation file, the sound or animation will play. If the package contains a picture, text, or spreadsheet, the program associated with that file type will open, displaying the information. For example, if the package contains a bitmap, *mspaint* opens, displaying the picture.

See Also

mspaint, wordpad

paint

See *mspaint*.

path   Internal to: \ *Windows\command.com*

Set or display the command search path

To Launch

path = [drive:][directory]; ... [drive:][directory]

Description

By default, DOS searches for executable files in the current directory only. The *path* statement is used to define additional directories to be included while searching for files. It is intended to be used in the *autoexec.bat* file, but can be used anywhere.

The path consists of a series of absolute directory pathnames, separated by semicolons. No spaces should follow each semicolon. If no drive letter is specified, all pathnames are assumed to be on the boot drive. There should be no semicolon at the end of the statement.

When you type the name of a command, DOS looks first in the current directory, then in each successive directory specified in the path. Within each directory, it will look for executable files by their extension, in the following order: *.com*, *.exe*, *.bat*.

The order of directories in the search path is thus quite important. For example, you might run MKS Toolkit, a set of third-party tools that brings Unix functionality to Windows systems. MKS normally stores its files in \ *MKSNT*.

If you have the path set as follows:

```
path=C:\;C:\MKSNT;C:\Windows;C:\Windows\Command
```

you won't be able to run a DOS command like *find* without typing its full pathname, because the MKS *find* command will be found and executed first.

Run *path* without options to display the current path.

Examples

Specify the directories *C:*, *C:\DOS*, *C:\Windows*, and *C:\Programs* in the path:

C:\>**path=c:\;c:\dos;c:\windows;c:\programs;**

A typical *path* statement in *config.sys* might be:

path=c:\;c:\windows

or in *autoexec.bat*:

set path=c:\;c:\windows;c:\windows\command

A useful batch file to add a directory to the front of the existing path is the one-line *addpath.bat*:

set path=%1;%path%

Or you can type something similar at the command line, putting the new directory at either the begining or end of the existing path:

C:\>**set path =%path%; c:\newdir**

Notes

- Type `path ;` to clear all search path settings and direct Windows to search only in the current directory.

- The *path=* statement is limited to 250 characters or less when set in *config.sys*. The *path=* statement is limited to 127 characters if set from a batch file (e.g., *autoexec.bat*) or from the command line.

- Use short names only (e.g., *C:\PROGRA~1* for *C:\Program Files*).

- When DOS or Windows 95 searches for a file, it first looks in the current directory, and then in the directories listed in the *path* statement in the order in which they are listed.

- To fit more directories in the search path, you can either shorten your directory names or use the *subst* command to assign directories to logical drives (which shortens the entries on the *path* command line).

- You might think that you could simplify your search path by putting a shortcut file to a program in a directory that is already in your search path, but DOS isn't smart enough to follow shortcuts. You could, however, create a batch file containing only the complete pathname of the program, and place that in one of the directories in your path.

pbrush

In Windows 3.x, *pbrush* was the Microsoft Paint Brush application. In Windows 95, it's just a stub loader for Microsoft Paint (*mspaint.exe*).

See *mspaint.*

phone dialer

See *dialer.*

pinball   *\Windows\Program Files\pinball.exe*

3D Space Cadet Pinball game.

To Install

pinball is installed by default with Microsoft Plus!

To Launch

Start → Run → `pinball`
Start → Programs → Accessories → Games → Space Cadet Table

Description

Space Cadet Pinball (see Figure 5-46) is a very popular 3D pinball game with a lot of great sounds.

Figure 5-46: 3D Space Cadet Pinball Game (pinball.exe)

See Also

For a reviewed list of other Win95 pinball games:

http://www.avault.com/pcrl/pinball.asp

ping

Verify connection to a remote TCP/IP host.

To Launch

ping [-t] [-a] [-n count] [-l size] [-f] [-i TTL] [-v TOS] [-r count] [-s count] [[-j host-list] | [-k host-list]] [-w timeout] destination-list

Description

This diagnostic command verifies connections to one or more remote hosts. If you can *ping* another host, it proves that you can communicate with it, that TCP/IP is configured correctly, and that the remote host is operating.

For example, if you've just tried to connect to a web site with Internet Explorer and were unable to connect, you might want to *ping* the site to find out if it is really not responding, or if the problem is on your end of the connection.

Like *tracert, ping* is also useful for taking a look "under the hood" of an Internet connection.

ping accepts the following parameters and options:

-a	Specifies not to resolve addresses to hostnames.

destination-list

Specifies the remote hosts to ping.

-f	Sends a Do Not Fragment flag in the packet. The packet will not be fragmented by gateways on the route.
-i *ttl*	Sets the Time To Live field to the value specified by *ttl*.
-j *host-list*	Routes packets by means of the list of hosts specified by *host-list*. Consecutive hosts may be separated by intermediate gateways (loose source routed). The maximum number allowed by IP is 9.
-k *host-list*	Routes packets by means of the list of hosts specified by *host-list*. Consecutive hosts may not be separated by intermediate gateways (strict source routed). The maximum number allowed by IP is 9.
-l *length*	Sends echo packets containing the amount of data specified by length. The default is 64 bytes; the maximum is 8192.
-n *count*	Sends the number of echo packets specified by count. The default is 4.
-r *count*	Records the route of the outgoing packet and the returning packet in the Record Route field. A minimum of 1 to a maximum of 9 hosts must be specified by *count*.
-s *count*	Specifies the time stamp for the number of hops specified by *count*.
-t	Pings the specified host until interrupted.
-v *tos*	Sets the Type Of Service field to the value specified by *tos*.
-w *timeout*	Specifies a time-out interval in milliseconds.

Examples

See why it's taking Yahoo! so long to respond:

```
C:\>ping yahoo.com

Pinging yahoo.com [204.71.177.35] with 32 bytes of data:

Reply from 204.71.177.35: bytes=32 time=144ms TTL=245
Reply from 204.71.177.35: bytes=32 time=138ms TTL=245
Reply from 204.71.177.35: bytes=32 time=136ms TTL=245
Reply from 204.71.177.35: bytes=32 time=139ms TTL=245
```

Notes

- The *ping* command verifies connections to a remote host or hosts by sending Internet Control Message Protocol (ICMP) echo packets to the host and listening for echo reply packets. By default, four echo packets containing 64 bytes of data (a periodic uppercase sequence of alphabetic characters) are transmitted.

- You can use the *ping* command to test both the hostname and IP address of the host. If the IP address is verified but the hostname is not, you may have a name resolution problem. In this case, be sure that the host name you are querying is in either the local *HOSTS* file or in the DNS database.

See Also

tracert

To use *ping* on the Web:

http://consumer.net/tracert.asp

---

poledit

\ *Windows\poledit.exe*

Standardize Windows 95 for a group of users.

To Install

Control Panel → Add/Remove Programs → Windows Setup → Have Disk →
\ *Admin\AppTools\Poledit* on the CD-ROM → OK → OK

To Launch

Start → Run → `poledit`
Start → Programs → Accessories → System Tools → System Policy Editor

Description

The System Policy Editor (Figure 5-47) allows you to create or edit system policies to standardize the appearance and capabilities of Windows 95 for a single user, a group of users, or the entire network.

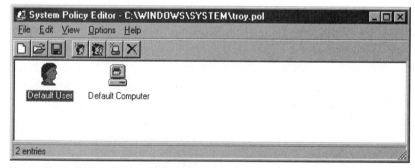

Figure 5-47: System Policy Editor (poledit.exe)

Once you've launched *poledit*, select File → Open Registry to customize settings on your computer. Two icons should be displayed: Local User (for user settings such as Control Panel and Desktop) and Local Computer (for system settings such as networking and sharing). Double-click each icon to view the profile listing of resources.

Each resource listed in the profiles has one of three possible settings:

Off (white)

When the button is white, the resource in question is available and/or ignored (whichever makes sense).

On (white with a checkmark)

When a resource is checked, that resource is restricted from the user or computer in question.

Use Registry Setting (grey)

When a resource box is grey, Windows 95 will use the default value for that resource as found in the Registry.

Examples

To disable the entire Display control panel, check off "Disable Display Control Panel." If you wish to disable individual pages found in Display properties, check off the appropriate page(s) listed under the "Disable Display Control Panel" option:

1. Local User → Control Panel → Display

2. Check the "Restrict Display Control Panel" box

3. Select any of the settings you wish to restrict

In a similar fashion, you can restrict the wallpaper used on the Desktop:

1. Local User → Desktop

2. Check the Wallpaper option and select the wallpaper from the drop-down list.

3. If you've created wallpaper in the form of a *.bmp* file, type the location in the "Wallpaper Name:" box. If you plan to implement a custom wallpaper company-wide, be sure to copy the custom bitmap file into the Windows directory of each computer.

Notes

* Changes made in *poledit* alter the Registry, so be sure to back up the Registry on your machine before using the program.

* When configured correctly, *poledit* allows you to use the Connect option to access the Registries of other computers on the network.

See Also

To download the System Policy Editor:

> *http://www.microsoft.com/windows95/info/admintools.htm*

---

powertoy *\Program Files\PowerToy\powertoy.exe*

A collection of PowerToys for Windows 95.

To Install

Download *powertoy.exe* from *http://www.microsoft.com/windows95/info/power-toys.htm* into a new directory (e.g., *\Program Files\PowerToy*). Run *powertoy.exe* to unzip all of the PowerToy tools, then install them individually by right-clicking

---

on each *.inf* file (when applicable) and selecting Install. Any of the tools that require a *.inf* installation can be uninstalled through Control Panel → Add/Remove Programs.

Description

powertoy.exe is a collection of utilities for Windows 95. These utilities were developed by Microsoft, but are unsupported. They let you change various Win95 settings, display a round clock, control CD-ROM drives from the Taskbar, exit to DOS from any folder, change screen resolution without rebooting, and perform other useful tasks.

Each utility in the PowerToy collection is listed here with a brief description about its use and installation instructions.

Desktop Menu   *deskmenu.exe*

deskmenu.exe puts in your System Tray an icon that provides quick access to all your Desktop items in a menu (see Figure 5-48). It also lets you minimize and maximize all of your windows.

Figure 5-48: A sample DeskMenu (deskmenu.exe)

To install, right-click *deskmenu.inf.* Select Install. Click OK, and when it tells you that you need the disk, browse to the directory where you downloaded the PowerToys. Once installed, double-click *deskmenu.exe*; a shortcut is put in the startup (*\Windows\Start Menu\Programs\StartUp*) directory so that *deskmenu* will be loaded every time you start Windows 95.

CabView
cabview.dll

CabView lets you browse any *.cab* file to see its contents and perform operations on the files inside (see Figure 5-49).

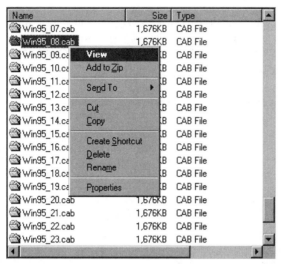

Figure 5-49: CabView modifies the .cab file context menu (cabview.dll)

To install, right-click *cabview.inf.* Select Install. Click OK, and when it tells you that you need the disk, browse to the directory where you downloaded the PowerToys. *cabview.dll* will always be running once installed, and is activated by right-clicking a *.cab* file.

QuickRes
quickres.exe

With QuickRes, you can click an icon in the System Tray and quickly change screen resolution and color bit depth without rebooting (see Figure 5-50).

Figure 5-50: QuickRes choices (quickres.exe)

To install, right-click *quickres.inf.* Select Install. Click OK, and when it tells you that you need the disk, browse to the directory where you downloaded the PowerToys. Double-click *quickres.exe*; a shortcut is placed in your startup directory.

CD AutoPlay Extender   *aplayext.dll*

This tool enables autoplay on non-audio CDs (see Figure 5-51).

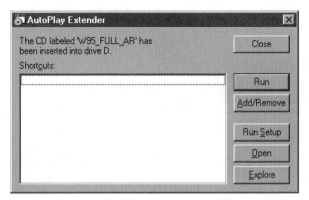

Figure 5-51: AutoPlay Extender for non-audio CDs (aplaytext.txt)

To install, right-click *aplayext.inf.* Select Install. Click OK, and when it tells you that you need the disk, browse to the directory where you downloaded the PowerToys. *aplayext.dll* will place a shortcut in your startup directory.

Round Clock   *clock.exe*

No installation is required on this tool, which provides you with a round analog clock. Double-click *clock.exe* to launch. See Figure 5-52.

Figure 5-52: Round clock display (clock.exe)

Contents Menu   *content.dll*

With Contents Menu installed, when you right-click on a folder or shortcut, you'll get a cascading menu that shows you the contents of the folder or shortcut one level deep. This tool is activated by right-clicking Contents in the context menu (see Figure 5-53).

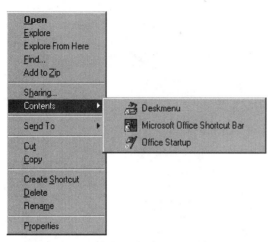

Figure 5-53: Contents menu (content.dll)

To install, right-click *content.inf.* Select Install. Click OK, and when it tells you that you need the disk, browse to the directory where you downloaded the PowerToys.

Explore From Here   *explore.exe*

This tool allows you to right-click on a folder and choose "Explore from Here" (see Figure 5-54). This option will create an Explorer window that has the target folder as its root.

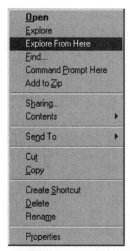

Figure 5-54: Explore From Here menu addition (explore.exe)

To install, right-click *explore.inf.* Select Install. Click OK, and when it tells you that you need the disk, browse to the directory where you downloaded the PowerToys.

FlexiCD   *flexicd.exe*

FlexiCD provides an icon in the System Tray that gives you audio CD control, play/pause control, a ToolTip showing the track and time of the song being played, and a right-click menu for starting, stopping, ejecting, and moving around tracks on the CD (see Figure 5-55). This will be used as the default CD audio control, rather than *cdplayer*. If you want *cdplayer* restored as the default player, select Explorer View → Options → Filetypes → Audio CD → Edit → Edit and type in the path to *cdplayer.exe*.

Figure 5-55: FlexiCD utility (flexicd.exe)

To install, right-click *flexicd.inf*. Select Install. Click OK, and when it tells you that you need the disk, browse to the directory where you downloaded the PowerToys.

Find X   *findx.dll*

This tool lets you customize your Find menu with drag-and-drop. It places all the shortcuts in your \ *Windows* \ *Start Menu* \ *Find* directory (see Figure 5-56).

Figure 5-56: Customize your Find menu with Find X (findx.dll)

To install, right-click *findx.inf*. Select Install. Click OK, and when it tells you that you need the disk, browse to the directory where you downloaded the PowerToys.

Send To X

sendtox.exe

Allows you to send items to any folder (see Figure 5-57).

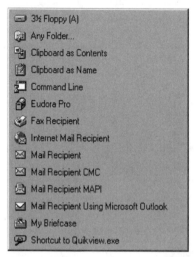

Figure 5-57: Customize your Send To menu with Send To X (sendtox.exe)

To install, right-click *sendtox.inf.* Select Install. Click OK, and when it tells you that you need the disk, browse to the directory where you downloaded the PowerToys.

Shortcut Target Menu

target.exe

This tool gives you the properties for a shortcut's target by right-clicking on the shortcut itself (see Figure 5-58).

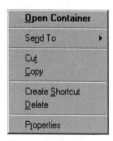

Figure 5-58: Shortcut target menu (target.exe)

To install, right-click *target.inf.* Select Install. Click OK, and when it tells you that you need the disk, browse to the directory where you downloaded the PowerToys.

Tweak UI   *tweakui.exe*

With Tweak UI, you can adjust your Windows interface, menu speed, window animation, and Internet Explorer. Once installed, click Control Panel → TweakUI to get to the TweakUI controls (see Figure 5-59).

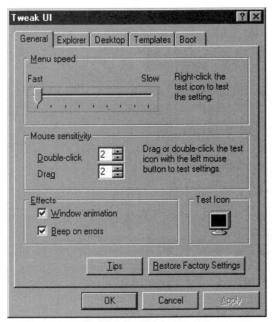

Figure 5-59: The General tab of TweakUI (tweakui.exe)

To install, right-click *tweakui.inf*. Select Install. Click OK, and when it tells you that you need the disk, browse to the directory where you downloaded the PowerToys.

XMouse   *xmouse.exe*

This tool causes the focus follow your mouse without clicking as in the Unix X Windows System. No installation is required. Just double-click *xmouse.exe* to activate this utility.

Command Prompt Here   *doshere.exe*

This tool lets you start a command prompt in the folder of your choice with the click of a button. Adds "Command Prompt Here" to the context menu (see Figure 5-60).

To install, right-click *doshere.inf*. Select Install. Click OK, and when it tells you that you need the disk, browse to the directory where you downloaded the PowerToys.

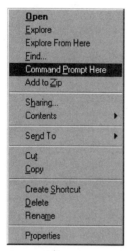

Figure 5-60: Command Prompt Here addition to the context menu (doshere.exe)

Telephony Location Selector *tapitna.exe*

This tool places an icon in the System Tray that allows you to quickly change dialing location for a mobile computer (see Figure 5-61). No installation is required; just double-click *tapitna.exe* and a shortcut is put in the startup directory.

Figure 5-61: Telephony Location Selector menu (tapitna.exe)

Notes

- Open the *readme.txt* file that is unzipped with each of the tools for more details about PowerToys and the use of the individual tools.

- These tools are not a part of Windows and are not supported by Microsoft. For this reason, Microsoft Technical Support is unable to answer questions about PowerToys.

---

progman

\Windows\progman.exe

The Windows 3.1 Program Manager, replaced by the Explorer in Win95.

To Launch

Start → Run → `progman`

Description

The Program Manager (*progman.exe*) was the Windows 3.1 shell, or interface between Windows and the user. In Windows 95, this role is played by the

---

Explorer (*explorer.exe*). Features of Windows 95 such as long filenames and short-cuts cannot be used within Program Manager.

If you run *progman* from the Explorer or DOS command line, you'll open up a Program Manager window, containing subwindows for each of the folders on the Start menu. (These correspond to Windows 3.1 program groups.)

If you actually prefer the Windows 3.1 interface, you can make it your default environment by modifying the shell= line in *system.ini*. Open *system.ini* with Notepad and change the line "shell=Explorer.exe" to "shell=Progman.exe". Once you reboot, the old Win3.1 Desktop will appear (see Figure 5-62).

Note, however, that if you do this, you will lose access to such Windows 95 features as the Taskbar, the Start menu, and the Recycle Bin, since these features are actually implemented as part of *explorer.exe*.

Figure 5-62: The Program Manager (progman.exe)

Notes

- *progman*'s behavior can be changed by modifying *progman.ini* (located in the \ *Windows* directory). Typically, this file contains two sections that define settings and groups found in the Program Manager.

- Under the [Settings] section you'll find the Order variable, which controls the order of groups in the Window menu, and the order of focus of switching between groups using `Ctrl-TAB`.

- Under the [Groups] section, you'll find a listing of pointers to the *.grp* files used by the Program Manager to display groups. You can hide any groups by removing them from the list. If you do so, remember to remove each unused group from the Order variable, found at the end of the [Settings] section.

- You can append a [Restrictions] section, where you can define the following variables:

  - *NoClose*, if set to 1, will disable the Exit Windows option from the File menu (Alt-F4 is deactivated, too).

  - *NoSaveSettings*, if set to 1, will disable the SaveSettings option from the Options menu.

  - *NoRun*, if set to 1, will disable the Run option from the File menu; this prevents users from running any programs other than those that are on your Desktop.

  - *NoFileMenu*, if set to 1, will disable the File menu altogether.

  - *EditLevel*, which can be set to a number between 1 (low security) and 4 (highest security).

Associated Files

progman.ini

See Also

command, explorer
Chapter 9

---

prompt

Internal to: \ *Windows\command.com*

Change the Windows command prompt.

To Launch

prompt [text]

Description

Run *prompt* without parameters to reset the prompt to the default setting: NG, current drive and the greater-than sign (>). A more useful setting is: PG, current drive and path, and >.

The $E code is typically used with *ansi.sys* escape sequences. See *prompt* /? for all $ codes.

The *prompt* options are:

text	Specifies a new command prompt. The prompt can contain normal characters and the following special codes:

$_	Carriage return and linefeed
$$	$ (dollar sign)
$b	| (pipe)
$d	Current date
$e	Escape code (ASCII code 27)
$g	> (greater-than sign)
$h	Backspace (erases previous character)

$l	< (less-than sign)
$n	Current drive
$p	Current drive and path
$q	= (equal sign)
$t	Current time
$v	Windows version number

Examples

Specify the current drive and directory followed by the greater-than sign (>):

```
C:\>prompt $p$g
```

Specify the drive and directory on one line, and the date followed by the greater-than sign (>) on another:

```
C:\>prompt $p$_$d$g
```

Notes

By adding the line "set winpmt=*text*" to your *autoexec.bat* file immediately after the *prompt* line, you can display a message on the DOS prompt in Windows, which won't appear in real mode.

---

pwledit
\Windows\pwledit.exe

Delete passwords from a stored password list.

To Install

Control Panel → Add/Remove Programs → Windows Setup → Have Disk → CD-ROM → *\admin\apptools\pwledit*

To Launch

Start → Run → **pwledit**
Start → Programs → Accessories → System Tools → Password List Editor

Description

The Password List Editor allows you to view the resources listed in your password files (*\Windows*.pwl*). It doesn't let you view the actual passwords, but you can remove specific password entries. (If you forget a password, deleting it and starting over with a new one is normally the way to go.) You can remove passwords for remote sharing if you're logged on to the computer on which the password was defined. The easiest way to clear a password is just to delete the *.pwl* file.

See Also

pwledit can also be downloaded from:

> *http://www.microsoft.com/windows95/info/admintools.htm*

qbasic

\Qbasic\qbasic.exe

Microsoft Quick Basic programming environment.

To Install

From the Windows 95 CD-ROM (in this example, drive *D*):

```
C:\>md \qbasic
C:\>cd \qbasic
C:\>copy d:\other\oldmsdos\qbasic.*
```

To Launch

qbasic [/b] [/editor] [/g] [/h] [/mbf] [/nohi] [[/run] [filename]

Description

The *qbasic* programming environment can be useful with batch files in Windows 95. See Figure 5-63. The /run option is especially interesting, because it allows *qbasic* to be used as a fully customizable calculator, or as a sort of batch language, if you end your program with the SYSTEM statement, and if you can tolerate a momentary screen flash. A QBasic program can't access command-line arguments, but it can access environment variables. See the following example.

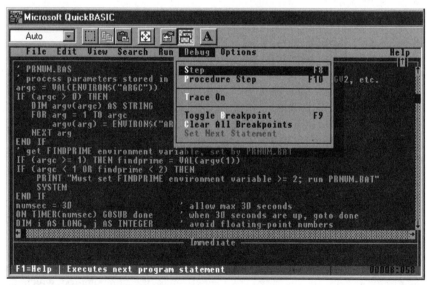

Figure 5-63: Quick Basic (qbasic.exe)

The *qbasic* options are:

/b	Allows use of a monochrome monitor with a color graphics card
filename	Specifies the program file to load or run
/editor	Starts the MS-DOS Editor (*edit.com*)
/g	Provides the fastest update of a CGA screen

/h	Displays the maximum number of lines possible for your hardware
/mbf	Converts the built-in functions MKS$, MKD$, CVS, and CVD to MKSMBF$, MKDMBF$, CVSMBF, and CVDMBF, respectively
/nohi	Allows the use of a monitor without high-intensity support
/run	Runs the specified Basic program before displaying it

Notes

- *qbasic* comes with a very large help file documenting the entire QBasic programming language. This help file is viewed within QBASIC itself; it does not work with WinHelp.

- *qbasic* comes with a decent editor and debugger.

Examples

Here's a small QBasic program that finds a prime number specified in an environment variable:

```
' PRNUM.BAS
' process parameters stored in environ vars ARGC, ARG1, ARGV2, etc.
argc = VAL(ENVIRON$("ARGC"))
IF (argc > 0) THEN
   DIM argv(argc) AS STRING
   FOR arg = 1 TO argc
       argv(arg) = ENVIRON$("ARG" + LTRIM$(STR$(arg)))
   NEXT arg
END IF

' get FINDPRIME environment variable, set by PRNUM.BAT
IF (argc >= 1) THEN findprime = VAL(argv(1))
IF (argc < 1 OR findprime < 2) THEN
    PRINT "Must set FINDPRIME environment variable >= 2; run PRNUM.BAT"
    SYSTEM
END IF

numsec = 30                       ' allow max 30 seconds
ON TIMER(numsec) GOSUB done       ' when 30 seconds are up, goto done
DIM i AS LONG, j AS INTEGER       ' avoid floating-point numbers
numpr = 1                         ' already have one prime: 2 (only even prime)
i = 3                             ' i holds odd numbers to test for prime
TIMER ON
WHILE (1)                         ' timer will break out of forever loop
    FOR j = 3 TO SQR(i) STEP 2    ' for each odd number up to square root
        IF ((i MOD j) = 0) THEN GOTO nexti    ' if evenly divisible, not prime
    NEXT j
    numpr = numpr + 1                         ' if get here, it's prime
    IF (numpr = findprime) THEN               ' is it the one they asked for?
        PRINT "Prime #"; findprime; "is"; i   ' if so, print it
        SYSTEM ' exit back to command prompt
    END IF
nexti:
    i = i + 2                     ' next odd number to test
WEND

done:
PRINT "Found"; numpr; "primes in"; numsec; "seconds"
PRINT "But didn't find prime #"; findprime
SYSTEM
```

A small batch file can then set the environment variable and call QBASIC:

```
C:\qbasic>type prnum.bat
@echo off
set findprime=%1
qbasic /run prnum.bas
set findprime=
echo.
```

```
C:\qbasic>prnum 100
Prime # 100 is 547
```

```
C:\qbasic>prnum 1000
Prime # 1000 is 7927
```

See also:

calc, jview

*http://www.yahoo.com/Computers_and_Internet/Programming_Languages/
BASIC/QBasic_QuickBasic/*

---

qfecheck   \ *Windows\qfecheck.exe*

Check versions of system files.

To Launch

Start → Run → qfecheck

Description

The Win95 Update Information Tool (*qfecheck*) allows you to find out which versions of updated system files are installed on your computer. You can also check to see whether the versions installed match the versions listed in your Registry.

There are two tabs in the *qfecheck* program: Registered Updates and Updated Files Found (see Figure 5-64):

Registered Updates

Displays the system file updates that are found in your Registry. If a file or component is designated as Invalid, the version of the file on your drive doesn't match the version in the Registry. If a file or component is designated as Not Found, either the file is not installed on your drive or *qfecheck* can't find the file on your computer.

Updated Files Found

To search for all system update files, whether or not they're in the Registry, click the Search Files button and specify the path you want to search. If a file appears on this list that does not appear on the Registered Updates list, it's probably because you installed an update without using the installation program or installed one of the early update releases.

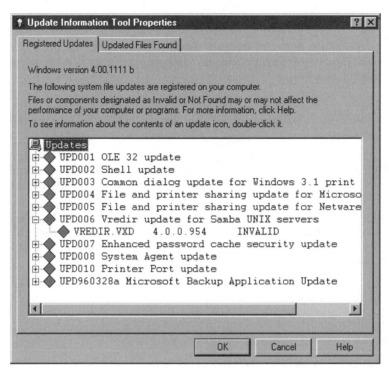

Figure 5-64: Win95 Update Information Tool: Registered Updates tab (qfecheck.exe)

Notes

- Once you've used the Search Files option in the Updated Files Found tab, you can right-click on any of the returned files and choose the Explore option. This opens the Explorer to the directory where the file is stored and highlights the actual file.

- You can find out the version for almost any *.dll* or *.exe* file by using the Version tab in the file's property sheet.

---

quickres   *\Program Files\PowerToy\quickres.exe*

Change monitor resolution and color depth without restarting Windows.

To Install

Install the Resource Kit tools, or, for the latest version, download the PowerToys (*quickres* is one component of the PowerToys—see *powertoy* earlier in this chapter), or download *quickres* separately from Microsoft's web site.

To Launch

    Start → Run → `quickres`

    Start → Programs → Resource Kit → Quick Resolution Changer

Description

The *quickres* application (Quick Resolution Changer) quickly changes the visible screen area (resolution and color depth) without restarting Windows. This tool is all but obsolete in OSR2, because you can configure the Display properties to change the resolution without rebooting.

Notes

- Put a shortcut to *quickres.exe* in the Start Up folder (\ *Windows\Start Menu\Programs\StartUp*) if you want *quickres* to start automatically.

- Once installed, the *quickres* icon can be found in the System Tray. By right-clicking the icon, you'll get a popup window with resolution and color depth options to toggle between (e.g., 640×480 pixels/256 color, or 800×600/256 color). Which options appear depends on your display adapter.

- To navigate to the Settings tab in Control Panel → Display, *quickres* has a "Properties for Display" option that automatically opens that tab for you. There you can alter any of the resolution or color options that aren't readily available with *quickres* since they require rebooting your machine.

- *quickres* is useful if you design web sites and need to check sites with different resolutions and color depths.

See Also

Chapter 4

For the most recent version of *quickres*:

http://www.microsoft.com/windows95/info/powertoys.htm

---

quikview   \ *Windows\System\ VIEWERS\quikview.exe*

View the contents of a file without launching the application.

To Launch

file → context menu → Quick View
```
C:\>\Windows\System\Viewers\quikview filename
```

Figure 5-65: Quick View addition to the context menu (qfecheck.exe)

Description

quikview (Quick View) lets you view the contents of a file without launching the associated application, if the file has a Quick View registered extension—see Figure 5-65.

Notes

There are several ways of registering Quick View with most of your applications, as listed here:

- Alter the Registry (see Chapter 10 for details about the Registry) to enable Quick View with most files:

    1. Start → Run → `regedit`

    2. Expand the branches to `HKEY_CLASSES_ROOT`

    3. Look for a key that reads *

    4. Under this key, add a new key, and call it QuickView

    5. Set the value of the (default) value to * and close *regedit*

    You should now be able to use Quick View for all types of files, except those that Quick View doesn't understand, such as *.pcx* files. If you use the Office Shortcut Bar, you will have a problem with registering Quick View in this fashion. When clicking on an Office Shortcut button, Quick View will attempt to read the *.lnk* file, which you clearly don't want it to do.

- Use the Send To menu with Quick View:

    1. Create a shortcut to *quickview.exe* (in \ *Windows*\ *System*\ *Viewers*) in your \ *Windows*\ *SendTo* directory.

    2. Now when you right-click on a file, you can "Send To" Quick View.

- Use the Desktop:

    1. Create a shortcut to *quickview.exe* on your Desktop.

    2. You can now drag any files you want to be viewed onto the shortcut.

See Also

Try Quick View Plus, which gives you the power to view, copy, and print almost any file or attachment:

http://www.inso.com

---

raplayer \ *Windows*\ *System*\ *raplayer.exe*

Real-time audio delivery system for the Web (RealAudio Player).

To Install

RealAudio Player can be downloaded for free:

http://www.realaudio.com

Run *raplayer_50.exe* to install it.

To Launch

raplayer.exe will launch automatically when you click on a RealAudio link on the Web. To launch it yourself:

> Start → Run → `raplayer`

Description

With *raplayer*, you can listen to live and pre-recorded audio clips on the Web.

Notes

- Using the RealAudio Player is straightforward. It should be quite obvious how to use the stop, pause, play, and volume controls, if you've ever played a tape or CD (see Figure 5-66).

Figure 5-66: RealAudio Player (raplayer.exe)

- You can adjust Audio Quality versus CPU Usage with a sliding bar in View → Preferences → General. If you notice a decrease in performance while playing a RealAudio file, just slide the bar. Experiment to discover the best setting for your machine and Internet connection.

- Make sure the Loss Correction box is clicked in View → Preferences → Network. When Loss Correction is unchecked, the lost packets are dropped, causing a skip in the audio stream.

- In View → Preferences → Network, you'll find the "Receive audio via UDP or TCP option." By default, *raplayer* receives data packets using UDP (User Datagram Protocol). If you are behind a packet-filtering firewall, you probably won't be able to receive UDP packets, so you should select the TCP (Transmission Control Protocol) instead. Keep in mind that if you use TCP with a modem, you may experience gaps in the audio stream.

- *raplayer* automatically comes with Internet Explorer 3.x, so there's no need to download *raplayer* unless you are looking for the most recent version.

- If you're on a local area network LAN, and your firewall is preventing the RealAudio stream from reaching you, it is possible to receive the audio stream without exposing your company's network to security risks. For more information, see:

  http://www.real.com/firewall

rd or rmdir
Internal to: \ *Windows\command.com*

Remove (delete) a directory.

To Launch
    rd [drive:]path
    rmdir [drive:]path

Description

The *rd* and *rmdir* commands are functionally identical. *rd* and *rmdir* will delete a directory containing no files or subdirectories only.

rmdir accepts the following options:

[drive:]path   Specifies the directory to delete.

Examples

Delete the empty subdirectory *test* within the current directory called *Temp* (\ *Windows\Temp*):

    C:\Windows\Temp>**rd test**

Delete the empty subdirectory called *newdir* located in the *C:\olddir* directory from any place other than *newdir*.

    C:\>**rd c:\olddir\newdir**

Notes

*   Attempting to delete a directory that is not empty will display the message:

        Invalid path, not directory
        or directory not empty

    If the directory appears empty, but still causes an error message, it may contain hidden files. Use the *dir* /ah command to view hidden files. To delete a directory or subdirectory containing files, either delete the files first with *del*, or use the *deltree* command (the files and the directory will be deleted). You can change the hidden attribute with the *attrib* command.

*   In Windows 95, *rd* can remove the current directory.

See Also
    attrib, deltree, dir

---

regclean
\ *Program Files\RegClean\regclean.exe*

Clean up the Registry.

To Install

Download RegClean 4.1 from:

   http://support.microsoft.com/support/kb/articles/Q147/7/69.asp

This downloads the file *regcln41.exe*. Launch this file; by default, RegClean will be installed in the directory \ *Program Files\RegClean*.

To Launch

Add *C:\PROGRA~1\RegClean* to the path= line in your *autoexec.bat* file to launch *regclean* from the command line or the Run prompt.

Start → Run → `regclean`
regclean [/a] [/s] [/d] [/l [file]]

Description

The *regclean* utility loads and scans your Win95 Registry for errors and other superfluous items. RegClean is designed to clean your Registry of all those unnecessary entries and orphaned files, saving them to an undo *.reg* file (see Figure 5-67). Unfortunately, if you find something you want returned to the Registry, you must return all of the entries in the *.reg* file.

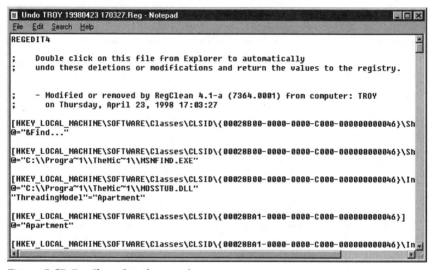

Figure 5-67: RegClean (regclean.exe)

It's not uncommon for *regclean* to remove Registry data that is used by programs, for example, license keys, causing the program to revert to a "demo" version or stop working. Therefore, it's important to save the undo *.reg* files until you're sure that the system is still working properly.

To run *regclean* in standard mode, type **regclean** without options.

The *regclean* options are:

/a	Automatic (standard mode only, no prompting).
/d	Detail mode (full UI).
/l *[file]*	Log all activity to file (the default file is *regclean.log*, stored in the same directory that *regclean.exe* resides in). A word of warning: if you choose this option, RegClean won't create the undo *.reg* file.
/s	Silent mode (no UI).

Notes

- Once you've run RegClean, you can view the entries that the program removed from the Registry by right-clicking on the undo *.reg* file in the Explorer and choosing Edit from the popup menu. If you see anything you don't want removed from the Registry, just double-click the *.reg* file and the entries will be placed back into the Registry.

- RegClean keeps your Registry uncluttered and allows your system to run smoothly and efficiently.

regedit
\ *Windows\regedit.exe*

View and modify the contents of the Registry.

To Launch

regedit [/c] [/e] [filename] [regpath] [/s]

Additional syntax (in MS-DOS 7 only, before the Windows GUI starts):

regedit [/?] [/l:system] [/r:user]

Description

regedit allows you to view and modify the contents of the Registry, the master file that stores configuration settings for Windows 95 and many of the applications on your computer (see Figure 5-68).

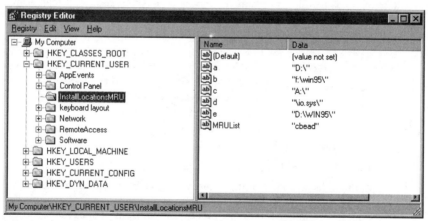

Figure 5-68: Registry Editor (regedit.exe)

regedit gives a two-pane view of the Registry, somewhat similar to the one in the Explorer, except that in this case, you're looking at the Registry database.

regedit takes the following options:

/c `filename`   Replace the entire Registry with the contents of `filename`

/e `filename [regpath]`
            Export a *.reg* file; if `regpath` omitted, exports entire Registry

---

filename	Import or merge a *.reg* file
/s	Run *regedit* silently, suppressing dialog boxes and messages (useful in batch files)

Additional options (only in MS-DOS 7, before GUI starts):

/?	Display RegEdit command-line syntax
/l:system	Path and filename of *system.dat*
/r:user	Path and filename of *user.dat*

Examples

Export Registry settings into a *.reg* file, modify the *.reg* file, and merge the new settings back into the Registry:

```
C:\>regedit /e run.reg
HKEY_LOCAL MACHINE\SOFTWARE\Microsoft\Windows\CurrentVersion\Run
echo "Fooble"="c:\\testing\\fooble.exe" >> run.reg
regedit /s run.reg
```

Notes

- *.reg* files are straight ASCII text (with the signature "REGEDIT4" as their first line). They can be viewed and modified with any text editor or word processor that can read and save plain text files. If modifying a *.reg* file with Word-Pad or Word, remember to save it as plain text.

- Rather than use *regedit*'s Edit → Find to search the Registry, export the entire Registry to a *.reg* file (for example, `regedit /e \reg.reg`), and then search the *.reg* file in a text editor: it's often faster.

- By default, Windows 95 associates *.reg* files with *regedit*: double-clicking on a *.reg* file's icon in the Explorer automatically imports the *.reg* file's contents into the Registry. This means that *.reg* files can be used as a sort of Windows 95 configuration-setting "batch language." But given Windows 95's reliance on the Registry, it also means that the mere act of double-clicking on a *.reg* file's icon can cause unwanted modifications to your system.

- *regedit* can be used to view and modify the Registry on other machines. See Registry → Connect Network Registry.

- Use of *regedit* can be disabled with *poledit*.

- If exporting a large chunk of the Registry, `regedit /e` will return before the file export actually completes; file writing takes place in the background. This can be important in batch files that process output from `regedit /e`. You can get around this by using *start* `/w` to wait for *regedit* to complete; for example:

```
start /w regedit /e \reg.reg
echo The \reg.reg file is now ready
```

See Also

poledit
Inside the Windows 95 Registry, by Ron Petrusha (O'Reilly & Associates), especially Chapter 2

---

ren or rename

Rename a file or directory.

To Launch

```
rename [filename1] [filename2]
ren [filename1] [filename2]
```

Description

The *ren* and *rename* commands are functionally identical. You can't specify a new drive or path for your destination when using *ren* or *rename*, and the renamed file remains in the same drive and path as the file or directory you are changing.

The *ren* options are:

[filename1]   The name of the current directory or file. '

[filename2]   The new name of the file. You can't move files to another directory with *ren*. You can rename a directory or files, but can't **ren** x*.* to y*.*. Use *move* instead.

Examples

Rename *myfile.txt* to *file.txt*:

```
C:\>rename myfile.txt file.txt
```

Rename *chap 5.doc* to *sect 5.doc*:

```
C:\>ren chap?5.doc sect?5.doc
```

Both *chap 5.doc* and *sect 5.doc* have spaces in the fifth character position, which are represented with the ? wildcard.

Change all filenames with *.txt* extensions in the current directory to *.rtf*:

```
C:\>ren *.txt *.rtf
```

Rename the files *chap1.doc*, *chap2.doc*, etc. to *revchap1.doc*, *revchap2.doc*, etc.:

```
C:\>ren chap*.doc revchap*.doc
```

Notes

- The file's creation date is not changed when using *ren*.
- Quotation marks are needed if the name of a directory or file contains a space. Or use ? as shown in the second example.
- Use wildcards (* and ?) to alter only part of a name in a series of files.

See Also

move

resource meter

See *rsrcmtr*.

route   *\Windows\route.exe*

Manipulate the TCP/IP routing table for the local computer.

To Launch

> route [-f] [command [destination] [mask netmask] [gateway]

Description

The route print command is useful if you are having a problem (e.g., "Host Unreachable" or "Request timed out") with the routes on your computer, since it will display all the different fields in the active route (see the following example).

command   Specifies one of four commands:

      print Prints a route

      add   Adds a route

      delete Deletes a route

      change Modifies an existing route

destination The host or network that is reachable via *gateway*.

-f   Clears the routing tables of all gateway entries. If this is used in conjunction with one of the commands, the tables are cleared prior to running the command.

gateway   The gateway to be used for traffic going to *destination*.

mask netmask Specifies the subnet mask for a *destination*. If not specified, a mask of 255.255.255.255 is used (i.e., a "host route" to a single host, not a network).

Examples

`C:\>route print`

```
Active Routes:
  Network Address          Netmask  Gateway Address       Interface Metric
         0.0.0.0          0.0.0.0      172.16.80.5    172.16.80.150      1
       127.0.0.0        255.0.0.0        127.0.0.1        127.0.0.1      1
    172.16.80.10    255.255.255.0    172.16.80.150    172.16.80.150      1
   172.16.80.150  255.255.255.255        127.0.0.1        127.0.0.1      1
   172.16.80.200  255.255.255.255    172.16.80.150    172.16.80.150      1
         224.0.0.0        224.0.0.0    172.16.80.150    172.16.80.150      1
 255.255.255.255  255.255.255.255    172.16.80.150          0.0.0.0      1
```

Add a default gateway:

> `C:\>route add 0.0.0.0 10.0.0.200`

Notes

- The fields in the previous example are as follows:

  Gateway Address
  > The IP address of the gateway for the route. The gateway will know what to do with traffic for the specified network address.

Interface

The IP address of the network interface that the route is going to use when leaving the local computer.

Metric

The hop count or number of gateways between the local computer and the gateway.

Netmask

The mask to be applied to the network address. If all ones (255. 255. 255. 255), the route is a host route and refers to a single machine, not a network.

Network Address

Any network matched by this address should use this route. The default route is all zeros and is used if no other route is found.

- All symbolic names used for destination or gateway are looked up in the network and hostname database files *networks* and *hosts*, respectively.

- If the command is print or delete, wildcards may be used for the destination and gateway, or the gateway argument may be omitted.

---

rsrcmtr   *Windows**rsrcmtr.exe*

Monitor the system resources programs are using.

To Install

Control Panel → Add/Remove Programs → Windows Setup → Accessories →
Details → System Resource Meter in the Components list → OK → OK

Windows 95 will prompt for the CD-ROM to complete the installation, unless the .*cab* files are stored on your hard disk (*Windows**Options**Cabs*).

To Launch

Start → Run → rsrcmtr
Start → Programs → Accessories → System Tools → Resource Meter

Description

When running, the Resource Meter places a small icon in the System Tray next to the clock. The Resource Meter monitors the resources for the following three areas of your running computer: *system resources, user resources,* and *GDI* (Graphics Device Interface) resources.

The percentage of each of these resources that is free is represented by the green lines on the icon in the System Tray. If resources drop dangerously low, the line turns yellow. If you see red lines, then your situation is near-critical.

For exact free resource amounts, hold your cursor over the icon for a moment, and a small ToolTip will appear with exact percentage free figures for System, GDI, and User resources.

You can obtain an even clearer display by double-clicking the icon (or right-clicking, and selecting Details). When you do this, a window will appear (see

*Commands &
Applications*

Figure 5-69). When any of the three graphs drops below 50 percent, you should close some programs to free resources.

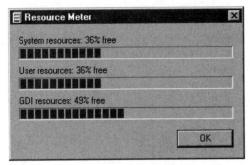

Figure 5-69: Resource Meter (rsrcmtr.exe)

Notes

To load the Resource Meter automatically when you run Win95, place a shortcut to *rsrcmtr* in the startup folder (*Windows\Start Menu\Programs\StartUp*).

---

rundll   *Windows\rundll.exe*

See *rundll32*.

---

rundll32   *Windows\rundll32.exe*

Provides "string invocation," command-line–based run-time dynamic linking.

To Launch

    rundll[32] dll_name,function_name [function arguments . . .]

Description

rundll32 provides dynamic linking to functions exported from Dynamic Link Libraries (DLLs). *rundll* is for 16-bit (Win16) *dlls*, and *rundll32* is for 32-bit (Win32) *dlls*.

rundll32 is used throughout Windows 95. For example, almost all of the Control Panel involves *rundll32*. Many GUI elements that appear to have no command-line equivalents actually employ *rundll32* behind the scenes. This means that these GUI elements can be semi-automated in a batch file.

The *rundll32* options are:

`dll_name`   The filename of a Dynamic Link Library (DLL)

`function arguments`
                Case-sensitive string parameters to the function being called

`function_name`   The case-sensitive name of a function exported from the DLL

Examples

Launch Dial-Up Networking from the command line or a batch file (the *type* command is used to show the contents of the batch file):

```
C:\>type dialup.bat
rundll32 \windows\system\rnaui.dll,RnaDial %1
C:\>dialup OReilly
```

Start the "Add New Hardware Wizard":

```
C:\>rundll32 shell32.dll,Control_RunDLL sysdm.cpl,Add New Hardware
```

Start the "OpenAs" dialog box for unknown file type *.xyz* without actually having a file of type *.xyz* handy:

```
C:\>type openas.bat
echo blah blah blah > foobar.%1
rundll32 shell32.dll,OpenAs_RunDLL foobar.%1
C:\>openas xyz
```

Notes

To locate many *rundll* and *rundll32* command lines, see the Registry:

```
C:\>regedit /e \reg.reg
```

(Wait while *regedit* command completes: it may take a few minutes!)

```
C:\>find /i "rundll" \reg.reg > rundll.log
```

See Also

While written primarily for Visual Basic programmers, this site provides an excellent listing of *rundll32* command-line examples:

http://home.sprynet.com/sprynet/rasanen/vbnet/code/systems/controlpnl.htm

Also see Microsoft's documentation ("The Windows 95 *rundll* and *rundll32* Interface"):

http://premium.microsoft.com/support/kb/articles/q164/7/87.asp

And "Starting a Control Panel Applet in Windows 95 or WinNT":

http://premium.microsoft.com/support/kb/articles/q135/0/68.asp

---

sage

See *sysagent*.

---

scandisk   \Windows\Command\scandisk.exe

Check the disk surface for errors.

To Launch

Start → Run → scandisk
Start → Programs → Accessories → System Tools → ScanDisk
scandskw [drive:] [/a] [/n] [/p] [dblspace.*nnn*] [drvspace.*nnn*]

Description

scandisk checks the disk surface, files, and folders of your computer for lost clusters, correcting them if they exist, thus freeing disk space by getting rid of unusable information. Checking for these errors ahead of time can prevent data loss problems. There are two separate versions of *scandisk*; one version is run in Windows, and the other from the real-mode command line (before Windows is launched, during startup). If you run *scandisk* from within Windows, you'll see a DOS box appear, then ScanDisk for Windows will be loaded and the DOS box will disappear.

Don't confuse running *scandskw* from the command line with running *scandisk* from the MS-DOS real-mode command line. There is a different set of options available for *scandisk* when running it from the command line in real-mode, which is described next.

When run from Windows, *scandisk* provides two processes to choose from:

Standard
> Checks your file allocation table, folders, and files for errors such as cross-linked files, lost file fragments, invalid file dates, and invalid file names. You also have the option to have *scandisk* automatically fix any problems. It's a good idea to run the Normal scan once a day. This can be accomplished by putting *scandskw* in the *StartUp* directory, or by configuring this in the System Agent if you have Plus!.

Thorough
> Checks the integrity of the hard drive surface. The Surface Scan finds potential bad sectors on your hard drive. The process then marks bad areas to prevent those sectors from being used. If data is saved to a bad area, you run the risk of losing that information.
>
> The surface scan can also give you the warning signs of hard drive failure by marking bad sectors on the drive. You might consider running the Thorough Scan about once a month.

Windows ScanDisk (*scandskw.exe*) can be run from a batch file or as a shortcut from the Target box of ScanDisk, if it's placed in the startup directory, and can also be run from the MS-DOS command line.

The following steps illustrate how to run *scandskw* in the *Windows* startup directory:

1. Copy a shortcut to *scandskw* from the *Windows* directory to your startup directory (*Windows**Start Menu**Programs**StartUp*) and right-click the icon.
2. Click Properties → Shortcut (see the dialog box in Figure 5-70).
3. After the text in the Target box (*C:**Windows**scandskw.exe*), specify one or more of the command-line options described later in this section.
4. Click OK, and the next time you start Windows, *scandisk* will automatically run in whatever fashion you've specified.

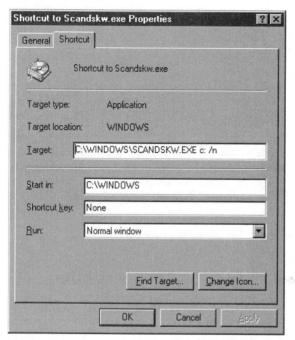

Figure 5-70: Windows ScanDisk properties (scandskw.exe)

scandskw options are:

/a   Checks all your local, nonremovable hard disks

dblspace.*nnn* *or* drvspace.*nnn*

Checks the specified unmounted DoubleSpace or DriveSpace compressed volume file, where *nnn* is the filename extension for the hidden host file

drive: Specifies one or more drives to be checked

/n *(or* /noninteractive*)*

Starts and closes ScanDisk automatically

/p *(or* /preview*)* Runs ScanDisk in Preview mode. ScanDisk reports errors but does not write changes to the disk

Examples

Check all nonremovable hard disks, but prevent ScanDisk from correcting any errors it finds, with text in the Target box similar to the following:

```
C:\windows\scandskw.exe /a /p
```

Force a batch file to wait for *scandskw* to run *scandisk* on the *C:* drive, starting and closing *scandisk* automatically:

```
start /w scandskw c: /n
```

Run *scandisk* in the Preview mode from the command line, forcing *scandisk* to start and close automatically:

```
C:\>scandskw /n /p
```

Notes

When running ScanDisk in Preview mode (scandskw /p), it appears as though the program is fixing errors, but it isn't. To determine whether *scandisk* is running in Preview mode, look for the Preview tag in the caption of the main ScanDisk window.

The following syntax applies only to running ScanDisk in real-mode MS-DOS. You won't be able to use this syntax from MS-DOS once Windows is running. (To execute real-mode MS-DOS, press F8 on startup when the "Starting Windows 95" bitmap is showing, then choose "Command Prompt Only.") To launch the DOS version of ScanDisk:

scandisk [drive: | /all] [/checkonly | /autofix [/nosave]] [/surface]
scandisk drive:\drvspace.nnn [/checkonly | /autofix[/nosave]]
scandisk /fragment [drive:][path]filename
scandisk /undo [drive:] (specify the drive containing your undo disk)

The options for the DOS version of ScanDisk are:

/all	Checks and repairs all local drives
/autofix	Fixes damage without prompting
/checkonly	Checks a drive, but does not repair any damage
/custom	Configures and runs ScanDisk according to *scandisk.ini* settings
/mono	Configures ScanDisk for use with a monochrome display
/nosave	With /autofix, deletes lost clusters rather than saving as files
/nosummary	With /checkonly or /autofix, prevents ScanDisk from stopping at summary screens
/surface	Performs a surface scan after other checks

Examples

(These apply only to *scandisk* in real-mode MS-DOS.)

Run *scandisk* on drive *C*:

```
C:\>scandisk c:
```

Run *scandisk* on all non-removable drives (e.g., hard disk drives):

```
C:\>scandisk /all
```

Run *scandisk* according the settings in *scandisk.ini* (\ *Windows*\ *COMMAND*):

```
C:\>scandisk /custom
```

Notes

- The DOS version of ScanDisk can also check unmounted drives compressed with DoubleSpace or DriveSpace, but it can't check for long filename integrity. As a rule, you should use the Windows version of ScanDisk first and then the MS-DOS version if you still need to correct other problems.

- You have the option to replace, append, or disable a log file that's created once ScanDisk has run. The name of the file is *scandisk.log*, stored in the root drive. *scandisk.log* will report all of the *scandisk* results.

---

scanpst

The Inbox Repair Tool.

To Launch

Start → Programs → Accessories → System Tools → Inbox Repair Tool

Description

If you use the Inbox, you might want to run *scanpst* periodically to prevent lockups and problems in the future. *scanpst* looks for errors in the *.pst* or *.ost* file, which stores all of your email messages. If you have a large number of messages stored in Windows Messaging/Exchange (or Internet Mail & News, Outloook, etc.), it will take *scanpst* longer to scan and repair them.

When the *scanpst* dialog box appears (see Figure 5-71), you must type the path of the personal folder file (*.pst*) or offline folder file (*.ost*) that you want to scan. Alternatively, you can use the Browse button to open the "Select File To Scan" dialog box, where you can locate the file you want to scan.

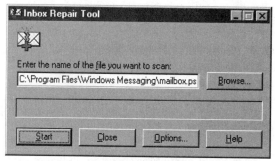

Figure 5-71: Inbox Repair Tool (scanpst.exe)

Before starting the scan, you can select the Options button and choose one of three options for handling the log file that records errors in case they are found: Replace Log, Append to Log, or No Log.

If, after the scan is complete, no errors are found, just click the OK button (you're finished). If, however, errors are found, you have the option of checking the "Make Backup Of Scanned File Before Repairing" box. If you check this box, then you must select the Browse button to specify the location where you'd like the backup file (e.g., *mailbox.pst*) to be placed.

Notes

- If you are using the original version of Windows 95, you will find *scanpst* at the following location: *\Program Files\Exchange\scanpst.exe*. The location listed above (*\Program Files\Windows Messaging*) is for OSR2, since the name changed from Exchange to Windows Messaging at that time.

- *scanpst* will perform eight different types of scans on the selected file. If errors are found during the scan and you decide to back up the file before having it repaired, you will need up to twice the available disk space of the *.pst* or *.ost* file size.

- If you are using OSR1, you will find the name of the postoffice (*mailbox.pst*) file in *Exchange*; if you have OSR2, you'll find it in *Program Files**Windows Messaging*. If you're having problems finding your postoffice file, simply use Find and search for **.pst*.

---

set   Internal to: *Windows**command.com*

Display, set, or remove MS-DOS environment variables.

To Launch
    set [variable=[string]]

Description

The *set* command is primarily intended for use in the *autoexec.bat* file or other batch files, but it can be used at the command prompt.

Environment variables are a simple means of interapplication communication, as well as a mechanism for storing data used repeatedly in a batch file.

Run *set* without options to display the current environment variables.

The *set* options are:

`string`   Specifies a series of characters to assign to the variable

`variable`   Specifies the variable name

Standard *set* environment variables include:

COMSPEC
    The location of the DOS command interpreter, if not in *C:*.

COPYCMD
    Whether *copy, move,* and *xcopy* should prompt for confirmation before overwriting a file. The default value is `/-y`. To stop the warning message, type `set copycmd=/y`.

DIRCMD
    Standard options for the *dir* command. For example, `set dircmd=/p` will cause *dir* to always pause after displaying a screenful of output.

PATH
    The sequence of directories in which the command interpreter will look for commands to be interpreted. Each additional directory in the path is separated by a semicolon. The path can also be set with the path command. See *path* for additional details.

PROMPT
    The format of the command-line prompt. This value can also be set with the prompt command. See *prompt* for details.

TMP, TEMP

The location where many programs will store temporary files. *TMPDIR* is also sometimes used.

WINDIR

The directory where Windows system files are found. Normally *C:\Windows*.

You can also display the value of any individual variable using the *echo* command, surrounding the variable name with percent signs. For example, echo %temp% will display the value of the temp variable. You can use the *%variable%* syntax to use environment variables in other ways as well:

```
C:\>set workdir="C:\Windows\Desktop\win95\tim's draft"
C:\>cd %workdir%
```

Here, the environment variable is used to store a long pathname, including spaces (which must be quoted), for quick navigation to a frequently used directory.

To clear the value of an environment variable, type set variable=, supplying no value.

Examples

Set the temporary files directory to *C:\temp*:

```
C:\>set temp=c:\temp
```

Set the *dir* command to display files in directories and subdirectories and sort by size with the largest first:

```
C:\>set dircmd= /s /o-s
```

A batch file to add directories to the front of the path:

```
C:\>set path=%1; %path%
```

Set the default DOS prompt to show the current time, followed by a right angle bracket:

```
C:\>set prompt=$t>
```

Notes

- The *set* command affects only the MS-DOS environment. To set master or global environment variables that will affect Windows, use *winset*.

- The total amount of memory allocated for environment variables is set with the /E switch to *command.com*. The default value is only 256 characters. If you use many environment variables, you may want to change this value. The maximum value is 32,768 bytes. You can set the environment in MS-DOS Prompt → Properties → Memory → Initial Environment, as shown in Figure 5-72. You can also set it in the shell= statement in *config.sys* (not to be confused with shell= in *system.ini*). For example:

```
shell=command.com /p /e:2048
```

See Also

echo, prompt, path, winset

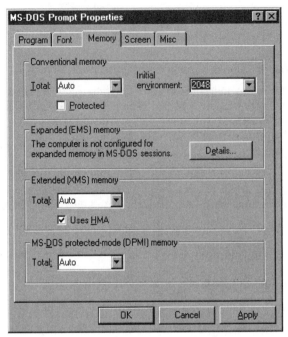

Figure 5-72: Setting MS-DOS prompt properties (scanpst.exe)

---

setup

Set options to customize and control a Win95 installation.

To Launch

setup [/c] [/d] [/id] [/it] [/ih] [/iq] [/is] [/l]

Description

You can use *setup* to customize your Windows 95 installation from the command line, from MS-DOS mode, or in a script from a network computer.

The *setup* options are:

/c	Prevents *setup* from running SmartDrive
/d	Prevents *setup* from using existing configuration files, such as *win.ini* and *system.ini*
/id	Prevents *setup* from checking for the minimum disk space required to install Win95
/ih	Runs *scandisk* in the foreground.
/iq	Prevents *setup* from checking for cross-linked files (if you use the /is option)
/is	Prevents *setup* from running ScanDisk

/it   Prevents *setup* from checking for TSRs

/l   Enables a Logitech mouse during *setup*

You must run *setup* from your previous version of MS-DOS or start Win95 in MS-DOS mode to enable the options in the following section.

To Launch

    setup [/n] [/p <string>] [-s] [/t:<dir>]

setup's options are:

/n   Allows *setup* to run without a mouse.

/p   Pass string(s) directly to the Detection Manager (*sysdetmg.dll*) during *setup*. The /p option isn't used by itself; it must be followed by a detection option or string. The string can contain one or more detection options separated by a semicolon (e.g., setup /p f;i). Some options are on/off switches; the absence implies off (a minus sign after an option also turns it off) and the presence turns the switch on:

    a   Enables safe detection (enabled by default).

    b   Enables the Prompt Before mode, allowing you to step through each detection module manually and decide if you want to skip it (disabled by default).

    c   Enables class detection for finding hints for a certain class of devices (enabled by default).

    d=*name*
       Detects the listed detection modules only, where *name* is a detection module name or a device class name.

    e   Enables *setup* mode detection (enabled by default).

    f   Enables Clean Registry mode, which cleans the root branch of the Registry before starting (disabled by default).

    g=*n*
       Specifies the verbose level, where *n* is 0 to 3, which can help identify which detection module causes a certain problem (disabled [0] by default).

    i   Tells *setup* not to report the existence of a Plug and Play BIOS. It is useful on systems that have a Plug and Play BIOS not reported in *machine.inf.*

    j   Tells *setup* to undo the results of *setup* /p i. This option should be used only after a machine that required *setup* /p i has the updated Plug and Play BIOS.

    l=*n*   Specifies the logging level for *detlog.txt*, where *n* is 0 to 3. (The default is maximum [3] logging).

m Enables Mini-Windows mode. This is enabled only when *setup* is run under MS-DOS.

n Enables No Recovery mode, which turns off the Windows 95 setup recovery mechanism (disabled by default).

o=*traceoutput*

Specifies the trace output, writing the information to the file *tracelog.txt* in the current directory. This option is available only in the Debug version of *sysdetmg.dll*.

p Enables performance logging, writing the performance timing information to the *detlog.txt* file (disabled by default).

r Enables Recovery mode, causing Detection to use the *detcrash.log* file, if found, for recovery. If this option is not enabled, Detection ignores and deletes *detcrash.log* even if it is found (used only if Safe Recovery is selected during setup).

s=*name*

Skips the listed detection modules or classes of detection modules, where *name* is a detection module name or a device class name.

t=*n* Specifies the trace level, where *n* is 0 to 9: disabled (0) by default. This option is available only in the Debug version of *sysdetmg.dll*.

v Enables Verify Only mode. Detection has two stages: verify existing devices in the Registry and detect new devices. This option tells Detection to perform only the first stage. This option is used by the PCMCIA Wizard to verify legacy devices in the Registry (disabled by default).

x=*res list*

Excludes the listed resources from detection, where *res list* is one of four possibilities:

io(*xxx-yyy*, *xxx-yyy*, . . .)

mem(*xxxxx-yyyyy*, *xxxxx-yyyyy*, . . .)

irq(*x,y,z*, . . .)

dma(*x,y,z*, . . .)

This option protects resources so that no detection modules can access them.

-s Specifies an alternative *setup.inf* file.

/t:*dir* Lets you specify where *setup* will copy its temporary files. Any existing files in this directory will be deleted.

Examples

Start Windows 95 *setup* from MS-DOS:

1. If you're installing from the CD-ROM, put the CD in the drive and make that the active drive.

2. If you're installing from source files on a network server, connect to that server and switch to the shared network directory that contains the Win95 source files.

3. At the command prompt, run *setup* and any options that you want configured, and then press Enter.

Start Windows 95 Setup from a network computer using a setup script:

1. Log on to the network, running the existing network client.

2. Connect to the server that contains the Win95 distribution files.

3. At the command prompt, type:

```
C:\>setup msbatch.inf
```

For example, type setup \\ntserver\win95\mybatch.inf to run *setup* using a setup script named *mybatch.inf* that is stored in the *win95* directory on a server named *ntserver.*

Notes

- If Win95 is installed from a server, the location of that network directory is stored in the Registry. When you add a device or require additional support files to run Win95, *setup* automatically attempts to retrieve the files from that same location on the server. This eliminates the need to maintain a permanent network connection on the computer and makes it easier to modify the configuration of a computer in a networked environment.

- You can use *batch* to create a setup script, or you can edit *msbatch.inf* with a text editor such as Notepad.

See Also

batch, notepad, scandisk

---

shortcut

Command-line tool for creating and maintaining Windows 95 shortcuts.

To Install

Copy *shortcut.exe* from the Win95 CD-ROM (\ *Admin\AppTools\EnvVars*) to your \ *Windows* directory.

To Launch

```
shortcut: [-h -f -c -r -s] [[-t] target [[-n] name]] [-d working directory]
       [-a arguments] [-i iconfile] [-x icon index] [-u {all | [natdix]}]
```

**Commands &
Applications**

Description

You can use *shortcut* to create a shortcut (*.lnk*) in DOS. For example, to create a shortcut named "email" to *exchg32.exe* on the Desktop:

C:\Windows\Desktop>**shortcut -t C:progra~1\window~1\exchng32.exe -n email**

(Note the use of 8.3 filenaming for DOS recognition.)

When you create a shortcut to a resource on a mapped network drive, and then remap the same drive to a different network resource, Windows attempts to connect to the original network resource when you access the shortcut. Also, when you re-establish the original connection, a different drive letter may be mapped to the original resource. This may then cause some programs to fail because the expected drive mappings are not present. This behavior is the result of Windows attempting to resolve and automatically maintain shortcuts to network resources.

Running *shortcut* with the −s option on a target shortcut file prevents the shortcut from finding the original server associated with the drive letter, since *shortcut* removes UNC (Universal or Uniform Naming Convention—*server-name\shared-resource-pathname*) path information from the shortcut.

The options for *shortcut* are as follows:

−a *arguments*	Specifies the arguments.
−c	Changes existing shortcut.
−d *directory*	Specifies the working directory.
−f	Forces overwrite.
−h	Displays short help.
−i *iconfile*	Specifies the icon file.
−n *name*	Specifies the shortcut.
−r	Resolves broken shortcut.
−s	Makes shortcut nontracking.
−t *target*	Specifies the target of the shortcut.
−u *[spec]*	Dumps the contents of a shortcut. *spec* can be any one of the option letters n (name), a (arguments), t (target), d (directory), i (icon file), or x (icon index). "all" is the same as "natdix", but the individual letters of "natdix" can be specified in any order to display specific fields in the shortcut (repeats allowed, and order followed).
−x *index*	Specifies the icon index.

Examples

Disable the link-tracking feature of the shortcut file *mylink.lnk*:

    C:\>**shortcut -c -s -n mylink.lnk**

Print the information about the shortcut "Pilot Desktop":

```
C:\Windows\Desktop>shortcut -u all "Pilot Desktop"

LinkName: Pilot Desktop.lnk
Arguments: <none>
Target: C:
ilot\PILOT.EXE
Working Directory: C:
ilot
Icon File: <none>
Icon Index: 0
```

Notes

- To run *shortcut* on each shortcut you create that accesses network resources, you must first find the location of each shortcut. One way is to locate them with the Explorer, and move all the shortcuts to an accessible directory, such as *Temp*. You can then use MS-DOS to run *shortcut* on each of the shortcuts and move the shortcuts back to their original location when you've finished.

- Network clients often have shortcuts to programs that reside on network servers. Although shortcut files support the use of variables in the working directory, they do not support variables on the command line. Before *shortcut*, this restriction prevented the use of network shortcuts for balancing server workloads. With *shortcut*, administrators can also use shortcuts to alternate drive mappings to different servers that are mirrors of each other. Because shortcut files track the links to the original network resource, this method was also previously unavailable.

---

sndrec32   *Windows**sndrec32.exe*

Record and play sound files with a *.wav* extension.

To Launch

Start → Run → sndrec32 [play] [/close] [filename.wav]
Start → Programs → Accessories → Multimedia → Sound Recorder

Description

sndrec32 lets you control recording and playback of sound files. It pops up a window with controls that should be familiar to anyone who has ever used a cassette tape recorder. The buttons across the bottom (see Figure 5-73) represent (from left to right) reverse, fast forward, play, stop, and record. The slider lets you postition the "playback head" anywhere within the sound file, with an immediate readout of the total length of the sound file in seconds and your position in the file. A waveform display gives a visual readout of the sound as it plays.

When running *sndrec32* from the command line, you can use the following options:

/play   Play the specified file (*filename.wav*). Without this option the file will be loaded but not played.

/close   Close when playing (the default is to remain open).

Figure 5-73: Record and play .wav files (sndrec32.exe)

The following are some of the tasks and options you can perform with *sndrec32*:

- File → New allows you to create a new, blank sound file (*.wav*). If your computer has a microphone, you can use these blank files to record your own sounds. Or just record a sound and then choose Save As. Note that *sndrec32* is unlike many Windows applications in that Save doesn't automatically call Save As if the filename isn't already known. The Save As dialog includes a Change button that lets you change the format of the saved data. You can get to this same format selection from File → Properties.

- The Effects → Increase Volume and Effects → Decrease Volume options work by increasing or decreasing the height of the recorded sound wave data. When you decrease the volume level of the recorded wave, you risk losing some of the wave, thus giving less audio detail and creating distortion. Increasing the volume of an ordinary speech file shouldn't affect the quality, but music files are less forgiving due to their wider dynamic range.

- The Effects → Increase Speed and Effects → Decrease Speed options are similar to the volume options, except that you are dealing with the speed in which the sound is being played, rather than the volume at which it's being played.

- The Effects → Reverse option reverses the order in which the *.wav* samples contained in the file are played.

- The Effects → Add Echo is fun to use, but the only way to remove the echo is to select Revert before you save the file.

- To mix sound files, move the slider to the place you want to overlay the second sound file, use Edit → Mix With File, and select the *.wav* file you want to mix.

Notes

- Really big *.wav* files take a long time to open in *sndrec32*, since it must read in the whole file before playing it. If this becomes a problem, use View → Options → File Types to change the default Play action for *.wav* files to Media Player (*mplayer.exe*), which "streams" the audio so it can start playing while the file is still loading. Alternatively, there is a Preview tab on the Properties dialog box for *.wav* files that lets you do a "quick listen."

- Note that there are two context menu actions for *.wav* files, Play and Open. Open loads the file but does not play it until you click the Play control. The Play action typically uses the `/play` and `/close` options to play the sound file and then exit. (Be sure to include these options if you change the play program to *mplayer.*)

- When editing a *.wav* file, you can return the file to its original condition (if you haven't saved it) by selecting File → Revert.

- You can mix only an uncompressed sound file. If you don't see a green line in Sound Recorder, the file is compressed and you can't modify it.

- You can open up as many copies of *sndrec32* as you like, up to the limits of your computer's memory. This comes in handy when editing many different *.wav* files.

You can record from your system's CD drive or from any external device you can hook up to "live in" on a multimedia sound card by turning off the system microphone and turning on the other input device using the volume control (*sndvol32* → Options → Properties → Recording). See *sndvol32* for details.

See Also

For details on mixing, inserting audio files and *sndrec32* audio properties and sound formats:

> *http://www.skwc.com/WebClass/Task-Sound1.html*

---

sndvol32   \ *Windows\sndvol32.exe*

Control volume and balance of the system's sound devices.

To Launch

    Start → Run → sndvol32
    Start → Programs → Accessories → Multimedia → Volume Control
    System Tray → Volume Control (if enabled via Control Panel)
    CDplayer → View → Volume Control

Description

sndvol32 pops up the Volume Control applet, which displays a series of sliders for controlling volume and balance of the system's sound devices, including speakers, microphones, the *.wav* file driver, and MIDI devices (see Figure 5-74). Volume Control offers sliders for both balance and volume. For mono devices (such as a simple built-in speaker), the balance control should be left in the middle.

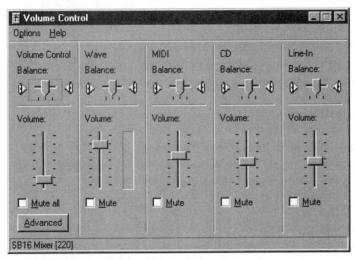

Figure 5-74: Volume Control (sndvol32.exe)

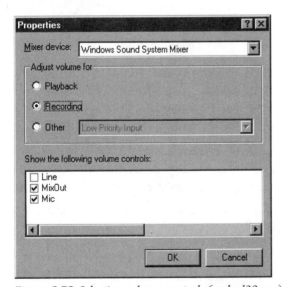

Figure 5-75: Selecting volume controls (sndvol32.exe)

To set which controls are displayed, go to Options → Properties and check off the controls you want (see Figure 5-75). Options include:

Volume control

Control for the system's built-in speaker. This control does not override the hardware volume dial (if present), but interacts with it. For example, if the hardware volume control is turned all the way down, the Volume Control applet won't have any effect. However, if it's turned all the way up, you can turn the volume down using the software control. If the hardware control is in the middle, you can go in either direction.

Line in

Control for recording volume for a direct line in from another device.

Wave

Sound going to or coming from a *.wav* file on disk. This control also displays a visual readout of frequencies much like that on many high-end audio devices. Use *sndrec32* (Sound Recorder) or one of the many commercial multimedia devices to create or play *.wav* files. Note that adjusting the volume for *.wav* file playback here adjusts the overall playback level for all *.wav* files. You can also adjust the volume for a single *.wav* file by opening it with *sndrec32*, adjusting the volume there, and saving the file with its new volume. So you really have three volume levels that are being mixed: the volume of the actual input (in this case, the *.wav* file), the software volume control (*sndvol32*), and the hardware volume control.

Microphone

The system microphone. Note that if both speaker (Volume Control) and Microphone volume are turned up all the way, you will probably get feedback.

CD Audio

Control the volume of CDs played with programs such as *cdplayer.exe*. Note that you can record from a CD into a *.wav* files using *cdplayer* and *sndrec32*, with *sndvol32* controlling the playback and recording levels of both.

Synthesizer

Control the volume of an attached synthesizer or other MIDI device.

You can check off a different set of controls to be displayed for recording, playback, or other purposes (such as voice input). The interface is a bit awkward, but once you've set up the chosen controls for each purpose, you can switch between the various sets of controls by going back to Options → Properties and choosing the radio button for recording, playback, or other. When recording is chosen, the titlebar shows the name Recording Control.

WARNING

A particular volume control can be enabled or disabled by checking or unchecking select at the bottom of each control area. This is effectively a "mute" checkbox during playback, although only the box under the master Volume Control slider is labeled as such. When the Volume Control is configured as a Recording Control, the checkboxes have the opposite function. A checkmark turns that function on rather than off.

Notes

- Check Control Panel → Multimedia → Show volume control on Taskbar for quick access to the volume control. Double-click on the indicator to pop up a full Volume Control application, or single-click to pop up a single slider for controlling only the speaker volume or temporarily muting the sound.

- If you want to be able to control both recording and playback volume at the same time, launch two instances of Volume Control, and choose Options → Properties → Recording for one, and Options → Properties → Playback for the other. You can arrange them one above the other on the screen for a complete audio control console.

- Control Panel → Multimedia → Audio gives access to a subset of the available volume controls. The Playback volume control corresponds to the Wave control here; and the Recording volume control corresponds to the Volume Control → Recording → Recording Volume control.

- The relationship between the various volume controls can seem mysterious if you don't have all the appropriate devices connected, since all of the controls are active, but some of them appear to do nothing. A common problem when trying to record and not getting any sound is that the devices in the "recording" section aren't "selected."

See Also

cdplayer, *sndrec32*, Control Panel → Multimedia

For links to freeware and shareware sound applications:

http://www.aclass.com/SOFT/sound.html

---

sol

\ *Windows\sol.exe*

The popular Microsoft Solitaire game.

To Launch

Start → Run → **sol**
Start → Programs → Accessories → Games → Solitaire

Description

The following are some options available when playing *sol* (see Figure 5-76 for a sample game):

- Draw one card at a time

- Draw three cards at a time

- Enable scoring

- Play Las Vegas–style, in which each card costs $1 ($52 per game); each card scored earns $5 (11 cards scored wins $3)

- Time the game

- Undo the last action only

- Choose a new deck back

Notes

You don't have to be limited by the deck back options available to you in *sol*. You can download many others from the URLs in the "See Also" section.

Figure 5-76: Solitaire (sol.exe)

> If you start a game drawing three cards at a time, trying to switch to Game
> → Options → Draw One will normally start a new game. However, you can
> temporarily switch to Draw One by holding down Ctrl-Alt- while clicking
> on the deck to turn over a new card.

See Also

freecell (the deterministic version of Solitaire)

For add-ons and downloadable Solitaire versions:

http://www.solitairecity.com/
http://www.solitairecentral.com/
http://www.goodsol.com/

---

sort   \Windows\Command\sort.exe

Sort text input in alphanumeric order.

To Launch

sort [/r] [/+n] [filenames]

Description

The *sort* command sorts text on a line-by-line basis. Each line of the input is
ordered alphanumerically and output to the screen. By default, sorting starts with
the character in the first column of each line, but this can be changed with the /+n
option. *sort* is often used in conjunction with either pipes or output redirection.
That is, you might want to sort the output of another command, and you will often
want to redirect the output to a file so that it can be saved.

sort takes the following options:

command	Specifies a command whose output is to be sorted
/+n	Sorts the file according to characters in column *n*
/r	Reverses the sort order; that is, sorts Z to A, then 9 to 0

Examples

Display an alphabetically sorted directory (similar to `dir /o`):

```
C:\>dir | sort
```

Sort the contents of a file starting with column 21:

```
C:\>sort /+21 txtfiles.log > txtfiles.srt
```

Notes

- The input to *sort* should be ASCII text, so that each line can be considered a record of data. For example, Notepad and *edit* produce text files, but Word-Pad and Word (by default) produce binary *.doc* files, not text.

- The lines (records) may be broken into fields, each beginning a fixed number of characters from the start of the line.

- *sort* is a real-mode program; it can handle files over 64K in size, but the maximum is about 640K. It may have problems with very long lines.

- Blank lines and leading spaces will be sorted. This can result in many blank lines at the top of the sorted output; you may need to scroll down in an editor to see non-blank lines.

- *sort*'s collating sequence is based on the country code and code-page settings. In particular, the sort order of characters greater than ASCII code 127 depends on the COUNTRY settings.

- If you do a lot of sorting, you may want to get a Windows version of the Unix *sort* utility, which is much more powerful. The Unix *sort* command lets you define and sort on fields within the line, ignore upper- and lowercase distinctions, and eliminate duplicate lines, among other things. See the MKS Toolkit:

  http://www.mks.com/solution/tk

  or the Hamilton C Shell:

  http://www.hamiltonlabs.com/cshell.htm

  If you have Unix access, you can also *ftp* your file to a Unix machine, use *telnet* to run the Unix *sort* command on it, and then *ftp* it back to your Windows machine.

See Also

find

---

sound recorder

See *sndrec32*.

---

start   *\Windows\Command\start.exe*

Start applications in a new window.

To Launch

start [/m][/max][/r][/w] program [arg...]
start [/m][/max][/r][/w] document.ext
start [/m][/max][/r][/w] url

Description

Normally, when you run a DOS program from the command prompt the command runs in the same window. If you want to open a new window for the command to run in, use *start*. Opening in a new window is the default behavior for Windows programs, but even with Windows programs, *start* is handy, because it lets you specify whether the program is run maximized or minimized. You can also open a file with its associated application by typing **start** followed by the filename. The *start* command also makes it possible to open URLs from a DOS prompt or from a DOS batch file.

start accepts the following options:

`arg`	Specifies the optional list of arguments for the program to run.
`document.ext`	Specifies a document to open. Windows will launch or open the appropriate program based on the filename extension associated with that file type.
`/m`	Runs the new program in a minimized window.
`/max`	Runs the new program in a maximized window.
`program`	Specifies the program to run. If the program is not in the current directory, a drive and/or path should be included.
`/r`	Runs the new program restored (in the foreground). This is the default behavior.
`url`	Specifies a URL (e.g., *http://www.oreilly.com*) to open.
`/w`	Specifies that control does not pass back to the window from which *start* was invoked until the new window is closed.

Examples

Run the Windows Notepad program, opening the window to full size:

    C:\>**start /max notepad.exe**

Run the DOS program *myprog.exe* in the *C:\DOS* directory, and wait until the window is manually closed:

    C:\>**start /w c:\dos\myprog.exe**

Run the Windows Notepad application to open the *readme.txt* file (by default, the file association *.txt* is run by Notepad, due to a setting made in the Registry, which any user can change):

    C:\>**start c:\windows\readme.txt**

Open a URL with the default browser:

```
C:\>start http://www.oreilly.com
```

Notes

- *start* will run executable programs with *.exe*, *.com*, and *.bat* extensions.

- Only one option can be specified when utilizing the *start* command. If more than one parameter is entered, they are ignored (no error message).

- To open folders quickly, use the *start* command followed by the folder's name at the MS-DOS Prompt. (Note that this works only if the folder is in the current path.) Windows will find the folder and open it on the Desktop.

If you want to be able to run a command in the background (i.e., do its thing without putting up a window), use `start /m`.

Typing `start .` will open the current directory in a Desktop folder view; `start ..` will open the parent directory, and so on.

If you want to "preload" a set of URLs into your browser for quicker performance (if there are a group of news sites you like to check every morning, create a batch file containing *start* commands for each URL, then execute it each morning while you go get your cup of coffee, or use *sysagent* (from Plus!) to schedule the batch file to run before you come in for work. Of course, this works best if you have a full-time Internet connection.

See Also

command, regedit

---

sys   *\Windows\Command\sys.com*

Create a bootable MS-DOS disk.

To Launch

sys [drive1:][path] drive2:

Description

sys is similar to `format /s`, except that *sys* works with already formatted disks, and *sys* lets you specify an optional location in which to find the system files.

Neither *sys* nor `format /s` do what's necessary to make Windows 95 bootable from a floppy: merely the MS-DOS 7.x portion is booted.

The *sys* options are:

[drive1:] [path]
Specifies the location of the system files

drive2:   Specifies the drive the system files are to be copied to

---

Examples

`C:\>`**sys a:**

Notes

- Besides the boot record (containing a bootstrap loader for *io.sys*), the "system files" are *io.sys, drvspace.bin,* and *command.com. sys* and **format** **/s** generate a small *msdos.sys* "on the fly." *msdos.sys* normally needs to be 1K in size for compatibility with some pre-Win95 DOS programs, but the *msdos.sys* file created by the Emergency Boot feature is only 9 bytes.

- Surprisingly, Windows 95's "Emergency Boot Disk" option (Control Panel →
Add/Remove Programs → Startup Disk) doesn't make a fully bootable Windows 95 disk either. To boot the full Win95 with a GUI from a floppy, the floppy needs *io.sys, msdos.sys,* and a *config.sys* that looks something like the following:

```
shell=c:\command.com /p /e:1024
device=c:\windows\himem.sys
device=c:\windows\ifshlp.sys
device=c:\windows\setver.exe
dos=high
```

If you want it to boot automatically into the Win95 GUI, then you also need an *autoexec.bat* with at least one line:

```
c:\windows\win.com
```

- Like *format,* the *sys* command doesn't work with *subst*ed or network drives.

- When *sys*ing a floppy, a new *msdos.sys* file is created. This means that if you then boot from the floppy, you won't be able to start Windows 95. The way around this is to copy the *msdos.sys* file from *C:* to the floppy after using *sys.*

See Also

format

---

sysagent

\Program Files\Plus!\sysagent.exe

System Agent for scheduling programs (Microsoft Plus!).

To Install

System Agent is installed by default once you install Plus!.

To Launch

Start → Run → **sysagent**

Start → Programs → Accessories → System Tools → System Agent

Description

System Agent is a general-purpose scheduler application that allows you to schedule Win95 programs to run at various times (e.g., schedule ScanDisk to run every evening). Unless it's disabled, System Agent places an icon in the System Tray. Double-click it to launch the System Agent user interface; right-click and select Suspend System Agent to suspend the program (the icon will still be in the System Tray, but it will have a big red "x" on it); right-click again and select Suspend System Agent to resume the program.

There are three separate files that make up System Agent: *sage.exe*, *sage.dll*, and *sysagent.exe*. When you log in to Windows 95, *sage.exe* runs automatically and then loads *sage.dll*, which actually monitors the Win95 system, running programs that have been designated in System Agent to run at their appointed times. The System Agent user interface is actually provided by *sysagent.exe* (see Figure 5-77).

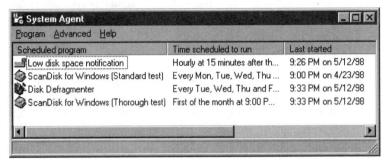

Figure 5-77: System Agent schedule (sysagent.exe)

By default, the System Agent dialog contains four scheduled programs:

Low disk space notification
ScanDisk for Windows (standard test)
Disk Defragmenter
ScanDisk for Windows (thorough test)

For each program, the following information is supplied by System Agent:

Time scheduled to run
Time last started
Time last ended
The last result

To change the schedule for any of these, select the program, context menu → Change Schedule. To get the details on a program, right-click → Properties. Of course, you can also use the menus to do the same thing. You can also disable or remove a program by right-clicking on it or using the menu (the Remove function deletes the schedule for the program).

Notes

- Program → Schedule a New Program will walk you through adding a new program to System Agent.

- Program → Run Now (or right-click → Run Now) on a selected program will run the program regardless of the scheduled time.

- Advanced → View Log provides an ASCII file (*sagelog.txt* stored in *Program Files\Plus!*) of all the recent programs that System Agent has run.

See Also

For information about the *sage* API:

http://www.eu.microsoft.com/win32dev/guidelns/sageapi.htm

---

sysedit

Edit system intialization files.

To Launch

Start → Run → `sysedit`

Description

sysedit (shown in Figure 5-78) opens the following files simultaneously in overlapping windows: *autoexec.bat*, *config.sys*, *system.ini*, *win.ini*, *protocol.ini*, and *msmail.ini*, using a Notepad-style text editor.

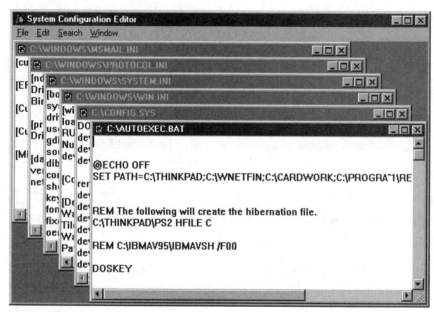

Figure 5-78: System Editor (sysedit.exe)

By automatically loading these system setting files, *sysedit* makes it quick and easy to view or make changes to them. If you select one of the files and make changes to it, make sure that you save it before closing the editor.

Notes

The Window → Tile option neatly arranges the system files into six equal sub-windows, making it easier to navigate among the files.

sysmon

Monitor memory functions and disk cache settings.

To Launch

Start → Run → `sysmon`
Start → Programs → Accessories → System Tools → System Monitor

Description

Using *sysmon*, you can monitor many functions and settings, such as current virtual memory and disk cache size, and max\min settings for virtual memory and disk cache (see Figure 5-79). For virtual memory, you'll see the actual virtual memory size go up as you open more applications.

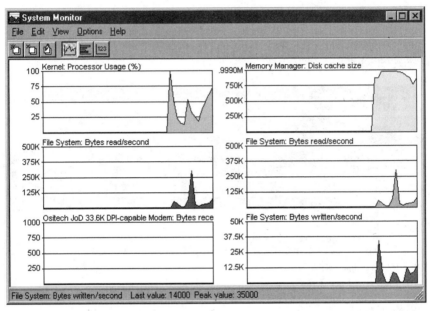

Figure 5-79: System Monitor (sysmon.exe)

When you first start the System Monitor, the display is blank. Click the first box on the toolbar, or Edit → Add Item; then, in the Category list, select the feature you want to monitor (e.g., File System). In the Item list, select the item or items you want to monitor (e.g., Bytes read/second or Bytes written/second).

You can display the same output in any one of three formats: Line, Bar, or Numeric Charts. Select the view with the last three toolbar buttons or the View menu.

Notes

- File → Connect lets you monitor a remote computer.
- The Explain button on the Add Item dialog gives an explanation of what each possible value means.

---

system policy editor

See *poledit*.

---

taskman

Display currently running programs.

Description

With *taskman* (Figure 5-80), you can start new programs and shut down individual programs or Windows itself. In the Options menu, you can select several different ways for the programs to be viewed in *taskman*. For example, you can select Always on Top, Text in Buttons, and Small Icons, to name a few. It is always available, even if you've changed your default shell.

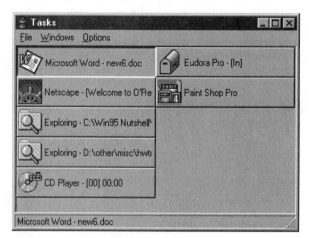

Figure 5-80: The Task Manager (taskman.exe)

taskman is the most privileged application in Windows 95. This means that if you substitute a shell (shell= in *system.ini*) and have no way of exiting out of Windows (shutting down), you can press Ctrl-Esc and shut down through the *taskman* menu option.

Notes

- *taskman* also has options to arrange ("tile" and "cascade") the windows of your currently running programs, thus bringing a bit of Windows 3.1 functionality back to the Windows 95 Desktop.

- *taskman* is the default Windows program that can run if nothing else is running. For example, if the Explorer crashes but Windows 95 itself is still running, you can press Ctrl-Esc to launch *taskman*.

- Because *taskman* can start new programs (see the File → Run Application menu item), it could be used as a minimalist alternative to the Explorer by putting shell=taskman.exe instead of shell=Explorer.exe in the [boot] section of *system.ini*.

See Also

Chapter 8

telnet

Create an interactive session on a remote computer using TCP/IP.

To Launch

telnet [host [port]]

Description

telnet (shown in Figure 5-81) is a Windows Sockets–based application that simplifies TCP/IP terminal emulation with Windows 95. Your host computer uses TCP/IP protocol to run the Client Telnet, negotiating a session with the other computer (the remote host or Server Telnet). Once the terminal settings are determined and set, you can log in to the other computer and access files. Each instance of the *telnet* application is limited to one connection. However, the application itself can be launched multiple times to create simultaneous connections to a single host or multiple hosts.

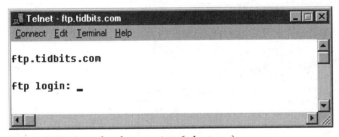

Figure 5-81: Sample telnet session (telnet.exe)

telnet is useful for connecting with a Unix shell account. In addition, there are many useful library catalogs and other services provided via *telnet*. See Figure 5-82.

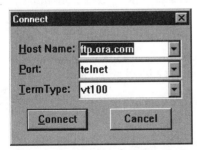

Figure 5-82: Initiating a telnet connection (telnet.exe)

telnet accepts the following options:

host
: Specifies the hostname or IP address of the remote system to which you want to connect.

| port | Specifies the remote name or number of the TCP port to connect to. The default value is specified by the *telnet* entry in the *services* file. If no entry exists in the *services* file, the default connection port value is decimal 23. The following port names are known by default in telnet.exe: *telnet, chargen, qotd, echo,* and *daytime.* (Each Internet server, such as ftp, *telnet,* or the Web [http] is assigned a standard port number, but it is also possible for alternative servers to be offered using other ports.) |

Associated files

\ *Windows*\ *services*

Examples

Connect to a library from the command line by typing:

```
C:\>telnet opac.sonoma.edu

Welcome to the Sonoma State University LIBAXP.
Username: OPAC
Welcome to OpenVMS AXP (TM) Operating System,
Version V6.2-1H3 on node LIBAXP
Last interactive login on Wednesday, 31-DEC-1997 10:52:39.10
Last non-interactive login on Tuesday, 30-DEC-1997 20:33:16.28
```

Notes

- Local Echo causes everything you type to be displayed in the *telnet* window.

- The Blinking Cursor option makes it easier for you to keep track of the cursor location in the window.

- The VT-100/ANSI setting will serve your purposes in most cases, unless the remote host instructs you differently when you log in.

- The Buffer Size setting (default: 25) specifies the number of lines of text the *telnet* window will maintain in its line buffer. Increasing this number allows you to scroll further back in the session to review previously displayed data.

- Start Logging allows you to save all data displayed in the *telnet* window to a file. You can review this file with a text editor.

- *telnet* provides Edit → Copy and Edit → Pause, but doesn't support the usual `Ctrl-C` and `Ctrl-V` keyboard accelerators.

- Adding "http 80/tcp" to the port number list in the *Services* file enables you to type `http` instead of 80 as the port when connecting.

- Various *telnet* settings (i.e., WinPosTop, Machine1, Rows, etc.) are stored in the Registry at:

`My Computer\HKEY_USERS\Default\Software\Microsoft\Telnet`

See Also

Internet in a Nutshell, by Valerie Quercia (O'Reilly & Associates)

For more information on using *telnet* for email:

http://faq.total.net/other/telnet/telnet.html

Commands & Applications

To download a shareware program that locates the appropriate address, login name, and port for libraries and *telnet* resources all around the world:

http://www.lights.com/hytelnet/

For a more sophisticated *telnet* program, try downloading Tera Term (Pro), a free software terminal emulator for MS-Windows:

http://spock.vector.co.jp/authors/VA002416/teraterm.html

---

time   Internal to: *\Windows\command.com*

Display or set the system time.

To Launch

    time [time]

Description

Run *time* without options to display the current time setting and a prompt for a new one. Press **Enter** to keep the same time.

The *time* options are:

time   To set the system time without a prompt: *hh*:*mm*:*ss* [A|P]

        hh   Hours: valid values = 0–23

        mm   Minutes: valid values = 0–59

        ss   Seconds: valid values = 0–59

        A|P   A.M. or P.M. (for 12-hour format). If a valid 12-hour format is entered without an A or P, A is the default.

Notes

- *time* and *date* affect all of Windows, not just the DOS box in which they are run. These commands can be used instead of Control Panel → Date/Time.

- The time format can be changed in Control Panel → Regional Settings → Time, but this doesn't affect the output of the DOS *time* command even though it has an instant effect on the time displayed in the System Tray. The format of *time* is set with the COUNTRY= setting in *config.sys*. You have to reboot after making this change.

- *time* always prompts for new time. If you want a batch file to display the time without prompting for a new one, create a tiny file with just a return/linefeed character in it, and redirect this to *time*, as shown in the following example. Here, *x* is a file created with *copy con* that contains a single carriage return/linefeed:

```
C:\>type timex.bat
@echo off
time < x | find "Current"
echo.
C:\>type x
C:\>timex
Current time is 9:56:54.33a
```

- Windows 95 has automatic changeover for daylight savings and a GUI interface for changing time zones (see Control Panel → Date/Time → Time Zone), so there is probably little reason to run *time* or *date*, except perhaps in a batch file to create a time or date stamp.

See Also

date
"Date/Time" in Chapter 4

---

tracert   \ *Windows\tracert.exe*

Internet trace route utility.

To Launch

tracert [-d] [-h max_hops] [-j ip-list] [-w timeout] target

Description

tracert displays the route that IP packets take between the local system and a remote system. This is handy if you want to know why a connection is slow (since it shows the time associated with each hop). But it's also just a great look "under the hood" of the Internet. Doing a *tracert* to frequently visited Internet sites will give a useful perspective on how the Internet works. When you connect to the Internet, your data is forwarded from one system to another via a series of "hops." Depending on your Internet service provider, the route from any one system to another can be long or short. Understanding just how your data gets from here to there can help you understand Internet connection or performance problems.

tracert accepts the following options:

-d	Do not resolve addresses to hostnames. This is helpful if there is also a problem with DNS.
-h *max_hops*	Maximum number (usually 30) of hops to search for target.
-j *ip-list*	Loose source route along *ip-list*; specifies a suggested route the packet should take.
target	Destination system whose connectivity you are checking. Can be either a TCP/IP hostname (such as *chinchilla.ora.com*) or an IP address (such as 130.132.59.234).
-w *timeout*	Number of milliseconds to wait for a reply before going onto the next hop.

Examples

```
C:\>tracert www.yahoo.com

Tracing route to www10.yahoo.com [204.71.200.75]
over a maximum of 30 hops:
  1    *        *        *      Request timed out.
  2  119 ms   118 ms   120 ms  e4-gw2.west.ora.com [192.168.50.5]
  3  122 ms   128 ms   125 ms  e3-gw.songline.com [10.0.0.1]
  4  124 ms   132 ms   120 ms  ans-gw.songline.com [172.16.30.4]
  5  165 ms   139 ms   134 ms  s2-5.cnss12.San-Francisco.t3.ans.net [192.103.60.61]
```

```
 6  137 ms  160 ms  133 ms  f2-1.t8-1.San-Francisco.t3.ans.net [140.222.8.222]
 7  144 ms  132 ms  136 ms  core5-fddi1-0.SanFrancisco.mci.net [206.157.77.1]
 8  148 ms  142 ms  145 ms  bordercore2.Bloomington.mci.net [166.48.176.1]
 9  149 ms  151 ms  155 ms  hssi1-0.br2.NUQ.globalcenter.net [166.48.177.254]
10  148 ms  151 ms  148 ms  fe4-0.cr1.NUQ.globalcenter.net [206.251.1.1]
11  171 ms  288 ms  231 ms  pos6-0.cr2.SNV.globalcenter.net [206.251.0.30]
12  166 ms  229 ms  228 ms  www10.yahoo.com [204.71.200.75]
Trace complete.
```

Notes

- *tracert* is a version of the Unix *traceroute* command.

- The remote system does not have to be a computer; it can be a router or any type of system that implements ICMP (Internet Control Message Protocol).

- Sometimes *tracert* can hang for several minutes while trying to resolve each IP address to its TCP/IP name. This can happen if DNS is not working properly on the local computer or if there are IP addresses on the route without proper DNS records. If this happens, you can turn off DNS with the –d option.

See Also

There are many web-based versions of *tracert* that show the route taken between the web server and another machine. You can find an example here:

> *http://www.yahoo.com/Computers_and_Internet/Software/Communications_ and_Networking/Networking/Utilities/Traceroute/*

Another such program is Yahoo! traceroute:

> *http://net.yahoo.com/cgi-bin/trace.sh*

---

type   Internal to: \ *Windows\command.com*

Display the contents of a text file.

To Launch

type filename

Description

The *type* command is useful if you need to quickly view the contents of any text file (especially short files). *type* is also useful for concatenating text files, using the >> operator.

Notes

- If the file is long and you'd like to quit displaying a file, press Ctrl-C to end the text display and return to the command prompt.

- To display binary (non-text) files (e.g., to search for strings), use *edit.com*.

See Also

more

---

tzedit \quad \Windows\tzedit.exe

Time Zone Editor.

To Install

Copy *tzedit.exe* and *tzedit.hlp* from the Win95 CD-ROM (*Admin\AppTools\Tzedit*) to your *Windows* directory.

To Launch

Start → Run → `tzedit`

Description

The Time Zone Editor lets you create and edit time zone entries for the Date/Time applet in the Control Panel (see Figure 5-83). *tzedit* is available on the OSR2 CD-ROM.

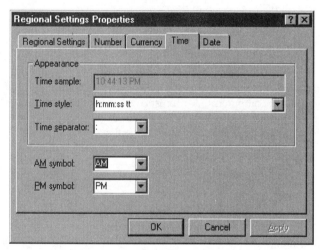

Figure 5-83: The Time Zone Editor (tzedit.exe)

tzedit has two main functions:

*   To edit a time zone name or adjust the start and end dates for daylight savings time

*   To create new time zone entries for the Date/Time tool

To edit a time zone:

1. Select a current time zone and then click Edit.

2. Change the time zone name, abbreviation, or the difference from Greenwich Mean Time.

3. If you want Daylight Saving Time to be enabled automatically for the time zone, click the "Automatically Set Daylight Saving Time" box. Then, in the boxes underneath the option, fill in the start and stop days and times.

4. In the Daylight Bias box, select the amount of time to move forward or backward from the Standard time for Daylight Saving Time.

To create a new time zone:

1. Click New.

2. In the Time Zone Name box, type a name to be displayed in the Date/Time applet.

   Time zone names should start with the general template GMT+\– 0x:00; they can't exceed 63 characters.

3. In the Abbreviation box, type a name for the Standard time zone name abbreviation. The name can't exceed 31 characters.

4. In the "Offset From GMT" box, select the time difference from Greenwich Mean Time.

5. If you want Daylight Saving Time to be enabled automatically for the time zone (if the area uses Daylight Saving time), click the "Automatically Set Daylight Saving Time" checkbox.

6. In the boxes underneath the option, fill in the start and stop days and times.

7. In the Daylight Bias box, select the amount of time to move forward or backward from the Standard time for Daylight Saving Time.

Notes

Changes made with *tzedit* affect the stored data for time zones in the Registry. If a time zone is already set on the computer, that data is saved in another location in the Registry. In order for the new information to be used, you must use the Date/Time applet in Control Panel and select or reselect the time zone.

---

ver   Internal to: *Windows\command.com*

Display the Windows 95 build number.

To Launch

ver [/r]

Description

ver shows the version of Windows 95 you're using. The following table lists all of the different Win95 versions:

Build/Revision	MS-DOS Version	Release Name	Date
950	7.0	original	August 1995
950A	7.0	SR1	December 1995
950B, 1111	7.10 (FAT32)	OSR2	August 1996
950C	7.10	OSR2.5	January 1998

ver takes the following option:

/r   This undocumented option also displays the revision number, and whether DOS is located in the high memory area (HMA; same as DOS=HIGH).

Examples

```
C:\>ver /r
Windows 95. [Version 4.00.950]
Revision A
DOS is in HMA
```

Notes

- Windows 95 is really MS-DOS 7.x + Windows 4.0.*xxxx*, where *xxxx* is the build/revision number.

- Windows 98 is really MS-DOS 7.10 + Windows 4.10.*xxxx*, where *xxxx* is the build/revision number.

- *ver* just shows the Windows 95 build number (such as 950 or 1111), not the DOS or Windows version number. To get the DOS version number (7.00 or 7.10 for the version that supports FAT32), you can use *debug* to call the internal "Get DOS version" function:

  To check the MS-DOS version number by calling INT 21h Function 3306h:

```
C:\>type dosver.dbg
a
mov ax,3306
int 21
ret

g 105
r bx

q
C:\>debug < dosver.dbg
....
BX 0007
```

  (The number after BX at the end is the hexadecimal DOS version number: 0007 for MS-DOS 7.0, 0A07 for MS-DOS 7.10.)

- For more information on what Windows updates, patches, and fixes you might be running, use *qfecheck* (Update Information Tool).

See Also

debug, qfecheck

---

volume control

See *sndvol32*.

---

wangimg   \ *Windows\wangimg.exe*

Read or import different types of image file formats.

To Install

If you don't have OSR2, download *wangimg.exe* from *http://www.microsoft.com/ windows95/info/wang.htm* and install it in your \ *Windows* directory.

To Launch

wangimg [file]

Description

With *wangimg.exe*, you can use your computer to transform any paper or fax-based information into an electronic image document that can be stored, filed, retrieved, edited, printed, faxed, and shared. *wangimg.exe* can even read or import several different types of image file formats, including *.awd* (Microsoft FAX), *.bmp*, *.dcx*, *.jpg*, *.pcx*, and *.tif*.

You can not only view an image, but you can zoom in and out, view certain portions, and even mark up the image with the Annotation Toolbox. You can also print the images on a laser printer with letter-size paper. The imaging software supports standard black and white, grayscale, and color image documents. The viewing and readability of black and white documents can be significantly enhanced by using the product's scale-to-gray technology (View → Scale to Gray). If you have a scanner, you can even use *wangimg.exe* to create, append, and edit scanned images.

Notes

- Before you can scan for the first time, you must specify a scanner with File → Select Scanner. Once you've selected a scanner, you can scan a new document by doing the following:

  1. File → Scan New

  2. Follow the instructions on the screen. See your scanner's help or documentation for more information.

  With a new scanned document or an active document on your screen, you can send it as a fax or an email by selecting File → Send.

See Also

faxview

---

win   \ *Windows\win.com*

Bootstrap loader for Windows 95.

To Launch

win [/d:[f][m][s][v][x]]

Description

win.com is the command that Windows 95 uses to start the Windows 95 GUI on top of MS-DOS 7.x. Normally it runs automatically after the processing of *autoexec.bat*. However, if you disable this default behavior (by placing BootGUI=0 in *msdos.sys*, for example, by booting Windows 95 from a floppy disk, or by pressing a function key during the boot process), you can then run *win* yourself from the DOS prompt. This is useful if you want to run some DOS commands before the Windows 95 GUI has started.

The *win* options are:

/d	Used for troubleshooting when Windows does not start correctly.
:f	Turns off 32-bit disk access. Equivalent to *system.ini* file setting: 32BitDiskAccess=FALSE.
:m	Enables Safe mode. This is automatically enabled during a Safe start (function key F5).
:n	Enables Safe mode with networking. This is automatically enabled during a Safe start (function key F6).
:s	Specifies that Windows should not use ROM address space between F000:0000 and 1 MB for the V86BreakPoint. Equivalent to *system.ini* file setting: SystemROMBreakPoint=FALSE.
:v	Specifies that the ROM routine will handle interrupts from the hard disk controller. Equivalent to *system.ini* file setting: VirtualHDIRQ=FALSE.
:x	Excludes all of the adapter area from the range of memory that Windows scans to find unused space. Equivalent to *system.ini* file setting: EMMExclude=A000-FFFF.

Notes

- If you try to run *win* when Windows 95 is already running, an error message will remind you that you are already running Windows.

- Windows 95's *win.com* will fail with an error message if the underlying DOS is not version 7.0 or higher. Some versions of *win.com* require DOS version 7.10 or higher. *win.com* also requires that the underlying DOS load (either implicitly or via DEVICE= in *config.sys*) appropriate versions of the XMS driver (*himem.sys*) and the Installable File System helper (*ifshlp.sys*).

- *win* is just a small bootstrap loader. Its main job is to run *vmm32.vxd*, which contains the Virtual Machine Manager (VMM) and virtual device driver (VxD) core of the Windows 95 operating system; *vmm32.vxd* in turn loads the Win16 and Win32 GUI.

See Also

sys

---

winchat

\Windows\winchat.exe

Conduct "chat" sessions with other Windows 95 users.

To Install

Control Panel → Add/Remove Programs → Windows Setup → Have Disk → (OSR2) CD-ROM *\Other\Chat* → Install → Chat

---

To Launch

Start → Run → winchat
Start → Programs → Accessories → Chat

Description

winchat allows you to conduct chat sessions with other Windows 95 users through your Internet connection, without using IRC (Internet Relay Chat) servers. *winchat* uses *netdde* as a communications mechanism.

You must be running *netdde* to run this program. It's a good idea to put it into your startup folder if you plan on using *winchat* frequently. *winchat* will automatically start when a Chat call is received by your computer, if the "Autostart Chat when called" box is checked in Options → Preferences (the box is checked by default).

To call someone using *winchat*:

1. On the Conversation menu, click Dial.

2. Specify the computer name of the person you want to chat with.

To hang up: click Conversation → Hang Up.

To answer a call with *winchat*:

1. Click the Chat button that appears on the Taskbar when someone uses Chat to dial your computer.

2. If your Chat window is already open, click the Conversation → Answer.

To hang up, click Conversation → Hang Up. See Figure 5-84.

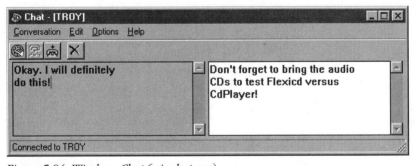

Figure 5-84: Windows Chat (winchat.exe)

Notes

- You can type your message in the Chat window before calling someone.

- To change the appearance of your Chat window, click Options.

- If you have several people you Chat with often, you might consider doing the following:

  1. Create a file called *lmhosts* in your *Windows* directory, if you don't already have one. (A sample *lmhosts* file is in *Windows**lmhost.sam*. You can view this file with Notepad or any other text editor.)

2. List those people you want to Chat with, in the following format:

   `IP_address computer_name`

   Be sure to use a separate line for each entry (each person to chat with).

   You can find the IP address of your own machine using *winipcfg*. You can find the name of your machine by opening Control Panel → Network → Identification. You can get the name of a remote machine by opening the Network Neighborhood and looking for likely names (or ask the other user to check Control Panel → Network → Identification on their machine). To find the IP address associated with the remote machine, use *tracert* or *ping*. (The IP address will be shown in brackets after the hostname.)

3. To enable the changes, either reboot the computer or run *nbtstat* -R (uppercase R, since a lowercase r is a different command switch).

See Also

nbtstat, netdde.exe

windows messaging

See *exchng32*.

winfile

\ *Windows* \ *winfile.exe*

The Windows 3.1–style File Manager.

To Launch

Start → Run → `winfile`

Description

If you're accustomed to Windows 3.1, you may want to use *winfile* instead of the Explorer, although there are some drawbacks (mentioned later). *winfile* (Figure 5-85) lets you rename file extensions and delete files without being prompted.

Notes

- *winfile* does have limitations that the Explorer doesn't. The most obvious ones are that *winfile* lacks support for long filenames and doesn't support context menus (right-click).

- Although you can select the "Indicate Expandable Branches" option, you can't toggle the plus and minus sign, as you can in the Explorer.

- If you maximize the entire *winfile* window, the Taskbar will be covered and you won't be able to access it.

See Also

explorer

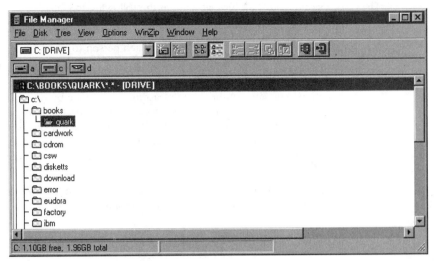

Figure 5-85: Windows 3.1–style file manager (winfile.exe)

winhelp

16-bit launcher for *winhlp32.exe*.

See *winhlp32*.

winhlp32
\ *Windows\winhlp32.exe*

WinHelp engine and viewer.

To Launch

Start → Run → winhlp32

There is no real reason to launch *winhlp32*, since it's automatically loaded whenever you double-click on any *.hlp* file or choose the Help menu in any application.

A dialog box pops up when you launch *winhlp32.exe*. The application needs you to select a *.hlp* file so it can execute.

Description

When you choose Help in a Win95 application, you are launching *winhlp32*, the WinHelp engine and viewer. *winhelp* is the 16-bit launcher for *winhlp32*.

The Help dialog in all Win95 *.hlp* files provides a consistent starting point and features three tabs: Contents, Index, and Find. They are designed to help users locate information in three different ways:

Contents

The outline that appears under the Contents tab is defined in a *.cnt* file, and is located in the same directory as the application's *.hlp* file. If you delete this file (the file must not be running) and select Contents from the application's Help menu, the Index tab will be selected instead of the Contents tab. However, if you double-click on the *.hlp* file after deleting the *.cnt* file, the help file's introductory page will be displayed instead.

Index

This is identical to any book index, and contains keywords listed alphabetically, with second-level entries indented. The Index can encompass multiple help files.

Find

The Find tab can perform a full text search on the entire *.hlp* file. The first time you click the Find tab, the Find Setup Wizard appears and prepares to generate a database of searchable text as an *.fts* (full text search) file, giving you three options. The default choice, "Minimize Database Size," produces the smallest word list. If, however, you have a fast machine and plenty of hard disk space, you may want to choose the "Maximize Search Capabilities" option. Luckily, *.fts* files can be deleted at any stage, provided their associated *.hlp* file isn't running and you're willing to rebuild it the next time you need to go hunting through the *.hlp* file. The final option choose is "Customize Search Capabilities," which allows you to select which topics you'd like included. This can obviously save you disk space by cutting down on the size of the *.fts* file that's generated (see Figure 5-86).

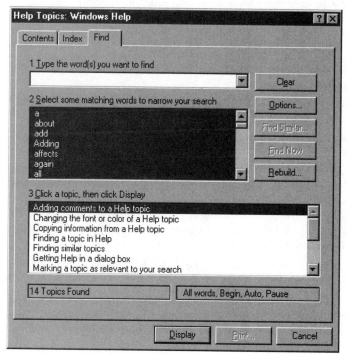

Figure 5-86: WinHelp (winhlp32.exe)

winhlp32 also supports five hypertext functions:

1. Links to other parts of the help document or other help files

2. Pop-up boxes, which provide definitions in a non-intrusive way

3. A history feature, so you can retrace your steps

4. A keyword search capability for finding specific information

5. A contents (*.cnt*) page designed as the starting point for help files

Associated Files

winhelp.ini (configuration file located in the \ *Windows* directory)

Notes

- If there is no *.cnt* file, *winhlp32* goes to a defined contents page which is the entry point to the help, bypassing the contents/index/find tabs. This is common for small help files, and is done deliberately.

- You can add your own annotations to any help topic. Pick Annotate from either the Options menu or the context menu; do the same to view any existing annotations. The menu also lets you print the help topic or copy it to the Clipboard.

- The Win95 *.hlp* files are located in the \ *Windows\Help* directory; however, all applications store their *.hlp* files in their own program directory. All *.cnt*, *.fts*, and *.gid* files reside in the same directory as their *.hlp* file. Annotation (*.ann*) files, on the other hand, are stored in the \ *Windows\Help* directory regardless of their origin.

- For help on using Help, open the *winhlp32.hlp* file located in the \ *Windows\Help* directory.

- Each *.hlp* file contains the "Stay on top" setting, which lets the Help window remain in view when working with other windows.

- The contents of *.hlp* files can be copied to the Clipboard for pasting into other applications.

- Brief notes or "annotations" (*.ann*) can be added to a help page, and are signified by a paper-clip icon appearing above the topic heading. To view comments, click on the icon. Annotations are saved in individual files, each with the same name as the annotated *.hlp* file, but bearing an *.ann* extension. Annotations made to the WordBasic help file *wrdbasic.hlp*, for instance, are stored in a file called *wrdbasic.ann*.

- A *.gid* file is created the first time the *.hlp* file is run, and lets Windows find the help file the next time. It can be deleted if the *.hlp* file isn't currently open.

- Bookmarks can be inserted anywhere into a *.hlp* file; they appear in the Bookmark menu. *winhelp.bmk*, located in the \ *Windows* directory, contains the combined bookmark pointers for all *.hlp* files.

- Microsoft is currently migrating toward HTML-based help. See the URL under "See Also" for more information.

- The *.cnt* file can be deleted to get rid of the silly "contents" window for a help system.

See Also

For information about HTML Help, and to download HTML Help 1.1:

http://www.microsoft.com/workshop/author/htmlhelp/home-f.htm

---

winipcfg

\Windows\winipcfg.exe

Display the current TCP/IP settings on your computer.

To Launch

Start → Run → winipcfg [/all] [/batch [filename]]

Description

winipcfg displays TCP/IP configuration information for your computer. It also allows you to release or renew a dynamically allocated IP address. With no arguments, *winipcfg* displays the dialox box shown in Figure 5-87.

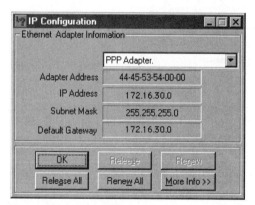

Figure 5-87: IP Configuration (winipcfg.exe)

The *winipcfg* options are:

/all   Displays all adapter information. The default action is to display or write the minimum amount of adapter information, depending on whether the /batch option was specified. This is the same as clicking More Info on the basic *winipcfg* dialog box. See Figure 5-88.

/batch [*filename*]
                Batch mode. The IP configuration information is written to a file called *winipcfg.out* in the current directory. If the optional filename is given on the command line, IP configuration information will be written to this file instead.

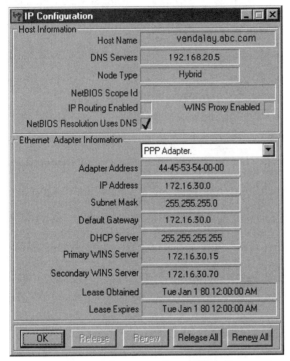

Figure 5-88: IP Configuration (winipcfg.exe)

Examples

Launch *winipcfg*, sending all of the IP information to a file named *ipconfig.out* in the root directory of the *C:* drive:

```
C:\>winipcfg /all /batch c:\ipconfig.out
```

Notes

- *winipcfg* is useful if you have two different ways of connecting to a network. For example, you might have two different kinds of modems (e.g., one ISDN or cable) for connecting to two different kinds of networks, or you might dial in on your laptop, and then connect it directly at the office. After you've used one, you need to clear the cache of network info in order to use the other without rebooting Windows. This is done by clicking "Release All" and then "Renew All."

- For more information on IP configuration values, see Control Panel → Network in Chapter 4. The Lease Obtained and Lease Expired fields will contain data only if you are using DHCP.

winmine   *Windows\winmine.exe*

Minesweeper game.

To Install

Minesweeper should be installed by default, but if not:

> Control Panel → Add/Remove Programs → Windows Setup → Accessories → Games

To Launch

> Start → Run → `winmine`
> Start → Programs → Accessories → Games → Minesweeper

Description

The object of Minesweeper (Figure 5-89) is to uncover "safe" areas on a playing field, without stepping on any landmines.

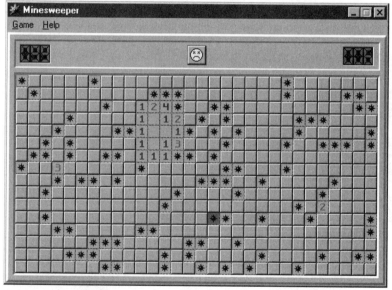

Figure 5-89: Minesweeper game (winmine.exe)

Associated Files

> *Windows\winmine.ini*

Notes

- The beginner game uses an 8×8 grid with 10 mines; intermediate uses a 16×16 grid with 40 mines; expert uses a 30×16 grid with 99 mines. You can also create custom games, such as an easy 30×30 grid with only 10 mines, or a difficult 8×8 grid with 60 mines.

- If a number appears on a square, it specifies how many mines are in the eight squares that surround the numbered square.

- The "XYZZY" cheat code does not work in the Windows 95 version.

See Also

See the Yahoo! Minesweeper page:

> *http://www.yahoo.com/Recreation/Games/Computer_Games/Titles/*
> *Strategy/Minesweeper/*

A web-based Java version is available at:

> *http://www-mtl.mit.edu/~aarong/java/Minesweeper.html*

---

winpopup
\ *Windows\winpopup.exe*

Send pop-up messages to other Win95 computers on your network.

To Launch

    Start → Run → `winpopup`

Description

In order to successfully send a *winpopup* message to another Win95 machine on your network, that machine must also be running *winpopup* (see Figure 5-90).

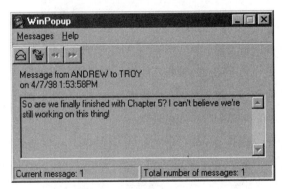

Figure 5-90: winpopup.exe

To send a message to an individual, click "User Or Computer" and type in the network name (a UNC path to the computer). To send a *winpopup* message: Click Messages → Send.

To send a message to everyone in your workgroup, click Workgroup and type in the workgroup name. Type your message and click OK.

Notes

- *winpopup* messages can't be saved.

- *winpopup* will say "Message successfully sent" even if *winpopup* is not running on the target machine. The message just disappears into the ether.

- If you plan on using *winpopup* on a regular basis, place a shortcut to the program in the startup directory (\ *Windows\Start Menu\Programs\StartUp*) so that it's always running. The reason for this is that if *winpopup* isn't running, you won't be able to receive any *winpopup* messages from anyone.

- You can configure *winpopup* with the following options:
  - Play sound when a new message arrives
  - Enable "Always on top"
  - Pop up a dialog on message receipt
- For more sophisticated options and ways of delivering messages, you might consider *winchat* or some type of email program such as Exchange/Windows Messaging.

See Also

exchng32, winchat

---

winset

\Windows\winset.exe

Set or remove global Windows environment variables.

To Install

Copy *winset.exe* from the CD-ROM (*\Admin\Apptools\Envvars*) to your *\Windows* directory. For example,

```
C:\>copy d:\admin\apptools\envvars\winset.exe c:\windows
```

To Launch

winset [variable=[string]]

Description

winset.exe does not set an environment variable in a batch file's environment, only in the Window's global environment.

When an MS-DOS box starts, it gets a copy of the global environment owned by Windows, but then the connection is broken. Changes made in the copy don't affect the global environment. They're not visible in other DOS boxes, and when the DOS box terminates, they're lost.

To view Window's global environment variables, start an MS-DOS Prompt (duplicating the global environment variables), then use the *set* command without options.

The *winset* options are:

string   Specifies a series of characters to assign to the variable

variable   Specifies the environment variable name

Examples

Keep a batch file in sync with the global environment:

```
C:\>WINSET foo=bar
C:\>SET foo=bar
```

See Also

set, wintop

wintop

A daemon that tracks all Win95 running applications; this is one of the components contained in Kernel Toys (a collection of utilities that you can download from: *http://www.microsoft.com/windows95/info/kerneltoys.htm*).

See *krnltoys*.

wordpad   *\Program Files\Accessories\wordpad.exe*

A simple word processor that comes with Windows 95.

To Launch
        Start → Run → **wordpad**
        Start → Programs → Accessories → WordPad

Description

Although *wordpad* lacks many of the features that come with Microsoft Word, it has many basic word processing features; you can:

- Set word wrap options: no wrap, wrap to window, or wrap to ruler
- Use Print Preview
- Apply 16 different colors to selected text
- Set the tab stop position and insert bullets
- Set the ruler to one of the following measurement units: Inches, Centimeters, Points, or Picas
- Automatically load the current WordPad document into Windows Messaging/Exchange for sending through email
- Save or open any of the following types of files: *.doc, .wri, .rtf,* and *.txt*
- Undo the last action (only one), and redo that same one action
- Choose from a wide selection of different fonts and font sizes
- Insert objects of your choice

Notes

- Unlike Notepad, WordPad doesn't have a 32K limit; this is why Win95 prompts you to open *.txt* files over 32K with *wordpad*).
- You can open Word 6.0 documents with WordPad, but you might lose some formatting. Before saving a Word 6.0 document, WordPad will display the following warning: "This document was created by Word 6.0. WordPad does not support all of the features provided by Word 6.0. Therefore, you may lose information by saving this file as a Word file with the same name."
- WordPad doesn't have spell-checking capabilities.
- WordPad's default font is Times New Roman, and there's no way for WordPad to open with any other default font. Once WordPad is running you can select all or some of the text and change the font.

- Beware of the following when dragging a file onto WordPad: be sure to drop the file icon onto the menu bar (or a blank part of the toolbar) if you want to view it or edit it, and drop it onto the open window if you want to embed the contents of the file into a WordPad document.

- To prevent WordPad from overriding your file extensions and adding its own when you save a file, place quotation marks around the name of the file you want to save (e.g., "read.me"), and click Save.

See Also

notepad

To download CWordPad, a freeware program similar to WordPad that does have spell-checker capabilities:

http://www.cetussoft.com/freeware.htm

---

write \ *Windows\write.exe*

write (Windows Write) is a stub that runs *wordpad*. Windows Write was prevalent in Win3.1, but in Windows 95, it has been replaced with WordPad.

See *wordpad*.

---

xcopy \ *Windows\Command\xcopy.exe*

Stub-loader for *xcopy32*

See *xcopy32*.

---

xcopy32 \ *Windows\Command\xcopy32.exe*

Copy files and directories, including subdirectories.

To Launch

xcopy source [destination] [/a | /m] [/d[:date]] [/p] [/s [/e]] [/w] [/c] [/i] [/q] [/f] [/l] [/h] [/r] [/t] [/u] [/k] [/n]

Description

xcopy32 provides more options and is often faster than *copy*. *xcopy* is just a stub-loader for *xcopy32* (which is not a DOS program, but a Win32 "Console" program).

The *xcopy32* options are:

/a   Copies files with the archive attribute set, but doesn't change the attribute of the source file.

/c   Continues copying even if errors occur.

/d:date   Copies only files changed on or after the specified date. If no date is given, copies only those source files that are newer than existing destination files.

`destination`	Specifies the location and/or name of new files. If omitted, files are copied to the current directory.
`/e`	Copies directories and subdirectories, including empty ones. Same as `/s /e`. May be used to modify `/t`.
`/f`	Displays full source and destination filenames while copying.
`/h`	Copies hidden and system files also.
`/i`	If a destination is not supplied and you are copying more than one file, assumes that the destination must be a directory. (By default, *xcopy* asks if the destination is a file or directory.)
`/k`	Copies attributes. (By default, *xcopy* resets read-only attributes.)
`/l`	Displays files that would be copied given other options, but does not actually copy the files.
`/m`	Copies files with the archive attribute set, then turns off the archive attribute of the source file.
`/n`	Copies files using short (8.3) file and directory names (for example, "PROGRA~1" instead of "Program Files").
`/p`	Prompts you before creating each destination file.
`/q`	Does not display filenames while copying.
`/r`	Overwrites read-only files.
`/s`	Copies directories and subdirectories, except empty ones. (Probably the most useful *xcopy* option.)
`source`	Specifies the file(s) to copy; must include either a drive or a path.
`/t`	Creates directory structure, but does not copy files. Does not include empty directories (use `/t /e` to include empty directories).
`/u`	Copies from source only files that exist on destination; used to update files.
`/v`	Ignored under Windows 95.
`/w`	Prompts you to press a key before copying.
`/y`	Overwrites existing files without prompting.
`/-y`	Prompts you before overwriting existing files. (This is default; overrides opposite setting in COPYCMD= environment variable.) Only COPYCMD=/y and –/y have an effect on *xcopy32* (and *copy*).

Exit codes (can be tested in batch file with ERRORLEVEL):

0	All files were copied without errors.
1	No files were found to copy.
2	*xcopy* was terminated by `Ctrl-C` before copying was complete.

4	An initialization error occurred. Such an error would generally be caused by insufficient memory or disk space, or an invalid drive name or syntax.
5	A disk-write error occurred.

Examples

Copy all the files and subdirectories, including any empty subdirectories and hidden files, from *C:\foobar* to the disk in drive *A*:

```
C:\>xcopy \foobar a: /s /e /h
```

Notes

It has been reported that the /s and /e options have bugs when used in conjunction with /d and /u.

See Also

copy, diskcopy

CHAPTER 6

The Batch Language

Most Windows 95 books treat batch files as if they were some kind of skeleton in the closet, or a crazy aunt you wouldn't want anyone to meet. While it's true that batch files are much less important than they were in DOS, they still crop up throughout the system. If you are in the unfortunate position of needing to write or understand one, you need documentation—perhaps even more than you need it for parts of the system that you use more often. What's more, even in the world of graphical user interfaces, scripting has an important place. The principal complaint about batch files should not be that they are obsolete, but that Windows 95 has done too little to integrate scripting into its interface. Fortunately, the Windows Scripting Host (WSH), which is a standard part of Windows 98, will make it easier to use much more advanced scripting languages such as Visual Basic, Perl, PerlScript, JavaScript, or Python.

A batch file is an ASCII text file containing a series of commands, each on its own line, which will be executed one line at a time. A batch file can't have the same name as a DOS internal command (such as *dir, copy,* or *cd*), and it must have a *.bat* extension.

Although any commands that you can type at the command line can be used in a batch file, there are several additional commands that can be used only in a batch file. These commands are used for loops, conditionals and other programming functions within the batch file and are explained in detail later in this chapter.

Creating Batch Files

You can create batch files with any text editor or word processor that can save plain ASCII text files, such as *notepad* or *edit.*

When naming a batch file, make sure you don't use a name that is already used by a DOS internal command or by a *.com* or *.exe* file in your search path. The reason for this is that when DOS executes programs, it first looks for the *.com* extension, then the *.exe* extension, before finally executing a file with the *.bat* extension. So, for instance, if you have a file called *work.exe*, and you create *work.bat* in the same directory, your batch file will not execute unless you type the full name, including the extension.

You can create and execute batch files from the current directory or any directory in your search path, or by specifying their complete pathname, just as with any other command. But if you're going to use batch files a lot, it makes sense to keep them all in one place. Create a directory called *\Batch* and add it to your search path. (See the *path* command in Chapter 5, *Commands and Applications*, and *autoexec.bat* in Chapter 9, *Windows Startup*.)

Some Rules of the Road

Here are the basics of batch file programming:

- Each command in a batch file must be on a separate line. The last command line in the file should end with a carriage return.

- You can use wildcards, pipes, and redirection inside a batch file, but you can't redirect or pipe the output of a batch file. If you type something like:

  ```
  myfile.bat > savefile
  ```

  the batch file will execute, but the redirection will be ignored. Put the redirection (using >> if there's output from multiple commands) on the command lines inside the batch file.

- A batch file can take arguments such as filenames or options. Up to nine arguments are stored in the variables %1 through %9. So, for example, the following line in a batch file:

  ```
  copy %1 %2
  ```

  would mean that the batch file would copy the filename specified in the first argument to the name specified in the second argument.

- The name of the batch file itself is stored in the variable %0. This allows you to do things like have a temporary batch file that deletes itself when done. The name is stored as it was typed at the command line, so if you had typed myfile.bat, %0 would be *myfile.bat*, but if you had typed C:\batch \myfile, %0 would be *C:\batch\myfile*.

- A batch file run from the command prompt or by double-clicking on its icon will open a DOS window while it is executing. (A batch file run from an existing DOS window will run inside that window, unless it contains an explicit command such as *start* that opens another window.) If you don't want this behavior, use the batch file's Properties → Program → Run to specify that the batch file should be run minimized rather than in a normal window. The property sheet lets you specify a working directory for the batch file, although you can also change the directory with a *cd* command within the batch file. If necessary, the property sheet also lets you specify that Windows exit before running the batch file and restart when finished. (See "Shortcut Properties of

DOS Programs" under the entry "Shortcuts" in Chapter 3, *The Windows 95 User Interface*, for details.)

- You can stop a running batch file by pressing `Ctrl-Break` or `Ctrl-C`; the following message will appear in its DOS window: "`Terminate batch job (Y/N)?`" Press `Y` to abort or `N` to continue running the batch file.

- By default, each command in a batch file is echoed to its DOS window. To execute a command silently, precede it with an @ symbol. Alternatively, you can turn command echo off with the command `@echo off`.

- A batch file can contain any command that you can type at the command prompt (i.e., anything described in Chapter 5, plus any third-party applications). However, keep in mind that each line in the batch file is executed sequentially, so there are a couple of gotchas, especially when the batch file runs programs that pop up a separate window. When you run a Windows program and it pops up its own window, control returns immediately to the batch file and the next line is executed. But what if you don't want that next command to run until the user is finished with the application in the popup window? In this case, you can make the batch file wait for completion of the Windows program by using *start* /w. But there's also the opposite problem, where you don't want the batch file to wait. Use *start* (without the /w) for that case. The *call* command performs the same function as *start* /w for DOS programs—i.e., it calls another command and waits for it to complete before continuing. A batch file can even call itself. (See *call* later in this chapter for an example.)

The following commands, described in Chapter 5, are particularly helpful in writing batch files:

cd	Change directory
cls	Clear the screen
exit	Exit from a command or batch file
for	Repeat a command for a set of variables
set	Set or clear the value of a variable
start	Start a command in a separate window, continuing execution in the current batch file

The following commands are normally used only in batch files, and are documented later in this chapter:

call	Invoke another batch file or external command and wait for it to finish before continuing
choice	Prompt the user for input
echo [on | off]	Turn on or off printing of batch file commands to the screen as they are executed; also, echo messages to the screen
errorlevel	Test return value of a command in an if statement
goto	Branch to another part of the batch file
if	Test a condition and act accordingly
pause	Wait before continuing

---

rem   What follows is a comment (remark), not a command to be executed

shift   Read and discard a command line argument, shifting over the remaining arguments

You can store temporary data in your batch file using environment variables created with the *set* command. To use the value of any variable, surround its name with % symbols. There is a limit on the size of the environment, which you can change in *config.sys*. See the discussion of *config.sys* in Chapter 9.

Looping constructs in batch files are extremely weak. There is no *while* or *until* loop, and the *for* loop and *if* conditional let you run only one command. There's no *else*. As a result, the only way to iterate is with a complex set of kludges too ugly to demonstrate. Users of Unix shells or AppleScript are likely to be really disgusted.

If you are serious about scripting repetitive tasks, get a real scripting language like Perlscript, which is freely downloadable from *http://www. activestate.com*. Perlscript not only gives you a much more robust programming environment, it even lets you access the internals of Windows programs like Microsoft Word via their COM objects. (For more information, see *Learning Perl on Win32 Systems*, by Randal L. Schwartz, Erik Olson, and Tom Christiansen (O'Reilly & Associates). With the Windows Scripting Host (WSH), you can also write programs in VBScript, Jscript, Python, or Tcl. WSH will be standard in Windows 98 and NT 5.0, but you can download it for Windows 95 from *http://www.microsoft.com/scripting/windowshost/*.

- A debugging environment can be created to test batch files by starting a new instance of *command.com*:

```
command /y /z /c batchfile.bat [arguments]
```

- /y will show each line of batchfile with % variable substitutions completed, followed by the prompt:

```
[Enter=Y,Esc=N]?
```

Enter or Y will execute the *.bat* file line. Esc or N will skip the *.bat* file line.

When to Use Batch Files

This section gives a few examples of when you might want to use batch files.

First, while Windows 95 no longer requires the use of an *autoexec.bat* file, if present, this file is executed whenever the system is booted before Windows itself is launched. Any commands you want to have executed automatically can be run from there. This is a batch file like any other, and the features described in this chapter can be used there. See Chapters 9 and 10 for additional details.

Second, if you still use older DOS programs on your machine, they sometimes require what is called MS-DOS mode, in which all Windows programs are shut down before the DOS program is run. (See "Shortcut Properties of DOS Programs" in Chapter 3.) When a program requires a switch to MS-DOS mode, the file *dosstart.bat* is executed (if found), and the file *winstart.bat* is executed when returning to Windows mode. These batch files let you run commands to customize your DOS environment and restore your Windows environment.

Third, if you look at Properties → Program for any DOS program, you'll see that you can specify the name of a batch file to be run whenever the shortcut is executed. This allows you to do things like set environment variables required by the program, change to a particular directory when the program is run, and so on.

But there's more to batch files than backwards compatibility with legacy DOS programs. Let's make a little digression about shortcuts. Since any shortcut, even a shortcut to a Windows program, actually specifies a command line as part of its properties, you can think of a shortcut as performing the same function as a one-line batch file. Typically, users simply create shortcuts that point to some program, and leave it at that. However, if the program supports any command line options, you can specify them on the shortcut's command-line as well. For example, when you run the Direct Cable Connection (*directcc*), you are prompted to specify whether the computer act as the host or the guest. Embedding the command line:

```
directcc connect
```

in the shortcut on the guest computer avoids the prompt and simplifies life all around.

As described in Chapter 4, *The Control Panel*, knowing the command line to complex dialogs such as control panel applets lets you build shortcuts directly to a specific tab in a dialog. A shortcut or batch file containing the following command line could replace the following five mouse clicks: Start → Settings → Control Panel → System → Device Manager:

```
control sysdm.cpl ,1
```

But sometimes a single line of stored commands is not enough. Let's say you occasionally play *mshearts* with a friend, or occasionally use *winchat*. *mshearts* and *winchat* both require *netdde* to be running before you can use them over the network. The conventional advice is to put *netdde* in your *Windows**Start Menu**Programs**StartUp* folder, so it is always running. But if you use these programs only occasionally, why have *netdde* running all the time? It might be better to create a batch file that always starts up *netdde* before running *mshearts* or *winchat*:

```
rem mychat.bat
netdde
winchat
```

One problem with a batch file like this is that it creates a DOS window, which by default will remain open even when the batch file completes. To make this window go away automatically, go to Properties → Program for the batch file, and click "Close on exit." (You probably also should select "Run minimized" from the drop-down box.)

Or suppose you are a big fan of the playlist feature of *cdplayer.exe*, so much so that you can't keep all of your playlists in *cdplayer.ini* due to its size limitations (see *cdplayer* in Chapter 5). You might want to organize your playlists into a series of *.ini* files, one per artist, for instance, or by music category. Then you might well want to run *cdplayer* from a batch file like this one, called *play.bat*:

```
@echo off
rem syntax:  play playlist, where playlist is rock,
rem country or classical
rem save the default cdplayer.ini file
rename \windows\cdplayer.ini \windows\cdplayer.save
rem replace cdplayer.ini with a custom playlist before
rem starting cdplayer
copy \myplaylists\%1.ini \windows\cdplayer.ini
start /w cdplayer.exe
rem save the ini file that's just been used, in case there
rem are changes
copy \windows\cdplayer.ini \myplaylists\%1.ini
rem restore the original cdplayer.ini
rename \windows\cdplayer.save \windows\cdplayer.ini
```

Batch files are particularly powerful for creating and moving files and directories. For example, when starting a new project, an author might always want to create the same directory structure and put some basic files into each directory. Here's the kind of batch file you might create for this kind of housekeeping:

```
@echo off
if "%1"=="" goto skip
mkdir %1\figures
mkdir %1\sources
mkdir %1\old
copy c:\templates\mainfile.doc %1
copy c:\templates\other.doc %1
copy c:\templates\image.tif %1\figures
:skip
```

Create a new folder in the Explorer, and then drag and drop it onto this batch file (or add the batch file to the SendTo menu). Subdirectories called *figures, sources,* and *old* will be created inside, and three template files are copied into the new directories. Voilà—you just saved about a minute of clicking and dragging.

The construct:

```
if "%1"=="" go to skip
```

is a useful error-checking technique. You can use an *if* statement to test for null arguments (or other similar conditions), and if encountered, either issue an error message or simply quit. (This example will exit after jumping to the `:skip` label, since there are no further commands to be executed.)

You can also use batch files to work around some of the limits of Windows 95. For example, the Explorer doesn't let you print out a hardcopy listing of the contents of a folder. You can do this simply from the command line by typing:

```
dir > lpt1:
```

but the following batch file does even better—you can drag and drop a folder icon onto it to get a printed directory listing:

```
@echo off
if "%1"=="" goto skip
dir %1 > lpt1:
:skip
```

You could, of course, replace lpt1: with, say, c:\windows\desktop\dir-list.txt to output the directory listing to a text file instead, or construct a loop so that the batch file could repeat itself automatically for multiple directory name arguments.

Alphabetical Reference

The following list contains descriptions of the commands that are used principally within batch files.

---

call
Internal to: *Windows\command.com*

Invoke a batch file from within another batch file, returning control to the original when the called file completes.

Syntax

    call [filename] [arguments]

Description

The *call* command lets you invoke a batch file from within another batch file and wait for it to finish before continuing. Once the called file has completed its execution, the control returns to the original batch file. *call* will also recognize executable programs, which can be useful if you've designed a batch file to launch a program (e.g., *regedit.exe*) and then continue with other DOS commands in the batch file.

call options can be passed on to the secondary batch file either as variables generated by the primary file or as replaceable variables holding data entered on the command line.

WARNING

If you run another batch file from within a batch file without using *call*, the control will never be returned to the parent batch file when the child process is finished. The whole thing just quits. Of course, this fact can be put to use; for example, it helps to avoid recursion when a batch file calls itself.

The options for *call* are as follows:

arguments   Specifies any command-line information required by the batch program, such as replaceable parameters.

filename   This can be a batch name or the name of any other executable program.

Examples

The following *sample.bat* calls *sample2.bat,* and then returns the control back to itself:

```
@echo off
rem this is a call test
call sample2.bat
cls
cd \windows\desktop
```

sample2.bat:

```
command /c
cd "c:\win95 nutshell\current\chap06"
start chap06.doc
cls
```

sample.bat launches *sample2.bat,* which opens *chap06.doc* after navigating to the proper directory. *sample2.bat* then returns to *sample.bat,* the DOS screen is cleared, and the directory is changed to *Windows\Desktop.*

The batch file *loop.bat* runs itself again and again, using *call* to start whatever external program and arguments are passed to it. (The following implementation is limited to a program name plus no more than eight arguments.)

```
@echo off
if (%1) == () goto usage
%1 %2 %3 %4 %5 %6 %7 %8 %9
loop call %1 %2 %3 %4 %5 %6 %7 %8 %9
:usage
echo Usage: loop [program] [args...]
```

---

choice

Ask for user input in a batch program.

Syntax

choice [options]

Description

choice provides a prompt string that waits for the user to choose one of a set of choices. The exit value of the command is used to decide which response was chosen.

If no alternate choices are specified with /c, the default choices are Y and N, and the prompt to the user will be "[Y,N]?". You can specify only single characters as choices; if you use /n to suppress the normal choice prompt and supply a longer prompt, you should be careful to supply a corresponding list of choices using /c.

choice recognizes the following options:

/c[:]choices	Specify allowable keys (default is YN).
/n	Do not display choices and ? at end of prompt string.

/s	Treat choice keys as case-sensitive. By default they are not.
/t[:]c,nn	Default choice to c after *nn* seconds (c must exist; *nn* must be in the range 0 to 99).
text	Prompt string to display.

Examples

If you'd like to have the option of running *defrag* on drive *C:* before logging in to Windows, the following lines could be added to *autoexec.bat*:

```
@echo off
choice run defrag /ty,10
if errorlevel 2 goto skipdefrag
defrag c:
:skipdefrag
```

If you press **N** within 10 seconds, *defrag* won't be launched and *choice* returns an errorlevel value of 2. If you don't press **N** within 10 seconds, or if you choose **Y**, *defrag* runs on drive *C*.

The following errorlevel values are used by the *choice* command:

0	*choice* was terminated by Ctrl-C before a choice was entered.
1	The key corresponding to the first choice was pressed.
n	The key corresponding to the *n*th choice was pressed.
255	An error occurred.

See Also

errorlevel, goto, if

---

echo   Internal to: \ *Windows\command.com*

Displays messages, turns command echoing on or off, or forces a blank line in a batch file.

Syntax

echo [on | off] [message]

Description

By default, each command in a batch file is echoed to the screen as it is executed. You can turn this behavior on and off with *echo*.

To display the current *echo* setting, type echo without any options. The following options can be used with *echo*:

| on | off | Toggles the *echo* command on or off |
| message | Type the message you'd like displayed |

To turn *echo* off without displaying the *echo* command itself, use *@echo off*. The @ symbol in front of any command in a batch file prevents the line from being displayed.

To force a blank line, use one of the following:

```
echo.
echo,
echo"
```

Note the absence of the space between the *echo* command and the punctuation. (You can also use a colon, semicolon, square brackets, backslash, or forward slash.)

Examples

Announce the success or failure of a condition tested in a batch file:

```
if exist *.rpt echo The report has arrived.
```

It's a good idea to give the user usage or error information in the event that they don't supply proper arguments to a batch file. You can do that as follows:

```
@echo off
if (%1) == () goto usage
. . .
:usage
echo You must supply a filename.
```

One handy use of *echo* is to answer **y** to a confirmation prompt such as the one *del* issues when asked to delete all the files in a directory. For example, if you wanted to clear out the contents of the *\temp* directory every time you booted your machine, you could use the following command in *autoexec.bat*:

```
echo y | del c:\temp\*.*
```

or even:

```
echo y | if exists c:\temp\*.* del c:\temp\*.*
```

This construct works because the pipe character takes the output of the first command and inserts it as the input to the second.

errorlevel

Although not a command, *errorlevel* is used with the *if* statement, since most batch files make decisions based on the errorlevel value returned from a program.

Description

When a program exits, it returns an integer value to the operating system which can be used by *errorlevel*. In a batch line, *errorlevel* is followed by a return code (number). If the return code from the application is greater than or equal to this number, then the condition is considered true and any action in the *if* statement is then taken (which is why you want to start with the highest number first when using *errorlevel* in a batch file). Normally, a return code of 0 indicates that the command was successful, with various errors receiving higher error codes. It's up to the program to define what error codes it uses.

If you're curious about the errorlevel number in any of the external DOS commands, just run *command.com* with the /z option. The *errorlevel* number will be displayed as follows once the command has been executed:

```
Return code (ERRORLEVEL): n
```

n is the errorlevel returned by the last executed external command.

Examples

The following batch file illustrates the use of *errorlevel* with the *find* command:

```
@echo off
find /i "98" c:\windows\desktop\win95.txt
if errorlevel 2 goto error
if errorlevel 1 goto nomatch
if errorlevel 0 goto match

:match
echo a match was found!
goto end

:nomatch
echo sorry, but a match wasn't found.
goto end

:error
echo sorry, but an error has occurred!

:end
pause
```

In this example, find searches for 98 in *win95.txt*, then, depending on the return code, displays the proper message before pausing at the end.

While the errorlevel varies from program to program, you don't necessarily have to use all the information provided. It's often enough simply to test:

```
if errorlevel 1   ...
```

after running a program (like *scandisk*), since if the program finds any errors, it will return a nonzero errorlevel.

See Also

choice, find, goto, if

---

for

Internal to: \ *Windows\command.com*

Run a specified command for each instance in a list.

Syntax

for %%variable in (set) do command [options] %%variable

in and *do* are not options, but a required part of the *for* command. If you omit either of these keywords, MS-DOS displays an error message.

Description

Use this command to create loops in a batch file. A *for* loop is a programming construct that allows you to repeat a command for a list of items (such as filenames). You specify an arbitrary variable name and a set of values to be iterated through. For each value in the set, the command is repeated.

The syntax for using for in a batch file is different from that used on the command line. You must specify %%*variable* instead of %*variable*.

When redirecting the output of a *for* loop to a file, you must use >> (append to a file) rather than >, or you will save only the last iteration of the loop. The values in the set are enclosed in parentheses, and should be separated by spaces. Wildcards can be used to supply a list of filenames.

Examples

Create a set of numbered directories (such as for chapters in a book):

```
@echo off
C:\>for %%n in (1 2 3 4 5) do md ch0%%n
```

Since the *for* loop works only for a single command (and it doesn't work well with *goto*), you need to do something like this to run multiple commands with *for*1 t:

```
for %%f in (1 2 3 4 5) do call loop1.bat %%f
echo done!
```

loop1.bat might then look like this:

```
if not exist file%1 goto skip
copy file%1 c:\backup
copy file%1 lpt1
del file%1
:skip
```

Or you could get really clever, and put it all in one batch file, creating the loop file dynamically with *echo* and then removing it before you exit:

```
echo if not exist file%1 goto skip > loop1.bat
echo copy file%1 c:\backup >> loop1.bat
echo copy file%1 lpt1 >> loop1.bat
echo del file%1 >> loop1.bat
echo skip >>loop1.bat
for %%f in (1 2 3 4 5) do call loop1.bat %%f
del loop1.bat
echo done!
```

---

goto   Internal to: \ *Windows\command.com*

Branches to a labeled line in a batch program.

Syntax

```
goto label
...
:label
```

Description

goto is typically used with an *if* or *choice* statement to branch to a particular part of a batch file depending on the result of the condition or the user response.

A label marks the beginning of a subroutine, letting the batch file know where to begin processing after it encounters a *goto* command.

The label value you specify on the *goto* command line must match a label in the batch program. The second instance of the label (at the location where execution should resume after the *goto* is executed) must be preceded with a colon.

The *goto* command uses only the first eight characters of a label. Therefore, the labels mylabel01 and mylabel02 are both equivalent to mylabel0. The label cannot include separators such as spaces, semicolons, or equal signs.

If your batch program doesn't contain the label you specify, the batch program stops and MS-DOS displays the message "Label not found."

Examples

Format a floppy disk in drive *A:* and display an appropriate message of success or failure:

```
@echo off
format a:
if not errorlevel 1 goto end
echo an error occurred during formatting.
:end
echo successfully formatted the disk in drive a.
```

See Also

if

---

if

Performs conditional branching in batch programs.

Syntax

if [not] errorlevel number command
if [not] string1==string2 command
if [not] exist filename command

Description

Conditional branching lets your batch file test to see whether a condition is true, and if it is, forces the batch file to execute a subroutine. By using the [not] option, you can force a batch file to execute a subroutine if the condition is false.

The following options can be used with the *if* command in batch files:

command	Specifies the command to be carried out if the condition is met.
not	Specifies that Windows should carry out the command only if the condition is false.

errorlevel *number*

>Specifies a true condition if the last program run returned an exit code equal to or greater than the number specified. See *errorlevel* earlier in this chapter.

exist *filename* Specifies a true condition if the specified filename exists. If the condition is true, the specified command is executed. The *not exist* condition is useful if you'd like a specified command to execute if the condition is false.

string1==string2

>Specifies a true condition if the specified text strings match. To test for an empty string (for example, the presence or absence of a command-line argument), use quotes or parentheses:
>
>```
>if "%1"==""
>```
>
>or:
>
>```
>if (%1)==()
>```

Examples

The following batch file checks the current directory for the file *form.bat*. If it finds it, the message "It exists!" is displayed, and if it doesn't, "The file doesn't exist" is displayed:

```
@echo off
if exist form.bat goto jump
goto stop

:jump
echo It exists!
pause
goto end

:stop
echo The file doesn't exist.
pause
goto end

:end
cls
```

See Also

goto

---

pause   Internal to: \ *Windows*\ *command.com*

Suspends processing of a batch program and displays a prompt in the DOS box to press any key to continue.

Description

The *pause* command causes the execution of the batch program to stop and display a message, prompting the user to press a key to continue. This allows users sufficient time to read menu options or displayed text.

The message "Press any key to continue..." is automatically displayed whenever the *pause* command is used. The comment line will not appear if *echo* is off.

At a *pause* point, a batch file may be terminated by pressing `Ctrl-C` or `Ctrl-Break`, at which point MS-DOS displays the following message:

```
Terminate batch job (Y/N)?
```

If you press `Y` (for yes) in response to this message, the batch program ends and control returns to the operating system. Therefore, you can insert the *pause* command before a section of the batch file you may not want to process.

Examples

Prompt the user to change disks in one of the drives in a batch program:

```
echo Insert next disk in drive A
pause
```

When this *pause* command is executed, the following message will appear.

```
Insert next disk in drive A
Press any key to continue ...
```

Something like this is also common:

```
Echo Press Ctrl-C to cancel, or
pause
```

---

rem

Internal to: \ Windows\command.com

Insert comments ("remarks") into a batch file. Lines beginning with *rem* will be ignored when the batch file is executed.

Syntax

```
rem [comment]
```

The comment can say whatever you want. It's a good idea to put comments in your batch file so that others (including you in the distant future) can figure out how it works.

The *rem* command is also useful for disabling commands. Just add *rem* right before the command to disable it.

Unlike other DOS commands, *rem* also works in the *config.sys* file.

Examples

A batch file that uses remarks for explanations and to disable a command:

```
@echo off
rem This batch program may one day change a directory.
rem But not until I remove the rem before the cd command.
rem It is called mydir.bat.
rem cd \batch\ch2
```

See Also

echo

---

shift

Deletes the variable that holds the first command-line argument (%1) and shifts over the remaining arguments. %2 becomes %1, %3 becomes %2, and so on. This is particularly useful when processing loops.

Examples

In the following batch file, *shift* is used so that each of the (unknown number of) command-line options becomes option #1 (%1) for processing within the loop:

```
@echo off
rem MTYPE.BAT
rem example: mtype foo.txt bar.txt *.bat
:loop
if (%1)==() goto done
for %%f in (%1) do type %%f
shift
pause
goto loop
:done
echo.
```

The *if* statement tests for an empty argument, and if it finds it, ends the loop. Otherwise, it repeats as many times as needed to use up all the arguments.

WARNING

If you use a wildcard on the command line, it is passed to the batch file as a single argument (e.g., *.*), which can be used as is. It isn't expanded first, as by Unix shells, so you can't pick it apart in the script and use each matched filename separately.

The Batch Language

CHAPTER 7

Dial-Up Networking

In the not-too-distant past, there was a major gulf between local area networks running high-speed networking protocols and dial-up "communications" applications for connecting to bulletin boards, online services, and other remote computers. The Internet changed all that, creating a common set of networking protocols for both dial-up and direct network connections. In Windows 95, Dial-Up Networking (DUN) allows you to dial in to an Internet service provider (or to a Windows NT or NetWare server), and, once the connection is made, to use the same kind of networking facilities as you can use on a local area network.

Many Microsoft networking applications, including Network Neighborhood, Internet Explorer, and the Microsoft Network, as well as many third-party networking applications, are able to work over Dial-Up Networking, although some are more tightly integrated than others. (For example, Internet applications will automatically start up a Dial-Up Networking connection if you start the application while you are not connected, while Network Neighborhood will work over an established connection but won't initiate one.)

Once you understand its architecture, configuring Dial-Up Networking is fairly clear-cut. But if you don't know how it hangs together underneath, the user interface can be quite confusing. Much as in the old Adventure game, "you're in a maze of twisty little passages, all alike." Figure 7-1 shows how all of the dialogs involved in configuring Dial-Up Networking fit together.

DUN stores information about how to connect into two separate "dialog trees":

1. Information about the site or service you're dialing *to*, such as an Internet service provider. This is referred to as a *connection* (or sometimes, a bit tongue-in-cheek, as a *connectoid*).

2. Information about the location you're dialing *from*, such as whether you need to dial 9 for an outside line, whether you need to use a calling card, and so on. This is referred to as a *location*. Laptop users in particular might need to define multiple locations.

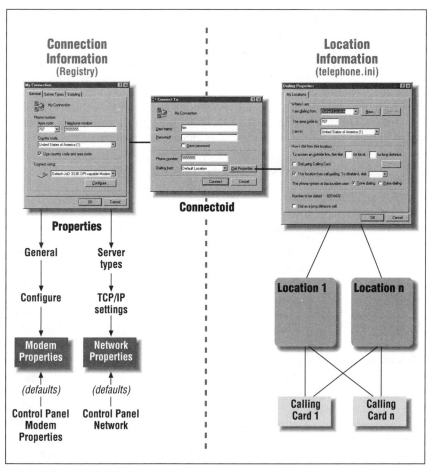

Figure 7-1: How Dial-Up Networking hangs together

This division seems fairly logical. Unfortunately, though, the two halves are not well integrated, leading to an unnecessarily confusing user interface. Connection information is stored in the Registry, but for backward compatibility with older applications, location information is stored in the file *Windows\telephon.ini*. A completely different set of dialogs is used to modify each one, and information that is set in the connection (such as the phone number) is presented as a read-only field in the location. So you can find yourself scratching your head and saying "why can't I change that here?"

What makes things even more complicated is that other dial-up applications that are not Internet-related and don't use Dial-Up Networking, such as HyperTerm, make their own connection-like objects, and even use the common pool of locations stored in *telephon.ini*. So once again, you may be faced with an interface that seems like it ought to be part of the same beast, but somehow isn't.

A brief aside about Microsoft's terminology: Strictly speaking, the facilities for establishing networking links with remote computers are referred to as Remote Network Access, or RNA. You'll see evidence of this in the names of the underlying DLLs used to provide the networking services—such as *rnasetup.dll* or *rnaui.dll*. On NT servers, the related facilities are referred to as Remote Access Services, or RAS. Dial-Up Networking is just the most visible RNA application, and there are some differences in the way that applications use RNA functionality. But we're not purists, and we think that referring to the system as Dial-Up Networking is more intuitive.

In the discussion that follows, we use Dial-Up Networking as the reference implementation of RNA, since it seems to use the most common features. Extrapolate from there if you are using an application that uses the facility slightly differently. Furthermore, the primary focus is on connecting to the Internet, rather than directly to a Windows NT or NetWare network. For more information, see "Server Types and Protocols" later in this chapter.

To top it off, many of the connection properties use exactly the same dialogs as Control Panel → Modem and Control Panel → Network, leading many a novice to try to change settings there. But these control panels set only the default values that will be used for new connections, and don't propagate to existing connections. You must edit a connection's properties to make any changes.

Here are some survival tips for navigating the maze:

1. Find the Dial-Up Networking folder. Unlike most other important objects, it isn't found on the Desktop or the Start menu. You have to go to My Computer. It should be there on the top level along with your disk drives, Control Panel and Printers folders. The reason probably is that you're expected to click on one of the Desktop icons such as Internet or Microsoft Network, and just use the facilities from there. But that's like one of those cattle chutes, herding you towards using Microsoft as your Internet service provider. We suggest you go directly to the Dial-Up Networking folder instead. (If it's not there, go to Control Panel → Add/Remove Programs → Windows Setup → Communications → Details and make sure it's installed. You might also want to go to Control Panel → Network, and see if you have TCP/IP bound to a Dial-Up Adapter. See Chapter 4, *The Control Panel*, for details.)

2. To create a new connection, use Dial-Up Networking → Make New Connection. If you've got only one modem installed, name the connection, enter the phone number to be dialed, and you're done. The wizard will create an icon in the Dial-Up Networking folder with the name you gave to the connection.

3. You can make a connection explicitly or implicitly. To use a connection explicitly, double-click on its icon. To use a connection implicitly, just start up any Internet-aware application. Applications such as Internet Explorer, which are designed to dial up automatically if they are not already connected to a network, will use the last active connection. Double-clicking these gives you a Connecting To dialog box.

---

4. To change any of the following information, you must use a connection's properties, including:

   – The area code and phone number to be dialed. (You can change the phone number on the Connecting To dialog, but the change won't be remembered.)

   – The country code, if any.

   – The modem to be used, and any specific modem settings.

   – The type of server you're dialing in to (PPP, NetWare, Windows for Workgroups, Unix, and so on). These are really just "aliases" for common settings required by this type of host.

   – Network properties such as IP addresses and DNS servers.

   – The script, if any, needed to dial in.

5. To change any of the following information, you must use the Dial Properties button on the connection, which brings up a dialog box with the tab My Locations:

   – The location you're dialing from, including a new location

   – A prefix needed to reach an outside line

   – Whether to use a calling card

   – The code to disable call waiting, if necessary

   – Tone or pulse dialing

   – Whether this is a local or long distance call (i.e., whether the country code and area code should be used)

6. To change options that apply to all connections, use Connection menu → Settings on the Dial-Up Networking folder:

   – Whether to show the Connect To dialog box, or just dial immediately (OSR2 only)

   – Whether to show a confirmation dialog after connecting

   – Whether to put a connection icon in the system tray (OSR2 only)

   – Whether to redial automatically after a failed connection

   – Whether applications that require network access should prompt to use Dial-Up Networking

The following section provides an alphabetical reference to some of the major elements you may want to configure. Because the dialogs aren't always logically organized, we work backwards from the element you want to configure, rather than following the structure of the dialogs.

The alphabetical reference includes the following sections:

Busy Signals
Call Waiting
Calling Cards
Dial Tone
Disconnecting

ISDN
Login Scripts
Long Distance (including dialing to and from foreign countries)
Modem and Port Settings
Passwords
Phone Numbers
Server Types and Protocols
Status Information
TCP/IP Settings (IP and DNS addresses)

Unlike in other parts of the book, multiple paths given in the heading of a section don't refer to alternate ways to reach the same point, but the path to multiple settings relevant to the topic.

Busy Signals

Dial-Up Networking → Connections menu → Settings → Redial

If you want the modem to redial automatically if a connection wasn't completed (e.g., upon receiving a busy signal), use the Connections menu on the Dial-Up Networking folder. Settings → Redial lets you set how many times to retry, and how long to wait between tries, in minutes and/or seconds.

This setting applies to all Dial-Up Networking connections; you can't specify it on a per-connection basis.

Call Waiting

connection → Dial Properties → This location has call waiting

If a location has call waiting (a telephone company feature that sounds a tone if there is another incoming call while you are on the phone), you should disable it. Some modems will drop the line in response to a call waiting signal. Even for those that are robust enough to ignore it, it is polite to disable call waiting, since if it is enabled, the calling party will hear the phone ring but no answer, while if it is disabled, the line will give a busy signal.

Check "This location has call waiting," and enter the code to disable call waiting. The most typical code in the U.S. is *70, but some regions use codes such as 70# and 1170. Any code you enter will be remembered in the drop-down list. Check with your local phone company if none of these codes works.

Call waiting is disabled only for the duration of the present call, and is re-enabled when you close the connection.

Calling Cards

connection → Dial Properties → Dial using calling card

If you are dialing from a location where you need to use a calling card to pay for the call, check "Dial using calling card," and select the appropriate card from the drop-down list. Enter your calling card number.

Note that a number of the defined calling cards are "pseudo cards" used to access an alternate long distance carrier. In these cases, no card number can be specified.

If your calling card is not in the drop-down list, you must create a new card. Click New, and give the card a name. The field for entering a card number will be blank. Click Advanced to define the dialing sequence used with the card (see Figure 7-2).

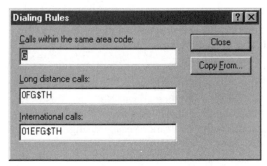

Figure 7-2: Advanced dialog box: Dialing Rules

In each of the three fields, you must define the sequence with which any dialing prefixes, area codes and phone numbers, and calling cards will be dialed. These Dialing Rules are defined using the arcane syntax shown in Table 7-1.

Table 7-1: Dialing Rules

Symbol	Description
0–9	Digit(s) to be dialed (e.g., 0 for Operator, 9 for an outside line, or perhaps a special phone company number you have to dial to use their credit card)
#	Touch tone pound sign key
*	Touch tone star key
!	Flash (briefly go on hook)
,	Wait two seconds
@	Wait for a ring, followed by five seconds of silence
$	Wait for the calling card tone (bong in the U.S.)
?	Prompt for user input
E	Country code
F	Area code
G	Local Phone number
H	Calling card number
P	Dial using pulse dialing
T	Dial using touch tone
W	Wait for a second dial tone

For example, the entry for Calling card via 0 (the most common sequence in the U.S.) defines the following three dialing rules:

- Calls within the same area code: G

  Simply issue the phone number. This is a local call, so no calling card is needed.

- Long distance calls: 0FG$TH

  0 for operator, then the area code, then the phone number. Wait for the bong, then send the calling card number. Use touch tone dialing for the credit card number even if the local phone system uses pulse dialing (see "Notes" below).

- International calls: 01EFG$TH

  0 for operator, then 1, then as for long distance above. Note that this is actually incorrect, since in the U.S., you typically need to type 011 to initiate an international call, not 01. Unfortunately, you cannot easily change the dialing rules for an existing credit card. See "Notes" below.

Notes

- Access numbers for many long-distance providers are defined as if they were credit cards. You can think of a long-distance provider's access number as a kind of calling card that just doesn't happen to require you to enter a card number. If your provider's access number is not already defined, you may want to add it as a new card type.

- Rather than constructing a new credit card entry from scratch, it's often easier to use the Copy From button to copy in the entry from one of the existing credit card definitions. This may also be the safest course if a predefined credit card entry is incorrect, since if a credit card's dialing rules are grayed out, this means that a flag has been set in *telephon.ini* to make them read only. You must edit *telephon.ini* directly in order to change this flag. (More on that below.)

- Some modems don't know how to wait for the bong tone, and foreign phone systems may not even use it. In such cases, the modem will send the calling card number right away. If this appears to be the case, try using @ instead, or several commas in a row, to make the modem wait. Experiment till you get the timing right.

- The length of time to wait for the credit card bong tone is set not in Dialing Properties, along with everything else about the Location, but perplexingly, in the connection Properties, at connection → Properties → Configure → Options → Wait for credit card tone.

- If a credit card type doesn't appear to work correctly, try placing a credit card call manually, and take note of the exact sequence of steps. Check this against the dialing rules to make sure they are correct. If they are not correct, create a new credit card and use Copy From to copy the dialing rules from the incorrect definition; then modify the rules until they are right.

Alternatively, edit the entry for that credit card in *Windows\telephon.ini.* The format of a card entry is as follows:

> card_index=card_id, "card name", "encrypted card number", "local calling rules", "long distance calling rules", "international calling rules", edit_flag

Quotes should be typed as shown. If a string argument is empty, use the null string ("").

For example, the offending "Calling Card via 0" entry looks like this:

> Card21=12,"Calling Card via
> 0","21217916228312","G","0FG$TH","01EFG$TH",0

The fields are as follows:

card_index=card_id
> Each new card is given a unique *card_index* number in sequence, using the next available index. The *card_id* is usually the same as the *card_index* (e.g., Card 15=15), but may be different, as in the previous example.

card name
> A quoted string containing the name that will appear in any drop-down list of available credit cards.

encrypted card number
> A quoted string containing the card number, if any, that has been entered, encrypted to protect it from view. If editing *telephon.ini* directly, do not enter anything in this field.

local calling rules
long-distance calling rules
international calling rules
> Quoted strings containing the Dialing Rules as defined previously.

edit_flag
> Whether this credit card entry is visible and/or editable. There are four values:

> *0*   visible and editable in application

> *1*   visible, but read-only

> *2*   hidden (not shown) but editable

> *3*   hidden (i.e., will not appear in the list)

0 is the value that will be given to any new card definitions you create. Theoretically, a value of 2 should produce an editable calling rule field that does not show the existing calling rules, but in practice, it seems to have the same effect as a value of 0. 1 grays out the dialing rules so they can't be edited. This is the default for all of the built-in card definitions. 3 causes the card entry not to be displayed at all.

Dial Tone

> *connection* → Properties → General → Configure → Connection → Wait for dial tone before dialing
> *connection* → Properties → General → Configure → Options → Operator assisted or manual dial
> *connection* → Dial Properties → To access an outside line...

With a telephone, you don't think about dial tone. You pick up the phone, and it's either there or it isn't. If you're in Germany, the dial tone sounds a bit different, but you're smart enough to figure that out. Many modems are not.

Dial-Up Networking gives you several settings for dealing with dial-tone problems.

WARNING

Given what we've said about the structure of Dial-Up Networking, you'd think that these settings would be in a location's Dialing Properties. After all, these settings all have to do with characteristics of the location you're dialing from. But as is often the case, things aren't where you expect them. Two of the three dial-control settings described here are in the properties for an individual connection.

Wait for dial tone before dialing

If you aren't dealing with a standard US dial tone, you may need to uncheck *connection* → Properties → General → Configure → Connection → Wait for dial tone before dialing. The modem will then dial whether or not it hears what it thinks of as a dial tone.

Operator assisted or manual dial

If you need to go through a switchboard or have a telephone that doesn't respond properly to auto-dialing, you can check *connection* → Properties → General → Configure → Options → Operator assisted or manual dial. When you initiate the connection, the dialog box shown in Figure 7-3 will appear.

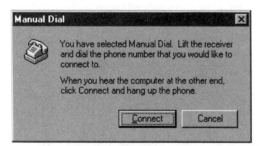

Figure 7-3: Manual dialing

In theory, just follow the instructions in the dialog, and this should work fine. In practice, the remote modem may be finicky, and if the timing isn't just right, the receiving modem will give up on you, cycling through non-matching modem tones, before your modem has a chance to go online.

To access an outside line...

In a hotel or corporate location, you may have two levels of dial tone. The first is the dial tone for the PBX; the second is the dial tone for the telephone network. Enter the number you need to dial to get an outside line in connection → Dial Properties → To access an outside line... In the U.S., 8 or 9 are the most common numbers to dial for an outside line.

There are a couple of "gotchas":

- If a second dial tone doesn't come quickly enough, your modem may dial before the phone system is ready. You can enter a comma after the outside line prefix to wait for two seconds. In fact, even though these look like one- or two-character fields, you can type in up to 28 digits here and the field will scroll.

- If you want to get a second dial tone from a specific long-distance company, it's better not to type the full access number in here. Instead, define the long distance company number as a calling card (see "Calling Cards") and check Dial using Calling Card. (In fact, many long-distance providers have access numbers already defined there.)

Disconnecting

Control Panel → Internet → *connection* → Disconnect if idle

Internet Explorer allows you to set a disconnect if you're idle for more than a set amount of time. Unfortunately, it doesn't recognize activity in other programs, so unless you're actually working in IE, you may be disconnected when you don't expect it. If this turns out to be a problem, turn off auto-disconnect in IE.

ISDN

ISDN, or "Integrated Services Digital Network," is a special type of digital service offered by your phone company. It requires an ISDN adapter and the service, and can offer speeds up to 128 kbps (more with compression).

Any ISDN adapter you install should come with the appropriate drivers and software. Microsoft offers the ISDN accelerator pack, but this should only be used if your ISDN adapter specifically requires it.

When setting up an ISDN adapter, it helps to know that external adapters (connected to your PC's serial port) are treated like standard external modems, while internal ISDN adapters are treated like network cards. The exception is external ISDN routers, which offer the speed of internal adapters (serial ports are limited to 112 kbps) with the flexibility and convenience of external adapters. The drivers and the DUN setup procedure will depend on which type of adapter you have—consult the installation instructions that accompany your adapter for more information. Any modem adapter should provide straightforward instructions for using it with Windows 95's Dial-Up Networking service.

See Also

Download the ISDN Accelerator Pack from:

http://www.microsoft.com/windows95/info/isdn4w95.htm

Login Scripts

connection → Properties → Scripting

If you are using PPP to connect to an ISP, or using Netware Connect or Windows for Workgroups, account authentication (login name and password) will be handled transparently. PPP uses either PAP (Password Authentication Protocol) or CHAP (Challenge Authentication Protocol), two authentication methods built in to PPP. However, if you are using SLIP to connect to a Unix host, or via older terminal servers, you may need to build an explicit login script and link it to your connection.

In older versions of Dial-Up Networking (before OSR2), you needed a special scripting tool (*dscrpt.exe*) to attach a script to a connection. This tool can be downloaded from *http://www.microsoft.com*, or loaded from the Win95 CD-ROM in *Admin\AppTools\Dscript*. It also is installed with Microsoft Plus!. *dscrpt* lists all of your dial-up connections: select a connection, and type a pathname for a script file. The filename you specify need not exist yet. An option allows you to step through the script one command at a time for debugging purposes.

In OSR2, scripting is built-in. *connection* → Properties → Scripting lets you enter the name of the script associated with the connection, or browse to locate a script file. Documentation on the scripting language can be found in *Windows* *script.doc*.

Script files have the extension *.scp*; they describe the various prompts and responses of the login process using a simple language.

For example, the following script (which is very similar to the *generic.scp* script that comes with the scripting package) waits for a login prompt (a string ending with the characters "ogin:"), and then sends the username from the Connecting To dialog box. It sends an explicit carriage return (<cr>), waits for a prompt ending with the characters "ssword:", sends the password from the Connecting To dialog box, followed by another carriage return:

```
proc main
waitfor "ogin:"
transmit $USERID
transmit <cr>
waitfor "ssword:"
transmit $PASSWORD
transmit <cr>
endproc
```

It's typical to search for only the end of a string ("ogin" rather than "Login" or "ssword" rather than "Password") because that insulates you from variations in the case of the prompt's first letter. This is particularly important when debugging new scripts—small differences in the prompt and the string you wait for can cause the script to keep waiting until the login attempt finally times out.

The best way to build a script is to log in manually by setting *connection* → Properties → Options → Bring up terminal window after dialing, and then firing up the connection. Write down exactly what prompts appear and how you respond, then build that into the script. If you can't get a script to work reliably, you can even leave this option set and do the login manually every time you connect. Just hit **F7** or click Continue after the login process is complete.

Some tips and gotchas:

- PCs and Unix systems use different conventions for ending lines. PCs use a carriage return and a line feed; Unix systems use only a line feed. You may need to specify an explicit return or line feed to proceed to the next step in the script.

- You need match only the end of a prompt string. The last five or six characters are sufficient. Keeping the matching string short helps avoid problems such as not matching case or spaces exactly.

- If you're having trouble with your script, check *connection* → Properties → Scripting → Step through script, and watch its progress during the connection, so you can see where it gets hung up.

- Don't confuse the connection's login with any network login required after the PPP session is started. *connection* → Properties → Server Type → Log on to network controls whether your system will log on to the remote Netware or NT network once the lower-level PPP login has taken place. See "Passwords" for additional details.

The Windows 95 Scripting Language

The scripting language is defined below:

Script Structure

All scripts must have a main procedure, delimited by **proc** and **endproc**, that can contain variable declaration and commands:

```
proc main
endproc
```

Variables

Variables are either user- or system-defined names for holding values during the execution of the script. Variable names must begin with a letter or underscore character, but can contain mixed-case letters, numbers, and underscores. Be sure to avoid using any of the scripting language commands as variable names. These are called "reserved words," in that they are unavailable for use within the script.

Variable Data Types

The Windows 95 scripting language variables support the concept of type, which defines the kind of data contained in the variable and operations that can be performed on it (see the following table).

Type	Description
Integer	A negative or positive number
String	One or more characters enclosed in double quotation marks
Boolean	Only possible values are TRUE or FALSE

Variable declaration and assignment

Variables are declared with a type the first time they appear in the script:

```
integer timeout
```

Variables are assigned values using an expression:

```
timeout = 10
```

Variables can also be declared and assigned in the same statement:

```
integer timeout = 10
```

Predefined variables

The system provides several variables as a way for scripts to check for a common condition at run-time. They are read-only, meaning that you can query their value, but not alter it (see following table).

Name	Type	Description
$USERID	String	The username of the account making the connection. This is taken from the User field of the Connect To dialog box.
$PASSWORD	String	The password of the account making the connection. This is taken from the Password field of the Connect To dialog box.
$SUCCESS	Boolean	If a script command succeeds, this is set to TRUE; otherwise, it is FALSE.
$FAILURE	Boolean	If a script command fails, this is set to TRUE; otherwise, it is FALSE.

String literals

String literals (see following table) are used to represent characters or strings that would be difficult to use because they contain nonprinting characters or characters that may be interpreted by the scripting language (instead of taken literally).

String	Name	Description
^ char	Caret translation	Used to represent nonprinting ASCII characters.
<cr>	Carriage return	
<lf>	Line feed	
\"	Double quotation mark	Protects or quotes the double quotation mark from being interpreted as the beginning or end of a string.
\^	Caret	Prevents character following caret from being interpreted as a caret translation.
\<	Less-than sign	
\\	Single backslash	

Expressions

Expressions are operations that yield a result which can be assigned to a variable or evaluated.

Operator	Type	Valid Data Types
–	Unary minus	
!	One's complement	
*/	Multiplicative	Integer
+–	Additive	Integer, string (+ only)
<><=>=	Relational	Integer
== !=	Equality	Integer, string, boolean
and	Logical AND	Boolean
or	Logical OR	Boolean

Comments

The comment character for scripts is the semi-colon. Anything following the comment character is ignored by the script processor.

Keywords

Keywords define the structure of the script and declare variable type:

proc *name*
> Beginning of procedure. Scripts must have at least a main procedure.

endproc
> End of procedure. Has effect of ending script processing.

integer *name [= value]*
> Declare *name* as type integer and optionally assign it a *value*.

string *name [= value]*
> Declare *name* as type string and optionally assign it a *value*.

boolean *name [= value]*
> Declare *name* as type boolean and optionally assign a *value*.

Commands

Commands control the flow of the script or perform some function on a variable.

if/then
> Execute *commands* if *condition* is TRUE.

goto *label*
> Jump to *label* and resume execution. Used to escape out of program flow structures.

delay
> Pause script execution for *seconds* seconds.

waitfor
> A form of a case statement that waits for output from remote device and jumps to labels based on the output or a timeout. The system variable

$SUCCESS is set to TRUE if a label is matched by output and set to FALSE if *time* expires before any output is received.

while/do

Execute *commands* while *condition* is TRUE.

halt

Cease executing script, without terminating terminal window.

Functions

getip *[value]*

Obtain IP address from remote device. If multiple IPs are received, parse output using *position* to index the list.

set port *[options]*

Set communications parameters of terminal window session, overriding current settings for phonebook entry.

set screen keyboard *value*

Either allow or disallow keyboard input in terminal window during script execution.

set ipaddr *value*

Set IP address for current session.

transmit *[string]*

Send *string* to remote device.

Reserved Words

The following reserved words are part of the script language and cannot be used as variable names:

```
and boolean databits delay do endif endproc endwhile even
FALSE getip goto halt if integer ipaddr keyboard mark
matchcase none odd off on or parity port proc raw string then
transmit TRUE until waitfor while
```

Long Distance

connection → Dial Properties → Dial as a long distance call

On the surface, long-distance dialing seems pretty simple. Unless *connection* → Properties → Use country code and area code is unchecked, simply check "Dial as a long distance call" in Dial Properties if you are dialing from outside the local area.

However, there are two areas in which "long distance" is not as simple as it appears:

1. If you want to use a specific long-distance carrier other than the default carrier for the current location, choose Dial Using Calling Card and select the direct dial access number there, if available (see "Calling Cards").

2. The prefix 1, which many Americans take to be a special code meaning "dial as long-distance" is actually the country code for the U.S.

If you want to dial a country whose country code is not in the drop-down list, you can simply embed the country code in the phone number field. However, if you do this, you will also need to embed the prefix to make a long-distance call to another country (e.g., 011 from the U.S.), because otherwise, when you select "Dial as a long-distance call," the dialer will embed whatever country code is currently selected.

Modem and Port Settings

> *connection* → Properties → Configure → Connection

If you need different modem or port settings on a per-connection basis, you can change them here.

See Control Panel → Modem for a discussion of the options. The settings are the same; however, any values set here will override the Control Panel settings for this particular connection.

The modem property sheet accessed here has one additional tab that is not accessible from the Control Panel. The Options tab lets you specify things like operator assisted dialing (see "Dial Tone"), but more importantly, in the context of modem settings, it lets you specify "Bring up terminal window before dialing." Use this option if you want to issue AT commands directly to your modem.

Passwords

> *connection* → Save password

It's convenient to enter your dial up password once and have it remembered. If you find that the Save password checkbox is grayed out, this is because you didn't supply a Windows password when you logged in.

Windows keeps a master password list of all your passwords in the file *<login-name>.pwl*. This list is loaded and consulted only if you supply a login password.

If you failed to supply a password to the initial Windows 95 login prompt, use Start Menu → Shut Down and then select "Close all programs and login as another user." Then, when the initial login box comes up again, log in as yourself, but this time supply a password.

Notes

- Don't confuse the connection's login with any network login required after the PPP session is started. *connection* → Properties → Server Type → Log on to network controls whether your system will log on to the remote NetWare or NT network once the lower-level PPP login has taken place. In theory, if the username and password are the same, you should be logged in automatically, with your login name and password automatically passed to any secondary login screens.

- Some applications (such as Microsoft Exchange or Eudora) do password caching independent of the system password caching. They will not be affected by the login password bug mentioned earlier.

Phone Numbers

Connect To: *connection* → Properties → General → Telephone number

The initial Connect To dialog box lets you enter a new phone number into any connection. This number will replace the stored number and will be dialed by the connection. Unfortunately, though, it will not be remembered. You must go to the connection properties to change the phone number permanently.

What's more, by a bizarre feat of user interface engineering, all area codes you enter in the connection properties will be remembered in a drop-down list, but only one phone number will be remembered. This means that if, for instance, you are calling in to a site with multiple phone numbers, you must create a separate connection for each one (or else remember the alternative phone numbers, and type one in if you want to try a different number).

Server Types and Protocols

connection → Properties → Server Type

What's on the other end of the connection, and what dial-up protocol does it support?

Options include:

PPP: Windows 95, Windows NT 3.51, Internet
> PPP stands for Point-to-Point Protocol, a flexible dial-up protocol that supports TCP/IP over dial-up, as well as NetBEUI and IPX/SPX. PPP is the server type of choice for most Internet connections, as well as for dialing in to NT or Windows 95 dial-up servers.
>
> For an Internet connection, you typically should turn off "Log on to network," "Enable software compression," and "Require encrypted password." Only the TCP/IP protocol should be enabled, and the others should be off.
>
> If the PPP server is actually a frontend to an NT or NetWare-based network, then "Log on to network," "Enable software compression," and "Require encrypted password" should probably be turned on, and any protocols used by your network should be turned on. Many NT networks support all three protocols.
>
> For information on TCP/IP Settings, see the section by that name later in this chapter.

SLIP (Unix Connection)
> Serial Line Internet Protocol is a predecessor to PPP that has fallen out of wide use.
>
> If you connect to a SLIP server, you can use TCP/IP only as a network protocol. NetBEUI and IPX/SPX are not supported over SLIP.

NRN: NetWare Connect
> When connecting to a NetWare server via dial-up networking, you will have a unique IPX address for each session.

Status Information

Dial-Up Networking → Connections menu → Settings

How you are prompted when making a connection and what kind of status indicators are available are controlled by the Connections menu on the Dial-Up Networking folder. You can:

Show an icon on the task bar when connected (OSR2 only)
(Actually, this goes in the System Tray, and shows an image of two PCs with a cable between them.) When the connection goes down, one of the PCs gets an X on it. Clicking on the indicator pops up a connection status dialog box.

Prompt for information before dialing (OSR2 only)
Check this if you want all connections to put up the Connect To dialog box before dialing. Otherwise, the system will just go ahead and dial. Note that if you aren't set up to remember passwords, you will need to see the Connect To dialog box.

Show a confirmation dialog after connected
The confirmation dialog box shows the speed of the connection, the number of bytes transferred, and the length of time you've been connected. When you minimizes the dialog box, it goes onto the Taskbar as a button. Maximize it to see the status information again.

You probably won't want both the confirmation dialog box and the System Tray icon.

TCP/IP Settings (IP and DNS addresses)

connection → Properties → Server Types → TCP/IP Settings

In dealing with most modern ISPs, TCP/IP (see Figure 7-4) settings are trivial, since if the ISP is running DHCP (Dynamic Host Configuration Protocol), IP address, DNS, and WINS fields will be filled in automatically when you make the connection. Simply choose "Server-assigned IP address" and "Server-assigned name server addresses."

However, if you are dialing in to a corporate site or an ISP that does not run DHCP, you may need to enter addresses manually. Ask the ISP or network administrator for the correct addresses to use.

Use IP header compression
This should be checked, unless your ISP tells you otherwise. Try turning it off if you have trouble connecting.

Use default gateway on remote network
This should be checked, unless your ISP tells you otherwise. If not checked, you must specify an explicit gateway address in Control Panel → Network.

Notes

- If the site you're connecting to is running DHCP, it will probably supply both the IP address for your machine and the server addresses for DNS and WINS servers. However, it is also possible that you might connect to a site that supplies a temporary address from a pool, but requires you to enter the server addresses manually.

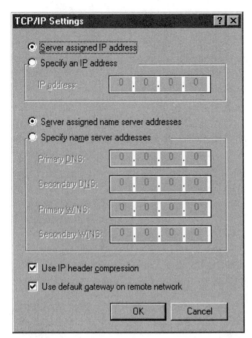

Figure 7-4: TCP/IP settings

- If you connect to multiple providers, all of whom use DHCP, you can specify "Server-assigned IP address" and "Server-assigned name server addresses" in Control Panel → Network, but if addresses are explicitly specified, you will need to enter separate IP addresses for each connection. Because an IP address includes information about the network as well as the specific host, you can't just "reuse" an IP address from one network on another.

PART III

Under the Hood

CHAPTER 8

Inside Windows 95

Windows 95 is big: the Windows 95 CD-ROM comes with over 2,500 files, and once installed on your hard disk, a typical Windows 95 installation contains well over a thousand files, distributed across more than a hundred subdirectories, such as these:

\Windows\System
\Windows\Desktop or *\Windows\Profiles\<your name>\Desktop*
\Windows\Start Menu\Programs\Accessories
\Program Files\Accessories

In fact, Microsoft has even boasted about the size of its operating system. According to one Microsoft employee quoted in the *Chicago Tribune* (August 19, 1995), Windows 95 contains almost 15 million lines of code, whereas "the flight control software for the entire U.S. Space Shuttle program is roughly 500,000 lines of code, or 1/29th the size of Windows 95."

It's difficult even for experienced computer users to wrap their minds around something so large and diffuse. Windows 95 may be easy to start using, but it's difficult to fully grasp; it's easy to come to depend on it, but hard to master. As a result, many (perhaps most) Windows 95 users employ only a small percentage of the system, and are cautious about trying out unfamiliar parts of Windows 95.

One way to take command of Windows 95 is simply to try things out. For example, once you're aware that clicking the right mouse button over the Desktop brings up a menu of options, you can try right-clicking other places to see what happens.

You'll soon find that right-click works all over the place in Windows 95. But not everywhere. Unfortunately, Windows 95's user interface has many inconsistencies: features that work only 90% or perhaps 95% of the places you would expect them to work. Conversely, it sometimes seems as if Windows 95 offers six different ways of doing the same thing.

Why is Windows 95 so inconsistent? One answer is that it isn't, really. Much of the inconsistency attributed to Windows 95 is actually based on a misunderstanding of what you're getting when you buy Windows 95 or (more likely) when it comes preinstalled on your computer.

Windows 95 isn't a single program. It's a large collection of smaller programs. Most of these programs are arguably not part of the operating system itself; they're applications that just happen to be shipped with the operating system. The fact that these applications are not 100% consistent wouldn't surprise anyone who had to go out and buy or download each one separately.

For example, the *telnet* program bundled with Windows 95 surprises users who find that it doesn't support the normal Ctrl-C and Ctrl-V keyboard accelerators for Clipboard copy and paste. But telnet isn't really "part of" Windows 95; it's just an application (*telnet.exe*) that happens to ship with every copy of Windows 95. While this sounds at first like a pedantic quibble, as we'll see, it's really an important distinction for several reasons, one of which is that understanding this distinction can make it easier to grasp and control this large system.

This distinction—between the operating system on the one hand, and the applications that come bundled with it on the other—extends to the Windows 95 user interface (UI) itself. Many of the things that users associate with Windows 95—the Desktop, Start menu, Taskbar, Programs menu, and so on—are really part of an application named *explorer.exe*. It just so happens that this application is the default "shell" that Windows 95 automatically runs when it starts up.

As it turns out, there's a single line in a configuration file called *system.ini* that determines which shell Windows 95 will use. Change this line to specify some program other than *explorer.exe*, and you've got a different user interface. The Desktop and Start button and things like that won't be available. Yet you've still obviously got Windows 95, in that you can start all your Windows programs—including even the one called *explorer.exe*.

In other words, the UI is not Win95. But so what? What does a Windows 95 user care that the Desktop is a feature, not of Windows 95 itself, but of an application called *explorer.exe*? Given that Windows 95 (unless you make that one-line change to *system.ini*) always starts *explorer.exe* as the shell, what difference does it make that the shell is distinct from the operating system? Your machine starts up, eventually the Desktop comes up: so as far as you're concerned the Desktop *is* Windows 95, right?

Well, this surface picture of Windows 95 does let you get started, but when things go wrong, it's hard to understand why. The user who understands that Windows is not one big piece of code, but rather a big collection of many medium-sized pieces of code, is in the same position as the driver who understands that his car is not a single seamless piece of metal, but a container for a set of discrete parts, including the engine, ignition system, and so on, each of which can be viewed somewhat separately. Rather than stare in bafflement at this "integrated product" when it stalls, they feel comfortable with popping open the hood and poking the engine, or perhaps even with buying and installing replacement parts.

This chapter will try to give you a "mental model" of the Windows 95 architecture, so that its behavior seems more predictable. Right now, many users of

Windows 95 probably picture it as something like a beast behind a wall. We're going to try to replace this vague image with something a bit more technical.

Unlike most of the chapters in this book, the discussion here isn't full of detailed documentation or practical tips. The purpose is simply to give you a look under the hood, and to provide some context that might eventually lead to an "aha!" when things don't work the way you expect.

Modularity

For a variety of reasons, Microsoft often refers to Windows 95 as an "integrated product." One reason is that its 1995 consent decree with the U.S. Department of Justice, while forbidding so-called "tying" arrangements, *does* allow Microsoft to build what the company's lawyers call "integrated" products. Though millions of dollars have been spent trying to determine the exact legal meaning of this phrase, from a layman's point of view, it seems to suggest a system whose individual pieces inextricably fit together in some way that they cannot be easily pried apart or replaced with substitute components. Indeed, Microsoft explicitly maintains that "Integration Isn't a Pick-and-Choose Proposition" (see *http://www.microsoft.com/ innovation/pick.htm* for a not-very-convincing explanation).

If you think about it, such an "integrated" product would not be all that desirable, at least from the user's point of view, in that it would violate the general principle behind "plug and play." Modularity is vastly preferable to "integration."

Fortunately, Windows 95 is fairly modular, and Microsoft's claims of integration seem strangely self-deprecating. By portraying Windows 95 as an integrated product from which pieces such as Internet Explorer cannot be easily removed, Microsoft seems to be seriously underselling the flexibility and modularity of its own product.

One reason Windows 95 *must* be modular is that it supports different hardware configurations. Users can run the same Windows 95 product on a wide variety of computers, with a huge variety of video displays, keyboards, mice, fixed and removable disks, networks, multimedia cards, and so on, from a wide variety of vendors. (With the exception of mice, Microsoft is not yet heavily involved in the hardware business.)

As a demonstration of modularity in action, consider that while the Windows 95 CD-ROM comes with about 700 Dynamic Link Libraries (DLLs; see explanation later in this chapter), a typical machine is likely to be running less than 100 of them at a given point in time. Similarly, the Windows 95 CD-ROM comes with over 200 Virtual Device Drivers (VxDs; see explanation later in this chapter), but a typical machine is likely to be running fewer than 100 VxDs.

As noted earlier, the entire Windows 95 product comes with over 2,500 files. But in a typical setup, less than half of these are copied to your hard disk. What then is the point of the other half? The idea, of course, is that each Windows 95 setup will likely contain a somewhat *different* subset of the entire Windows 95 product. It's as if when you bought a car, you were shipped a huge box of parts, with some sort of setup device that semi-automatically turned them into a usable car, based on your local terrain and projected routes. Compared with the sorts of things consumers are used to buying, Windows 95 (like most software) isn't prefabricated or integrated at all.

Some of the component nature of Win95 is visible through Control Panel → Add/Remove Programs → Windows Setup (see Chapter 4, *The Control Panel*). Many pieces included with Windows 95 are not installed by default, and many pieces that are installed can subsequently be removed in some way.

Windows 95 is a much nicer system—more flexible and configurable—than it at first appears, or than Microsoft lets on. Almost all of the company's documentation for users seems based on the idea that "what you see is what you get," i.e., that Windows 95 *is* whatever set of features it appears to come with. In fact, a lot of what you see at first glance in Windows 95 can be dispensed with, and, conversely, it provides a lot more than you typically see.

The non-integrated, component-based architecture of Windows also helps explain how Microsoft can keep expanding the Windows operating system into what was formerly considered the domain of application software: just keep adding on more DLLs and VxDs. If Microsoft is "taking over the world," as seems to be the widespread perception in popular culture, then it's worth noting that one technical explanation for this is the component-based kitchen-sink design of Windows, into which more and more functionality can be dumped.

So what are the different pieces you get when you buy Windows 95?

Modules and APIs

As noted earlier, Windows 95 isn't a single large program: it contains a large collection of small and medium programs. But more than that, Windows 95 is really a collection of *modules*.

Modules are files with extensions such as *.dll* (Dynamic Link Libraries), *.vxd* (32-bit Virtual Device Drivers), *.drv* (16-bit Windows device drivers), and *.sys* (DOS device drivers). Together, these make up the actual Windows 95 operating system itself, upon which applications—such as *notepad.exe, telnet.exe, winword.exe,* and even *explorer.exe*—rely.

The Windows 95 CD-ROM contains about 120 megabytes of code and data; this includes about 46 megabytes worth of DLLs, 19 megabytes of EXEs, 7 megabytes of VxDs, 5 megabytes of DRVs, one megabyte of SYS files. In other words, here's one way to think about Windows 95:

> Windows 95 = DLL + EXE + VXD + DRV + SYS

Incidentally, this gives us a handle on Microsoft's claim that Windows 95 is more manly than the U.S. space shuttle. If 500,000 lines of code are "1/29th the size of Windows 95," then Windows 95 is supposedly 15 million lines of code. We've just seen that Windows 95 consists of about 46+19+7+5+1=68 megabytes of executable code. Figuring maybe 9 bytes of object code per line of commented C or assembly source code, it works out to almost 8 million lines of code. Well, whether it's 8 or 15 million, Windows 95 is a mammoth ongoing project, one that rivals such feats of engineering as Stonehenge and RMS Titanic.

If you use the Explorer to open the *Windows\System* folder, or use the MS-DOS prompt and type `dir /s /os \windows\system`, you'll see a long list of file-names, such as *shell32.dll*, *vmm32.vxd*, *user.exe*, *krnl386.exe*, *kernel32.dll*, *gdi.exe*, *user32.dll*, *pscript.drV*, and so on. These files are what really constitute Windows 95. The user interface, the ability to play Solitaire, the ability to mess with settings in Control Panel—all that is simply a reflection of these underlying files.

A module is a somewhat discrete component that provides an "interface"—not a user interface, but a programmatic interface, also called an Application Program-ming Interface (API). An API gives access to subroutines in modules such as DLLs, VxDs, and DRVs. Generally (though by no means always), Microsoft documents these APIs in products sold to software developers, such as the Windows Soft-ware Development Kit (SDK) and Windows 95 Device Driver Kit (DDK).

Windows 95, more than anything else, is a collection of APIs, which developers use as a platform upon which to build applications. Of course, for better or for worse, many of these developers work for Microsoft, and many of these applica-tions come with Windows 95 or Microsoft Office. This can make it difficult to see the real API core of Windows 95. Windows 95 has come to seem more like a fixed set of features than like an open-ended base for applications that haven't been written yet.

As an example of how applications rely on APIs, consider the Solitaire program, *sol.exe*. *sol* needs to display the bitmapped images of playing cards in a window on the screen. *sol* calls a subroutine to do this. But the subroutine—the code that knows how to display bitmaps on the display—is *not* "integrated" into *sol.exe*. It's inside the Windows Graphical Device Interface, provided by *gdi.exe* and *gdi32.dll*.

One file (such as the Solitaire program) can call subroutines in another file (written at a different time by a different programmer) because Windows provides a mechanism for doing just that. This mechanism is called *dynamic linking* and is one of the key features of Windows 95. Users don't see it (except via the *rundll* and *rundll32* programs; see Chapter 5, *Commands and Applications*), but it's far more part of Windows 95 than, say, the Explorer or Control Panel.

Just as Solitaire doesn't contain the actual code that puts an image on the display and relies instead on GDI to do this, likewise GDI actually doesn't contain the actual code to put bits on the display. If this were the case, then every time a new type of video display came out, *gdi.exe* and *gdi32.dll* would have to be upgraded. That way, obviously, lies madness. Instead, modules rely on services provided by separate device drivers such as—to pick some video-specific examples—*supervga.drv*, *chips.drv*, *s3.drv*, and *cirrus.drv*. These in turn interact with VxDs such as *vdd.vxd* (built into *vmm32.vxd*), *s3.vxd*, and so on.

So modules rely on services provided by other modules. Eventually one gets to a module that actually knows how to *do* something. (There's a lot of buck-passing in Windows; this is the price paid for a modular architecture.) This will likely be a low-level device driver that knows the specifics of a particular device.

This is a somewhat idealized picture. The term "module" implies a cleaner separa-tion between these components than always exists. Some of the components that make up Windows 95 use undocumented backdoor interfaces into other components. For performance reasons, upper-level modules may sometimes bypass lower-level helpers, and talk directly to the hardware. Microsoft frequently modifies upper-level modules such as GDI to accommodate lower-level device drivers. Modules at a lower level often call back up into modules at a higher level. And, as many Windows users know from the headaches created by multiple vendor implementations of WinSock (the Windows Internet "sockets" DLL), Windows components are sometimes less interchangeable in practice than in theory. But they remain individual components that can be understood somewhat separately.

Layers

Notice that we're beginning to have a sense of *layers*: EXEs generally rely on DLLs, which rely on DRVs, which rely on VxDs, and so on. As noted earlier, sometimes code in one layer can bypass lower layers; for example, the VxD layer often (though not always) bypasses DOS, and talks directly to the hardware.

Figure 8-1 shows how Windows 95 looks from this perspective. The diagram uses some terms (Win16, Win32) that may not be familiar; they'll be explained later on, in the blow-by-blow description of each layer.

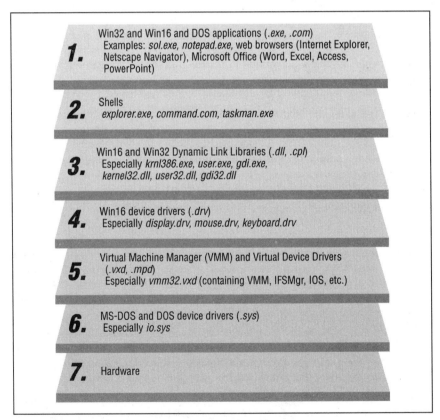

Figure 8-1: A seven-layer perspective on Windows 95

As you can see, from this perspective Windows 95 looks a bit like an archaeological site: the layers that make up Windows 95 reflect the history of PC operating systems, with MS-DOS at the bottom, then 16-bit Windows, 32-bit Windows, with the Web at the top of the pile. Interestingly, a book published by Microsoft for programmers (*Systems Programming for Windows 95*, by Walter Oney) contains a similar description, likening Windows to a bulletin board on which notices are constantly posted, but from which no notices have ever been removed.

So here's another way to look at Windows 95:

Windows 95 = MS-DOS + VMM/VxD + Win16 + Win32 + shell + applications

Let's look at some of these layers in more detail.

Applications

The big application (or suite of applications) that many users care about is Microsoft Office: Word, Excel, Access, PowerPoint, and Outlook. It comes preinstalled on many machines along with Windows 95 itself, so it could perhaps be seen as part of the operating system. The executables that comprise Microsoft Office are 32-bit programs that employ the Win32 API (see layer 3, later in this chapter, in "Dynamic Link Libraries (DLLs)"). Microsoft Office also comes with its own DLLs. There are developers who write software add-ins to Word and Excel; for them, Microsoft Office effectively is the operating system.

Growing in importance is the web browser, such as Netscape Navigator or Communicator, Microsoft Internet Explorer, or the small, fast Opera. Web browsers for Windows almost always use the Win32 API. Like Office, web browsers also typically come with their own DLLs, in addition to using the ones that are available with every copy of Windows 95. Sometimes they use their own DLLs even when Windows 95 provides similar functionality of its own. For example, Netscape does not use the web-related DLLs that come with Windows; given the relative simplicity of web protocols such as HTTP and HTML, Microsoft probably exaggerates the value of its own web APIs.

However, Netscape does rely on other DLLs that are part of the system. For example, if you use Netscape Navigator over a dial-up link, you'll find yourself working with the familiar Dial-Up Networking dialog boxes—they are provided by a file called *rnaui.dll.*

While most large new applications use a set of APIs collectively known as Win32, the older 16-bit Windows API (Win16) still sees full employment. Many of the smaller applications that come with Windows 95, such as *sol* and *notepad,* use Win16. If a program uses a fairly small amount of code and data, and does not manipulate a lot of large integers, Win16 may actually be preferable to Win32.

Windows 95 also comes with a large set of DOS programs. These can have surprising advantages over the fancier and more sophisticated Win16 and Win32 applications. For example, Windows 95 comes with no fewer than three different editors: not only the Win32-based WordPad and Win16-based Notepad, but also the DOS-based *edit.com.* You can usually edit small files a lot more efficiently in the DOS-based *edit.com* than you can in the Win16-based *notepad.exe,* and this in turn is often much faster than the Win32-based *wordpad.exe.* In general, many features available in the Windows GUI are duplicated at the DOS command line, and the command-line versions may prove more efficient for power users.

Incidentally, Windows 95 also provides developers with a way to write Win32-based "console" programs that *look* like DOS programs, that is, that produce white-on-black output in a DOS window, expect to receive input from the DOS prompt, and/or have no user interface at all besides the command line. Good examples are *start.exe* and *xcopy32.exe* (see Chapter 5). These examples show that how a program looks tells you little about what type of program it really is, i.e., which API is relies on. If you run *xcopy* in a DOS box (see the following explanation), you're still running a 32-bit Windows program.

It's worth noting an important distinction between DOS programs on the one hand and Win16 and Win32 programs on the other. DOS programs run in one or more of what are usually called *DOS boxes*. A DOS box is actually a *virtual machine* (VM). You can have multiple DOS boxes open at the same time, each with its own DOS "state" (current drive, directory, etc.). In contrast, all Win16 and Win32 programs run in a single VM, called the System VM; this is really just a DOS box with special privileges. (The file *winstart.bat*, noted in Chapter 9, *Windows Startup*, is a sort of "autoexec" for this special DOS box.) Those odd Win32 console applications, such as *start.exe*, also run in the System VM, but they send their output to a separate DOS box.

Not only Win16 and Win32 applications, but also all the Win16 and Win32 DLLs and DRVs (layers 3 and 4), are loaded into the System VM. However, the VMM and VxDs (layer 5) and MS-DOS (layer 6) sit beneath *all* the VMs. Perhaps we need to redraw the earlier diagram (see Figure 8-2). (Not all of this will make sense right now; you might want to come back to this diagram as you read about the other layers below.)

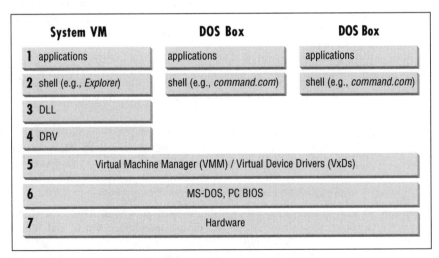

Figure 8-2: A revised seven-layer perspective

Two more points before moving down to the next layer.

First, the web browser seems destined to become a new layer in its own right, and it is tending to diminish the importance of the other Windows 95 layers. The Web represents a new paradigm not only for information distribution, but for software development as well. New "APIs" such as HTTP, HTML, JavaScript, and CGI are so compelling that it seems inevitable that more and more applications will be written to these APIs rather than to Win32. This becomes obvious if you look at web sites like *http://www.amazon.com*, *http://altavista.digital.com*, and *http://www.yahoo.com*— these represent a new type of application, one that may be far more relevant to the actual needs of users than the traditional Desktop applications that Microsoft has made its specialty.

Second, the line between layers 1 and 2 is somewhat arbitrary. As noted later in this chapter, any Win32, Win16, or even DOS application can be selected as your Windows "shell." Conversely, the default Windows shell, *explorer.exe*, can be run as an application.

Shells

Because the default Windows 95 shell, *explorer.exe*, provides the familiar user-interface elements such as the Desktop, Taskbar, Start menu, and so on, many users would identify this layer as Windows 95 itself.

But ironically, far from being synonymous with Windows 95 itself, this layer is, from a technical perspective, arguably the *least* important one in Windows. The shell is really just another application. This application is no more essential to running Windows 95 than is Solitaire or Notepad. It's like your car's dashboard: useful, necessary perhaps, but hardly synonymous with the car itself.

Windows 95 gets its characteristic look and feel because, by default, the [boot] section of *system.ini* contains a line that reads:

```
shell=explorer.exe
```

By providing a different shell= line in *system.ini*, you can see that the Desktop, Taskbar, and so on, are part of the Explorer, not Windows 95 itself. The shell= setting is one of several *seams* in the supposedly seamless Windows 95; shell= is a seam between layers 2 and 3. By editing this line, you can designate any other Win32, Win16, or even DOS application as the shell.

Windows 95 comes with two "legacy" shells: the File Manager (*winfile.exe*) and Program Manager (*progman.exe*). However, neither of these programs has been updated to know about long filenames. All long filenames have short 8.3-style aliases (arguably, the short names are the genuine ones, and the long names are the aliases); the short names are all the File Manager and Program Manager see.

For that matter, you can even say:

```
shell=c:\command.com
```

This sets the DOS command shell as the shell for all of Windows 95. If you try this, notice that the familiar UI elements such as the Desktop and Start menu are gone. However, the ability to start all your Windows 95 programs from the C:\> prompt shows that this is indeed still Windows 95. In addition, *command.com* (unlike the File Manager and Program Manager) knows all about long file and directory names.

You're not restricted to using the Explorer, File Manager, or Program Manager as your Windows 95 shell. It really can be any Win32, Win16, or DOS program. For example, in a kiosk or trade show demo situation, you might want to set shell= to the name of a specific application to keep people from doing anything with the machine other than running the desired program.

The dependence of the shell on this single setting also means that it is theoretically possible for third parties to offer alternative shells. For example, the Macintosh Finder interface could perhaps be ported to Windows 95, or Netscape Navigator could be extended (especially now that the source code is available) to provide additional access to the local disk.

Almost any alternative application you designate as the shell will have one significant difference from *explorer.exe* when it is run as a shell: these applications allow you to exit without also shutting down Windows. If no other programs are running, and you exit the shell, you are faced with a blank screen. You can then shut down Windows 95 with Ctrl-Alt-Esc, which will bring up the familiar "Close Program" dialog box with its "Shut Down" option. But how do you *start* any other programs?

Similarly, what if you choose as your shell something like *sol.exe* that has no option for launching other programs? Unless your goal is to produce a dedicated machine that does nothing other than run *sol* (and we've all seen people who seem to use Windows 95 in this manner), what good is this?

It turns out that Windows 95 has a good built-in solution: press Ctrl-Esc even when Explorer is not running, and Win95 still brings up the Task Manager (*taskman.exe*), which has the ability to start applications. It also has a menu item to shut down Windows. (See *taskman* in Chapter 5.)

Thus it seems that if we're looking for a privileged Windows 95 application, it's not *explorer.exe*, but *taskman.exe*. This program is hard-wired into the Win16 *user.exe*. We might then consider *taskman* the only genuinely "integrated" Win95 executable. However, even this is really just another seam: you can designate any program as the "task manager" with the taskman.exe= setting in the [boot] section of *system.ini*. Perversely, you can even make taskman.exe=sol.exe. (Once you start looking at these settings, Windows 95 appears almost infinitely configurable.) The default, of course, is taskman.exe=taskman.exe.

Dynamic Link Libraries (DLLs)

Windows applications are written, either by Microsoft or by third-party developers, using a set of functions called the Windows Application Programming Interface. (These are actually a set of interrelated APIs—even at the API level, Windows is not monolithic.) These functions have names such as WinExec, CreateWindow, and TextOut. Programs that you use to get real work done, such as Word and Excel, are written using these APIs. When talking about Windows, most software developers are really referring to the code in Windows that provides these APIs, which are provided by Dynamic Link Libraries (DLLs).

The central DLLs in Windows 95 are *krnl386.exe* (Win16 kernel), *kernel32.dll* (Win32 kernel), *user.exe* (Win16 user interface APIs), *user32.dll* (Win32 UI), *gdi.exe* (Win16 Graphic Device Interface), and *gdi32.dll* (Win32 GDI).

Does any of this matter to users? Unfortunately, it does. DLLs are components, but unfortunately they are not quite interchangeable: many applications are overly dependent on the precise characteristics of a particular DLL. What's more, because of the modular nature of Windows 95, an application can't always depend on a particular DLL being installed. As a result, many applications install their own copy of a required system DLL or VxD. Unfortunately, if two applications each depend on a slightly different version of the same file, the last one installed wins, and an application that used to run just fine mysteriously stops working.

So then you try to uninstall the new application, and sure enough, it deletes the offending module, but fails to replace the original that it had overwritten.

For this reason, it's a good idea to do a complete backup before installing any new program. Then use *attrib* to clear the archive bit from all files (in case the backup program didn't do this). After the install, type:

```
C:\>dir /aa /s
```

at a DOS prompt to get a list of all the files that have been replaced or changed on your system. You might be surprised how many "system" files have been replaced.

Third-party applications may also include their own DLLs or VxDs. Once installed, these modules are pretty much indistinguishable from ones shipped by Microsoft as part of Win95—they can even be used by other applications if their APIs are published. Applications often dump them right into the same directory where most of the system files are kept—\ *Windows\System.*

Effectively, applications become part of the operating system.

Microsoft Versus the DOJ: Integrated Applications

This discussion sheds an interesting sidelight on the dispute between Microsoft and the Department of Justice. It's legitimate to argue, as Microsoft does, that Internet Explorer *is* integrated, in that it depends on specific DLLs within Windows 95, and that, conversely, it provides some DLLs that other programs might rely on. But that is no different from any other application that Microsoft or a third party might provide. Any application is integrated into Win95 in this sense. Third-party DLLs are indistinguishable from ones that happen to come with the operating system. In this sense, *any* application added to Win95 becomes an "integrated application." Is Netscape Navigator any less integrated than IE once it's installed? The answer, of course, is no.

Win16 Device Drivers (DRVs)

16-bit drivers (DRVs) are holdovers from earlier incarnations of the operating system. Rather than providing equivalent functionality from the ground up,

Microsoft has "embraced and extended" its own history. These modules (which used to talk directly to the hardware) have often been "tricked" into thinking they are still doing so by lower-level VxDs.

The Virtual Machine Manager (VMM) and Virtual Device Drivers (VxDs)

The Virtual Machine Manager/VxD layer is the core of the Windows 95 operating system: this is where the code that provides process and thread control and manages access to memory, the file system, and disk really lives.

Much as VxDs "hook" the 16-bit driver APIs, so too they hook a lot of the DOS API. What appears to be DOS is now actually handled by VxDs rather than by the original DOS code. This is why, for example, a built-in DOS command like *dir* can now recognize long filenames. But the relationship between VMM and DOS is more complicated than that.

Each DOS box actually runs in a separate virtual machine. As noted earlier, all programs built with Win16 and Win32 APIs run in a single virtual machine called the System VM. (In many ways, the System VM is really just a privileged DOS box.) This is why setting environment variables such as the path in one DOS box won't affect the search path in another DOS box, nor will it affect the search path at the Run prompt. To affect the System VM, path settings must be made in *autoexec.bat*, which is executed as part of the boot process before the Win16/Win32 parts of Windows 95 are loaded. (See Chapter 9 for additional details.)

In theory, the fact that each DOS box is a separate VM means that DOS applications can coexist with Windows applications. In practice, as noted elsewhere in this book (see "Shortcut Properties of DOS Programs" in Chapter 3, *The Windows 95 User Interface*), some ill-behaved DOS programs will require you to enter "MS-DOS mode," in which you close down Windows and all other applications before running the program.

Some of the baroque complications in the Windows 95 architecture come from the historical burden of backward compatibility. Each new version of the operating system, from DOS through Windows 3.1 through Windows 95, has had to maintain compatibility with applications that ran on the earlier system.

Unfortunately, the chain of backward compatibility leads all the way back to a fundamental weakness in the design of the original Intel 8086 processor. It was able to address memory only in 64K segments, limited to 16 segments, or a total of 1 megabyte of memory. In DOS, that memory is subdivided into 640K of "conventional" memory and 384K of "high" memory. (Conventional memory was originally used for applications, and high memory for system data.)

In order to be backward-compatible with the 8086 and 80286, the Intel 386 and later Intel processors were designed to support two basic modes of operation: so-called Real mode, which emulates the original 8086 behavior, and Protected mode (also called Enhanced mode), which addresses memory in a linear fashion (rather than in segments) and eliminates the 1 MB limit.

In Real mode, applications are not cleanly separated from each other or from the operating system, allowing a poorly designed application to overwrite portions of memory used by other applications, or even by the operating system itself.

Protected mode allows (but does not enforce) memory protection for the OS and applications. The 386 and later Intel processors implemented three levels of memory protection within Protected mode, referred to as Rings 0–3. Ring 0 is the most privileged and least protected area; Ring 3 is the least privileged and most protected.

As it turns out, the VMM/VxD layer is the only part of Windows 95 that runs in Ring 0. The Virtual Machine Manager (VMM) and VxD layer is arguably therefore the real heart of the operating system.

This is an important fact about the Windows DLLs that is missed even by many hard-core Windows programmers: these DLLs and the APIs they provide run in Ring 3, which is the *least* privileged (outermost, most protected) level in Protected mode, and provides the same protection level used by Windows applications. Everything done by these system DLLs—even the so-called "kernel"—is based on, and subject to control by, the VMM and VxDs running in Ring 0.

In this interpretation, Windows has a so-called "microkernel" architecture. The VMM/VxD layer is actually fairly small.

When looked at in this light, even the core of the operating system is flexible. Any third party can make a Ring 0 VxD, which is indistinguishable from Microsoft's operating system. Ironically, most of the "operating system" software shipped by Microsoft belongs to Ring 3, the user application level.

MS-DOS and DOS Device Drivers (.SYS)

While Windows 95, like Windows for Workgroups 3.11, does provide 32-bit file access that bypasses DOS for file I/O, it still uses MS-DOS for many other non-file operations.

DOS is part of Win95, not simply as a convenient place from which to "boot," nor simply for "compatibility." Every Windows program, even the newest Win32 program, requires a DOS data structure, the Program Segment Prefix (PSP), which must be allocated in conventional memory and initialized with a DOS call (INT 21h function 55h).

What's more, it has been demonstrated that overwriting DOS, albeit from a "contrived" example program, brings down the entire system. Win95 can't survive without working DOS code underneath it—even if you never run any DOS programs.

You could argue that Windows 95 really is just MS-DOS 7 (7.0, 7.10) plus Windows 4 (4.0, 4.10), with a block and tackle used to hoist one on top of the other and a small amount of glue to keep it there. But that would be something of an oversimplification. As noted earlier, the VMM/VxD layer takes care of many operations that in Windows 3.1 were done by DOS. But *io.sys* and DOS device drivers like *himem.sys* and *ifshlp.sys* are still critical parts of the system. It's more like ancient Troy as unearthed by Schliemann: we see the remains of one city after another built on the ruins of its predecessor, reusing many of its building blocks.

Note that *command.com* (which puts up the C:\> prompt) is the DOS shell, not MS-DOS itself. In fact, at this point, it's just an application like any other. Because it's sitting on top of the VMM/VxD layer, which can in turn call back up to the DLL layer, it is able to employ all three. That's why, if you type the name of a Windows application from the DOS prompt, it runs. This works fine even when the Explorer is not the shell.

Is This Overkill?

If most users run only a word processor or a web browser, there seems to be something almost perverse about the complexity of the operating system. It's a massive foundation for a relatively small building. This is the problem not only with Windows 95's archeological heritage but also with its tremendous modularity. It's a superset of all possible configurations, so by definition it's overkill for any given configuration.

There may be a further element to the complexity of Windows 95. Microsoft learned an important lesson from DOS, and the ease with which it was cloned by competitors. How do you manage to be ubiquitous, but not a commodity? Keep the operating system a moving target. Why has something as ubiquitous and profitable as Windows not been cloned? It's not primarily a matter of legal protection. It's the sheer complexity of Windows, and the rate at which it changes. Any attempt to compete with Windows has been a grueling treadmill.

The problem with this approach is that an operating system, like a civilization, eventually topples from the weight of its own accumulated institutions.

Microsoft has told us that Windows 98 will be the last generation in the DOS → Windows → Win95 family tree. But the switch to Windows NT, with its fresher kernel architecture, will not entirely solve the problem.

In the end, it may be that the entire desktop-oriented computing metaphor is running its course. If you look at the most exciting applications being created today, they aren't traditional desktop applications at all. What is a web site like *http://www.amazon.com* or Microsoft's own *http://www.expedia.com*, but a new kind of information application? What's more, it's increasingly becoming possible to decipher the implicit API that a web site uses so that you can create web applications that draw their data not just from the local machine or a back-end database, but from other web servers. (For more information on this fascinating concept, see *http://www.webmethods.com*.)

If most of what users need could be done inside a web browser, then that obviously makes a much leaner basis for an operating system. The APIs on which the Web is built are orders of magnitude simpler than the Win32 APIs. What's more, they are significantly more capable, allowing you to build true distributed applications in only a few lines of code.

But even if the Windows API turns out to have been a massive detour, with the main line of future software development represented by HTTP, HTML, and so on, Intel and Microsoft still got millions of cheap boxes out there, with modems and with a TCP/IP stack, ready for the Web revolution.

Whatever happens in the future, though, the increasing complexity of Windows has helped to destroy the sense of mastery and control that was one of the original attractions of the so-called "personal" computer.

Still, to the extent you realize that Windows 95 is not monolithic, and its behavior is not hard-wired but rather endlessly mutable, you can regain that original sense of power over your computer.

Inside Windows 95

CHAPTER 9

Windows Startup

The process of starting up a computer is called *bootstrapping*, because it's analogous to the proverbial "pulling yourself up by your own bootstraps"—only in this case, that's really what happens. A very small piece of code is loaded, which then loads the next piece, which loads the next, and so on, until the entire system is up and running. The Windows 95 boot process involves the loading of literally hundreds of files. At the risk of gross over-simplification, though, we can say that it consists of six major phases:

1. Hardware startup. The BIOS (Basic Input-Output System) stored in ROM runs a hardware self-test (sometimes called the POST, or Power On Self Test), and then loads the software it finds in the boot sector on the startup disk drive. If the BIOS can't find system software in the boot sector (for example, because you've left a non-system disk in the floppy drive), you'll get a message such as "Invalid System Disk." Pressing F1 during this stage will normally enter the BIOS's setup mode. In modern systems, with larger ROM chips, this can be a fairly substantial environment, in which you can make detailed system configuration decisions. Most users need never enter this setup mode.

2. MS-DOS 7.x is loaded. The *io.sys* file contains the Real mode operating system. *io.sys* in turn loads a number of other programs and startup files, including *msdos.sys*, *logo.sys* (the screen that says "Starting Windows"), *drvspace.bin* or *dblspace.bin* (if present), the system portion of the Registry (*system.dat*), *config.sys*, and *autoexec.bat*. In so-called "Safe mode" (accessible via startup function keys, as described later in this chapter), *config.sys* and *autoexec.bat* are bypassed.

3. The Windows VxD layer is loaded. This starts with *win.com*, which under Windows 95 is just a stub loader for the VxDs that follow, rather than the Windows Desktop environment that it contained in Windows 3.1. The real work at this stage is done by *\Windows\System\vmm32.vxd*, the Virtual Machine Manager.

4. The DLLs that provide the raw material for the GUI are loaded, starting with *Windows\System\krnl386.exe*, which loads the Win16 environment. It is at this stage that the user portion of the Registry (*user.dat*) is first loaded. If present, the file *winstart.bat* is executed. Then *Windows\System\kernel32.dll* loads the Win32 environment. It is at this point that keyboard, mouse, and display drivers are loaded, as well as many system fonts. *Windows \System.ini* is first consulted at this stage. While most of what used to be stored in the *system.ini* file has been moved to the Registry, there is a minimal set of device settings that are required, and the shell= line specifies which command interpreter is to be provided as the overall system shell.

5. If multiple users or networking passwords are configured, the login screen is shown. The user actually logs in. The user's password file (*Windows \username.pwl*) is consulted. If user profiles are enabled, the user portion of the Registry is reloaded, this time from the file *Windows\Profiles\<username>\user.dat*.

6. The Explorer (or other shell specified by the shell= line in *system.ini*) is loaded. The Explorer uses the user Registry data to build the Desktop and other remembered states.

Portions of this sequence are recorded in the file *bootlog.txt* the first time Windows is started. Thereafter, a new bootlog file will be created only if you specifically ask for it during a manual startup, using the option keys described in the next section.

While you probably don't want to look at every detail of the boot sequence—it really is quite remarkable just how many files are loaded—it's definitely useful to have a rough idea of what happens at each stage, because it makes sense out of some of your available options. Especially if you are familiar with DOS or Windows 3.1, you may have to throw some of your assumptions out the window. For example, you are used to having *autoexec.bat* executed each time you log in. So when you select "Close all programs and login as a different user" you might think that *autoexec.bat* will be executed again. But it is read all the way back at the initial loading of DOS. If you make changes there and want them recognized, you must do a full reboot.

Each of the options to the Shut Down command on the Start menu simply restarts the process at one of the stages in the boot process:

Shut down the computer?
Any software loaded in steps 3–6 is removed from memory, and the "It is now safe to turn off your computer" screen is shown. On systems with Advanced Power Management enabled, the system will simply shut down without the warning screen.

Restart the computer?
Any software loaded in steps 3–6 is removed from memory, and the process starts over with step 2. However, if you hold down the Shift key when selecting this option, only the software loaded in steps 4–6 is removed from memory, and you start over at step 4. This isn't a real reboot; it saves time, but is sometimes insufficient to clear any problems.

Cold Boot Versus Warm Boot

A *cold boot* is what happens when you turn off the computer, wait at least 10 seconds, and then turn the computer back on. A cold boot is required to change any hardware settings.

A *warm boot* is what happens when you hit the reset button on the computer (if there is one), or when you select Restart from the Shut Down dialog box. The only difference is that invoking Restart from the Shut Down screen closes Windows 95 gracefully, and pressing the hardware Reset button does not.

Restart the Computer in MS-DOS Mode?
> Any software loaded in steps 4–6 is removed from memory, and an MS-DOS screen is displayed. Note however that the step 3 Windows/VxD bootstrap layer remains in memory, and when you type exit, Windows restarts. (At least this is the way it works in OSR2; in the original release, typing exit does a full reboot before loading Windows.)

Close all programs and log on as a different user?
> Only the software loaded in steps 5 and 6 is unloaded from memory; you start over again at step 5. Logging back in as the same user is thus a way to do a "local reboot" of the Explorer without going all the way back to the beginning and restarting all of Windows 95. Note that this option is only visible in the Shut Down dialog box when network drivers are loaded (including Dial-Up Networking)—its presence, oddly, doesn't have much to do with the existence of multiple users.

For further details on various configuration files used in the boot process, see the alphabetical reference later in this chapter. The next section focuses on the ways you can intervene in the boot process.

Startup Option Keys

The following keys may be pressed during Windows startup (when the "Starting Windows" message appears) to invoke special startup options:

Esc	Disables logo (the logo is not shown; the screen displays the progress of startup).
F4	Starts previous version of MS-DOS (if available). BootMulti=1 must be specified in *msdos.sys.*
F5	Initiates Safe mode startup, without networking support.
F6	Initiates Safe mode startup, with networking support.
F8	Displays Windows Startup menu. See "Windows Startup Menu" for more information.

Windows Startup Menu

In normal operation, Windows 95 loads and runs automatically. However, additional load-time options are available. Many of these options are useful when troubleshooting Windows startup malfunctions.

To initiate the load-time options menu, press F8 at any time after the various hardware BIOSes have loaded (a good time is when you see the "Starting Windows" message). A menu will then be displayed, giving you several options as follows:

Normal
> Normal start.

Logged
> System starts, creates *bootlog.txt* file.

Safe mode
> Starts Windows, bypassing startup files and using only basic system drivers. No network support. Same as pressing F5 or typing win /d:m at the command prompt. See "Safe Mode Startup" later in this chapter for more information.

Safe mode with network support
> Starts Windows, bypassing startup files and using only basic system drivers, including basic networking. Same as pressing F6 or typing win /d:n at the command prompt. See "Safe Mode Startup" for more information.

Step-by-step confirmation
> Starts Windows, confirming startup files line by line. Same as pressing F8 when the Startup menu is displayed. For more information, see "Step-by-Step Confirmation" later in this chapter.

Command prompt only
> Starts the operating system with startup files and Registry, displaying only the command prompt. Allows for starting Windows using *win.com* command-line switches. See "win.com Startup Switches" for more information.

Safe mode command prompt only
> Starts the operating system in Safe mode and displays only the command prompt, bypassing startup files. Same as pressing Shift+F5. See "win.com Startup Switches" for more information.

Previous version of MS-DOS
> Starts the operating system that was installed on your computer before you installed Windows 95. Same as pressing F4 during startup. This option is available only if the line BootMulti=1 is in *msdos.sys*.

Step-by-Step Confirmation

Step-by-step confirmation allows you to accept or skip one or more startup options, and is useful when troubleshooting startup errors. You will be given the following options (press Enter to confirm; Esc to skip):

1. Load DoubleSpace (or DriveSpace) driver?

2. Process the system Registry?

3. Create a startup log file (*bootlog.txt*)?

4. Process your startup device drivers (*config.sys*)?

   config.sys options will be displayed (Enter=Yes; Esc=No; Tab to accept all options).

5. Process your startup command file (*autoexec.bat*)?

   autoexec.bat options will be displayed (Enter=Yes; Esc=No; Tab to accept all options).

6. Run *win.com* to start Windows 95?

7. Load all Windows drivers?

Answering Yes (or pressing Enter) to each prompt results in the same operating environment as starting Windows 95 normally, except that the logo does not appear.

Answering No to "Load All Windows Drivers?" runs Windows 95 in Safe mode.

Safe Mode Startup

Safe mode startup provides an alternative boot process for Windows should normal startup fail. Normal startup may fail for any of a number of reasons, including:

- One or more drivers are incompatible with Windows or the system.

- The Registry is corrupted.

- An application requests Safe mode startup (which may occur if you prematurely quit Windows before it has completely started).

Safe startup loads only the minimal drivers necessary for using the Windows GUI. These drivers include:

- Mouse

- Keyboard

- Standard VGA

- Device Manager drivers

There are two forms of Safe mode startup: with and without networking support.

You may start Windows in Safe mode in any of the following ways:

- Press F8 during system startup to display the Windows Startup menu. Choose Safe mode or Safe mode with network support.

- Press F5 when the "Starting Windows" message appears during system startup for Safe mode startup without network support.

- Press F6 when the "Starting Windows" message appears during system startup for Safe mode startup with network support.

Safe mode, non-network

There are actually three variations of Safe mode without networking support, invoked by **F5**, **Ctrl-F5**, and **Shift-F5**, respectively. The differences are shown in Table 9-1.

Table 9-1: Safe Mode Options (Non-Network)

Function	F5	Ctrl-F5	Shift-F5
Process *config.sys* and *autoexec.bat*	N	N	N
Load networking drives	N	N	N
Load *himem.sys* and *ifshlp.sys*	Y	N	N
Process Registry information	N	Y	N
Load *command.com*	N	Y	Y
Load DoubleSpace or DriveSpace if present	Y	N	Y
Start Windows 95 GUI (run *win.com*)	Y	N	N

Safe mode, network

For those computers connected to a network, it may be necessary to establish basic connection with the network for even rudimentary maintenance of the Windows 95 system. (A standalone computer has a full copy of Windows 95 on the local hard disk; a shared installation runs a shared copy of Windows 95 from a server.) Windows 95 supports Safe mode startup with network driver support.

Safe startup with networking performs the following functions:

- Load *himem.sys* and *ifshlp.sys*, regardless of *config.sys* settings
- Process Registry information
- Load DoubleSpace or DriveSpace if present
- Load Windows 95
- Load network drivers

Safe startup with networking does not process *config.sys* or *autoexec.bat*. The *command.com* command-line interpreter is not processed.

win.com Startup Switches

The Windows 95 GUI can be started using switches (options) from the command prompt. This is useful if you need to troubleshoot a balky system.

To run *win.com* manually using these switches, press **F8** at startup and choose either command prompt only, or Safe mode command prompt only.

Syntax

win [/b] [/d:[options]

Options

/B	Creates a *bootlog.txt* file that records operating-system messages generated during system startup.
/D:	Used for troubleshooting when Windows 95 does not start correctly. Combine this switch with one or more of the following options:

F	Turns off 32-bit disk access. Equivalent to setting 32BitDiskAccess=FALSE in *system.ini*.
M	Starts Windows 95 in Safe mode. Same as pressing F5.
N	Starts Windows 95 in Safe mode with networking support. Same as pressing F6.
S	Specifies that Windows 95 should not use the ROM address space between F000:0000 and 1 MB for a break point. Equivalent to setting SystemROMBreakPoint= FALSE in *system.ini*.
V	Specifies that the ROM routine will handle interrupts from the hard disk controller. Equivalent to setting Virtual-HDIRQ=FALSE in *system.ini*.
X	Excludes all of the adapter area from the range of memory that Windows 95 scans to find unused space. Equivalent to setting EMMExclude=A000-FFFF in *system.ini*.

Examples

Start Windows in Safe mode (non-network):

```
C:\>win /d:m
```

System Configuration Files and Commands

This section describes the contents of various system configuration files, especially those used during the startup process. (See Appendix C, *System File and Directory Organization,* for a list of other important files whose contents we don't document in detail.) The files are listed in alphabetical order for easy reference, but it is wise to understand just where they are consulted in the boot process. Since there is some overlap in the settings that can be stored in some of the files, a setting in a later file can override one stored earlier. See Chapter 10, *The Registry,* for information about the Registry (*system.dat* and *user.dat*).

Files are used in the following order:

> *io.sys*
> *msdos.sys*
> *logo.sys*
> *system.dat* (Registry)
> *config.sys*
> *autoexec.bat*

user.dat (Registry)
system.ini
user.dat (Registry) again
winstart.bat
win.ini
system.ini (again)
Password file (<username>.pwl)
user.dat (again)
system.dat (again)
system.ini (again)

This alphabetical reference section also lists the following commands, which can only be invoked from system startup files:

emm386
loadhigh
setver

autoexec.bat *autoexec.bat*

Windows 95 does not require the *autoexec.bat* startup batch file. *autoexec.bat* is supported for backward compatibility, and as a means to run DOS-based programs at startup.

autoexec.bat is not read each time you create a new DOS window, unless you create the window with command /p (permanent). Neither is *dosstart.bat* (for "MS-DOS Mode"; see MS-DOS → Properties → Program → Advanced). Each new DOS window inherits its environment and other settings from the *autoexec.bat* file run at startup, but it is not rerun. If you have a batch file that you want to run for each new DOS window, specify it in MS-DOS Prompt → Properties → Program → Batch File.

IO.SYS Equivalent Commands

The *io.sys* file is a binary file, but it contains various settings that can be overridden in *autoexec.bat*. Table 9-2 lists variables that you can set in *autoexec.bat* to override the defaults in *io.sys*. The examples in the table show the format of each possible entry, but actually just reset the default value in *io.sys*.

Table 9-2: io.sys Variables That Can Be Overridden in autoexec.bat

Entry	Description	Example Showing Default Setting
tmp	Path for temporary files	set tmp=c:\windows\temp
temp	Path for temporary files	set temp=c:\windows\temp
prompt	Command prompt	prompt=pg
path	Search path for executable files	path=c:\windows;c:\windows\command
comspec	Name and location of command-line interpreter	set comspec=c:\windows\command.com

Network Settings

Windows 95 runs the following network command, which may be overridden in the *autoexec.bat* file:

net start   Binds the real-mode network components and validates the binding

Notes

Observe the following rules when editing the *autoexec.bat* file:

- The *autoexec.bat* file should not include a path to other versions of Windows that may be on the system.

- Do not alter the path to the previous MS-DOS directory, if any.

- The path= statement line should begin with the following: *C:\Windows;C:\Windows\Command.* (Use the actual paths for Windows 95 on your hard disk.)

- Use a batch file in *\Windows\Start Menu\Programs\StartUp* to connect to a network server upon startup rather than putting networking commands into *autoexec.bat.*

- Remove unnecessary statement lines from *autoexec.bat.* When possible, specify initializing parameters for applications in the System Properties sheet in the System Control Panel.

- Do not use long filenames. *autoexec.bat* is processed before *vmm32.vxd* is loaded, so long filenames are not yet supported.

- If present, *autoexec.bat* is executed just before *win.com* is loaded. Windows 95 effectively acts as though *win.com* were the last line of *autoexec.bat,* so if you put the *pause* command as the last line of *autoexec.bat,* the boot process will pause before loading the GUI portion of Windows 95. Press Enter to continue the boot, or press Ctrl-C to cancel the GUI boot, leaving you at the DOS 7 C:\> prompt.

---

config.sys   *config.sys*

The *config.sys* file may contain drivers and configuration information needed by certain hardware or software installed on the computer. Windows 95 does not require the *config.sys* file. *config.sys* is supported as a means for backward compatibility with MS-DOS applications, as well as for computers that require special drivers, or that require special setup (such as double-buffering for SCSI drives).

Windows 95 provides default values for most configuration settings that can be specified in the *config.sys* file (see *io.sys* for more details on these default values). However, you may override any of these default values by inserting a new value in the *config.sys* file. The *config.sys* file may also contain application- or driver-specific information, as required. Examples include drivers for special memory or network managers.

You can add DOS application-specific commands using the Properties → Program → Advanced dialog box for the application in question. (Navigate to the program

---

using the Explorer, then right-click on the program icon for access to the Properties sheet.)

Notes

- Under Windows 95, the *config.sys* file should *not* contain the following:

  – Command line for loading the *smartdrv* driver. Windows 95 includes built-in disk-caching.

  – Command line for loading a mouse driver or drivers for other pointing devices. Windows 95 includes built-in mouse support.

- Many of the commands that require some allocation of memory have two forms (e.g., *buffers* and *buffershigh*). The "high" form of each command stores its information in high memory. The limit on high memory is 64K, so depending on the amount of memory required, you may not be able to get all the data structures into high memory.

Commands Used in config.sys Files

The following commands are allowed in *config.sys* files under Windows 95. Note though that even though they are allowed, they may affect only DOS applications.

accdate=*drive1*+|- [*drive2*+|-]

For each drive, specifies whether to keep track of the last access date for all files (+) or not (–). Last access dates are turned off for all files when in Safe mode, and are off by default for floppy drives. They are on by default for hard disks.

break

Sets or clears extended Ctrl-C checking. Normally, DOS checks for Ctrl-C only when reading from the keyboard or writing to the screen (or a printer). With extended checking, it checks for Ctrl-C during disk read and write operations as well.

buffers=*n*[,*m*] and buffershigh=*n*[,*m*]

Allocates memory for a specified number of disk buffers when the computer starts. *n* must be from 1 to 99 (default is 30). An optional second value (*m*) specifies the number of buffers in the secondary cache, and must be from 0 to 8 (default is 0).

country=*xxx* [[, *yyy*] [, *path*]]

Enables the operating system to use country-specific conventions for displaying dates, times, and currency; for determining the order by which characters are sorted; and for determining which characters can be used in filenames. *xxx* specifies the country code and *yyy* (optionally) the character set. Path specifies the drive and path of the file containing country information. The following is an example:

```
country=049,437,c:\windows\command\country.sys
```

Country codes are usually the same as international telephone dialing prefix (e.g., 44 for UK). See *http://www.memoware.com/country.txt*. The character set value 850 applies to most countries.

`device=driver` [options] *and* `devicehigh=driver` [options]

Loads the device driver you specify into memory. *options* specifies any parameters required by the device driver command line. See \ *Windows\config.txt* for a description of additional options for *devicehigh*.

The following device drivers can be loaded in *config.sys* using a device= statement:

display.sys

Displays international character sets on EGA, VGA, and LCD monitors.

driver.sys

Creates a logical drive that you can use to refer to a physical floppy disk drive.

emm386.exe

Provides support for loading real-mode device drivers in the UMBs (dos=high) if both *emm386.exe* and *himem.sys* are loaded with device= commands in *config.sys*. See *emm386* later in this chapter for details.

himem.sys

Loads *himem.sys*, an extended memory manager. This command line must come before any commands that start applications or device drivers that use extended memory.

keyboard.sys

Enables the operating system to use a keyboard other than the standard U.S. QWERTY keyboard layout.

mscdex.exe

Provides DOS access to CD-ROM drives.

The file \ *Windows\ios.ini* is a text file that contains a list of drivers known to be safe or unsafe for use in *config.sys*. Drivers that are listed in the "unsafe" portion of this file will cause Windows 95 to use a 16-bit MS-DOS compatibility mode for file access and virtual memory. Check Control Panel → System → Performance to make sure you are in 32-bit mode. If you are in 16-bit mode, and your driver is simply not listed in *ios.ini*, try adding them to the safe list and see if Windows 95 still runs normally. Don't try this with disk compression utilities, DOS disk caching utilities, or VESA and PCI disk drivers.

The following device drivers should not be used under Windows 95, either because of incompatibility reasons, or because the device drivers are not included in Windows 95:

–ega.sys

–printer.sys

–ramdrive.sys

–romdrive.sys

dos=[high|low][, umb|noumb][, auto|noauto]

Specifies that the operating system should maintain a link to the upper memory area (UMA), load part of itself into the high memory area (HMA), or both.

high

Loads part of DOS into high memory

low   Keeps all of DOS in conventional memory (default)

umb   Manages upper memory blocks created by a program like *emm386.exe*, if they exist

noumb

Does not manage upper memory blocks (default)

auto

Loads *himem.sys*, *ifshelp.sys*, *dblbuff.sys* and *setver.sys*, and automatically use *buffershigh*, *fileshigh*, *fcbshigh*, *last-drivehigh*, and *stackshigh* (default)

noauto

Does not do all of the things listed under auto automatically

drivparm=*options*

Defines parameters for devices (e.g., disk and tape drives) when the operating system starts. Options include:

/D:*n* Specifies the physical drive number. Values for *n* must be in the range 0 through 255 (for example, drive number 0 = drive A, 1 = drive B, 2 = drive C, and so on). This parameter is required, since it specifies which drive the following parameters refer to.

/C   The drive can detect whether the drive door is closed.

/F:*n* Specifies the drive type ("factor"). The default value for *n* is 2. Values include:

0   160K/180K or 320K/360K

1   1.2 MB

2   720K (3.5-inch disk)

5   Hard disk

6   Tape

7   1.44 MB (3.5-inch disk)

8   Read/write optical disk

9   2.88 MB (3.5-inch disk)

/H:*heads*

> Specifies the maximum number of heads. Values for heads must be in the range 1 through 99. The default value depends on the value you specify for /F.

/I Specifies an electronically compatible 3.5-inch floppy disk drive. (Electronically compatible drives are installed on your computer and use your existing floppy disk drive controller.)

/N Specifies a nonremovable block device.

/S:*sectors*

> Specifies the number of sectors per track that the block device supports. Values for sectors must be in the range 1 through 99. The default value depends on the value you specify for /F.

/T:*tracks*

> Specifies the number of tracks per side that the block device supports. The default value depends on the value you specify for /F.

fcbs=*n* *and* fcbshigh=*n*

> Specifies the number of file control blocks that the operating system can have open at the same time. *n* must be between 1 and 255 (default is 4).

files=*n* *and* fileshigh=*n*

> Specifies the number of files that the operating system can access at one time. *n* must be between 8 and 255 (default is 8).

install progname [*options*]

> Loads a memory-resident program into memory. This works only for programs that have no user interface, such as *keyb.com*.

Lastdrive=*x* *and* Lastdrivehigh=*x*

> Specifies the maximum number of drives you can access. *x* must be a letter between A and Z (default is Z).

Numlock=[on|off]

> Specifies whether the Numlock setting on the numeric keypad is set to on or off.

rem Comments out a line and prevents it from executing.

set var=[*string*]

> Sets an environment variable (see set in Chapter 5, *Commands and Applications*, for details).

shell=command [*options*]

> Specifies the name and location of the command interpreter for use with Windows 95. Most often used to specify additional options for *command.com*, such as /e (to increase the size of the environment). For example:

```
shell=/command.com /e:1024
```

`stacks=`*n, s* *and* `stackshigh=`*n, s*

Supports the dynamic use of data stacks to handle hardware interrupts. *n* is the number of stacks, and can be 0 or a value from 8 to 64. *s* is the size in bytes of each stack, and can be 0 or a value from 32 through 512.

switches   Specifies special startup options for DOS. See the file \Windows\config.txt for available options.

dosstart.bat   \Windows\dosstart.bat

This is an optional DOS batch file that, if present, runs when you exit Windows 95 into real-mode "MS-DOS Mode." (You can enter MS-DOS mode via Start → Shutdown → Restart in MS-DOS mode, or by running an MS-DOS program with the setting Properties → Program → Advanced → MS-DOS Mode.) The file *winstart.bat* is executed when you re-enter Windows GUI mode.

Normally, you will use *dosstart.bat* to run *mscdex.exe* for CD-ROM access from DOS and a mouse driver for mouse support. The default *dosstart.bat* contains only a set of comments describing its intended use.

emm386   \Windows\emm386.exe

Used to display the current status of *emm386.exe* expanded memory support and to turn the device driver on or off.

Description

The *emm386.exe* device driver is different from the *emm386* command used from the command line. In order to use the *emm386* command from the command line, you must have an 80386 or higher processor, and you must have the *emm386.exe* device driver installed in the *config.sys* file by using the *device* command. The device driver is loaded by the execution of *config.sys*; without it, the *emm386* command is thus inoperable. The *emm386* command, issued at the command-line prompt, enables or disables support for expanded memory services. Expanded memory allows compatible DOS programs to run in expanded (1 MB and beyond) memory.

emm386.exe has the folllowing syntax:

    emm386 [on | off | auto] [w=on | w=off]

The *emm386.exe* options are:

on   Turns the *emm386* device driver on. This is the default setting.

off   Turns the *emm386* device driver off.

auto   Enables expanded memory support only when a program calls for it.

w=on   Enables support for the Weitek co-processor.

w=off   Disables support for the Weitek co-coprocessor. This is the default setting.

Notes

- To display the current status of *emm386* expanded memory support, type emm386 at the command prompt.

- In order to use the *emm386* command, you must load the *emm386.exe* device driver from within the *config.sys* file, using the syntax:

  ```
  device=x:\path\emm386.exe
  ```

  where *x:\path* is the drive and path to the directory containing the *emm386.exe* program.

---

io.sys   /Windows/io.sys

The *io.sys* file contains the real-mode MS-DOS 7.x operating system. This is a binary file; it is no longer an editable text file. The Windows 95 *io.sys* file is renamed to *winboot.sys* when you start the computer using the previous version of MS-DOS.

io.sys loads several system drivers by default, if they are found:

- *himem.sys*
- *ifshlp.sys*
- *setver.exe*
- *dblspace.bin* or *drvspace.bin*

WARNING

io.sys does not load *emm386.exe*. If any of your applications require expanded memory or load data into high memory, you should run *emm386.exe* in *config.sys*.

---

autoexec.bat and config.sys Defaults

io.sys contains default values of setup switches and command parameters that can be overridden in *config.sys* and *autoexec.bat* (see the entries for those files for additional details):

himem.sys	Enables access to the high memory area. Loads and runs the real-mode Memory Manager, typically *himem.sys*. (The Windows GUI won't load without it.) Compatibility: used by Windows 95; loaded by default.
ifshlp.sys	Loads the Installable File System Helper, which allows the system to make file system calls. Only the minimal file system from *io.sys* is used if this driver is not loaded. (The Windows GUI won't load without it.) Compatibility: used by Windows 95; loaded by default.

---

setver.exe	Loads optional TSR-type program for compatibility with older MS-DOS–based applications that require a specific version of MS-DOS to be running. When queried by an application, *setver.exe* responds with the appropriate version number for that application. Compatibility: used by Windows 95; loaded by default.
dos	Loads MS-DOS into the high memory area. *umb* setting is used only if *emm386.exe* is loaded in *config.sys*. Default value: dos=high,umb. Compatibility: used by Windows 95; loaded by default.
files	Specifies the number of file handle buffers to create under MS-DOS. Default value: files=60. Compatibility: not required by Windows 95; included for compatibility with MS-DOS applications.
lastdrive	Specifies the last drive letter available for assignment. Default value: lastdrive=z. Compatibility: not required by Windows 95; included for compatibility with MS-DOS applications.
buffers	Specifies the number of file buffers to create. Default value: buffers=30. Compatibility: not required by Windows 95; included for compatibility with MS-DOS applications.
stacks	Specifies the number and size of stack frames. Default value: stacks=9,256. Compatibility: not required by Windows 95; included for compatibility with MS-DOS applications.
shell	Indicates the command process to use. (The /p switch indicates that the command process is permanent and should not be unloaded; when /p is not specified, the command process can be unloaded when exiting the system.) Default value: shell=command.com /p. Compatibility: not required by Windows 95; included for compatibility with MS-DOS applications.
fcbs	Specifies the number of file control blocks to be created. Default value: fcbs=4. Compatibility: not required by Windows 95; included for compatibility with MS-DOS applications.

You may override the default values in *io.sys* by inserting an entry in *config.sys*. Override values for files, buffers, and stacks must be equal to or greater than the default values specified in the previous list.

---

loadhigh or lh Internal to: \ *Windows\command.com*

The *loadhigh* command loads a program into the upper memory area. The command can be used in the *config.sys* file or the *autoexec.bat* file to load programs when the computer starts. The *lh* command is a shortcut name for *loadhigh*.

loadhigh has the following syntax:

    loadhigh [filename] [options]
    loadhigh [/L:region1[,minsize1][;region2[,minsize2]...] [/S]] filename [options]

Options

filename   Specifies the location and name of the program you wish to
                         load.

/l:*region1[,minsize1] [;region2[,minsize2]]*
                         Specifies the region(s) of memory into which to load the
                         program. You can specify as many regions as you want.

region1   Specifies the number of the first memory region.

minsize1   Specifies the minimum size, if any, for *region1*.

region2   Specifies the number of the second memory region, if any.

minsize2   Specifies the minimum size, if any, for *region2*.

/s   Shrinks a UMB (Upper Memory Block) to its minimum size
                         while the program is loading.

Associated Files

config.sys
autoexec.bat

Examples

In *config.sys*:

```
C:\device=c:\windows\himem.sys
C:\device=c:\windows\emm386.exe
DOS=high,umb
fileshigh=16
buffershigh=50
devicehigh=mscdex.exe
```

In *autoexec.bat*:

```
lh c:\windows\command\doskey
lh mscdex.exe
```

Notes

- Using Upper Memory Blocks (UMBs) is a way to free conventional memory
  for use by MS-DOS–based applications and thus improve performance. In
  conventional memory, UMBs are the unused part of upper memory from
  640K to 1 MB (the old system area, in earlier versions of DOS), where information can be mapped to free memory below 640K.

- Before you can load a program into the upper memory area, you must install
  an upper memory area manager. You can use *emm386.exe*, which manages
  the upper memory area for computers with an 80386 or higher processor. To
  install *emm386*, add a *device* command to your *config.sys* file.

logo.sys, logos.sys, and logow.sys

\logo.sys,
\ Windows\logos.sys,
\ Windows\logow.sys

\logo.sys contains the startup image with the Microsoft Windows logo. If not present, *io.sys* uses a built-in logo. \ *Windows**logow.sys* and \ *Windows**logos.sys* contain the shutdown screens that read "Please wait while your computer shuts down" (*logow.sys*) and "It is now safe to turn off your computer" (*logos.sys*). These files are just bitmaps, so you can substitute other bitmap files if you like, provided that you get the aspect ratio and number of colors right. The files must be 256-color (8-bit) Windows bitmaps, 320×400 pixels in size. You should make copies of the existing files before replacing them. See *Windows Annoyances*, by David Karp (O'Reilly & Associates), for a detailed description of how to replace these files.

msdos.sys

Startup information for Windows 95. This file, located in the root directory of the computer's boot drive, may be edited to alter the boot or run-time behavior of Windows. In DOS 6 and earlier, *msdos.sys* was a binary file, part of the MS-DOS kernel. The entire DOS kernel is now stored in *io.sys* (with the installation version on the Windows 95 CD-ROM called *winboot.sys*). *msdos.sys* is now a text file containing configuration settings.

On machines with compressed hard disks, the entire version of *msdos.sys* is stored on the non-compressed (host) drive.

The *msdos.sys* file is editable; however, in normal use, the file is hidden and read-only. These attributes should be changed prior to editing.

Use the following command at the command line to make the *msdos.sys* file editable:

```
C:\>attrib -s -h -r \msdos.sys
```

After the desired changes have been made, use the following command to restore *msdos.sys* to its normal attributes:

```
C:\>attrib +s +h +r \msdos.sys
```

Restart Windows to have your changes take effect.

Important note: for compatibility with MS-DOS and some older applications, *msdos.sys* must be at least 1024 bytes in length. The file may contain the following remarked lines, which should not be removed:

```
;The following lines are required for compatibility with other programs.
;Do not remove them (MSDOS.SYS needs to be >1024 bytes).
;xxxxxxxxxxxxxxxxxxxxxxxxxxxxxxxxxxxxxxxxxxxxxxxxxxxxxxxxxxxxxxxxxxxxxxxa
;xxxxxxxxxxxxxxxxxxxxxxxxxxxxxxxxxxxxxxxxxxxxxxxxxxxxxxxxxxxxxxxxxxxxxxxb
;xxxxxxxxxxxxxxxxxxxxxxxxxxxxxxxxxxxxxxxxxxxxxxxxxxxxxxxxxxxxxxxxxxxxxxxc
 . . .
```

Among the information stored in *msdos.sys* is the path to critical Windows files. The *msdos.sys* file contains two sections, [Paths] and [Options], and one or more keys defined under each section. Following is a description of the sections and keys found in the *msdos.sys* file.

[Paths] Section

`HostWinBootDrv=path`
> Points to the boot disk (optional). Default: HostWinBootDrv=C.

`UninstallDir=path`
> Points to the directory that will be used for Uninstall (optional). Default: UninstallDir=C:\.

`WinDir=path`   Points to the main Windows directory, as specified during Windows Setup (required). Default: WinDir=C:\Windows.

`WinBootDir=path`
> Points to the main Windows directory, specifically for files needed to start Windows (optional). Default: WinBootDir= C:\Windows.

[Options] Section

`AutoScan=n`   In OSR2 only, specifies whether *scandisk* should be run automatically after improper shutdown. Values for n include:

0   No scanning

1   Prompt the user, but scan automatically if no response within 60 seconds (default)

2   Scan automatically without prompting

Example:

Autoscan=0.

`BootDelay=r`   Sets initial startup delay to the number of seconds; the default is 2 seconds. Examples:

Set to 1 second delay: BootDelay=1
Set to no delay: BootDelay=0

`BootFailSafe=n`
> Enables/disables Safe mode startup. Examples:

Disable: BootFailSafe=0
Enable (default): BootFailSafe=1

`BootGUI=n`   Enables/disables automatic graphical startup. If BootGUI=0, the system boots only to the DOS 7 prompt. Type **win** at the DOS prompt to start the Windows 95 layer. If Windows 95 is started manually in this way and then shut down, typing **MODE CO80** followed by the **Enter** key when the "It is now safe to turn off your computer" screen is displayed will return you to the MS-DOS prompt. Examples:

Disable: BootGUI=0
Enable (default): BootGUI=1

BootKeys=*n*   Allows/prevents special option keys (e.g., F5, F6, and F8) from functioning during Windows startup. Note that if Bootkeys=0 is set, BootDelay will be ignored. (That is, the system will assume BootDelay=0.) Examples:

Prevent: BootKeys=0
Allow (default): BootKeys=1

Bootmenu=*n*   Displays/skips Windows startup menu. By default, you must press F8 within the time specified by BootDelay to see the startup menu. Set Bootmenu=1 to always display the menu. Examples:

Displays: Bootmenu=1
Skips (default): Bootmenu=1

BootMenuDefault=*n*
Sets the default menu item on the Windows startup menu. The default is normally 1, but is changed to 4 if the system hung on the last reboot. Example:

Set default to item 3: BootMenuDefault=3

BootMenuDelay=*n*
Specifies number of seconds to display the Windows startup menu before running the default menu item. Examples:

Delay for three seconds: BootMenuDelay=3
No delay (default): BootMenuDelay=0

BootMulti=*n*   Enables/disables dual-boot capabilities. This allows you to boot multiple operating systems, such as Windows 95 and Linux, or Windows 95 and 98, or Windows 95 and Windows NT, from separate partitions on the same boot disk. If BootMulti=1, the *boot.ini* file gives additional boot instructions. Examples:

Disable (default): BootMulti=0
Enable: BootMulti=1

BootWarn=*n*   Enables/disables Safe Start warning and menu. Examples:

Disable: BootWarn=0
Enable (default): BootWarn=1

BootWin=*n*   Enables/disables Windows 95 as the default operating system (used when another operating system is also available on the computer).

Note: pressing F4 inverts the default if BootMulti=1. (For example, pressing the F4 key when BootWin=0 forces Windows 95 to load.) Examples:

Disables: BootWin=0
Enables (default): BootWin=1

DblSpace=*n*   Prevents/allows automatic loading of *dblspace.bin*. Examples:

Prevent: DblSpace=0
Allow (default): DblSpace=1

`DisableLog=n`   Enables/Disables creation of *bootlog.txt*. Examples:

Disable (default): DisableLog=0
Enable: DisableLog=1

`DoubleBuffer=n`

Enables/disables double-buffering for SCSI controller. A value of 1enables double-buffering for controllers that need it (such as SCSI controllers). A value of 2 enables double-buffering regardless of whether the controller needs it. Examples:

Disables: DoubleBuffer=0
Enables (default): DoubleBuffer=1

`DrvSpace=n`   Prevents/allows automatic loading of *drvspace.bin*. Examples:

Prevent: DrvSpace=0
Allow (default): DrvSpace=1

`LoadTop=n`   Enables/disables loading of *command.com* and/or *drvspace.bin* at the top of 640K memory. If you are having problems with software that makes assumptions about the available memory, try setting this to 0. Examples:

Disable: LoadTop=0
Enable (default): LoadTop=1

`Logo=n`   Hide/show the animated Windows logo (during logo display, Windows loads interrupt drivers that can cause incompatibility with some memory managers; hiding the logo prevents the loading of these drivers). Examples:

Disable: Logo=0
Enable (default): Logo=1

`Network=n`   Specify whether Windows 95 network software components were installed. If installed, Network will be set to 1 and "Safe startup with networking" will appear on the startup menu. Examples:

Off (default for non-network): Network=0
On: Network=1

`SystemReg=n`   Load/don't load Registry. Examples:

Load registry (default): SystemReg=1
Don't load registry: SystemReg=0

Registry

system.dat, *user.dat,*
\ *Windows**Profiles**<username>**user.dat*

The Registry provides Windows 95 and applications with a hierarchically-organized database of settings and configuration information. While initialization files such as *config.sys, system.ini,* and *win.ini* do remain important in Windows 95, the Registry holds a lot of the information that previous versions of Windows kept in separate *.ini* files.

For more information on the Registry, see Chapter 10.

---

setver

Lie about the MS-DOS version number on a program-by-program basis.

Description

Some Windows and DOS programs (including ones written by Microsoft) check the DOS version number incorrectly: for example, the program will actually run properly in any DOS version greater or equal to 5.0, but it instead checks to see whether the DOS version is exactly 5.0. To allow such programs to be run under Windows 95 (which includes MS-DOS 7.00 or 7.10), *setver* can be used to fake the DOS version number that Windows 95 reports to that program. For example, *winword.exe* apparently has to be told that it's running under DOS version 4.10.

setver has the following syntax:

    setver [drive:path] filename n.nn
    setver [drive:path] filename /delete [/quiet]

By using *setver* without any options, the current version table is displayed. The *setver* options are:

`[drive:path]`   Specifies location of the *setver.exe* file (*not* of the program for which you want to change the DOS version number).

`filename`   The filename of the program. No drive or path can be specified.

`n.nn`   Specifies the MS-DOS version to be reported to the program.

`/delete` *or* `/d`   Deletes the version-table entry for the specified program.

`/quiet` *or* `/q`   Hides the message typically displayed during deletion of version-table entry.

Examples

Tell Win95 to report DOS version 5.0 to *myprog.exe*:

    C:\>setver myprog.exe 5.00

Delete *myprog.exe* from the version table:

    C:\>setver myprog.exe /d

Notes

- Changes to the *setver* table don't take effect until the system is restarted.

- *setver* displays a dire-sounding warning message when a change is made to the version table.

- `drive:path` in the *setver* syntax specifies the location of *setver.exe* itself, not the location of the program for which the DOS version number is being set. The `drive:path` of *setver* itself can be specified because the version table is stored within the *setver.exe* executable file. Drives and paths cannot be specified for the program to be given a fake DOS version number: thus, setting the version number for *foobar.exe* sets it for any *foobar.exe* on any drive or directory.

- To load the version table stored in *setver.exe*, the Windows 95 boot process performs a device=setver.exe, whether or not *config.sys* actually contains an explicit statement.

system.ini   *\Windows\system.ini*

Most configuration information that used to be stored in the *system.ini* file has been moved to the Registry or is no longer valid. However, the file is still required, and there is a minimal set of essential entries, perhaps most importantly shell=, which specifies the overall operating system shell (not to be confused with the shell= command in *config.sys*, which specifies the DOS command line interpreter). This is normally specified as *explorer.exe*, but could be changed to *taskman.exe, command.com*, or a standalone application for kiosk for demo use.

While *system.ini* is a text file and can be edited with any text editor, large parts of its format are poorly documented, so tread with caution.

The continuing use of *system.ini* and other *.ini* files as a data storage area for system programs indicates once again that Windows 95 is not an integrated system, so much as a collection of independent applications, some of which have been updated to take advantage of newer system services, and some of which have not. (See Chapter 8, *Inside Windows 95.*)

win.ini   *\Windows\win.ini*

As with *system.ini*, many of the functions that were formerly performed by *win.ini* have migrated to the Registry. Still, a surprising amount of data is stored there. For example, Desktop settings from Control Panel → Desktop, such as the colors of various user interface items and the pathname and tiling options of Desktop wallpaper can be found in the [Colors] and [Desktop] sections, respectively. Regional settings are also stored here, in the [Intl] section. While you can change these values with a text editor, you're far better off using the GUI Control Panel interfaces.

win.ini is also used for storing font substitution information (i.e., what Microsoft fonts correspond to various PostScript fonts), as well as information about ports and printers.

Additional information about other Control Panel settings is stored in the file *\Windows\control.ini*.

Probably the most useful statements in *win.ini* are load= and run=. These statements can be used to specify programs that will be run automatically upon system startup. Specify the complete pathname of any program(s) to be run, separated by spaces. (Programs specified with load= are run first, then run=.)

Generally, though, it's easier to run programs automatically by putting shortcuts into *\Windows\Start Menu\Programs\StartUp*, especially since there are limits on the length of the run= and load= statements. These statements can each contain only 128 characters. By the time you specify a set of program pathnames (especially if they are in out-of-the-way places), you can fill up these statements pretty quickly. Note that if you exceed 128 characters, any programs specified beyond that limit will be silently ignored. What's more, there are documented cases of programs run with load= and run= statements not running properly, or having unintended side effects. (You can also specify programs to be run automatically at startup in the Registry at the key HKEY_LOCAL_MACHINE\SOFTWARE\Microsoft \Windows\CurrentVersion\Run and the corresponding keys RunOnce, RunServices, and RunServicesOnce.)

winstart.bat

\ *Windows\winstart.bat*

This is a regular DOS batch file that the DOSMGR VxD (inside *vmm32.vxd*) runs (if present) when starting up the System Virtual Machine in which all Win16 and Win32 apps run. In other words, the System VM is really a DOS box in which you can start DOS TSRs, etc. just before the GUI appears.

winstart.bat also runs when you exit from MS-DOS mode to normal Windows 95. (See *dosstart.bat*.)

CHAPTER 10

The Registry

The Registry provides Windows 95 and applications with a hierarchically organized database of settings and configuration information. While initialization files from earlier versions of Windows such as *config.sys*, *system.ini*, and *win.ini* do remain important in Windows 95, the Registry holds a lot of the information that previous versions of Windows kept in separate *.ini* files.

An amazing amount of what you assume is "hardwired" into Windows—the location of key directories, the names of objects such as the Recycle Bin, even the version number of Windows 95 reported on Control Panel → System—is actually the product of data stored in the Registry. Change the Registry data and key parts of your system can be affected. For this reason, Microsoft provides only minimal user documentation on *regedit*, the Registry Editor, preferring to leave such things in the hands of experienced system administrators and programmers.

Despite the enormous potential for harm, the Registry is fairly robust, and for every entry that you can wreak havoc by changing, there are hundreds that you can change with impunity. Nonetheless, you should back up the Registry files before making significant changes with *regedit*. See "Backing Up the Registry" later in this chapter for details.

The Registry is normally consulted silently by the programs (such as the Explorer) that build the Windows 95 user interface, as well as by most applications. Programs also write data to the Registry when they are installed, when you make changes to configuration settings, or just when they are run. For example, a game like Freecell keeps statistics in the Registry on how many games you've won and lost. Every time you play the game, those statistics are updated. For that matter, every time you move an icon on your Desktop, the position is recorded in the Registry.

You can view and modify the contents of the Registry with *regedit*. This program is not visible on the Start Menu. To run it, you either need to navigate to *Windows\\regedit.exe* in the Explorer, or (more practically), type the command name at the Run or Command prompt. When you first start the program, you'll see the display shown in Figure 10-1.

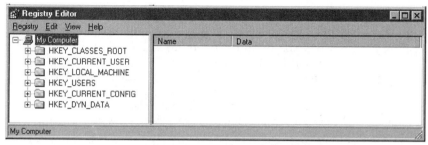

Figure 10-1: The Registry Editor dialog box

This interface looks familiar, even if the "folders" shown have strange names. (In the Registry, these folders are referred to as *keys*.) As in the Explorer, you have a two-pane view. Click on any item in the left pane to navigate, and click on the tiny plus signs or double-click on the folders to expand and collapse branches. View the results on the right. Given the familiar interface, you might hope just to start clicking away and see something familiar, like you do in the Explorer. Unfortunately, you can soon find yourself lost in a bewildering morass of tantalizing but ultimately meaningless data. You need to arm yourself with a few basic concepts, and then back up a few steps and start over with the big picture. That's what we'll do in the next two sections.

What's in the Registry

The Registry contains keys (represented in *regedit* by folder icons, even though they are nothing of the sort) and values. Keys can contain other keys, and/or values. That keys can in turn contain other keys establishes a hierarchy; a key with all its subkeys and values is often called a *branch*.

For example, information about the current user's configuration is kept in the key `HKEY_CURRENT_USER`. This key includes many subkeys, including one called `Software`, which includes keys for each vendor whose software is installed on the machine. In turn, each vendor will probably have a further key for each individual product, and then additional keys for whatever amount of data they want to store for the application. This can be a single value or an entire hierarchy of additional keys. What the authors of any program store in the Registry is entirely up to them.

Backslashes are used to represent the key/subkey hierarchy, much as they are used to represent the directory/subdirectory hierarchy in the file system.

For example, Netscape Navigator keeps information in the Registry about where to find my bookmark folder in the key `HKEY_CURRENT_USER\Software\Netscape\Netscape Navigator\Bookmark List`

The contents of this key on my machine are shown in Figure 10-2.

Speeding Up Registry Navigation

As in the Explorer, it's wise to train yourself to use the keyboard rather than the mouse. Typing the first letter of a Registry key is a quicker way to navigate to it than scrolling and clicking with the mouse.

When the focus is in the left (navigation) pane, you can also use the Back-space key and the arrow keys to navigate through the Registry hierarchy. Backspace will pop you up to the top of the next level in the key hierarchy but will not collapse any expanded keys. The left arrow will actually collapse the branch while moving back a level. The right arrow will expand the current key if it's collapsed. The up and down arrows will simply move vertically through any expanded keys. This is harder to explain precisely than it is to do; experiment, and you'll quickly get a feel for how it works.

Other useful navigation tools are Edit → Find (Ctrl-F) and Find Next (F3). You can search for a particular key, value, or value data, or can look in all three. One thing that's a bit confusing, though, is that Find starts its search from the currently highlighted Registry key and doesn't wrap around to the beginning. So if you want to search the entire Registry, be sure to start by highlighting the My Computer icon at the top of the Registry tree. Alt-Home will take you right there, as long as the focus is in the left pane.

Conversely, if you want to speed up your searches, first move down the navigation tree closer to where you think the target may be.

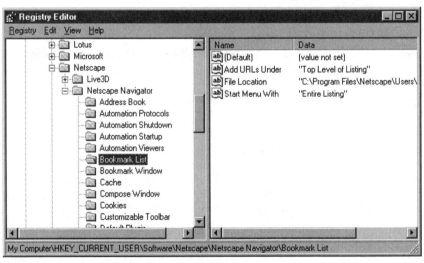

Figure 10-2: The Registry Editor illustrating values of Netscape Navigator's Bookmark List key

---

WARNING

It's easy to get confused about keys and values. You might be tempted to refer to a value name (e.g., "File Location" in Figure 10-2) as a key, and think of its associated data as the value, but in fact, the final item in any path is referred to as a value, whether or not it contains any data. It has two components: the value name and the value data. Anything that appears in *regedit*'s left pane is considered a key, while anything that appears in the right pane is considered a value.

Every key contains the value whose name shows up as (`Default`). If there is no default value for the key, you'll see the value data (`value not set`), as in Figure 10-2. You'll also see this in the right pane whenever you open a key that contains one or more subkeys with no values. But in other cases, you'll see the value name (`Default`) with an actual data value. See the discussion of `HKEY_CLASSES_ROOT` later in this chapter for an example.

With the exception of (`Default`), all of the value data shown in Figure 10-2 is in string format—text enclosed in quotes. To change a value, simply double click on it or select it and choose Modify from the Edit menu. An edit dialog box will be displayed. For example, if I wanted to change the location of my bookmark file (something I can't do with Navigator's Edit → Preferences menu), I could double click on File Location to see the edit dialog box shown in Figure 10-3. The current value is highlighted in the dialog box; simply replace the entire value by typing over it, or click to move to a particular point in the value to edit it.

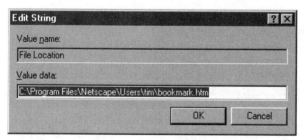

Figure 10-3: Editing a string value to change Netscape's bookmark directory

There are two other formats commonly found in the Registry—binary and DWORD (32-bit unsigned integer)—as well as three other internal formats that can't be modified by *regedit* and so are not discussed here.

Note that "string" values might be real text strings, such as pathnames, text messages, and so forth, or numeric values. It's up to the program that stored them to interpret them correctly. So-called binary values are actually stored as hexadecimal numbers, shown as four pairs of digits. As these are hex values, the digits range from 0 to F rather than from 0 to 9.

For example, the FreeCell game keeps its statistics in the Registry in binary format. Figure 10-4 shows the FreeCell statistics, plus a new value that was added to the FreeCell key for demonstration purposes.

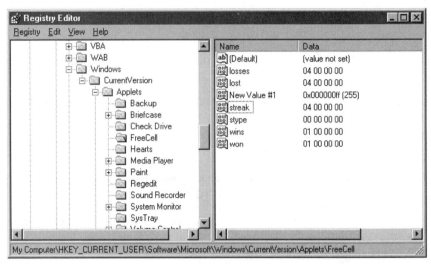

Figure 10-4: The Registry Editor illustrating values of the FreeCell key

In general, if a value is stored in binary or DWORD format, you can guess that it was either programmatically generated or the program's author wished to make the value a little more obscure and difficult to edit. However, if you know what you are doing, you can edit binary or DWORD values almost as easily as you can string values. For example, if I want to lie to my friends to tell them I've won 435 games of FreeCell rather than just one, I simply need to double-click on "won" and edit the value as shown in Figure 10-5.

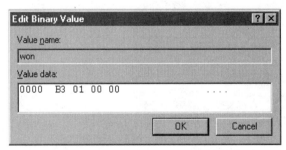

Figure 10-5: Editing the DWORD "won" value to alter the number of games won in FreeCell

Even if you're not a programmer, you can figure out hexadecimal values pretty easily with *calc* (see Chapter 5, *Commands and Applications*). Just enter the number you want to convert and click the Hex radio button to see the hexadecimal equivalent: 435 is 1B3. Note, however, that the hex values stored in a binary Registry value are in a somewhat unexpected format. The two low-order digits appear in a pair on the left, followed by the next two digits, and so on. The hex value 1B3 thus needs to be entered as B3 01.

If you want to convert a binary value shown in *regedit* to decimal, you have to reverse this notation. For example, if I wanted to find the decimal equivalent to a value shown as 47 00 65 6e, I'd set *calc* to hexadecimal mode, enter the digits 6e650047, and then switch to decimal mode to find out that the equivalent decimal number is 1,852,112,967. Of course, if the numbers get that big, it's likely that they have a meaning you might not want to muck with. If the purpose was simply to encode a value to make it harder to edit, you'll probably see smaller numbers, using only the leftmost pairs of digits, as in the FreeCell example.

> If you aren't sure about the meaning of a specific Registry value, don't be afraid to experiment. Experimenting might include editing a value with *regedit*, but it might be easier or safer to work from the other end: open the application whose data is stored there (e.g., a Control Panel applet), change a setting, and watch how the Registry data changes. In this way, you can get a sense of the meaning of many binary encoded values. Note that the Registry data may change immediately, but in order to update the view in *regedit*, you need to press F5 (Refresh).
>
> It's a good idea, though, to make a backup copy of a registry key before making any changes. See "Editing the Registry" and "Exporting and Importing Registry Keys" later in this chapter for details.

Figure 10-4 showed an additional value, called New Value #1, which I entered into the FreeCell key using *regedit* → Edit → New → DWORD Value. This example makes two points:

1. The DWORD format is also a hexadecimal number, but this time in a more conventional representation. The leading 0x is a standard programmer's notation for a hex value, and the number can be safely read from left to right. The equivalent decimal value is shown in parentheses following the hex value. What's more, when you edit a DWORD value, the edit dialog box gives you a choice of entering the new value in decimal or hex notation.

2. A Registry entry is meaningless unless a program actually reads it. You can enter new keys or values all you like, with the only consequence being that you've bloated your Registry. The chief danger is in deleting or modifying existing entries. (Note that there are sometimes undocumented Registry values that are meaningful to a program but that are not normally present. Adding them to the Registry can make useful changes; see *Windows Annoyances* by David Karp (O'Reilly & Associates) for several examples. However, the chance of hitting upon such a value at random is vanishingly small!)

This last point is critical. You can use a tool such as *regedit* to add, rename, and delete values and keys (except for the very top-level keys such as HKEY_CURRENT_USER or HKEY_LOCAL_MACHINE, which cannot be deleted, supplemented, or renamed). If you modify the FreeCell statistics in *regedit* to say so, FreeCell will dutifully report that you've won 1,000 games and lost none. On the other hand, if you add some new Registry keys and values that no program ever looks for, then these new keys and values will have no effect. Conversely, if you change some Registry setting without understanding how the system relies on the setting, this change can have a disastrous, unintended effect. It's worth noting that in some cases, the mere presence or absence of a key (without any value) may have meaning to some program.

A final note: Don't confuse *regedit* with the Registry itself. *regedit* is just one program that displays and modifies the Registry. (In fact, almost all Windows 95 programs rely on and modify the Registry in some way). The Registry itself is typically loaded from two files, \ *Windows\system.dat* and \ *Windows\user.dat*, which Windows 95 loads into memory when it boots up. While Windows 95 is running, it modifies this in-memory version; whenever the system is idle, and when you shut down, it automatically writes the Registry back out to *system.dat* and *user.dat*, saving the previous version in the files \ *Windows\system.da0* and \ *Windows\user.da0*. These backups are used in the event that the Registry gets corrupted. If user profiles are enabled, a separate *user.dat* file for each profile is typically stored in \ *Windows\Profiles\<username>\user.dat*.

The fact that Registry changes are applied immediately is one reason why editing the Registry is considered dangerous. There's no "save" and no "undo" in *regedit*. Any changes you make are applied immediately. (If you've saved Registry patches as described later in this chapter, you can apply them for a limited form of undo.)

Organization of the Registry

The Registry is enormous and complex; a full Registry might easily contain 15,000 keys and 35,000 values. Entire books have been written about it, and we can't do it justice here. Our purpose in this section is to arm you with a basic understanding of how the Registry is organized, not to document individual values in detail or suggest changes you might want to make with *regedit*.

David Karp's book *Windows Annoyances* provides many tips and tricks that rely on the Windows 95 Registry. Ron Petrusha's book *Inside the Windows 95 Registry*, while aimed primarily at software developers, contains several chapters aimed at experienced users. In particular, see Chapters 1 to 3, which give a good overview of the Registry and a detailed description of how to use *regedit*, and Chapter 8, *What Goes in the Registry: System Settings*.

http://142.104.153.201/www/Registry.html also contains a number of useful Registry tips.

As was shown in Figure 10-1, the top level of the Registry is organized into six main branches. By convention, the built-in top-level keys are always shown in all caps, even though the Registry itself is case-insensitive. (For example, HKEY_ CURRENT_USER\SOFTWARE\MICROSOFT\Windows is identical to HKEY_CURRENT_ USER\Software\Microsoft\Windows.) For convenience in referring to them in documentation (though not in the actual software), the names of the top-level keys are often abbreviated as shown in Table 10-1.

Table 10-1: Registry Key Abbreviations

Key	Abbreviated Name
HKEY_CLASSES_ROOT	HKCR
HKEY_CURRENT_USER	HKCU
HKEY_LOCAL_MACHINE	HKLM
HKEY_USERS	HKU
HKEY_CURRENT_CONFIG	HKCC
HKEY_DYN_DATA	HKDD

The function of each of these branches is briefly summarized in the following list. Subsequent sections go into their contents in more detail.

HKEY_CLASSES_ROOT (HKCR)

Contains file types, filename extensions, URL protocol prefixes, and OLE and DDE information. This information is the "glue" that ties Windows 95 together. It is critical to drag-and-drop operations, context menus, double-clicking, and many other familiar user interface semantics. The actions defined here tell Windows 95 how to react to every file type available on the system.

This entire branch is a mirror of HKLM\SOFTWARE\Classes, provided purely for convenience. Because the information here is accessed so frequently, it is made available at the top level.

HKEY_CURRENT_USER (HKCU)

Contains user-specific settings for the currently logged-in user. This entire branch is a mirror of HKEY_USERS*login-name*, or, if profiles aren't enabled, of HKEY_USERS\.Default. An application that keeps information on a per-user basis should store its data in HKCU\Software, and put information that applies to all users of the application in HKLM\SOFTWARE.

However, it is somewhat arbitrary what Windows applications seem to consider user-specific, and what is for all users on the machine. Like many aspects of Windows 95, the Registry provides a mechanism for applications to store configuration data, but does little to enforce any policies about how and where it will actually be stored.

HKEY_LOCAL_MACHINE (HKLM)

Contains information about hardware and software on the machine, not specific to the current user. The values in this branch are loaded from *Windows\system.dat.*

HKEY_USERS (HKU)

Stores underlying user data from which HKEY_CURRENT_USER is drawn. The values in this branch are loaded from *Windows\user.dat* and, if present, *Windows\Profiles\<login-name>\user.dat.*

HKEY_CURRENT_CONFIG (HKCC)

Much as Windows 95 can handle multiple users on a single machine, and therefore preserves individual users' settings within the Registry, so too it supports multiple hardware configurations, which are also preserved within the Registry, under the HKEY_CURRENT_CONFIG branch.

This key is loaded from HKLM\Config*xxxx*, where *xxxx* is a subkey representing the numeric value of the hardware configuration currently being used by Windows 95. On a system with only a single hardware configuration, its value is 0001. The name of the configuration that is current—and therefore the subkey of HKLM\Config to which this key points—is stored in the CurrentConfig value entry of the HKLM\System\CurrentControlSet \control\IDConfig key.

HKEY_DYN_DATA (HKDD)

> This branch contains dynamic data, only in-memory, not associated with *system.dat* or *user.dat*. Used in Plug and Play (Configuration Manager); also for performance monitoring statistics.

As noted above, HKEY_CLASSES_ROOT is identical to HKEY_LOCAL_MACHINE \Software\Classes, HKEY_CURRENT_USER is identical to HKEY_USERS\.Default and HKEY_USERS*xxxx* (where *xxxx* represents the currently logged-in user), and HKEY_CURRENT_CONFIG is identical to HKEY_LOCAL_MACHINE\Config*xxxx* (where *xxxx* represents the current hardware configuration).

HKEY_CLASSES_ROOT (HKCR)

On the surface, Windows 95 seems very object-oriented. Files, folders, and devices are represented by icons that respond differently to various actions such as single or double clicks, right clicks, and left clicks. But in a true object-oriented system, the object itself contains the knowledge of how to respond to events such as mouse clicks.

By contrast, Windows 95 performs much like the Wizard of Oz, not with true object-oriented magic, but with a complex machinery hidden behind a screen. The knowledge of how the Explorer should treat each object is stored in the Registry, in a complex chain of interrelated keys.

Much of the system's behavior depends on file extensions. It's quite important that file extensions (almost always the old DOS-style three-letter extension) accurately reflect the file type. There is nothing in the system that enforces this relied-upon connection between file extensions and file contents. It's purely a convention, but one that much of Win95's behavior depends upon. That's why it's so stupid that the Explorer hides them by default.

When you open HKCR, the first thing you'll see is a very long list of file extensions known to the system, from *.acp* (Office Actor Preview) to *.zip* (WinZip or other similar compressed "zip" archive file). The subkeys and values associated with each extension vary. In some cases, the application that opens a file with the specified extension is named directly, but in others, there's just a pointer to another key elsewhere in the list.

Following the list of extensions, you'll see a set of keys that are sometimes referred to as *class definition keys* or *document type keys*. These keys provide a level of indirection that lets one extension point to one of several possible applications.

For example, should a file with the *.doc* extension be opened by Word 6 or Word 8? When you upgrade from Word 6 to Word 8, the installation program simply needs to change the key that describes the *.doc* file extension so that it points to Word.Document.8 instead of Word.Document.6.

Should a file with the *.htm* extension be opened by Netscape Navigator or Microsoft Internet Explorer? If you use Navigator, the *.htm* key will have the value name (Default) with the data "NetscapeMarkup". If you use Internet Explorer, the value name (Default) will have the value data "htmlfile". If you then look at either of those two class definition keys (NetscapeMarkup or htmlfile), you'll see a different chain of subkeys. While both Navigator and Internet Explorer know how to handle HTML files, they use a different set of internal instructions for figuring out how to display or edit the files, what icon to display for the file, and so on.

The detailed subkeys and values that appear under the class definition and document type keys start to get really confusing. Because each program may record and retrieve different keys, it's very hard to generalize about them. The best we can do is to mention some of the kinds of keys you might see associated with a particular file extension subkey or class definition subkey. Here are some of the most common:

CLSID

> Class Identifier for OLE (Object Linking and Embedding) services. This is a randomly generated 16-byte number in the following format: {aaaaaaaa-bbbb-cccc-dddd-ffffffffffff} where each letter represents a hexadecimal digit. (That's a sequence of eight, four, four, four, and twelve hex digits, with a hyphen between each group of digits and the whole thing enclosed in curly braces.) Only Microsoft could come up with an identifier as obscure as this one.

> CLSID appears both as a subkey of many class definition keys and as a class definition key in its own right. That is, the key HKCR\NetscapeMarkup might have a subkey CLSID with the data value {61D8DE20-CA9A-11CE-9EA5-0080C82BE3B6}, but there's also a key called HKCR\CLSID with the subkey {61D8DE20-CA9A-11CE-9EA5-0080C82BE3B6}, which in turn has the data value "Netscape Hypertext Document". The first entry is simply a pointer to the second, which contains the actual class data. You must always be on the lookout for this kind of indirection.

> There are some CLSID keys that don't correspond to any particular extension. The CLSID itself represents the file type. This is the case for various system objects such as the Recycle Bin, Control Panel, and so forth. This is the source of the tips you will frequently encounter on the Net telling you how to rename or relocate these system objects by typing the new name followed by the long and seemingly incomprehensible CLSID as an extension.

Content Type

> This is the MIME (Multipurpose Internet Mail Extension) type corresponding to this file type. This key will typically exist for Internet-related file types such as GIF and JPEG. Email programs that support attachments and web browsers such as Netscape Navigator use MIME Content Types as well as or instead of extensions to recognize the format of a file.

DefaultIcon

> The location (usually a pathname and an optional "icon index" within the file) of the file containing the default icon to be used for this file type. If you see the value data "%1", that means that the file will act as its own icon.
>
> Note that there may be more than one default icon for a given file type. A good example is the Recycle Bin, which shows a different icon when it is empty and when it is full. In cases like this, what happens is that the program knows to copy its icon for the appropriate state to the DefaultIcon (Default) value. In other cases, though, a DefaultIcon may be specified in more than one place (e.g., under a document type key and under an associated CLSID key).

Shell

> Contains subkeys that define actions (open, edit, print, play, and so forth) that may be available for the object. These are some of the items that will appear on the context menu for the associated file type. The shell keys under file extension keys sometimes seem to be empty. Look under the file class definition key for more information (e.g., look under HKCR\NetscapeMarkup \Shell, not HKCR\.htm\Shell).
>
> Note that you might find a subkey sequence like Shell\Open\Command, where the value for Command is the command that will be used to open the file, or the command line including options to perform other operations. As in batch files, the syntax %1 represents the first argument to the program (typically the filename).
>
> You might also find something like Shell\Open\ddeexec, where the value is the DDE (Dynamic Data Exchange) subroutine call for performing the specified operation. (For example, Windows might send a DDE message to an application to tell it to print a file after opening it.) DDE is supposedly obsolete, supplanted in Microsoft's toolkit by ActiveX (the API formerly known as OLE), but you wouldn't know it from the number of ddeexec keys in the Registry.
>
> You'll see the same split between command-line options and DDE using the Explorer interface to file associations, via the View → Options → File Types menu on any folder. Some actions will list a command line; others will use DDE. If you're not a programmer with access to the DDE documentation for a particular application, you may find this difficult to follow at times.
>
> What's often a little perplexing is why a given file type's subkeys don't seem to show a particular action, even though you know that action is supported for the file type. There's such a maze of indirection that the key you expect to find in one place just isn't there. It's somewhere else in the chain of associations.

ShellEx

> Shell Extensions. These keys, usually via subkeys called ContextMenuHandlers, define actions that are added only in specific contexts. For example, files and folders have an "Update" action on their context menu only when they are within a Briefcase. As often as not, ContextMenuHandlers involve some further redirection, usually involving a CLSID. There is also sometimes a

PropertySheetHandlers subkey under ShellEx, which defines cases where a file type has a special property sheet associated with it. This is how applications add their own specific tabs to the property windows for a given file type.

ShellNew

Defines whether the file type will appear on the context menu → New menu. The value name may be Command, Filename, NullFile, or Data. In most cases, this key will be empty, if it exists at all. (Contrast the enormous number of file types defined in the Registry with the much smaller number that appear on the New menu.)

Command contains a command line to create the new file. (This is used only for the *.bfc* and *.lnk* extensions.)

Filename contains the name of a file "template" to be copied to the new location. Its value data may contain a complete pathname, but if it's just a filename (e.g., *netscape.html, winword.doc,* or *winword8.doc*) it will be found in the directory \ *Windows\ShellNew.* (Of course, like almost everything else in Windows 95, this location is itself subject to a Registry setting (HKCU\Software\Microsoft\Windows\CurrentVersion\Explorer\ShellFolders\Templates) and can therefore be changed.)

Some file types (such as *.bmp* files, which may contain data in any one of a number of related formats, as specified by binary header data within the file itself) are described by the value NullFile. NullFile has the empty string (" ") as its value data. An application that opens a new file of this type will write out any necessary format data only when the file is first saved.

Data contains binary data that needs to be written to the new file. This might, for example, be some kind of binary header data.

Before leaving HKCR, two other keys are worthy of note.

HKCR* contains information that will be applied to all files, regardless of their extension.

HKCR\Unknown describes, via its Shell\OpenAs\Command subkey, just what will happen to a file whose type is unknown. As we know from Chapter 3, *The Windows 95 User Interface*, it will pop up the Open With dialog box. It is here that the *rundll32* command line to bring up that dialog box can be found. (It's amazing just how many system behaviors that don't seem to have a command line associated with them actually do. Quite often, you'll find a magical incantation starting with *rundll32* somewhere behind the scenes.)

HKEY_CURRENT_USER (HKCU)

The Registry separates user settings from global machine settings. In the FreeCell example earlier in this chapter, each user of the machine can have his or her own separate won/lost statistics because the program keeps these statistics in the HKCU branch of the Registry. If it instead used HKEY_LOCAL_MACHINE, all users would share the same statistics.

Information for all users is kept in HKEY_USERS (HKU), and the information for the current user is mirrored to HKCU. If there is only one user of the machine, the mirror is from HKU\.Default. If profiles are enabled, the mirror is from HKU*login_name*. (The preceding statement is a bit of an oversimplification. See the discussion of HKU later in this chapter for the full story.)

There are seven top-level subkeys: AppEvents, ControlPanel, InstallLocationsMRU, keyboard layout, Network, RemoteAccess, and Software. Note the inconsistent capitalization, which illustrates once again how the Registry is not a monolithic structure managed by one program or individual, but rather an inconsistent repository for whatever data the author of a particular program or subsystem chose to put there.

HKCU\AppEvents

This is where the associations between events and system sounds are kept. (See "Sounds" in Chapter 4, *The Control Panel*.) There are two branches here: EventLabels and Schemes. EventLabels contains the labels that will be used for the sounds; Schemes contains the pointers to the actual sounds.

Schemes has two main subkeys: Apps and Names.

Applications that use sounds can create their own subkey under Schemes \Apps, or they can add sounds into the default list, which is kept in the subkey Apps\.Default. If they add their own subkey, the sounds will show up in a separate section of the sounds list in Control Panel → Sounds. So you might see a subkey such as Mplayer, or Office97, since these applications add some of their own sound events in addition to the default sounds.

Schemes\Names is used to list named sound schemes like Jungle, Musica and so forth. When you change the sound scheme using the drop-down Scheme list on Control Panel → Sounds, the appropriate scheme is copied into .Default. (That's why, if you've made changes to your system sounds, you must save them as a new scheme before switching to another scheme.)

HKCU\ControlPanel

This is where data from several of the Control Panel applets is stored, particularly Accessibility and some (but not all) of the Display settings. (Additional Display settings are still stored in *.ini* files.) The names don't match up cleanly to the names used in the Control Panel, but you can usually figure out what's what by going back and forth between *regedit* and the target Control Panel applet. For example; HKCU\ControlPanel\Accessibility maps directly to Control Panel → Accessibility, but HKCU\ControlPanel\Cursors maps to Control Panel → Mouse → Pointers.

As is typical in the convoluted world of the Registry, some entries point somewhere else entirely. For example, HKCU\ControlPanel\International simply defines a Locale value, such as "00000409", which is the standard code for what the Control Panel calls "English (United States)". If you use *regedit*'s Find function to trace this value, you'll eventually find the scattered locations of many of the individual values that Control Panel → Regional Settings brings together in one place.

> This example illustrates a key point: there's little reason to poke around in the Registry for values that have a convenient user interface in the application. The point is to understand the overall structure of the Registry so that you can find and manipulate entries for which the application developer has provided no user interface.

HKCU\InstallLocationsMRU

This key lists the last five locations from which software has been installed. MRU stands for "MostRecentlyUsed"; whenever you see a drop-down list showing recent commands or actions, there's likely a *something*MRU key somewhere behind it. The five entries in this MRU list are stored in values named a, b, c, d and e, with their order in the list specified by the value MRUList (e.g., "dceba"). It's usually safe to erase this type of list.

HKCU\keyboard layout

This key is used only if you have installed more than one keyboard layout via Control Panel → Keyboard → Language. A Preload subkey lists a separate subkey for each installed language, with subkey 1 specifying the default language.

HKCU\Network

This key lists Network connections you've made. Persistent lists the UNC paths for connections for which you've mapped a local drive letter (using Explorer → Tools → Map Network Drive) and checked Reconnect at logon. Recent lists network connections you've made recently, regardless of whether they've been made persistent.

The format of the names shown in Recent seems a little odd. While Persistent uses UNC paths, Recent changes the leading \\ to ./././ when representing the network name, and inserts a . before every additional / in the path. What's more, it truncates any name to 12 characters.

HKCU\RemoteAccess

This key lists various types of information used by Dial-Up Networking, including the default connection to be used by Internet applications. The Implicit subkey lists the UNC path of any shared folders or printers that are accessed over a particular Dial-Up Networking connection. The Profile subkey stores information specific to each connection, such as the saved login name that will be supplied automatically when you make the connection.

HKCU\Software

This key contains subkeys for each vendor whose software is loaded onto the machine, and, within each vendor's area, subkeys for each product. The keys stored here contain only user-specific settings for each software application. Other settings, which are common to all users of software on the machine, are stored in HKLM\SOFTWARE. (Note the difference in capitalization between HKCU\Software and HKLM\SOFTWARE. Even though a search of the Registry and other Registry operations are case-insensitive, case can be used like this to make references to similarly named keys a little more distinguishable.)

The structure of these interrelated Registry branches (and particularly of the
Microsoft\Windows\CurrentVersion branch under both) is described later
in this chapter, in the section "HKCU\Software and HKLM\SOFTWARE."

HKEY_LOCAL_MACHINE (HKLM)

HKLM describes the configuration of your machine. It has eight top-level subkeys:
Config, DesktopManagement, Enum, hardware, Network, Security, SOFTWARE,
and System. (DesktopManagement will not be present on all systems.)

HKLM\Config

Hardware profiles (Control Panel → System → Hardware Profiles) are stored
in this branch. If hardware profiles are enabled, each profile will be stored in
a key with a four-digit name starting with 0001. If hardware profiles are not
enabled, only the key 0001 will appear. The current profile is mirrored to
HKEY_CURRENT_CONFIG (HKCC); the details will be discussed there.

HKLM\DesktopManagement

This branch provides information used by Microsoft's Desktop Management
Interface (DMI).

HKLM\Enum

This branch "enumerates" every device known to the system. It is the heart of
the Plug-and-Play (PnP) system. It contains an entry ("node") for each device
or bus controller (SCSI, etc.). From this list, the Windows 95 Configuration
Manager (a set of core routines in the Ring 0 portion of the operating system)
builds the list of currently active device nodes in HKEY_DYN_DATA\Config
Manager\Enum.

Plug and Play is a set of architecture specifications that allow a PC, its operating system, and any add-in hardware devices and associated device drivers
to work automatically without user intervention. PnP enumeration happens
whenever the system is booted, as well as when Windows 95 is notified that
you've changed the hardware (e.g., by swapping out a PCMCIA card, or by
docking or undocking a laptop that supports so-called "hot docking" rather
than requiring a reboot). Drivers are automatically loaded or unloaded from
memory; a static set of drivers does not need to be loaded at boot time. (At
least that's the theory.)

PnP is not something that Windows 95 can implement perfectly by itself, since
it requires that not only the operating system but also the underlying PC BIOS
and any add-in devices support the PnP specification.

PnP devices include PCMCIA cards and devices that attach to PCI or ISAPNP
buses. Advanced Power Management (APM) is also a Plug-and-Play feature. If
you have a Control Panel → Power applet, or a Suspend item on your Start
menu, APM is installed.

In cases where Windows 95 is running on legacy (pre-PnP) hardware or with
legacy devices, it goes through a process called hardware detection. This
process is initiated from Control Panel → Add New Hardware, rather than
being carried out automatically during the boot process. The Add New Hardware wizard creates a log file called *detlog.txt*, which can be helpful for
debugging purposes.

The Plug-and-Play BIOS specification is available at *http://www.microsoft.com/hwdev/*.

Walking through the Enum key in detail would require covering more hardware concepts than we have space for in this book. What's more, much of the information in this branch may be irrelevant to you, since it lists all devices known to your system, rather than what's currently installed. To see what devices are actually active in your system, go to HKEY_CURRENT_CONFIG. However, since this is where you'll see the complete list of available entries, we'll list some of the top-level subkeys you may find here.

Basically, the devices are listed by the buses they are attached to, much as they are in Control Panel → System → Device Manager when you select View devices by connection. Each device node is identified by a branch made up of three subkeys, effectively giving each device a three level name. The first subkey is the enumerator—the portion of the Configuration Manager that tracks this type of device—the second subkey is the device-id, and the third subkey is the instance of the device (in case there is more than one). The format of the last two subkeys depends on the enumerator. The instance is usually a sequence number, the position on a bus (PCI), or the combined enumerator, device-id, and instance of the parent device concatenated and separated by &.

Example names are:

```
BIOS\*PNP0C04\00
ESDI\GENERIC_IDE__DISK_TYPE<7_\BIOS&*PNP0600&0800
PCI\VEN_8086&DEV_1234\BUS_00&DEV_01&FUNC_00
```

If you're not a hardware jockey, this stuff can get pretty stiff. Even Device Manager (which is a lot friendlier than looking at this stuff in *regedit*) can be tough to follow if you don't really know much about hardware.

BIOS

A key found on systems with a Plug-and-Play BIOS (Basic Input/Output System) for devices found on the motherboard. On systems without a PnP BIOS, many of the same entries will be found in the Root key.

ESDI

Lists Enhanced System Device Interface devices. This is a hard disk device type. A CurrentDriveLetterAssignment value name contains the drive letter assigned to the drive. If a disk is partitioned, there may be more than one drive letter shown.

FLOP

Lists information about your floppy drive controller and attached floppy drives. There is one subkey below this one for each installed floppy drive.

HTREE

Stands for "Hardware Tree." We're not sure what this one does, although it seems to be referred to by a number of the other keys. We suspect it has something to do with the generation of the dynamic hardware tree in HKDD.

LPTENUM

Appears if a Plug-and-Play printer is configured for a parallel port.

MF

Stands for Multifunction PCI devices. The parent device is elsewhere in the tree, and the individual child devices appear separately here. An example might be the OSI Trumpcard, which combines a modem and Ethernet controller on a single PCMCIA card.

Monitor

Lists available monitors. The `Default_Monitor` subkey doesn't always indicate which monitor is currently in use. Instead, look at `HKDD\Config Manager\Enum\Monitor`.

Network

Specifies some parameters related to any network hardware. It doesn't list the actual hardware.

PCI

Stands for Peripheral Component Interconnect, Intel's 1992 local bus standard. The naming convention for keys here is pretty funky. You'll see names like `PCI\VEN_8086&DEV_1234\BUS_00&DEV_01&FUNC_00`.

Each vendor, device, bus, and function has a unique identifier. If you get to the end of the branch, you'll find some identifying data. But the Device Manager is a lot easier to use.

PCMCIA

Stands for Personal Computer Memory Card International Association. These days, PCMCIA cards are often called PC cards.

Root

Lists any non-PnP devices. For example, printer drivers may be listed here. Bindings will list protocols bound to a network adapter. (See "Network" in Chapter 4.)

SCSI

Stands for Small Computer System Interface.

Serenum

Lists any devices installed on a serial port.

HKLM\hardware

According to the Microsoft Windows 95 Resource Kit, the `devicemap\serialcomm` key is used by HyperTerminal. It lists values for COM1 and COM2 on my system. The `System\CentralProcessor` and `System\FloatingPoint-Processor` branches tell me that my CPU is "GenuineIntel." I hope the thought police aren't checking this key.

HKLM\Network

The `Logon` subkey tracks information for Dial-Up Networking, such as your username and whether to process a login script. The username is the name of the user who last successfully logged in. So, for example, if you logged in by pressing **Esc** at the initial Network logon prompt, this key will show the name of the last person who logged on with a valid name.

HKLM\Security

If remote administration is enabled, this subkey apparently contains information about the computer that will be used for administration. The format is obscure.

HKLM\SOFTWARE

This is the big one. It lists all of the software installed on your system. HKEY_CLASSES_ROOT is mirrored from the Classes subkey. As noted earlier, there is a subkey for each vendor. The Microsoft branch is discussed later in this chapter, in the section "HKCU/Software and HKLM/SOFTWARE."

HKLM\System

This branch contains a subkey called CurrentControlSet, which in turn has the two subkeys Control and Services.

The Control key contains a CurrentUser value as well as numerous subkeys. The CurrentUser value is the same as HKLM\Network\Logon*username*. It will exist only on a networked system. However, if the username was bypassed for the current login (by pressing Esc at the initial login prompt), this branch will not exist.

HKLM\System\Control

Some of the interesting subkeys in the Control branch include:

ComputerName

> Stores the name you give your system in Control Panel → Network → Identification.

InstalledFiles

> Seems to include a list of *.exe* and *.dll* files relating to networking that are installed on your system.

Keyboard Layouts

> Lists all of the available keyboard layouts, with pointers to the associated *.kbd* file.

Media Resources

> Lists multimedia drivers.

NLS

> Defines the code page values that are used to associate languages with keyboard layouts and other regional settings.

Perfstats

> Stores information about performance data that is kept in HKDD.

Print

> Lists keys for each of the printers in your *Printers* folder and pointers to the associated drivers. Also keys for the FAX: and PUB: virtual print devices.

SecurityProviders\SCHANNEL

> Lists certification authorities known to your system, as well as Ciphers, Hashes, and KeyExchangeAlgorithms (if any). Also lists the security protocols known to your system, such as SSL 2.0 or SSL 3.0.

SessionManager

Contains lots of tantalizing but obscure subkeys with names like `AppPatches`, `CheckBadApps`, `CheckVerDLLs`, `Known16DLLs`, and `WarnVerDLLs`. They are presumably of use to software developers who want to check what DLLs and application patches are installed in your system, and for Windows 95 to patch applications dynamically, but there may be some meat for browsing power users in here as well.

TimeZoneInformation

Stores the data set as a result of Control Panel → Date/Time → Time Zone.

VMM32Files

Lists all the *.vxd* files that have been incorporated into \ *Windows\System\VMM32.vxd.*

HKLM\System\Services

The Services branch gets into a miscellany of hardware- and system-related services, including:

Arbitrators

Subkeys here store reserved system addresses for legacy hardware with fixed hardware address, DMA addresses, I/O port addresses, and IRQ assignments. This is the information that shows up in Control Panel → System → View Resources.

Class

Subkeys here provide information on current devices. The information here is at a much higher level than that provided in `HKLM\Enum`. For example, the `Modem` key might list the Hayes commands to be used for each class of modem command. The `Display` key might include subkeys for available resolutions and the currently selected resolution.

RemoteAccess

Includes some information used by Dial-Up Networking.

VxD

Lists the installed Virtual Device Drivers.

HKCU\Software and HKLM\SOFTWARE

As noted earlier, both `HKEY_CURRENT_USER` and `HKEY_LOCAL_MACHINE` include a similarly structured Software branch (although in the first case, it is spelled with only an initial capital, where in the latter it is in all caps). Each has a branch for each vendor who has software installed on the system.

In theory, the `HKCU` branch should include information that is configurable on a per-user basis (which would be the case, for instance, with a software package with a per-user license, or per-user customization). The `HKLM` branch should include software that is standard for all users. In practice, though, it doesn't seem to be as consistent as that. The information that is stored in each branch sometimes overlaps (or doesn't overlap) in unexpected ways. So if you're looking for something, look in both branches. In the discussion that follows, we will try to compare and contrast what you will find in each branch.

Because this is a book about Windows 95, and not about the third-party applications that might be installed in it, the primary focus of this discussion is on the `Microsoft\Windows\CurrentVersion` branch. Except for the first entry, all the entries are relative to that key.

Microsoft\Windows\CurrentVersion

HKCU shows no data for this key at the top level. HKLM is where the goodies are: lots of information about the system configuration, including the registered owner of the software and his or her organization, and the version and sub-version of Windows 95. (See Chapter 2, *Versions of Windows 95*, for information on how to intepret what you see there.) And obviously, since this is just an editable Registry entry, be wary of what you find. The *ver* command is a safer way to find out your system version.

App Paths

HKLM only

This branch lists a path for many applications that are installed in nonstandard locations (i.e., not in \, *Windows*, or *Windows\Command*). It is the reason why you can successfully type a command name like *excel* or *winword* at the Run prompt, but not at the command prompt, unless you add *Program Files\Microsoft Office\Office* to your search path. They have listed their path individually under this key.

Note that in contrast to many of the keys in HKLM/SOFT-WARE/Windows/CurrentVersion, this branch includes references for non-Microsoft applications. The reason is that it's an information area to be used by a Microsoft application (to wit, the Explorer's Run prompt). Some, but not all, applications install a path here.

If you have an application that installs a shortcut on the Start menu, but doesn't let you type its name at the Run prompt, add a key for it here. It's fairly easy to duplicate the format of the existing keys. For example, I added a *PSP.EXE* key, with the values:

```
(Default)     "C:\Program Files\Paint Shop Pro\PSP.EXE"
Path          "C:\Program Files\Paint Shop Pro"
```

And now I can type *psp* at the Run prompt when I want to start up Paint Shop Pro (see *http://www.jasc.com*) to make a new screen capture for this book.

Applets

HKCU stores settings here for Backup, Briefcase, Check Drive, FreeCell, Hearts, Media Player, Paint, RegEdit, Sound Recorder, System Monitor, SysTray, Volume Control, and WordPad. Most of the values are encoded binary or DWORD values that you probably don't want to mess with, but there are some values that may prove of interest. For example, both Paint and WordPad keep a `Recent File List` key here.

`HKLM` includes subkeys for `Backup`, `Check Drive`, and `Popup`. The values stored for `Backup` and `Check Drive` do not overlap.

Explorer

This is where you hit pay dirt. There are many MRU lists, paths to system folders, and so forth. Here are some of the interesting subkeys in `HKCU`:

DeskView
> Contains the state of the Desktop as an encoded binary value. ExpView does the same for other Explorer states.

Doc Find Spec MRU
> Contains the last ten names you searched for using Find → Files or Folders. These are the items that appear in the drop-down list in the Find dialog box. While this may seem somewhat useless, you can imagine, for instance, writing a Registry editing script that would preload the Find drop-down list with a set of long names you wanted to search for repeatedly.

> As with all MRU lists, the value names are a series of letters; there is also a value called `MRUList` that specifies the order in which the entries should be displayed. That is, if you've just typed in the filenames *.dll* and then *.exe* into the Find dialog box, they might appear as items h and i in the list. But then, if you picked *.dll* again from the list, the `MRUList` would show "ijabcdefgh". The list is updated only when you actually execute a find, not when you type in a new filename to search for or pick an item from the drop-down list. In addition, when you quit Find, value j, which always contains an empty string, rotates to the front of the list.

FindComputerMRU
> Contains the MRU list for Find → Computer. It operates just like the previous example and most MRU lists in the Registry.

RecentDocs
> Contains an encoded version of the contents of *Windows**Recent*, the list of the twenty most recently opened files. The values are in binary format. The function of this data is unclear, since if you delete all the shortcuts in *Windows**Recent*, the Start → Documents list will indeed be empty, but the Registry entry will be unchanged.

RunMRU
> Stores the last 26 commands you issued at the Run prompt. The 26-command limit comes stems from MRU's use of lowercase letters of the alphabet as value names for each command.

ShellFolders
> Specifies the location of many of the standard Windows system folders, including Desktop, NetHood, Programs, Send To, Start Menu, Startup, and Templates (see the discussion of ShellNew earlier in this chapter in "HKEY_CLASSES_ROOT (HKCR)").

This branch really brings home the extent of Win95's mutability. Even the directory names that the Explorer relies on, such as \ *Windows\Desktop*—even these are not hard-wired. So the Explorer doesn't know anything about *C:\ Windows\Desktop*. All it knows is that it can get the name of the folder it's supposed to use as the Desktop from the Registry. Most of these values probably shouldn't be changed.

`User Shell Folders`

Supposedly stores the location of application-specific folders that are personal to each user. For example, you'll see Microsoft Office's Personal again here, as well as IE's Favorites. Note, however, that both of these also appear in the Shell Folders key. It's not immediately clear if this is a belt-and-suspenders kind of thing, or just an oversight. If you want to make changes, either change both or experiment to see which setting takes precedence. Whenever a key seems to be duplicated in more than one place, it's good practice to make changes in both places.

The `Explorer` branch in `HKLM` contains very different information. Here are some of its subkeys:

`Desktop\NameSpace`

Contains keys named with the CLSID of system folders that appear on the Desktop such as the Recycle Bin, Inbox, and Microsoft Network. Anything involving CLSIDs in the Registry is usually a maze of indirection.

`LastBackup`

Contains a value for each disk drive letter, with the data being the number of days since the last backup of that drive. The data is binary encoded; there's probably more than just the number of days in there, but that's what you see when you go to the *drive* → Properties → Tools tab. Similar keys exist for LastCheck (length of time since the last *scandisk*) and LastOptimize (length of time since the last *defrag*).

`mycomputer\NameSpace`

Contains a key named with the CLSID of Dial-Up Networking.

`Tips`

This is a good one. It contains the text of the system startup tips. If you wanted to provide your own tips, you could do so. Obviously, there's also extreme potential for misuse!

HKEY_USERS (HKU)

If there is only one user of a machine, `HKU` will contain only a branch labeled `.Default`. (Note the leading period.) If Profiles are enabled, there will be a second branch named after the currently logged-in user.

If it exists, the branch named after the currently logged-in user is mirrored to `HKEY_CURRENT_USER`; if not, the `.Default` branch is mirrored there.

Why is it that there are never more than two profiles contained here, even if there are multiple users? Basically, when you create a second username on the machine, the current contents of the Registry are written to a *user.dat* file in the directory \ *Windows\Profiles\<username>*. That file contains as its `.Default` branch the user data as of the time the profile was created. This is copied verbatim to the second branch, named after that user. As the new user makes configuration changes, the two branches gradually diverge. The .Default branch remains an unchanged copy of the settings that were in effect when the user's profile was first created.

During system idle time, and when the user logs out, any changes are written back to the *Windows\Profiles\<username>\user.dat* file.

This process is repeated for each user who logs in to the machine. When they log back in, only their own *user.dat* file is loaded, which is why multiple users don't show up in the active Registry.

This design prevents one user from easily viewing or changing another user's settings.

HKEY_CURRENT_CONFIG (HKCC)

As noted earlier, HKCC is mirrored from the HKLM\Config\000x key, where 000x is the name of the current hardware profile. If hardware profiles are not enabled, the source will be HKLM\Config\0001.

HKEY_DYN_DATA (HKDD)

HKDD contains two main branches: Config Manager and PerfStats.

Config Manager\Enum reflects the hardware devices for which drivers are actually loaded in memory. The HardWareKey value points to the corresponding path for each entry in HKLM\enum.

PerfStats contains pointers to the routines that gather the source data for the statistics displayed by the System Monitor (*sysmon*).

Backing Up the Registry

As noted earlier, the Registry is backed up automatically every time you boot the machine. The files *Windows\system.dat*, *Windows\user.dat*, and (if present) *Windows\Profiles\<username>\user.dat* are copied, respectively, to *Windows \system.da0*, *Windows\user.da0*, and *Windows\Profiles\<username>\user.da0*. (Note that the names *system.da0* and *user.da0* contain the number zero, not the letter O.) This means that you should always be able to go back to a workable version of the Registry by booting into DOS only (see Chapter 9, *Windows Startup*), and copying the *.da0* file to the corresponding *.dat* file.

The Registry files are hidden, read-only, system files. You'll need to change those attributes with *attrib* before you can see or copy them. You should reset the attributes when you're done, but if you don't, Windows will do it for you when it restarts.

Here's the procedure to follow if you think you've screwed up your Registry and want to get back to the last known good version:

1. Click Start → Shut Down.

2. Click Restart the computer in MS-DOS mode → Yes.

3. Type the following commands at the DOS prompt:

```
C:\>cd c:\windows
C:\Windows>attrib -h -r -s system.dat system.da0
C:\Windows>copy system.da0 system.dat
C:\Windows>attrib -h -r -s user.dat user.da0
C:\Windows>copy user.da0 user.dat
```

4. Restart your computer.

Of course, this procedure assumes that you haven't already restarted your computer since you made the damaging changes to your Registry.

In addition, the file *System.1st* contains the contents of HKLM immediately after your system was first installed. It's not much of a backup, since it is probably fairly out of date. But it may be better than nothing if you have lost everything.

If you're planning to do any serious Registry hacking, you may want to create additional backups. Simply copy the files in the previous list before making any major changes.

You can also export the branch of the Registry you're working on (see "Exporting and Importing Registry Keys" later in this chapter for details), and re-import it, overwriting your changes if you don't like what you've done. This is probably the simplest form of backup if you are making only small changes.

Editing the Registry

As we've suggested earlier, editing the Registry with *regedit* is fairly simple.

To create a new key or value, use Edit → New. The key or value is created within the currently selected key. A new string value will have the null string as its value; a new binary value will show the following message in parentheses: (zero length binary value). A new DWORD value will show up as zero: 0x00000000 (0). You can then edit that value (see following description) to change it.

To delete a key or value, select it and click Edit → Delete, or simply press the Del key. But be warned, there's no undelete, so you might want to first write out the branch containing the key you're about to delete as a *.reg* file (see following instructions). Or you can simply use Edit → Rename to rename the key. This disables it while preserving its data. (A key in the Registry that no program looks for does take up space, but otherwise has no effect.)

To edit a value, select it by clicking on the icon beside its name, and then choose Edit → Modify. Or just double-click on the icon. Enter the new value. Within the edit dialog box, you can select data, copy and paste in the normal way, dragging the cursor over data to select it, and using the Ctrl-C, Ctrl-X, and Ctrl-V keyboard accelerators to copy, cut, and paste.

These selection and copying techniques don't work for key names or other information on the left (navigation) pane in *regedit*. However, in OSR2, there's a Copy Key Name command on the Edit menu. This simply copies the full path to the key to the Clipboard. It doesn't copy the contents of the key. It's useful mainly for documentation purposes, since you can paste the key name into an external text file. (You can also paste it into *regedit*'s Find dialog box using Ctrl-V, even though there isn't a Paste command on the Edit menu. Of course, if you're already at the key, why search for it? I suppose you could edit down the path to the terminal component, and then look for other keys with the same name. This is handy if you're looking for other instances of a complex name like a CLSID key.)

If you want to copy an existing value, double-click on it and select all of the data in the edit window, as shown in Figure 10-6.

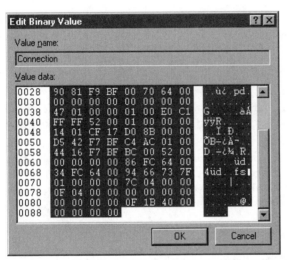

Figure 10-6: Copying an existing Registry value

Ctrl-C will copy the data to the clipboard. Then create a new value, being sure to match the type (string, binary, or DWORD) of the original value. Double-click on the new value to edit it. Use Ctrl-V to paste the copied data into the edit window.

This is a handy thing to do not only when using an existing value as a template for a new value, but also whenever you're going to make changes to an existing value. You can make little "inline backups" by creating a new value (*whatever.bak*, for instance) and pasting in the old value data before you change it. This might seem a little tedious, but it might prevent future headaches if you're about to change a complex value whose format you aren't completely sure you understand.

To copy a value name to the Clipboard, you can use a similar workaround. Ctrl-C won't work in the normal *regedit* window, but if you select Edit → Rename (or press F2), you can copy the name from there.

Unfortunately, there's no easy way to copy a key and all of its contents within *regedit*. If you want to copy an entire key and all its values, you'll have to do it one value at a time. It's usually much easier to export the key, edit the resulting file with a text editor, and then import the edited file. (See "Exporting and Importing Registry Keys" later in this chapter.)

In addition to the Edit menu, you may find it handy to use *regedit's* context menus. Right-clicking on a key in the left pane gives a context menu with Expand or Collapse, New, Find, Delete, Rename, and Copy Key Name. (Expand opens a

Registry key with subkeys. It will be grayed out if there are no subkeys below the selected key. If the branch is already expanded, the first item on the menu will be Collapse instead of Expand.)

Right-clicking with a value selected in the right pane gives a context menu with Modify, Delete, and Rename. Right-clicking in the right pane with no value selected gives a context menu with New (to create a new string, binary or DWORD value). You can also get to the New menu by pressing Shift-F10.

Exporting and Importing Registry Keys

You can export an ASCII copy of the entire Registry or any branch. Highlight the key you want to export and select Registry → Export. You'll get the standard Save As box. The selected key, any subkeys, and all their data will be saved in a file with the *.reg* extension. You probably don't want to select My Computer to export the entire Registry, since HKDD is huge and can't be re-imported in any case.

Exporting Registry files is a great idea. They are saved in text format, and they are generally easier to search, examine and edit with your favorite text editor (especially if you have a powerful one) than in *regedit*.

> Before making any changes to a Registry key, do a quick backup by exporting the key. Depending on what changes you've made, the Registry might not be identical after re-importing the key (see later explanation), but at least you'll have a record of what the key looked like before the changes.

Importing *.reg* files is more dangerous. The contents are merged into the Registry, overwriting the current contents. Especially if you've gone at the exported file with a text editor, which does less to ensure data integrity than *regedit*, you could potentially cause major harm. Note that the imported file is merged into the current Registry, not copied over it. This means that modified keys and values replace their equivalents, and new keys and values are added, but old keys that don't have a corresponding value in the saved *.reg* file are not deleted.

So, for example, if you export a branch, delete a few keys from the *.reg* file, and then import the file, the Registry will be unchanged. On the other hand, if you delete keys in *regedit*, then change your mind and import a *.reg* file you created before the deletions, the original keys will be restored.

You can also import and export Registry branches from the command line using the command-line options documented in Chapter 5.

The format of data values in *.reg* files is not identical to the way they are shown in *regedit*. The key name is printed first, enclosed in brackets. This is followed by a list of values for that key.

If set, the (Default) value shows up as @="somevalue"; if not set, it is omitted. Binary values are shown prefixed with the keyword hex:, and backslashes (for filenames in data values) are doubled to distinguish them from the backslashes in

---

Stop! Do Not Double-Click on This File!

The default value for double-clicking on a *.reg* file is not to edit the file, as you might expect, but to merge it into the Registry. This is a stupid and dangerous association, and one you should change immediately if you plan to work with *.reg* files. Before you do your first export, go to any folder's View → Options → File Types dialog box as described in Chapter 3, and edit the association for Registration Entries. Highlight the Edit verb and click Set Default, so that Edit rather than Merge will be the default action for files with the *.reg* extension. If you have a favorite text editor, you might want to edit the Edit verb as well, so that it points to your text editor rather than to Notepad.

---

key names. In addition, the file opens with the string REGEDIT4, followed by two carriage-return/linefeed pairs. This header must be preserved if you want to re-import the *.reg* file.

Here are the contents of a sample key from my system.

```
REGEDIT4

[HKEY_LOCAL_MACHINE\SOFTWARE\Microsoft\Windows\CurrentVersion]
"InstallType"=hex:03,00
"SetupFlags"=hex:04,01,00,00
"DevicePath"="C:\\WINDOWS\\INF"
"ProductType"="9"
"LicensingInfo"=""
"SubVersionNumber"=" B"
"InventoryPath"="C:\\WINDOWS\\SYSTEM\\PRODINV.DLL"
"ProgramFilesDir"="C:\\Program Files"
"CommonFilesDir"="C:\\Program Files\\Common Files"
"MediaPath"="C:\\WINDOWS\\media"
"ConfigPath"="C:\\WINDOWS\\config"
"SystemRoot"="C:\\WINDOWS"
"OldWinDir"="C:\\WINDOWS"
"ProductName"="Microsoft Windows 95"
"FirstInstallDateTime"=hex:e1,73,4a,22
"Version"="Windows 95"
"VersionNumber"="4.00.1111"
"PiFirstTimeOnly"="1"
"AuditMode"=hex:00,00,00,00
"OtherDevicePath"="C:\\WINDOWS\\INF\\OTHER"
"BootCount"="3"
"RegisteredOwner"="user"
"RegisteredOrganization"=""
"ProductId"="11197-OEM-0021533-28231"
```

PART IV

Appendixes

APPENDIX A

Keyboard Accelerators

This appendix lists many useful keyboard accelerators. The listings are organized both by type (alphabetically within groups such as function key, Alt-key combination, and so forth) and then by function or context (during startup, in the Recycle Bin, for managing windows, and so forth). The first section lists the key, and then the function. The second section lists the desired function, and then the required key(s).

Note that in addition to the standard keyboard accelerators, you can define additional accelerators of your own. For example, you can define a Ctrl-Alt combination to invoke any shortcut, whether it's on the Desktop, in the Start menu, or in any other folder. On the property sheet for any shortcut, go to the Shortcut tab, and in the Shortcut key field, hold down Ctrl, Alt, or both Ctrl and Alt, and then enter the additional key you'd like to have invoke this shortcut. You can use any key except Esc, Enter, Tab, the spacebar, PrintScreen, BackSpace, or Delete. If it conflicts with an accelerator used by any existing application, the accelerator you've just defined will override the existing accelerator. To clear an existing shortcut's accelerator, just go to the field on the property page and press Ctrl or Alt again, with no following key.

Keyboard Accelerators Listed by Key

Function keys have special meanings while Windows 95 is starting up. See "Startup Mode Keys" later in this appendix for details. In addition, there may be hardware-specific functions, often activated on laptops by pressing the Fn key plus a numbered function key. For example, on most laptops, pressing Fn-F7 will toggle between the built-in screen and an external monitor. Note that the following accelerators work in the Explorer and most of the applets that come with Windows. However, some applications don't always follow the rules.

In addition, Alt can be used to generate non-ASCII characters in fonts such as Wingdings. Open the Character Map (*charmap.exe*) and select any cell to see its Alt-key combination down in the status bar. While you can then simply select a non-keyboard character to be pasted into another application, it's quicker to hold Alt and type the four-digit ASCII code with the numeric keypad; example: Alt-0169 for the copyright symbol. This will of course produce the requisite character only in applications that have the ability to display different fonts, such as Notepad.

Table A-1: Function Keys

Key	Action
F1	Start Help.
F2	Rename selected item.
F3	Find files or folders.
F4	Open a drop-down list.
F5	Refresh Desktop, explorer or folder view.
F6	Move focus between panes in Explorer.
F10	Select first item on menubar.

Table A-2: Miscellaneous Keys

Key	Action
Arrow keys	Move through a drop-down menu, extend selection, and so on.
Backspace	Move up one level in folder hierarchy.
Delete	Delete selected item(s) or selected text.
End	Go to end of line (in Word, Notepad, etc.), or end of file list.
Enter	Activate highlighted choice in menu or dialog box.
Esc	Close dialog box or menu without activating any choice, goes up one level in menus.
Home	Go to beginning of line (in Word, Notepad, etc.), or beginning of file list.
Page Down	Scroll down one screen.
Page Up	Scroll up one screen.
PrtSc	Copy entire display as a bitmap to Clipboard.
Spacebar	Toggle a choice that is selected in a dialog box, or activate a command button.
Tab	Move focus to next control in a dialog box or window.

Table A-3: Alt Keys

Key(s)	Action
Alt	Select first item on menubar of current window.
Alt-*x*	Activate menu or menu item where letter *x* is underlined. Some of the more interesting combinations are summarized later in this appendix.

Table A-3: Alt Keys (continued)

Key(s)	Action
Alt-double-click (on icon)	Display Properties sheet.
Alt-down arrow	Drop down a drop-down list.
Alt-Enter	Display Properties sheet for selected icon. Switch DOS application between window and full screen.
Alt-Esc	Drop active window to bottom of pile, which, in effect, activates next open window.
Alt-F4	Close current window; if Taskbar or Desktop has the focus, exit Windows.
Alt-hyphen	Pull down document's system control menu in an MDI application.
Alt-PrtSc	Copy active window as a bitmap to Clipboard.
Alt-Shift-Tab	Same as Alt-Tab, but in the opposite direction.
Alt-spacebar	Pull down system control menu for a window.
Alt-Tab{+Tab}	Switch to next running application via Task Manager—hold Shift while pressing Tab to cycle through running apps.
Alt-S	Bring up Start menu (if no windows are open and nothing is selected on Desktop).

Table A-4: Ctrl Keys

Keys	Action
Ctrl-A	Select All.
Ctrl-Alt-*x*	User-defined accelerator for a shortcut, where *x* is any key.
Ctrl-Alt-Del	Close a wedged program, or reboot from DOS mode.
Ctrl-arrow key	Scroll without moving selection.
Ctrl-C	Copy to Clipboard. Interrupt a DOS program.
Ctrl-click	Select a new item without deselecting currently selected items.
Ctrl-drag	Copy a file.
Ctrl-End	Move to end of a document (in Word, Notepad, etc.).
Ctrl-Esc	Bring up Start menu. If Explorer is not running, bring up Task Manager.
Ctrl-Esc Esc Tab	Move focus to Taskbar.
Ctrl-Esc Esc Tab Tab	Move focus to Desktop.
Ctrl-F4	Close a document window in an MDI application.
Ctrl-F6	Same as Ctrl-Tab.
Ctrl-G	In Explorer, Go To.
Ctrl-Home	Move to start of document (in Word, Notepad, etc.).

Table A-4: Ctrl Keys (continued)

Keys	Action
Ctrl-Shift-drag	Display right-drag context menu without having to use right mouse button.
Ctrl-Tab	Tab through dialog pages or multiple document windows in same application. In Word, you must use Ctrl-F6 instead.
Ctrl-Shift-Tab	Same as Ctrl-Tab, but in reverse.
Ctrl-V	Paste contents of Clipboard.
Ctrl-X	Cut to Clipboard.
Ctrl-Z	Undo text just entered, or undo last file operation in Explorer. Insert an End of File when using *copy con* in DOS.

Table A-5: Shift Keys

Key(s)	Action
Shift	While inserting CD, hold to disable autoplay.
Shift-click	Select all items between first selected item and item on which you're clicking.
Shift-click on Close	Close current folder and all parent folders.
Shift-Del	Delete a file without putting in Recycle Bin.
Shift-double click	Open folder in two-pane Explorer view.
Shift-Tab	Same as Tab, but in reverse order.

Startup Mode Keys

Table A-6 lists special key combinations work while Windows is booting—while the message "Starting Windows 95" is displayed, but before splash screen is shown.

Table A-6: Startup Mode Keys

Key(s)	Action
F4	Boot into DOS instead of Windows 95.
F5	Start Windows 95 in Safe mode. Bypass *autoexec.bat* and *config.sys*, use VGA driver only for the screen, and do not load networking software.
Ctrl-F5	Start DOS without compressed drives.
Shift-F5	Start DOS in Real mode (loaded in conventional memory), without executing *autoexec.bat* or *config.sys*.
F6	Safe mode plus networking.
F8	Open startup menu (see Chapter 9, *Windows Startup*).
Shift-F8	Go through *config.sys* and *autoexec.bat* one line at a time, with confirmation before executing each command.

Doskey Accelerators

Table A-7 lists keystrokes that work when *doskey.exe* has been enabled in a DOS window.

Table A-7: Doskey Accelerators

Key(s)	Action
Left/Right arrow	Move cursor back/forward one character.
Ctrl + Left/Right arrow	Move cursor back/forward one word.
Home/End	Move cursor to beginning/end of line.
Up/Down arrow	Scroll up (and back) through list of stored commands. Each press of the "up" key recalls the previous command and displays it on the command line.
Page Up/Down	Recall oldest/most recent command in buffer.
Insert	Insert text at cursor.
Delete	Delete text at cursor.
F1	Copy next character from template to command line. This works with/without *doskey*.
F2 + *key*	Copy text from template up to (but not including) *key*.
F3	Copy template from present character position to command line. This works with/without *doskey*.
F4 + *key*	Delete characters from present character position up to (but not including) *key*.
F5	Copy current command to template and clear command line.
F6	Place an end-of-file character (^Z) at current position of command line.
F7	Display a numbered list of command history.
Alt-F7	Delete all commands stored in buffer.
chars + F8	Entering one or more characters *chars* followed by F8 will display the most recent command beginning with *chars*. Pressing F8 again will display the next most recent command beginning with *chars*, and so on. If no characters are specified, F8 simply cycles through existing commands in buffer.
F9 + *command#*	Display designated command on command line.
Alt-F10	Delete all macro definitions.

Keyboard Accelerators Listed by Function

The following keys operate in most contexts—i.e., on the Desktop, in the Explorer, and within most applications and dialogs. Functions are listed alphabetically, except where a logical order might make more sense.

Note also that many of the keystroke commands listed here are really just selections from the context menu or various window menus and dialog boxes, with navigation via keystrokes. The list is far from complete. For instance, Ctrl-Esc will bring up the Start menu, and `Alt` will take you to the menubar of the currently active window; thereafter, you can choose any item by typing a character sequence. And so `Ctrl-Esc+S+C+R` is really just another way of saying Start → Settings → Control Panel → Regional Settings, and `Alt+F+O` is another way of saying File → Open. Similarly, once you right-click on an item to get its context menu, you can pick from that menu by typing the underlined character. (Note that this is not always the first character of the menu item name.) So right-click+R is another way of saying context menu → Properties.

Table A-8: Miscellaneous

Action	Key(s)
Get help on selected item	F1
Bypass CD or CD-ROM autoplay	Shift while inserting disc
Cut selected item	Ctrl-X
Copy selected item	Ctrl-C
Jump to a Desktop, Explorer, or menu item	Type initial characters
Paste copied or cut item	Ctrl-V
Undo last command	Ctrl-Z

Table A-9: File Management

Action	Key(s)
Copy a file	Right-click drag file+C or hold Ctrl key
Create a shortcut	Ctrl-Shift drag file+S
Create a shortcut	Right-click-drag an item+S
Delete an item to Recycle Bin	Drag to Recycle Bin, or press Del, or right-click+D
Delete an item to Recycle Bin	Del
Delete an item with no undelete	Shift-Del
Delete an item with no undelete	Shift-right-click+D
Delete an item with no undelete	Shift-drag item to Recycle Bin
Find a file or folder	F3
Rename an item	F2
Undo any file operation	Right-click on Desktop+U
View an item's Properties sheet	Alt-Enter
View an item's Properties sheet	Alt-double-click

Table A-10: Menus

Action	Key(s)
Display 1 menu for selected item	Shift-F10, or context menu key on Win95 keyboard
Display Start menu	Ctrl-Esc, or Windows logo key on Win95 keyboard
Display current window's system menu	Alt-spacebar
Display current document's system menu	Alt-hyphen
Select first item on menubar	F10
Select first item on menubar	Alt
Move through menu headings	Left arrow, right arrow
Activate menu item where letter x is underlined	Alt-x if menu doesn't have focus, x by itself if menu has focus
Drop down selected menu	Alt-down arrow or F4
Move through menu items	Up arrow, down arrow
Go up a level in menu	Esc
Cancel current selection on menu bar	Alt or F10

Table A-11: Dialog Box Navigation

Action	Key(s)
Move focus forward through dialog box options	Tab
Move focus backward through dialog box options	Shift-Tab
Move forward between tabbed pages	Ctrl-Tab
Move backward between tabbed pages	Ctrl-Shift-Tab
Activate an option with the letter x underlined	Alt-x
Open a drop-down list box	Alt-down arrow
Go to top of a list box	Home
Go to bottom of a list box	End
Move to item in list box starting with letter x	x
Select or deselect items in a checkbox or list box	Spacebar
Select or deselect one item at a time in a list box	Spacebar while navigating with Ctrl-up arrow or Ctrl-down arrow
Make noncontiguous selections from list box	Ctrl-left-click

Table A-11: Dialog Box Navigation (continued)

Action	Key(s)
Open Look In list (Open dialog box)	F4
Open Save In list (Save as dialog box)	F4
Go to parent folder	Backspace
Create a new folder	Right-click+W+F

Table A-12: Windows, Icons and Desktop Layout

Action	Key(s)
Turn on/off Toolbar in Explorer and some Windows applets	Alt-V+T
Cascade all windows	Right-click on Taskbar+C
Close current application window	Alt-F4
Close current document window	Ctrl-F4
Close parent folders	Shift-click on Close button
Cycle through open applications	Alt-Tab (hold Alt while pressing Tab)
Line up icons	Right-click on empty area of Desktop or Explorer +E
Minimize all windows	Right-click on Taskbar+M Windows logo key+D
Quit a program	Alt-F4
Switch to last window used	Alt-Tab or Ctrl-Esc
Switch to next document window	Ctrl-F6 or Ctrl-Tab
Tile all windows horizontally	Right-click on Taskbar+H
Tile all windows vertically	Right-click on Taskbar+V
Toggle maximized and windowed displays	Alt-spacebar, or right-click on titlebar
Turn on (or turn off) icon autoarrange	Right-click on empty area of Desktop or Explorer+I+A

Table A-13: Taskbar

Action	Keys
Turn on or off Taskbar autohide	Ctrl-Esc, Alt-Enter, U, Enter
Remove clock from System Tray	Ctrl-Esc, Alt-Enter,+R+C, Enter
Cascade all windows	Ctrl-Esc, Alt-Enter,+C, Enter
Tile all windows horizontally	Ctrl-Esc, Alt-Enter,+H, Enter
Tile all windows vertically	Ctrl-Esc, Alt-Enter,+V, Enter
Undo last Desktop command	Ctrl-Esc, Alt-Enter,+U, Enter
Reduce size of icons in Start menu	Ctrl-Esc, Alt-Enter,+R+S, Enter

Table A-13: Taskbar (continued)

Action	Keys
Clear contents of Documents menu	Ctrl-Esc, Alt-Enter,+R, Ctrl-Tab+C, Enter
Add item to Start menu	Ctrl-Esc, Alt-Enter,+R, Ctrl-Tab+A+Alt-B, Enter

Table A-14: Start Menu

Action	Keys
Activate Start menu	Ctrl-Esc
Activate Start menu from Desktop	Alt-S
Add item to Start menu	Ctrl-Esc, Alt-Enter +R, Ctrl-Tab+A+ Alt-B
Remove item from Start menu	Right-click on Start menu+ O+P+Enter
Reduce size of icons in Start menu	Ctrl-Esc, Alt-Enter+R+S
Clear contents of Documents menu	Ctrl-Esc, Alt-Enter+R, Ctrl-Tab+C
Bring up Find utility	Right-click on Start button+F

Table A-15: Recycle Bin

Action	Keys
Empty Recycle Bin	Right-click+B
Cancel delete confirmation dialog box	Right-click+R+D
Reinstate delete confirmation dialog box	Right-click+R+D
Cancel undelete option for every deletion	Right-click+R+R

Table A-16: Explorer

Action	Key(s)
Open Explorer	Right-click on Start menu, My Computer, or any folder icon+E
Refresh a window	F5
Go to a named folder (two-pane Explorer only)	Ctrl-G+enter name
Jump to a folder (two-pane explorer only)	Tab or F6 to activate tree, type its initial character(s)
Jump to a file	Tab or F6 to activate file list, type its initial character(s)
Undo	Ctrl-Z
Select all (file list only)	Ctrl-A
Move to parent folder (one level up)	Backspace

Table A-16: Explorer (continued)

Action	Key(s)
Close selected folder and its parents (folder windows only)	Shift-click on Close button
Rename selected item	F2
Find a file or folder	F3
Cut selected item	Ctrl-X
Copy selected item	Ctrl-C
Paste copied or cut item	Ctrl-V
Cancel copy/cut operation	Esc
Delete an item to Recycle Bin	Del, or right-click+D
Delete an item with no undelete	Shift-Del or Shift-right-click+D
View an item's Properties sheet ·	Alt-Enter, or Alt-double-click
Copy a file	Ctrl-drag file
Create a shortcut	Ctrl-shift-drag file, select "Create Shortcut here"
Switch between left and right panes	F6 or Tab
Expand current folder's subfolders	Tab or F6 to activate tree, * on numeric keypad
Expand selected folder	Tab or F6 to activate tree, + on numeric keypad
Collapse selected folder	Tab or F6 to activate tree, – on numeric keypad
Expand current selection	Right Arrow
Select first subfolder (if expanded)	Right Arrow
Collapse current selection	Left Arrow
Select parent folder (if collapsed)	Left Arrow
Change icon size to small	Alt-V+M, or right-click on empty area of file list+V+M
Change icon size to large	Alt-V+G, or right-click on empty area of file list +V+G
Change icon view to a list	Alt-V+L, or right-click on empty area of file list +V+L
Change icon view to a detailed list	Alt-V+D, or right-click on empty area of file list +V+D
Arrange icons in alphabetical order	Alt-V+I+N, or right-click on empty area of file list +I+N
Arrange icons by size	Alt-V+I+S, or right-click on empty area of file list +I+S
Arrange icons by type	Alt-V+I+T, or right-click on empty area of file list +I+T

Table A-16: Explorer (continued)

Action	Key(s)
Arrange icons by modification date	Alt-V+I+D, or right-click on empty area of file list +I+D
Line up icons	Alt-V+I+A, or right-click on empty area of file list +I+A
Add Toolbar to any Windows applet or folder	Alt-V+T
Activate Toolbar's List box	Tab, or F4

APPENDIX B

Filename Extensions

This appendix lists many of the most common filename extensions that you'll find on your system or that you might download or have sent to you over the Internet.

Extensions were universally used on DOS and Windows 3.1 files, but Microsoft has gone to some difficulty to hide them in Windows 95. This is unfortunate, since they play a major role in the way Windows 95 decides what application will be used to open a file, as well as which files will be visible when opening files in a given application. While direct associations are made between some files without extensions and the applications needed to open them, in most cases, the association is between an extension and a Registry setting that tells the system what application to use.

If you double click on an unknown file type, the Open With dialog box (see Chapter 3, *The Windows 95 User Interface*) appears, allowing you to make a new association. However, to change an association once it has been made, you need to go to View → Options → File Types on any folder.

We've tried to list the most common system extensions, but there are literally hundreds of file formats used by third party applications. With the expansion of the Web, you may even find yourself trying to open files in formats native to other operating systems.

Some of these file types can be opened only if you have the appropriate application. However, especially with the growth of the Web, there are often viewers available that allow you to at least view the contents of the file, even if you can't change them. There's a very large list of file extensions and Win95 file viewers at *http://webhost.btigate.com/~russell/W95FV/all.html*. The viewer download links are not always up to date, but you can often figure out an alternative by modifying the download address that shows up in the status bar of your browser. A good technique is to back up each element of the URL path until you find something recognizable. (For example, change *http://www.fineware.com/peeper32.zip* to *http://www.fineware.com*.) If the address is given as an ftp address, you can also change it into an equivalent *www* address and see what happens. (For example, change *ftp.jasc.com/somepath* into *www.jasc.com*, and start browsing till you find what you need.)

For more details on dealing with downloads and file formats found on the Net, see *Internet in a Nutshell*, by Valerie Quercia. For details on the internals of many graphics file formats, see *The Encyclopedia of Graphics File Formats* by James Murray and Bill van Ryper.

Note that file types can be registered with QuickView as well, and if so, a Quick View option will appear on the file's context menu.

Extension	Description
.386	Windows Virtual Device Driver.
.3gr	Screen grabber for MS-DOS applications.
.aam	MacroMedia Shockwave.
.acm	Audio Compression Manager Driver.
.adf	Admin config files.
.arc	Archive file (obsolete). Open with PKZip or WinZip, available from *http://www.winzip.com*.
.avi	Video clip. Open with *mplayer*, IE, or Navigator with plugin.
.bak	Backup file; used by many applications.
.bas	Visual Basic code module.
.bat	Batch File. Run with double-click, or type filename and optional arguments at command line. Edit with Notepad.
.bfc	Briefcase file. Left off of most system-created Briefcases (never visible).
.bmp	Windows bitmap. Open with MS Paint or many third-party graphics programs.
.c	C compiler source file.
.cab	Cabinet file. A compressed format used to store Windows files on the Win95 CD and in \ *Windows\Options*.
.cdb	Clipboard file.
.cfg	Configuration file.
.chk	ScanDisk file.
.chm	Compiled HTML Help file.
.cis	CompuServe mail file.
.clp	Clipboard file.
.cls	Visual Basic class module.
.cnt	Help system table of contents file.
.com	MS-DOS executable file. Run with double-click, or type filename and arguments.
.cpi	International Code Page information.
.cpl	Control Panel applet. Normally stored in \ *Windows\System*. Double-click to open applet, or use *rundll32* command line. (See Chapter 4, *The Control Panel*, for details.)

Extension	Description
.cpp	C++ compiler source file.
.cpx	Control Panel control file. Internal.
.csv	Comma-delimited text file.
.cur	Windows cursor file. Open with icon or cursor editor.
.dat	Data file. Used by several applications and system functions, notably the Registry (loaded from *system.dat* and *user.dat*). Not to be opened directly.
.dbf	Dbase/FoxPro database file.
.dcr	MacroMedia Shockwave.
.dcx	FaxView document.
.dll	Dynamic Link Library. Internal, but can run with *rundll32*.
.doc	MS Word document.
.dos	MS-DOS file. May contain text. DOS versions of system files— important when setting up a dual-boot with WinNT.
.dot	Microsoft Word template.
.drv	Device driver.
.dwg	AutoCad file.
.dxb	AutoCad database file.
.dxf	AutoCad drawing interchange file.
.eps	Encapsulated Postscript. Printable, or open with postscript viewer or publishing program.
.exe	Executable file. Run with double-click or type filename and arguments.
.faq	Frequently Asked Questions. Almost always a text file.
.fon	Bitmapped font file. Used by many applications, but viable with *fontview* or *charmap*. Normally stored in \ *Windows\System\Fonts*.
.fot	Font metric for TrueType font.
.fpx	Kodak FlashPix.
.frm	Visual Basic form file, Adobe FrameMaker document.
.fts	A full text search file. The find wizard prepares this database of searchable text on setup when using the Find tab in a Help file.
.fxd	Winfax file. Also *.fxr* and *.fxs*.
.g3	Group 3 fax file.
.gif	Graphics Interchange Format—a common image format, especially on the Web. Open with IE, Netscape Navigator, other web browser, or most graphics editing programs.
.gr3	Windows 3.0 screen grabber.
.gz	Gzip file.
.h	C programming header file.
.hlp	Help data file. Double-click or open with *winhlp32 filename*.
.htm	Same as *.html*.

Extension	Description
.html	HyperText Markup Language file, the base format of the World Wide Web. Open with IE, Netscape Navigator, or other web browser. Editable with any text editor.
.hqx	BinHex archive format (Macintosh).
.ico	Windows icon. Open with icon editor.
.inf	Setup Information file, edit with text editor—sometimes used by right-clicking and selecting Install to set up drivers or shell extensions.
.ini	Configuration settings file. Edit with any text editor.
.jpg	Same as *.jpeg* (*.jpg* is more common).
.jpeg	Joint Photographics Expert Group format, an image file format widely used for high-resolution images. View with web browser or image editing program.
.kbd	Keyboard layout data.
.lgo	Windows logo driver.
.lib	Static-link library file.
.lnk	A Desktop shortcut. Double-click to open linked application or file, or type filename at command line. This extension can be viewed in the Properties sheet of a shortcut or in a DOS box.
.log	A log file. Created by many applications. Typically readable with any text editor.
.lst	Audio playlist, sometimes text file.
.lzh	LHArc compressed file (use WinZip).
.mak	C/C++ make file.
.mdb	Microsoft Access database.
.mid	MIDI Sequence.
.mif	MIDI Instrument File.
.mov	QuickTime movie. View with Apple QuickTime player, IE (with QuickTime ActiveX control), or Netscape with QuickTime plug-in.
.mpg	Motion Picture Experts Group video format (MPEG). Open with MPEG player or in IE/Netscape with plug-in.
.msc	Microsoft compressed archive.
.msg	CompuServe message file.
.msp	Microsoft Paint (obsolete).
.ocx	ActiveX Control (32-bit version of *.vbx*).
.nls	Natural Language Services driver.
.pcd	Kodak PhotoCD file. Open with most image editors.
.pcx	PC Paintbrush. Open with most graphics programs.
.pdf	Portable Document Format. A PostScript derivative viewable with Adobe Acrobat. Download viewer from *http://www.adobe.com /prodindex/acrobat/readstep.html*.
.pdx	Paradox database.

Extension	Description
.pif	PIF file. Shortcut to MS-DOS program; used to provide Windows context information for character-mode applications. Edit with Properties sheet of associated application. Extension invisible in Win95.
.pj	HP PaintJet file.
.pot	PowerPoint template.
.ppd	PostScript Printer Description file.
.ppt	PowerPoint Presentation file.
.ps	PostScript output file. Printable. Edit with vector graphics program.
.pwl	Password list. Can clear data with *pwledit*.
.qt	QuickTime movie. Viewable by *mplayer*, Apple QuickTime player, web browser with QuickTime plug-in.
.ra	Real Audio data file—read automatically when corresponding *.ram* file is launched.
.ram	Real Audio file. Can be listened to via web browser with Real Audio plug-in. *http://www.realaudio.com*
.reg	Exported Registry patch file. Double-click to import data into the Registry, or type *regedit filename*. Can be viewed and edited with any text editor. Create with *regedit /e* or *regedit* → Registry → Export menu item.
.rle	Picture file, Run Length Encoded (compressed) format (obsolete).
.rtf	Rich Text Format file, exported by Microsoft Word. Load with *winword.exe /n*.
.scp	Dial-Up Networking script.
.scr	Screen Saver file. Run automatically if set up in Control Panel → Display; double-click on filename to run, or type *filename /s*. (Typing filename without */s* will open Control Panel applet.)
.shs	Scrap object.
.sig	Signature file. Appended to outgoing mail messages by many email programs. Usually editable with text editor.
.sit	Stuffit archive (Macintosh).
.spd	PostScript Printer Description file.
.spl	Shockwave Splash file. Also used as extension for temporary printer spool files in Win95.
.swp	Swap file, used for virtual memory storage—no need to open or edit.
.sys	*config.sys* driver.
.tar	A Unix archive format. Open with WinZip.
.tif	Tagged Image File Format. Open with graphics editing program. Also *.tiff*.
.tmp	Temporary file. Could be used by any program. Usually found in *\ Windows\ Temp*.
.tsp	Windows Telephony Service Provider.

Extension	Description
.ttf	TrueType Font. Used by many applications. View with *fontview* or *charmap*.
.txt	Text file. Typically opened by default with Notepad by double clicking, or typing *notepad filename.txt* at command line. Can be imported into word processors and edited with any text editor.
.url	Internet shortcut (Universal Resource Locator)—edit with Properties sheet or in text editor.
.uu	UUencoded file. Open with WinZip.
.vbx	Visual Basic Custom Control (16-bit) File.
.vxd	Virtual device driver.
.wav	Waveform file. Contains sound data, including system sounds stored in *\Windows\System\Media*. Open with double-click or *sndrec32* filename.
.wdb	Microsoft Works database.
.wks	Lotus 1-2-3 worksheet. Also *.wk1* through *.wk4*.
.wll	Microsoft Word add-in.
.wmf	Windows MetaFile.
.wp	WordPerfect file. *.wp4*, *.wp5*, *.wp6* refer to WordPerfect versions.
.wpg	WordPerfect bitmap.
.wps	Microsoft Works text file.
.wpt	WordPerfect template.
.wri	WordPad file.
.xbm	X Window System bitmap (Unix)—view with web browser.
.xlm	Excel macro file.
.xls	Excel worksheet.
.xlt	Excel template.
.xlw	Excel workspace.
.xwd	X Window System dump (Unix).
.z	Compressed Unix file. Open with WinZip.
.zip	Compressed archive file. Open with WinZip.

Filename Extensions

APPENDIX C

System File and Directory Organization

The following directories and files play a significant role in Windows. The lists are not complete, but may be helpful in understanding where certain types of information are stored.

Note that the locations are generally accurate, but represent only the default values. For example, it is possible for Windows 95 to be installed in a directory other than \ *Windows*, and many of the locations are defined in the Registry. If you change a single Registry setting, Windows programs won't know where to look for these directories.

Dragging and dropping certain Windows folders in the Explorer will cause Windows to update automatically its location in the Registry. For example, if you drag *Desktop* from *C:\ Windows* to *C:\ Windows\ Start Menu*, it will still work. Your Desktop items will also be accessible from the Start menu.

Also, these folders don't all need to be on the same disk—for example, your setup might include *D:\ Windows* and *E:\ Program Files*.

System Directories

Directory	Description
\	Root directory of the file system on any disk
\Program Files	Default installation directory for third-party and Microsoft applications
\Recycled	The Recycle Bin
\Windows	Core Windows 95 files and directories, *.ini* files, screen savers, some components, such as Notepad
\Windows\Command	DOS commands
\Windows\Config	*general.idf*, the MIDI instrument definition

Directory	Description
\Windows\Cookies	Temporary files placed on your hard disk by web sites you visit, so they can identify you on future visits (only if IE is installed)
\Windows\Cursors	Standard and optional cursors
\Windows\Desktop	Whatever files and folders appear on the Desktop
\Windows\Favorites	Internet Explorer sites you've asked to remember; applications such as Word use it to remember documents
\Windows\Fonts	System and application font files
\Windows\Help	System and application Help files
\Windows\History	Shortcuts to web pages you've recently visited
\Windows\Inf	Device driver installation and setup files
\Windows\Java	The Win32 Java Virtual Machine
\Windows\Media	Sound and video files; used by Control Panel → Sounds (can safely be deleted)
\My Documents	A standard place for applications (especially MS Office) to save documents
\Windows\Nethood	Pointers to systems in the Network Neighborhood
\Windows\Options	In OSR2, the *.cab* files from the Windows 95 CD-ROM. Allows Control Panel → Add/Remove Programs → Windows Setup to be run without a physical CD-ROM. (This is subject to OEM installation.)
\Windows\Recent	Shortcuts to recently opened files; this is the list that appears on Start → Documents
\Windows\Sendto	Shortcuts and folders here appear on the SendTo menu
\Windows\Shellnew	Templates for the Explorer to use when creating new files with Context Menu → New
\Windows\Spool\Fax	Storage area for temporary fax files (only when Exchange and Windows Fax Services are installed)
\Windows\Spool\Printers	Storage area for temporary printer files
\Windows\Start Menu	Shortcuts and folders here appear on the Start menu
\Windows\Start Menu\Programs	Shortcuts to programs that will appear in the Programs section of the Start menu
\Windows\Start Menu\Programs\Startup	Shortcuts, programs, and batch files stored here will be run automatically every time Win95 boots

System Files & Directories

Directory	Description
\Windows\Sysbckup	Backup versions of system drivers and DLLs (hidden by default)—Windows will use these to replace important files that get over-written
\Windows\System	Drivers, DLLs, OCXs, VxDs, CPL files, and other system files
\Windows\System\Viewers	QuickView viewers (if installed)
\Windows\System\Vmm32 and \Windows\System\iosubsys	VxDs added after installation
\Windows\System\Shellext	Any installed Shell Extensions
\Windows\Temp	Scratch file area for Windows system and applications

System Files

Chapter 9, *Windows Startup*, gives a degree of detail on some of the most impor-tant system configuration files. The following files may also be of interest.

File	Description
\command.com	The DOS command-line shell.
\io.sys	Essential system file for starting DOS and loading Windows (hidden).
\msdos.sys	Settings for loading Windows (hidden).
\autoexec.bat and \config.sys	Startup files for legacy support.
\Windows\win386.swp or \win386.swp or 386spart.par	The swap file, used for storing virtual memory data on disk. Make sure your swap file is on a partition with enough space to grow as needed, or performance will suffer (hidden).

Log files

The following log files are found in the root directory of whatever disk is used to start up the system.

File	Description
\bootlog.txt	Log of Win95 startup process
\detlog.txt	Hardware detection log
\scandisk.log	Log from the last time Scandisk was run
\setuplog.txt	Log of the setup process

Setup Files

File	Description
\Windows\msbatch.inf	Master setup information file (only seen sometimes when the system was set up by OEM).
\Windows\control.ini	Initialization file for control panel.
\Windows\hosts	Mapping of IP addresses to host names. Not required if DNS is running but can help with quick lookup. A sample file showing the format is found in \Windows\Hosts.sam. (very obscure).
\Windows\lmhosts	Mapping of IP addresses to NetBIOS host names. A sample file can be found in \Windows\LMhosts.sam.
\Windows\protocol.ini	Initialization file for some networking protocols.
\Windows\system.ini	Initialization file for Windows. Largely but not entirely superseded by the Registry.
\Windows\telephon.ini	Initialization information for modem dialing.
\Windows\win.ini	Initialization file for Windows. Largely but not entirely superseded by the Registry.

Registry

File	Description
\Windows\system.dat	System portion of Registry
\Windows\system.da0	Current backup of system portion of Registry
\system.1st	System portion of Registry first created by setup
\Windows\user.dat	User portion of Registry—may exist in \Windows\Profiles\<username>
\Windows\user.da0	Current backup of user portion of Registry—may exist in \Windows\Profiles\<username>
\Windows\user.man	If present, user cannot change Registry settings (rename to user.dat to make changeable again)

Other Files Worth Knowing

File	Description
\Windows\programs.txt	Release notes for third-party apps under Windows 95 (yawn)
\Windows\readme.txt	Master readme file pointing to many subsidiary readme (release notes) files

File	Description
\Windows\System*.cpl	Control Panel applets
\Windows*.scr and \Windows\System*.scr	Screen saver files

APPENDIX D

Special/Reserved Characters

The characters listed here have special meaning to the system.

Character	Use
$	*prompt* command; *doskey* macros; also used internally (DOS device names, NetDDE shares)
%	Batch files; *for* command; shell command lines in Registry
>	DOS command-line output redirection; use >> rather than > to append to a file
<	DOS command-line input redirection
|	DOS pipe symbol
*	Used as a wildcard to represent any number of characters in a filename
.	Separates a filename from its extension; can also be used as a directory name to indicate the current directory, parent directory, grandparent, greatgrandparent (., .., ..., etc.) in *cd*, *md*, *rd*, commands and at the Run prompt
\	Directory paths; Registry key hierarchy; \\UNC names; also used as escape sequence in the Registry (e.g., \" for quotes and \\ for backslash)
/	Command-line switches (options); a few programs use –
"	On command line to hold together long filenames (LFNs) containing spaces; used in *regedit* to surround string values
~	In 8.3 aliases for LFNs, but not a reserved character
:	Separates drive letter from path; also batch file label (target for *goto*)
?	As a wildcard to represent a single character
=	Set environment variables, in *config.sys* settings
;	Separate parts of *path*; also as comment in *config.sys*, **.ini* files

APPENDIX E

Task Index

This appendix provides a quick reference to many common tasks in Windows 95. The list is far from comprehensive. We've tried to stay away from really obvious or well-known tasks, but what is obvious to one person may not be so to another; we've also tended to stay away from tasks that have an associated keyboard accelerator, since Appendix A, *Keyboard Accelerators*, gives a comprehensive list of those tasks. You'll find this appendix most useful for finding out where certain settings are buried in the Control Panel, or what DOS program or program option might help you do something you think you ought to be able to do but can't quite figure out.

In many cases, we're just trying to compensate for the haphazard organization of many Windows 95 functions. For example, if you want the system clock to display the time in 24-hour format, you might make the obvious assumption that the control would be in Control Panel → Date/Time; alas, we have to tell you to go to Control Panel → Regional Settings instead.

We've divided the listings into the following categories to make it easier to find what you need:

Applications	Files	Opening
Audio	Finding	Passwords
Booting Windows	Focus, changing	Printers
Briefcase	Folder contents	Sharing
Clipboard, accessing	Folders	Shortcuts
Date and time	Hardware	System Tray
Deleting	Help	Taskbar
Desktop	Icons and image files	Text and fonts
Disks	Keyboard, configuring	Troubleshooting
Display	Memory	Users
DOS window	Menus	Video
Email	Mouse	Web
Explorer	Networking	Windows
Faxing		

Applications (see also Files)
  adding to Office shortcut bar
    Office shortcut bar → system menu → customize → buttons
  adding to Start menu
    drag-and-drop onto Start menu
    put shortcut in \Windows\Start Menu\Programs
    Taskbar → context menu → Properties → Start menu Programs
  changing associations between file types and applications
    any folder → View → Options → File Types
  installing/uninstalling
    Control Panel → Add/Remove Programs → Install/Uninstall
    Control Panel → Add/Remove Programs → Windows Setup (for Windows
       components)
  Internet-related, configuring
    Control Panel → Internet → Programs
  linking icons to
    Folder → View → Options → File Types
  monitoring
    C:\>rsrcmtr
    Start → Programs → Accessories → System Tools → Resource Meter
    C:\>sysmon
    Start → Programs → Accessories → System Tools → System Monitor
  scheduling to run at a specific time
    C:\>sysagent
    Start → Programs → Accessories → System Tools → System Agent
  shortcuts to (see Shortcuts)
  starting
    application context menu → Open
    double-click associated file
    double-click program selection (.exe file)
    file context menu → Send To → application name
    C:\>start *program*
    Start → Programs → ...
    Start → Run → *program*
  stopping/interrupting
    Ctrl-Alt-Del
    Ctrl-C (for DOS programs or batch files)
    close box on window
    File → Exit
    right-click on respective button on Taskbar, select Close
  switching between
    Alt-Tab and Alt-Esc (Shift-Alt-Tab for reverse)
    C:\>progman
    C:\>taskman

Audio
  associating sounds with system events (or turning off system sounds)
    Control Panel → Sounds
    Control Panel → PC Card (PCMCIA) → disable sound effects

    audio CDs, playing
        C:\>cdplayer
        insert CD into drive (Shift+insert disk disables autoplay)
        Start → Programs → Accessories → Multimedia → CD Player
    playing and recording sounds
        C:\>sndrec32
        Start → Programs → Accessories → Multimedia → Sound Recorder
    replacing sound events with visual cues
        Control Panel → Accessibility Options → Sounds
    volume control
        Control Panel → Multimedia → Audio → Playback volume
        Control Panel → Multimedia → Audio → Show volume control
        C:\>sndvol32
        speaker icon in tray
        Start → Programs → Accessories → Multimedia → Volume Control

Booting Windows
    during the first few seconds of system boot only
        F4 (boot into real-mode DOS)
        F5, Ctrl-F5, Shift-F5, or F6 (for Safe mode options if the boot menu is
            shown)
        F8 (for startup options)
    from the DOS 7 Real mode prompt
        C:\>win
    starting programs automatically each time you boot
        put shortcut in \Windows\Start Menu\Programs\StartUp
        put start *programname* in *autoexec.bat*

Briefcase
    creating new Briefcase
        Desktop context menu → New → Briefcase
    creating sync copy for a file or folder
        drag file or folder to (or Send To) My Briefcase (if available)
    installing
        Control Panel → Add/Remove Programs → Windows Setup → Accessories
            → Details → Briefcase
    showing status and sync copy location for files
        My Briefcase → View → Details

Clipboard, accessing
        C:\>clipbook
        Start → Programs → Accessories → ClipBook Viewer
        C:\>clipbrd
        Start → Programs → Accessories → Clipboard Viewer

Date and time
    changing date or time display format
        Control Panel → Regional Settings

displaying clock in system tray
>Taskbar context menu → Properties → Taskbar Options → Show Clock

displaying date
>hold pointer over clock in System Tray
>double-click on clock in System Tray
>C:\>date

file/folder properties
>context menu → Properties
>Alt-double-click
>Alt-Enter selected item

finding files by
>Start → Find → Files or Folders → Date Modified

listing files by date modified
>click Modified column header in Explorer's or folder's details view or in find results
>C:\>dir /od

scheduling programs
>C:\>sysagent
>Start → Programs → Accessories → System Tools → System Agent

setting
>C:\>date
>C:\>time
>Control Panel → Date/Time → Date & Time
>double-click System Tray clock

synchronizing with another system
>C:\>net time

time zones and daylight savings
>Control Panel → Date/Time → Time Zone
>Control Panel → Regional Settings
>C:\>tzedit

Deleting

devices (see Hardware)

files (sending to Recycle Bin)
>context menu → Delete
>drag to Recycle Bin
>Del with selected files
>File → Delete
>file or folder context menu → Send To → Recycle Bin (add Recycle Bin shortcut to \Windows\SendTo—avoids notification)

files (deleting from Recycle Bin)
>Recycle Bin context menu → Empty Recycle Bin
>Recycle Bin → File → Empty Recycle Bin

files (without sending to Recycle Bin)
>C:\>del *filename*
>Shift-Del

folders (directories)
>C:\>rd *foldername* (rd and rmdir are functionally identical)
>C:\>deltree *foldername* (deletes all files and subdirectories)

---

compressing/uncompressing drives
    C:\>drvspace
    C:\>cmpagent (from Plus!)
    Start → Launch → Accessories → System Tools → Compression Agent
copying floppies
    C:\>diskcopy
    Explorer → floppy drive context menu → Copy Disk
creating/preparing for use
    C:\>fdisk
    C:\>format
finding amount of free space
    My Computer → View → Details
    My Computer → *drive* → Properties
    C:\>dir \
improving performance
    C:\>defrag
    Start → Programs → Accessories → System Tools → Disk Defragmenter
labeling
    C:\>label *drive* and *labelname*
    drive or disk context menu → Properties → Label
mapping network folder to drive letter
    Explorer → Tools → Map Network Drive
    C:\>net use
moving items to drive
    drag object to folder or icon in My Computer window
    object context menu → Send To → drive name
sharing on LAN
    context menu → Sharing
    context menu → Properties → Share
startup disks, creating
    Control Panel → Add/Remove Programs → Startup Disk
    C:\>sys (to convert existing floppy into startup disk)
troubleshooting
    C:\>scandisk (when Windows is not running)
    C:\>scandiskw (when Windows is running)
    Start → Programs → Accessories → System Tools → ScanDisk

Display
configuring
    Control Panel → Display
    Desktop context menu → Properties
    Start → Programs → Resource Kit → Quick Resolution Change (if installed)
configuring accessibility
    Control Panel → Accessibility Options → High Contrast
    Control Panel → Mouse → Mouse Trails
screen saver
    Control Panel → Display → Screen Saver

displaying/hiding file extensions
    Explorer → View → Options → View → Hide MS-DOS file extensions
opening at a particular folder, in two-pane view (/e option)
    Start → Run → explorer /e *foldername*
    Shift-double-click selected folder
    folder or Start menu context menu → Explore
showing all files, including hidden and system files
    Explorer → View → Options → View → Show all files

Faxing

cover pages
    C:\>faxcover
    Start → Programs → Accessories → Fax → Page Editor
requesting
    C:\>awsnto32
    Start → Programs → Accessories → Fax → Request a Fax
    Tools → Microsoft Fax Tools → Request a Fax (Windows
        Messaging/Exchange)
sending
    C:\>awsnto32
    Compose → New Fax (Windows Messaging/Exchange)
    Start → Programs → Accessories → Fax → Compose New Fax
viewing .dcx and .awd files
    double-click .dcx or .awd file (SR1)
    C:\>faxview

Files

comparing
    C:\>fc
copying
    Ctrl-drag
    C:\>copy
    C:\>diskcopy (entire diskette contents)
    Edit → Copy; open target folder; Edit → Paste
    right-drag file → Copy
    C:\>xcopy
copying to floppy disk
    context menu → Send To → 3 1/2 Floppy (A:)
    drag to My Computer → 3 1/2 Floppy (A:)
creating new
    File → New → File type
    C:\>copy con *filename.txt* → enter text → Ctrl-Z → Enter (creating a
        small ASCII file)
deleting (sending to Recycle Bin)
    context menu → Delete
    drag to Recycle Bin
    select files, Del
    File → Delete
    folder → File → Delete

restoring from deletion
> double-click Recycle Bin → select item → File → Restore
> drag file from Recycle Bin

shortcuts to (see Shortcuts)

showing all files (including system and hidden files)
> any folder → View → Options → View

viewing contents without opening
> context menu → Quick View
> C:\>type (text files only)
> C:\>extract /d *cabfilename.cab* (displaying *.cab* file contents)

viewing list of
> context menu → Explore
> C:/>dir
> double-click folder selection
> C:/>explorer
> right-click Start menu → Explore
> Shift-double-click on any folder
> Start → Programs → Windows Explorer
> View → Options → View

Finding

computers
> Start → Find → Computer

files and folders (see files, finding)

Registry keys
> C:\>regedit → Edit → Find

saving search criteria
> Start → Find → File → Save Search

shortcut's original file, folder, or application
> context menu → Properties → Find Target

text in files
> Start → Find → Files or Folders → Advanced

Focus, changing

between applications
> Alt-Esc
> Alt-Tab and Alt-Shift-Tab

between document windows
> on Desktop: left-click on window
> in programs: Ctrl-Tab (or Ctrl-F6) and Ctrl-Shift-Tab

to Desktop
> Ctrl-Esc Esc Tab Tab

to Taskbar
> Ctrl-Esc Esc Tab

within windows
> Tab and arrow keys

Folder contents (see also Files)
    changing list order
        clicking column headers
        C:\>dir
    deleting (see Deleting)
    listing/viewing (with the Explorer)
        context menu → Explore
        C:/>explorer
        right-click Start menu → Explore
        Shift-double-click on any folder
        Start → Programs → Windows Explorer
        C:\>start *foldername*
    listing/viewing (without the Explorer)
        C:/>dir
        double-click folder selection
    shortcuts for (see Shortcuts)

Folders (see also Folder contents)
    attributes
        C:\>attrib
        context menu → Properties
    behavior of
        View → Options → Folder
    closing folder and all parents
        Shift-click Close button
    copying
        C:\>copy
        folder context menu → Copy
        C:\>xcopy
    creating
        Desktop context menu → New → Folder
        File → New → Folder
        C:\>md (md and mkdir are functionally identical)
    current directory, changing
        C:\>cd (cd and chdir are functionally identical)
    deleting
        folder context menu → Delete
        select folder in Explorer → File → Delete
        C:\>rd
        C:\>rmdir
    finding
        any folder context menu → Find
        Ctrl+F in open folder window
        Explorer → Tools → Find → Files or Folders
        F3 while focus is on Desktop
        right-click in Explorer left pane
        Start → Find → Files or Folders

moving (see also Explorer)
    drag folders
    Edit → Cut, open target window, Edit → Paste
    C:/>move
moving items to (see also Explorer)
    drag object to folder
    object context menu → Send To → folder name
opening
    double-clicking icons
    folder context menu → Open
opening each folder in its own window/same window
    any folder → View → Options → Folder
properties
    Alt-double-click
    Alt-Enter selected item
    folder context menu → Properties
renaming
    folder context menu → Rename
    File menu → Rename
    C:\>rename
    select item → click on name → type new name
    select item → F2
restoring from deletion
    double-click Recycle Bin → select item → File → Restore
sharing
    folder context menu → Properties → Share
    folder context menu → Sharing
shortcuts for (see Shortcuts)
users of
    C:\>netwatch

Hardware
configuring
    Control Panel → System → Device Manager
disks (see Disks)
installing
    Control Panel → Add New Hardware
keyboard (see Keyboard, configuring)
modem, configuring
    Control Panel → Modems
    Control Panel → Power → PC-Card Modems
    Control Panel → System → Device Manager → Modems
monitor (see Display)
mouse (see Mouse)
PC Cards
    Control Panel → PC Card (PCMCIA)
    Control Panel → Power → Disk Drives
power management
    Control Panel → Display → Screen Saver
    Control Panel → Power → Show Battery Control

profiles
> Control Panel → System → Hardware Profiles

video driver
> Control Panel → Display → Settings → Advanced Properties
> Control Panel → System → Device Manager → Display adapters

Help
> ? icon on titlebar
> /? parameter for most commands in DOS window
> Alt-H
> double-click on .hlp file
> F1 (context-sensitive help)
> Start → Help

Icons and image files
arranging
> context menu → View
> Desktop context menu → Arrange Icons → Autoarrange
> Desktop context menu → Line Up Icons

copying to Clipboard
> Alt-PrtSc (capture active window)
> PrtSc (capture entire display)

creating or modifying
> C:\>imagedit (if installed)
> C:\>mspaint
> Start → Programs → Accessories → Paint
> Start → Programs → Resource Kit → Image Editor (if installed)

logo files for Windows
> \logo.sys, \Windows\logo.sys, \Windows\logow.sys (edit with MSPaint)

scanning
> C:\>wangimg

shortcuts, editing
> Properties → Shortcut → Change Icon

size to use
> folder → View → Large Icons | Small Icons

viewing
> context menu → QuickView

Keyboard, configuring
> Control Panel → Accessibility Options → Keyboard
> Control Panel → Keyboard

Memory
for hardware
> Control Panel → System → Performance

monitoring
> Control Panel → PC Card (PCMCIA) → Global Settings
> Control Panel → System → Performance → Virtual Memory
> C:\>rsrcmtr

Start → Programs → Accessories → System Tools → Resource Meter
Start → Programs → Accessories → System Tools → System Monitor
C:\>sysmon

Menus

context menus, accessing
    right-click
    Shift-F10
context menus, configuring
    View → Options → File Types → Edit
help (see Help)
Start menu, accessing
    Ctrl-Esc
    Start
    Windows logo key on Win95 keyboards
Start menu, managing contents of
    drag-and-drop onto Start menu
    put shortcut in \Windows\Start Menu\Programs
    Taskbar context menu → Properties → Start Menu Programs
startup menu, Windows
    F8 at "Starting Windows" message
system menu
    Alt-space in open window

Mouse

changing pointer images
    C:\>aniedit (if installed)
    Control Panel → Mouse → Pointers (if installed)
    C:\>imagedit (if installed)
    Start → Programs → Resource Kit → Image Editor (if installed)
configuring
    Control Panel → Accessibility Options → MouseKeys
    Control Panel → Mouse
    Control Panel → Mouse → Mouse Trails
configuring button functions
    Control Panel → Mouse → Buttons → Button configuration
setting double-click speed
    Control Panel → Mouse → Buttons → Double-click speed

Networking (see also Sharing; Web)

access control
    Control Panel → Network → Access Control
    Network Neighborhood → Properties → Access Control
accessing remote computers
    C:\>ftp (for file transfer)
    C:\>hypertrm (terminal access)
    C:\>iexplore (for Web pages)
    C:\>telnet (for interactive sessions)

Printers

> *accessing, configuring, managing*
>> click printer icon in Taskbar (only during print job)
>> Control Panel → Printers → *printer* → Properties
>> My Computer → Printers → *printer* → Properties
>> Start → Settings → Printers → *printer* → Properties
>
> *cancelling printing*
>> double-click printer icon → Document → Cancel Printing
>
> *printing a test page*
>> printer → Properties → General → Print Test Page
>
> *printing files*
>> context menu → Print
>> drag object to printer icon or shortcut
>> File → Print
>
> *setting default printer*
>> printer icon context menu → Set As Default
>
> *sharing*
>> printer icon context menu → Sharing
>> C:\>net print
>
> *viewing or changing the printer's job queue*
>> double-click printer icon or shortcut

Sharing

> *breaking the connection to a shared disk or folder*
>> Explorer → Tools → Disconnect Network Drive
>> C:\>net use /delete *UNC-path*
>
> *creating a shortcut to a shared network printer*
>> Control Panel → Printers → Add Printer → Network
>
> *data between applications*
>> C:\>netdde
>
> *enabling file or printer sharing*
>> Control Panel → Network → Configuration → File and Print Sharing
>
> *mapping a shared disk on another machine to a local drive letter*
>> Explorer → Tools → Map Network Drive
>> C:\>net use *drive:* *UNC-Path*
>
> *mapping a shared printer on another machine to a local printer port*
>> C:\>net use *port:* *UNC-Path*
>> Network Neighborhood → *select printer* → File → Capture Printer Port
>
> *opening a shared folder on another machine*
>> Network Neighborhood
>> Start → Run → *UNC path*
>
> *printers*
>> context menu → Sharing
>> Control Panel → Network → Configuration → File and Print Sharing
>> Control Panel → Printers → Add Printer → Network
>> C:\>net print
>
> *seeing what shared resources are available on another computer*
>> C:\>net view *UNC-path*

seeing who is connecting to shared resources on your computer
    C:\>netwatch
    Start → Programs → Accessories → System Tools → Net Watcher
setting or finding name of your own computer
    Control Panel → Network → Identification
setting shared status of specific files or folders
    context menu → Properties → Share
    context menu → Sharing
synchronizing clocks
    C:\>net time
synchronizing computers (see Briefcase)

Shortcuts

creating
    Ctrl-Shift-drag
    Desktop context menu → New → Shortcut
    File → Create Shortcut
    right-drag → Shortcut
    object context menu → Create Shortcut
icons for choosing
    Properties → Shortcut → Change Icon
finding original file
    context menu → Properties → Find Target
to recently opened files
    Start → Documents
    Taskbar context menu → Properties → Start Menu Programs → Documents
        menu
    C:\Windows\Recent

System Tray

Audio volume display
    Control Panel → Multimedia → Audio → Show Volume Control
Clock
    Taskbar → Properties → Taskbar Options → Show Clock
Desktop color palette, resolution and font size
    Control Panel → Display → Settings → Show settings
Dial-up connection
    Dial-Up Networking → Connections menu → Settings → Show an icon on
        Taskbar after connected
FilterKeys
    Control Panel → Accessibility Options → Keyboard → FilterKeys → Settings
Language
    Control Panel → Keyboard → Language
MouseKeys
    Control Panel → Accessibility Options → Mouse
Power status
    Control Panel → Power → Show Battery Meter

Task Index

Users
configuring
Control Panel → Users
network
C:\>net logon
C:\>netwatch
C:\>poledit
Start → Programs → Accessories → System Tools → System Policy Editor
passwords for (see Passwords)
profiles
Control Panel → Passwords → User Profiles
shared folders
C:\>netwatch

Video
configuring
Control Panel → Multimedia → Video
driver for
Control Panel → Display → Settings → Advanced Properties
playing
double-click on .avi files
C:\>mplayer

Web (see also Networking)
Internet caching
Control Panel → Internet → Advanced
Internet Explorer, starting
Desktop → Internet
double-click Internet shortcut
C:\>iexplore
Start → Programs → Internet Explorer
Start → Run → specific URL
Internet security (see also Passwords)
Control Panel → Internet → Security
Internet settings
Control Panel → Internet
TCP/IP settings, monitoring
Control Panel → Network → Confirmation
C:\>nbtstat
C:\>ping
C:\>route
C:\>tracert
C:\>winipcfg

Windows (see also DOS window)
cascading or tiling all open windows
Taskbar context menu

Index

RemoteAccess key (HKLM\System
\Services), 426
remoteshell command (FTP), 203
ren, rename commands, 277
rename command (FTP), 204
renaming files/folders, 148, 277
reordering text input, 299
repair (see debugging)
repetitive tasks (see batch files)
"Require encrypted password", 364
reserved characters (Win95), 459
reserved words (Win95 scripting
language), 362
Reset button (Joystick), 101
resolution, display
color palette and, 89
managing from System Tray, 256, 269
resource meter (rsrcmtr.exe), 279
restarting computer, 385
Restore (System menu item), 10
"Restore settings on startup" option, 65
right mouse button (context menu), 5,
33–35
.rle filename extension, 86
rmdir command (DOS), 273
rmdir command (FTP), 204
RNA (Remote Network Access), 350
rnaui.dll icon library, 46
root directories, 19
Root key (HKLM\Enum), 424
route.exe program, 278
RSACi content advisor, 97
rsrcmtr.exe program (resource meter),
279
"rubber band" outline, 6
Rudder checkbox (Joystick), 101
Run (shortcut property), 63
Run... option (see command line)
Run prompt (see command line)
run= statement (win.ini), 406
rundll32.exe program, 280
RunMRU key (Software\Explorer), 428

S

Safe mode startup, 384, 387–389
Safety Level button (Internet panel), 99
sage (see System Agent)

Save Results (File menu, Find dialog
box), 45
Save Search (File menu, Find dialog
box), 45
saving search criteria, 45
scandisk.exe program, 281
scanpst.exe program (inbox repair
tool), 285
SCHANNET key (System\Control
\SecurityProviders), 425
scheduling programs (sysagent.exe),
303
.scp filename extension, 358
screen savers, 87
DOS programs and, 65
passwords for, 114
Screen tab (.pif file properties), 65
scripts
dial-in login, 358
for repetitive tasks (see batch files)
Windows 95 language for, 359–362
scrollbars, 10
SCSI key (HKLM\Enum), 424
search path, 58–59
managing, 249
Run prompt, 125
searching (see finding)
security
https servers, 99
Internet Explorer, 97–99
passwords (see passwords)
system policies, 253
Security key (HKLM), 425
Security tab (Internet panel), 97–99
SecurityProviders\SCHANNET key
(HKLM\System\Control), 425
self-test, hardware, 384
send command (FTP), 204
Send To (context menu item), 60
Send To menu, customizing, 260
Send To X (sendtox.exe), 260
SendTo folder, 60
Serenum key (HKLM\Enum), 424
SerialKey devices, 80
servers
dial-in connections and, 364
fax (awsnto32.exe), 138
proxy servers, 95–96
Service Pack/Release 1, 24

User Shell Folders key
(Software\Explorer), 429
user.dat file, 429
user.exe, icons on, 46
$USERID variable, 360
users
accessibility options, 77–80
Registry settings for, 419–422
sharing directories, viewing, 245
system policies for, 253
user-level network access, 112
Users control panel, 121

V

variables
environment (DOS), setting, 286
shifting command-line arguments,
347
Windows 95 scripting language, 359
vendor information (software), 421
ver command, 25, 314
verbose command (FTP), 204
verifying/testing
batch files, 335
deletion from Recycle Bin, 56
dial-in connections, 365
hardware connections, 233
network connections (pinging), 251
startup, 387–388
(see also debugging;
troubleshooting)
versions
DOS, setver.exe for, 405
system files, checking
(qfecheck.exe), 268
Windows 95, 24–26, 314
workgroup redirector, 241
video
Multimedia control panel, 105–107
video player (mplayer.exe), 226
(see also multimedia)
video adapter, configuring, 90
video RAM, 89
Video tab (Multimedia), 106
viewing
available memory (mem.exe), 222
build number, Win95, 314

.cab files, 256
Desktop folder contents, 58
fax documents (faxview.exe), 190
file contents without opening, 270
files and folders, 37–40
folders, 16
font lists, 91
log files (logview.exe), 220
printer's job queue, 54
programs currently running, 307, 378
Registry contents, 275, 409
shared directory users, 245
system clock, 73
text file contents, 312
time (see clock; date/time)
toolbars, 16
TrueType fonts (fontview.exe), 195
workgroups computers, 241
virtual device drivers (VxDs), 380, 384
Virtual Machine Manager (VMM), 380
virtual machines (VMs), 376
Visto Briefcase, 32
VMM (Virtual Machine Manager), 380
VMM32Files key (HKLM\System
\Control), 426
VMs (virtual machines), 376
voice telephone calls, 169
volume control (sndvol32.exe), 295
volume labels (see disks, labels)
VxD key (HKLM\System\Services), 426
VxDs (virtual device drivers), 380, 384

W

"Wait for dial tone before dialing", 104,
356
waitfor command (Win95 scripts), 361
wallpaper, Desktop, 86
wangimg.exe program, 315
warnings
visual, instead of audio, 78
"Warn about invalid site certificates",
99
"Warn before accepting cookies", 99
"Warn before sending over an open
connection", 99
"Warn if still active" (shortcut
property), 66

About the Authors

Tim O'Reilly is founder and president of O'Reilly & Associates. He has written numerous books on computer topics, and as an editor, has had a hand in the development of many of the company's bestselling titles. Tim also conceived the award-winning series of travel books published by O'Reilly affiliate Travelers' Tales. He graduated from Harvard College in 1975 with a B.A. *cum laude* in classics. Tim is well known for his advocacy of "open source" software and the importance of open Internet standards. He is on the board of trustees of both the Electronic Frontier Foundation and the Internet Society.

Troy Mott is an associate editor for O'Reilly & Associates. He has played an integral role in managing many Windows books through the publishing process, from conception to release. He has degrees in English from California Polytechnic University and Sonoma State University. He is also a freelance writer for a Santa Rosa–based finance company and enjoys writing fiction in his spare time.

Colophon

Our look is the result of reader comments, our own experimentation, and feedback from distribution channels. Distinctive covers complement our distinctive approach to technical topics, breathing personality and life into potentially dry subjects.

The animal appearing on the cover of *Windows 95 in a Nutshell* is a frog (order *Salientia*). There are more than 2600 species of frog and toad, all easily distinguishable as members of this order. Frogs differ generally from toads in that they jump (toads tend to walk), are more dependent on access to water, and are slimy (as opposed to dry and warty).

Frogs range in size from less than half an inch to almost a foot in length (plus leg length). Despite their dependence on environmental conditions, frogs live in many different surroundings, including water, semi-deserts, and mountains. The only conditions in which they cannot exist are salt water and the iciest and driest frontiers. Frogs undergo a metamorphosis from swimming tadpole larvae to adult form; tadpoles are more subject to predation than are adults. Adult frogs rely on various methods of defense, including flight, poison, and many patterns and colors of camouflage.

Frogs breathe and absorb water through their skin, which is periodically shed. Most are nocturnal or twilight animals, and rely more on their sense of vision and smell than hearing. Many species hibernate through the winter months. Almost all male frogs produce a noise amplified by vocal sacs on the floor of the mouth. Females are frequently somewhat larger than the male, but have a more limited and quieter repertoire of calls. Despite fairy tale claims, it has not yet been proven that frog-kissing produces princes.

A group of frogs is called an *army*. The worldwide frog population has for some years been declining at unprecedented rates, causing speculation about the overall health of the biosystems from which they are disappearing.

Nancy Kotary was the production editor and copyeditor for *Windows 95 in a Nutshell*; Sheryl Avruch was the production manager; Ellie Maden, Ellie Cutler, and Jane Ellin provided quality control. Robert Romano created the illustrations using Adobe Photoshop 4 and Macromedia FreeHand 7. Mike Sierra provided FrameMaker technical support. Seth Maislin wrote the index, with additional index work done by Marie Rizzo.

Edie Freedman designed the cover of this book, using a 19th-century engraving from the Dover Pictorial Archive. The cover layout was produced with Quark XPress 3.32 using the ITC Garamond font. Whenever possible, our books use RepKover™, a durable and flexible lay-flat binding. If the page count exceeds RepKover's limit, perfect binding is used.

The inside layout was designed by Nancy Priest and implemented in FrameMaker 5.0 by Mike Sierra. The text and heading fonts are ITC Garamond Light and Garamond Book. This colophon was written by Nancy Kotary.

More Titles from O'Reilly

All the Facts. Not the Frills.

Director in a Nutshell

By Bruce A. Epstein
1st Edition September 1998 (est.)
450 pages (est.), ISBN 1-56592-382-0

Director in a Nutshell is the most
concise and complete guide available
for Director®. The reader gets both the
nitty-gritty details and the bigger context
in which to use the multiple facets of
Director. It is a high-end handbook, at
a low-end price—an indispensable
desktop reference for every Director user.

Internet in a Nutshell

By Valerie Quercia
1st Edition October 1997
450 pages, ISBN 1-56592-323-5

Internet in a Nutshell is a quick-moving
guide that goes beyond the "hype" and
right to the heart of the matter: how to get
the Internet to work for you. This is a sec-
ond-generation Internet book for readers
who have already taken a spin around the
Net and now want to learn the shortcuts.

Java Examples in a Nutshell

By David Flanagan
1st Edition September 1997
414 pages, ISBN 1-56592-371-5

From the author of Java in a Nutshell,
this companion book is chock full of
practical real-world programming
examples to help novice Java programmers and experts alike explore what's
possible with Java 1.1. If you learn best
by example, this is the book for you.

Java in a Nutshell, Second Edition

By David Flanagan
2nd Edition May 1997
628 pages, ISBN 1-56592-262-X

This second edition of the bestselling
Java book describes all the classes in
the Java 1.1 API, with the exception of
the still-evolving Enterprise APIs. And it
still has all the great features that have
made this the Java book most often recommended on the Internet: practical
real-world examples and compact reference information. It's
the only quick reference you'll need.

Lingo in a Nutshell

By Bruce Epstein
1st Edition September 1998 (est.)
650 pages (est.), ISBN 1-56592-493-2

This companion book to Director in a
Nutshell covers all aspects of Lingo,
Director's powerful scripting language,
and is the book for which both Director
users and power Lingo programmers
have been yearning. Detailed chapters
describe messages, events, scripts,
handlers, variables, lists, file I/O, Behaviors, child objects,
Xtras, browser scripting, media control, performance
optimization, and more.

Linux in a Nutshell

By Jessica P. Hekman &
the Staff of O'Reilly & Associates
1st Edition January 1997
438 pages, ISBN 1-56592-167-4

Linux in a Nutshell covers the core
commands available on common Linux
distributions. This isn't a scaled-down
quick reference of common commands,
but a complete reference containing
all user, programming, administration,
and networking commands. Also documents a wide range of
GNU tools.

O'REILLY™

TO ORDER: **800-998-9938** • **order@oreilly.com** • **http://www.oreilly.com/**
OUR PRODUCTS ARE AVAILABLE AT A BOOKSTORE OR SOFTWARE STORE NEAR YOU.
FOR INFORMATION: **800-998-9938** • **707-829-0515** • **info@oreilly.com**

All the Facts. Not the Frills.

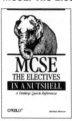

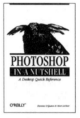

All the Facts. Not the Frills.

WebMaster in a Nutshell

By Stephen Spainhour &
Valerie Quercia
1st Edition October 1996
374 pages, ISBN 1-56592-229-8

Web content providers and administrators have many sources for information, both in print and online. WebMaster in a Nutshell puts it all together in one slim volume for easy desktop access. This quick reference covers HTML, CGI, JavaScript, Perl, HTTP, and server configuration.

Windows 95 in a Nutshell

By Tim O'Reilly &
Troy Mott
1st Edition June 1998 (est.)
550 pages (est.), ISBN 1-56592-316-2

This book systematically unveils the Windows 95 operating system and allows the user to modify any aspect of it, using the Command Line from the DOS or Run prompt, the Explorer, the Registry, the Control Panel, or any other tool or application that exists in Windows 95.

Windows NT in a Nutshell

By Eric Pearce
1st Edition June 1997
364 pages, ISBN 1-56592-251-4

Anyone who installs Windows NT, creates a user, or adds a printer is an NT system administrator (whether they realize it or not). This book features a new tagged callout approach to documenting the 4.0 GUI as well as real-life examples of command usage and strategies for problem solving, with an emphasis on networking. Windows NT in a Nutshell will be as useful to the single-system home user as it will be to the administrator of a 1,000-node corporate network.

Annoyances

Excel 97 Annoyances

By Woody Leonhard,
Lee Hudspeth & T.J. Lee
1st Edition September 1997
336 pages, ISBN 1-56592-309-X

Excel 97 Annoyances uncovers Excel 97's hard-to-find features and tells how to eliminate the annoyances of data analysis. It shows how to easily retrieve data from the Web, details step-by-step construction of a perfect toolbar, includes tips for working around the most annoying gotchas of auditing, and shows how to use VBA to control Excel in powerful ways.

Office 97 Annoyances

By Woody Leonhard,
Lee Hudspeth & T.J. Lee
1st Edition October 1997
396 pages, ISBN 1-56592-310-3

Office 97 Annoyances illustrates step-by-step how to get control over the chaotic settings of Office 97 and shows how to turn the vast array of applications into a simplified list of customized tools. It focuses on the major components of Office 97, examines their integration or lack of it, and shows how to use this new Office suite in the most efficient way.

Word 97 Annoyances

By Woody Leonhard,
Lee Hudspeth & T.J. Lee
1st Edition August 1997
356 pages, ISBN 1-56592-308-1

Word 97 contains hundreds of annoying idiosyncrasies that can be either eliminated or worked around. Word 97 Annoyances takes an in-depth look at what makes Word 97 tick and shows you how to transform this software into a powerful, customized tool.

Annoyances

Windows Annoyances

By David A. Karp
1st Edition June 1997
300 pages, ISBN 1-56592-266-2

Windows Annoyances is a comprehensive, detailed resource for all intermediate to advanced users of Windows 95 and NT version 4.0. This book shows step-by-step how to customize the Win95/NT operating systems through an extensive collection of tips, tricks, and workarounds. Covers **Registry**, **Plug and Play**, networking, security, multiple-user settings, and third-party software.

Outlook Annoyances

By Woody Leonhard,
Lee Hudspeth & T. J. Lee
1st Edition June 1998
400 pages, ISBN 1-56592-384-7

Like the other Microsoft Office-related titles in the Annoyances series, this book points out and conquers the annoying features of Microsoft Outlook, the personal information management software included with Office. It is the definitive guide for those who want to take full advantage of Outlook and transform it into the useful tool that it was intended to be.

How to stay in touch with O'Reilly

1. Visit Our Award-Winning Site

http://www.oreilly.com/

★ "Top 100 Sites on the Web" —*PC Magazine*
★ "Top 5% Web sites" —*Point Communications*
★ "3-Star site" —*The McKinley Group*

Our web site contains a library of comprehensive product information (including book excerpts and tables of contents), downloadable software, background articles, interviews with technology leaders, links to relevant sites, book cover art, and more. File us in your Bookmarks or Hotlist!

2. Join Our Email Mailing Lists

New Product Releases

To receive automatic email with brief descriptions of all new O'Reilly products as they are released, send email to:
listproc@online.oreilly.com
Put the following information in the first line of your message (*not* in the Subject field):
subscribe oreilly-news

O'Reilly Events

If you'd also like us to send information about trade show events, special promotions, and other O'Reilly events, send email to:
listproc@online.oreilly.com
Put the following information in the first line of your message (*not* in the Subject field):
subscribe oreilly-events

3. Get Examples from Our Books via FTP

There are two ways to access an archive of example files from our books:

Regular FTP

* ftp to:
  ftp.oreilly.com
  (login: anonymous
  password: your email address)
* Point your web browser to:
  ftp://ftp.oreilly.com/

FTPMAIL

* Send an email message to:
  ftpmail@online.oreilly.com
  (Write "help" in the message body)

4. Contact Us via Email

order@oreilly.com
To place a book or software order online. Good for North American and international customers.

subscriptions@oreilly.com
To place an order for any of our newsletters or periodicals.

books@oreilly.com
General questions about any of our books.

software@oreilly.com
For general questions and product information about our software. Check out O'Reilly Software Online at **http://software.oreilly.com/** for software and technical support information. Registered O'Reilly software users send your questions to:
website-support@oreilly.com

cs@oreilly.com
For answers to problems regarding your order or our products.

booktech@oreilly.com
For book content technical questions or corrections.

proposals@oreilly.com
To submit new book or software proposals to our editors and product managers.

international@oreilly.com
For information about our international distributors or translation queries. For a list of our distributors outside of North America check out:
http://www.oreilly.com/www/order/country.html

O'Reilly & Associates, Inc.
101 Morris Street, Sebastopol, CA 95472 USA
TEL   707-829-0515 or 800-998-9938
         (6am to 5pm PST)
FAX   707-829-0104

O'REILLY™

Titles from O'Reilly

International Distributors

UK, EUROPE, MIDDLE EAST AND NORTHERN AFRICA (except France, Germany, Switzerland, & Austria)

INQUIRIES
International Thomson Publishing Europe
Berkshire House
168-173 High Holborn
London WC1V 7AA, UK
Telephone: 44-171-497-1422
Fax: 44-171-497-1426
Email: itpint@itps.co.uk

ORDERS
International Thomson Publishing Services, Ltd.
Cheriton House, North Way
Andover, Hampshire SP10 5BE,
United Kingdom
Telephone: 44-264-342-832 (UK)
Telephone: 44-264-342-806 (outside UK)
Fax: 44-264-364418 (UK)
Fax: 44-264-342761 (outside UK)
UK & Eire orders: itpuk@itps.co.uk
International orders: itpint@itps.co.uk

FRANCE
Editions Eyrolles
61 bd Saint-Germain
75240 Paris Cedex 05
France
Fax: 33-01-44-41-11-44

FRENCH LANGUAGE BOOKS
All countries except Canada
Telephone: 33-01-44-41-46-16
Email: geodif@eyrolles.com

ENGLISH LANGUAGE BOOKS
Telephone: 33-01-44-41-11-87
Email: distribution@eyrolles.com

GERMANY, SWITZERLAND, AND AUSTRIA

INQUIRIES
O'Reilly Verlag
Balthasarstr. 81
D-50670 Köln
Germany
Telephone: 49-221-97-31-60-0
Fax: 49-221-97-31-60-8
Email: anfragen@oreilly.de

ORDERS
International Thomson Publishing
Königswinterer Straße 418
53227 Bonn, Germany
Telephone: 49-228-97024 0
Fax: 49-228-441342
Email: order@oreilly.de

JAPAN
O'Reilly Japan, Inc.
Kiyoshige Building 2F
12-Banchi, Sanei-cho
Shinjuku-ku
Tokyo 160 Japan
Tel: 81-3-3356-5227
Fax: 81-3-3356-5261
Email: kenji@oreilly.com

INDIA
Computer Bookshop (India) PVT. Ltd.
190 Dr. D.N. Road, Fort
Bombay 400 001 India
Tel: 91-22-207-0989
Fax: 91-22-262-3551
Email: cbsbom@giasbm01.vsnl.net.in

HONG KONG
City Discount Subscription Service Ltd.
Unit D, 3rd Floor, Yan's Tower
27 Wong Chuk Hang Road
Aberdeen, Hong Kong
Telephone: 852-2580-3539
Fax: 852-2580-6463
Email: citydis@ppn.com.hk

KOREA
Hanbit Publishing, Inc.
Sonyoung Bldg. 202
Yeksam-dong 736-36
Kangnam-ku
Seoul, Korea
Telephone: 822-554-9610
Fax: 822-556-0363
Email: hant93@chollian.dacom.co.kr

TAIWAN
ImageArt Publishing, Inc.
4/fl. No. 65 Shinyi Road Sec. 4
Taipei, Taiwan, R.O.C.
Telephone: 886-2708-5770
Fax: 886-2705-6690
Email: marie@ms1.hinet.net

SINGAPORE, MALAYSIA, AND THAILAND
Longman Singapore
25 First Lok Yan Road
Singapore 2262
Telephone: 65-268-2666
Fax: 65-268-7023
Email: daniel@longman.com.sg

PHILIPPINES
Mutual Books, Inc.
429-D Shaw Boulevard
Mandaluyong City, Metro
Manila, Philippines
Telephone: 632-725-7538
Fax: 632-721-3056
Email: mbikikog@mnl.sequel.net

CHINA
Ron's DataCom Co., Ltd.
79 Dongwu Avenue
Dongxihu District
Wuhan 430040
China
Telephone: 86-27-3892568
Fax: 86-27-3222108
Email: hongfeng@public.wh.hb.cn

AUSTRALIA
WoodsLane Pty. Ltd.
7/5 Vuko Place, Warriewood NSW 2102
P.O. Box 935,
Mona Vale NSW 2103
Australia
Telephone: 61-2-9970-5111
Fax: 61-2-9970-5002
Email: info@woodslane.com.au

ALL OTHER ASIA COUNTRIES
O'Reilly & Associates, Inc.
101 Morris Street
Sebastopol, CA 95472 USA
Telephone: 707-829-0515
Fax: 707-829-0104
Email: order@oreilly.com

THE AMERICAS
McGraw-Hill Interamericana Editores,
S.A. de C.V.
Cedro No. 512
Col. Atlampa 06450
Mexico, D.F.
Telephone: 52-5-541-3155
Fax: 52-5-541-4913
Email: mcgraw-hill@infosel.net.mx

SOUTHERN AFRICA
International Thomson Publishing Southern Africa
Building 18, Constantia Park
138 Sixteenth Road
P.O. Box 2459
Halfway House, 1685 South Africa
Tel: 27-11-805-4819
Fax: 27-11-805-3648

O'REILLY™

TO ORDER: **800-998-9938** • **order@oreilly.com** • **http://www.oreilly.com/**
OUR PRODUCTS ARE AVAILABLE AT A BOOKSTORE OR SOFTWARE STORE NEAR YOU.
FOR INFORMATION: **800-998-9938** • **707-829-0515** • **info@oreilly.com**

O'REILLY™

O'Reilly & Associates, Inc.
101 Morris Street
Sebastopol, CA 95472-9902
1-800-998-9938

Visit us online at:
http://www.ora.com/
orders@ora.com

O'REILLY WOULD LIKE TO HEAR FROM YOU

Which book did this card come from?

_____

Where did you buy this book?
- ❏ Bookstore
- ❏ Direct from O'Reilly
- ❏ Bundled with hardware/software
- ❏ Computer Store
- ❏ Class/seminar
- ❏ Other _____

What operating system do you use?
- ❏ UNIX
- ❏ Windows NT
- ❏ Macintosh
- ❏ PC(Windows/DOS)
- ❏ Other _____

What is your job description?
- ❏ System Administrator
- ❏ Network Administrator
- ❏ Web Developer
- ❏ Programmer
- ❏ Educator/Teacher
- ❏ Other _____

❏ Please send me O'Reilly's catalog, containing a complete listing of O'Reilly books and software.

Name _____ Company/Organization _____

Address _____

City _____ State _____ Zip/Postal Code _____ Country _____

Telephone _____ Internet or other email address (specify network) _____

Nineteenth century wood engraving
of a bear from the O'Reilly &
Associates Nutshell Handbook®
Using & Managing UUCP.

BUSINESS REPLY MAIL
FIRST CLASS MAIL   PERMIT NO. 80   SEBASTOPOL, CA

Postage will be paid by addressee

O'Reilly & Associates, Inc.
101 Morris Street
Sebastopol, CA 95472-9902